When Soldiers Fall

When Soldiers Fall

How Americans Have Confronted Combat
Losses from World War I to Afghanistan

STEVEN CASEY

OXFORD
UNIVERSITY PRESS

Oxford University Press is a department of the University of Oxford.
It furthers the University's objective of excellence in research,
scholarship, and education by publishing worldwide.

Oxford   New York

Auckland   Cape Town   Dar es Salaam   Hong Kong   Karachi
Kuala Lumpur   Madrid   Melbourne   Mexico City   Nairobi
New Delhi   Shanghai   Taipei   Toronto

With offices in

Argentina   Austria   Brazil   Chile   Czech Republic   France   Greece
Guatemala   Hungary   Italy   Japan   Poland   Portugal   Singapore
South Korea   Switzerland   Thailand   Turkey   Ukraine   Vietnam

Oxford is a registered trademark of Oxford University Press
in the UK and certain other countries.

Published in the United States of America by
Oxford University Press
198 Madison Avenue, New York, NY 10016

Library of Congress Cataloging-in-Publication Data
Casey, Steven.
When soldiers fall : how Americans have confronted combat losses
from World War I to Afghanistan / Steven Casey.
pages   cm
Includes bibliographical references and index.
ISBN 978-0-19-989038-5 (alk. paper)
1. Casualty aversion (Military science)—United States.
2. War casualties—United States—Public opinion.
3. War casualties—United States—History—20th century.
4. War casualties—United States—History—21st century.
5. War and mass media—United States.
6. Public opinion—United States. I. Title.
U163.C265   2013
355.4'22—dc23   2012045613

1 3 5 7 9 8 6 4 2

Printed in the United States of America
on acid-free paper

For Lauren

CONTENTS

ACKNOWLEDGMENTS

This book emerged partly from my earlier work on World War II and the Korean War, and so I must begin by thanking those organizations who made my research into these wars possible: the British Association of American Studies, which awarded me a Cunliffe grant; and the Truman Library, which gave me a Travel grant. More recently, I have been the recipient of a Matthew Ridgway grant, which enabled me to visit the U.S. Military History Institute; a Moody grant, which funded my trip to the Johnson Library; and a British Academy Small Grant, which allowed me to undertake research at a host of archives scattered across the United States. A Marshall-Baruch Fellowship also helped me get to some of the smaller archives in the Midwest.

At the London School of Economics, I have been extremely fortunate that successive heads of department have given me time to undertake the research and writing. I would like to express my warmest thanks to Arne Westad, David Stevenson, Dominic Lieven, and Nigel Ashton. My friends in the International History Department have also taken time out of their busy schedules to read through the manuscript and provide penetrating comments. I am particularly grateful to Kristina Spohr, who commented on earlier drafts with her customary sparkle and thoroughness, and Tim Hochstrasser, who provided numerous invaluable insights from the perspective of a nonspecialist. A number of colleagues have also read earlier versions of the manuscript. I would like to thank in particular Michael Pearlman, Ken Osgood, and Richard Lachmann.

Teaching students on my two LSE courses, HY311 and HY422, has shaped my approach to the issues in this book in countless ways. So has the support, encouragement, and advice of a number of people over the years, including Richard Crockatt, Roberto Franzosi, William Stueck, Ralph Levering, James Matray, Louise Fawcett, and Matthew Jones. I also owe a large debt to all the staff at so many archives, especially Michael Devine, Randy Sowell, and Lisa Sullivan at the Truman Library; James Zobel at the MacArthur Memorial Archives; Richard Sommers at the U.S. Military History Institute; Allen Fisher at the Johnson Library; and Valerie Comor and Francesca Pitaro at the AP Archives. I have been particularly fortunate to work for a third time with Susan Ferber at Oxford University Press, and I am extremely grateful for her continued support, advice, and editing expertise. I would also like to thank Mary Sutherland for her thorough copyediting and Joellyn Ausanka, who skillfully shepherded the book through the various production stages.

An earlier version of chapter 4 was published as "Casualty Reporting and Domestic Support for War: The U.S. Experience during the Korean War," *Journal of Strategic Studies* 33 (2010): 291–316, © Taylor & Francis.

My final and most important acknowledgments are to my family. My parents, Terry and Margaret, have provided boundless support for as long as I can remember. My wife, Gemma, has had to live with my repeated absences, both physical and mental, as I've traveled to countless archives or spent evenings bashing away at the keyboard. My lovely daughter, Lauren, has suffered most from these absences. She is a talented young writer, and I can only hope that this book provides an inspiration for her to one day get into print. It is with greatest pleasure—and love—that I dedicate this book to her.

When Soldiers Fall

Introduction

In the early hours of a chilly fall morning nine months into his first term as president, Barack Obama stood rigidly to attention on the runway at Dover Air Force base. Clad in a dark suit, he saluted solemnly as eighteen coffins were unloaded from a C-17 transport plane and slowly shifted to a waiting mortuary van. These returning bodies—of fifteen soldiers and three Drug Enforcement Administration agents—were just a few victims in the bloodiest month yet of the nine-year war in Afghanistan. And the president, who was nearing the end of a major policy review, was eager to emphasize that such losses were casting a long shadow over his new approach to the nation's Afghan strategy. But Obama's Dover visit had another goal. The president was aiming to underline the major difference between the way he and his predecessors treated returning American combat casualties, and he knew that his tribute to the fallen would dominate the airwaves and front pages the next day.

Almost twenty years earlier, during the Persian Gulf War, President George H. W. Bush had banned the media from covering the return of dead U.S. soldiers to American soil. During the Iraq War, his son George W. continued this ban, claiming that it was the most solicitous way of protecting the bereaved families' privacy. But many in the media were skeptical. In their view the Bushes were less worried about the families and more intent on "shielding the American public from the costs of war." Obama agreed. Soon after entering office he ostentatiously ended this contentious policy. Now his visit to Dover was clearly designed to demonstrate that change had come to the way the government dealt with this, the most heartrending consequence of war.[1]

Obama's action did not go unchallenged. While widely applauded by liberals, the reaction on the Right was inevitably far more caustic. "What President Bush used to do," observed Liz Cheney, a State Department official in the previous administration, "is to do it without the cameras. And I don't understand sort of showing up with the White House Press Pool with photographers and asking family members if you can take pictures. That's really hard for me to get my head around." Right-wing bloggers were less baffled. Obama was simply engaged in a "carefully choreographed cynical, ploy," declared one, "using our fallen troops as a campaign-like photo-op to make look like he actually gives a damned about our troops dying." "It was a photo op," agreed Rush Limbaugh in an interview on Fox News. "It was a photo op precisely because he's having big-time trouble on this whole Afghanistan dithering situation."[2]

That Obama and the Right would approach the same issue from diametrically opposed positions is scarcely surprising. But this particular round in their on-going fight fails to recognize that combat casualties have been an enormously contested part of U.S. wartime debates for many decades. This book traces the history of these American casualty debates from World War I, when the U.S. government first accepted full responsibility for reporting casualties, to the recent War on Terror. Based on a vast array of primary sources, many of them previously untapped, it integrates military, political, and media history to offer a new picture of how the American home front has dealt with this tragic dimension of war.

What results is often a dark tale of censorship and suppression, propaganda and spin—of the government trying desperately, on occasion, to mute or mask the human cost of bloody battles. But it has another side too. In all its wars since 1917, the U.S. government has encountered numerous practical problems in publicizing casualty information, from the basic difficulty of ascertaining who has fallen to the need to protect military security and family sensibilities. It has also worked hard to integrate casualty calculations into both its military and rhetorical strategies, sometimes in ways that have been excessively open rather than brazenly dishonest. And, as Obama discovered in 2009, at all times it has faced partisan opponents and scoop-seeking journalists eager to challenge its information or look elsewhere for more eye-catching headlines.

With the exception of Korea, the United States entered its twentieth-century wars after a protracted domestic debate in which casualties loomed large. During the two world wars, the public's basic hostility toward direct intervention was often sharpened by media stories of big, bloody, European battles. In the slow buildup to the major American intervention in Vietnam, the public's reluctance to fight an Asian land war was intermittently intensified by reports that U.S. military advisers were sustaining casualties. Faced with a home front clearly reluctant to spill American blood in faraway conflicts, presidents had to maneuver carefully—and sometimes unscrupulously—as soon as they decided that the United States had to wage war. Their attempt to convince compatriots to fight, and perhaps die, is the first theme of this book.

Having taken the country to war, these presidents and their senior advisers then had to decide how to fight it. Although weighing numerous factors, the home front's likely reaction to high casualties often loomed large. From Franklin Roosevelt to Donald Rumsfeld, some senior players advocated "technowar": using new innovations, from air power to smart bombs, in order to avoid the high casualties associated with deploying a massive ground army. But their generals frequently dissented. The men charged with commanding troops in battle invariably sought to deploy "overwhelming force" in order to place "unrelenting pressure" on the enemy. Yes, they conceded, such operations might result in high casualties at the outset, but this was the only way to weaken the enemy and force it to surrender. In most wars, then, there was an ongoing contest between two concepts, each with a competing vision of how casualties should fit into American military strategy. How the resulting strategy was connected to prospective U.S. casualties is the book's second theme.

Technowar was not the only method for keeping American casualties low. In World War II Roosevelt also turned the United States into the "arsenal of democracy," mass producing weapons that could be sent to allies such as the Soviet Union, whose larger army then bore the brunt of fighting Nazi Germany. In the latter stages of the Vietnam War Nixon likewise shifted the burden of the ground campaign onto America's South Vietnam ally, withdrawing U.S. troops and Vietnamizing the fight. While these initiatives helped to keep American casualties lower, they inevitably came at a cost to other belligerents. While Soviet and South Vietnamese losses far outweighed those sustained by the United States, technowar took an enormous toll on enemy civilians, especially the massive air campaigns over Germany and Japan in World War II, and in Vietnam during the 1960s and 1970s.

Although this book concentrates principally on American responses to its own casualties, these other deaths cannot be ignored. On some occasions, senior officials have worried about the public's squeamishness and its willingness to support a war when the human cost on both sides is so high. They have therefore sought to downplay or conceal the destructiveness of America's own military capabilities. For the most part, however, the U.S. government has not had to work too hard to suppress this information, for invariably the press, politicians, and public have been willing accomplices in a tacit conspiracy of silence. As presidential candidate George McGovern acidly observed toward the end of the Vietnam War, at a time when Richard Nixon had withdrawn U.S. troops from the South while unleashing American airpower on the North, "When the corpses changed color, American interest diminished."[3]

Despite the strategists' attempts to keep U.S. casualties low, America's twentieth-century wars were still costly. Since the 1970s political scientists have intensively debated the impact that these losses have had on the public's support for war. Leading the way, John Mueller has argued that "as casualties mount, support decreases."[4] In response, many of Mueller's colleagues have developed numerous refinements and challenges to his simple and powerful formulation. Some have

Table I.1 **U.S. Combat Casualties, 1917–2012**

	KIA	*WIA*	*Total*
World War I	53,402	204,002	257,404
World War II	291,557	670,846	962,403
Korean War	33,739	103,284	137,383
Vietnam War	47,434	303,644	351,078
Iraq War	4,804	32,223	37,027

Source: Anne Leland and Mari-Jana Oboroceanu, "American War and Military Operations Casualties: Lists and Statistics," *Congressional Research Service*, February 26, 2010; iCasualties.org, website.

undertaken research into whether certain groups in American society are less casualty averse or whether the public is more likely to accept high casualties in certain types of conflict.[5] Others have explored such variables as the perceived benefits of a war, the prospects for success, and the level of elite consensus or discord.[6] Still others have emphasized the importance of "marginal casualties" after particularly bloody battles, rather than the cumulative totals over the course of an entire war.[7]

What is lacking, however, is a detailed historical reconstruction of precisely how casualty information enters the political debate.[8] Such a reconstruction is this book's third and overarching dimension. Whereas the political science debate begins with the simple elegance of Mueller's influential thesis, the following pages provide a much richer, nuanced, and complex picture.

My own starting point is the process by which the public learns about U.S. combat casualties once the fighting begins. Here the government is in control. It decides what to release, and when, which inevitably raises the prospect that the public can be misled—that rather than receive accurate casualty information, it is the victim of spin, suppression, or even deception. Politicians and generals, after all, have an obvious incentive to bury bad news. With men like Franklin Roosevelt, Douglas MacArthur, Lyndon Johnson, Richard Nixon, and Donald Rumsfeld at the helm, the U.S. government has certainly succumbed to the temptation to play down the cost of particular battles, divert attention to other issues, or exploit casualty news for electoral gain. But casualty reporting has been politicized in others ways too. Often, officials have integrated casualties into their overall propaganda campaigns, publicly referring to battlefield sacrifices when insisting that they are necessary to make the world a better place. At one crucial moment in World War II, senior figures even emphasized, and in one instance actually exaggerated, casualty figures in order to demolish what they thought was the public's excessive complacency about ultimate victory.

Exaggeration has been unusual, however. The norm has been for official casualty totals to be much lower than the reality. Although propaganda and politics have been a clear cause of such underreporting, the main reason has often been more practical and prosaic. The grim task of reporting losses is simply tough and time-consuming. It contains three different facets: announcing cumulative totals of all Americans killed in action (KIA), wounded in action (WIA), and missing in action (MIA); releasing regular name lists of those who have recently died; and attempting to control how the media covers death in its accounts of particular battles. Each facet is beset by sensitive problems. First, there is the grim and laborious task of recovering the dead. Then the military has to take enormous care to make sure that the correct identification is made and the right family notified. It also has to be sensitive to security concerns on the battlefield, especially the censors' fear that if total losses are released too soon the enemy might be able to gauge the success of an operation. On occasion, it has even needed to listen to allies, particularly during the two world wars when European partners fretted that vital secrets would appear in the excessively open American press.

All these pressures tend to result in delays, but they are by no means the only practical problems. The government also has to decide what to include in each casualty category. Table I-1 illustrates some of the difficulties. Absent from its fatality totals are those killed in noncombat incidents, which would inflate the totals for World War I, World War II, Korea, and Vietnam by thousands in each conflict. In this table, moreover, the number of Vietnam wounded includes those personnel who did not require hospitalization. In Korea and the two world wars, by contrast, such light wounds were not always included in the official published figures. As a result, the Vietnam wounded total is about double what it would have been had a different standard been used—a fact that would cause quite a stir at a crucial moment in that controversial war.[9]

Then there is the term "casualty" itself. In this book, the word is used as shorthand for all those in the KIA, WIA, and MIA categories. In the emotive context of a charged wartime debate, however, the term has sometimes been conflated or confused with the number of fatalities—with potentially disastrous results. In 1952, for instance, the Truman White House was so worried that the public was getting the misleading impression that the 125,000 men listed as casualties were all dead (the actual KIA figure was less than twenty thousand) that it instructed the Defense Department "to correct an apparent widespread and popularly accepted impression that 'casualty' means 'fatality.'"[10]

Because of all these calculations and complications, the public has rarely received clear, timely, and accurate casualty figures. It has often been bombarded instead with official announcements that are unclear, out of date, or even deliberately misleading. Crucially, though, such official announcements have rarely gone unchallenged. Although wartime administrations wield enormous propaganda power, especially in the early days of a crisis when pressure on the media and op-position to rally 'round the flag is intense, they have never been all powerful. During the Vietnam War, in particular, the government faced intensive opposi-tion from an antiwar movement, which claimed that tens of thousands of young American lives had been thrown away for an immoral and illegal cause. But even during less polarizing wars, the government has still faced the two powerful groups that have had particular incentives to debate and dispute official casualty figures.

The opposition party, for obvious reasons, has generally been the most vocal focal point of dissent. For the Republicans who opposed the two world wars, Korea, and Vietnam, casualties were a particularly promising issue. Many truly thought that Democratic incompetence had either mired the nation in an un-necessary war or was the cause of costly defeats. Many more espied potential partisan gain in the charge that Democrats were concealing the true cost of the war—just as Democrats did when they were in opposition during Nixon's war in Vietnam and Bush's war in Iraq—charges that gained traction amid a general sense in both conflicts that the government had lied the country to war in the first place.

The media, for its part, has often regurgitated these allegations, and not just because of a partisan bias. Editors and reporters have invariably framed a large part of their war coverage around the number of American casualties. Convinced that war sells, small-town newspapers have been eager to print the names of local dead to increase circulation. For their part, the big-city organs have recognized that although most battles are newsworthy, those with a large American stake—including, however tragically, large numbers of American losses—will shift a large number of that day's edition. As well as reporting partisan casualty charges, big-city editors have sent war correspondents to the front to try to piece together what is going on. All these reports have then been published beneath headlines that tend to simplify information, stressing, for example, the overall total of ca-sualties, instead of just fatalities, especially when this total has passed a clear benchmark figure.

Driven by these clear incentives to publish or broadcast casualty stories, the media has often balked at the military's attempt to restrict the flow of informa-tion from the war zone. The worst moments have come when the government has ordered a complete clampdown, as it did during the Ludendorff Offensive in 1918 or after Pearl Harbor in 1941. Rather than recognize the legitimate security reasons for cutting copy about recent losses, reporters and editors have tended to view such strict censorship as an attempt to cover up incompetence. Often, they have also been exasperated by delays in publishing casualty information, even if such delays have been the result of legitimate practical problems. And their response has been telling. Desperate to print something in the next edition, the media has speculated or pedaled rumor. On occasion it has even turned to enemy sources, even though enemy propaganda has invariably offered a greatly inflated total of American losses.

Since 1917, then, the interaction among the government, press, and politicians over casualties has contained consistent ingredients, but the relationship has not remained static. The government's domestic audience has certainly changed in various ways. The media, most obviously, has evolved technologically, from its newspaper and magazine roots to the radio and television era, and finally to the modern landscape of cable broadcasting and the Internet. With the addition of each new media form, the government has faced fresh challenges related to coordination, speed, and packaging. In World War I, for instance, the War Department handed out press releases to print journalists who had two daily deadlines. Almost a hundred years later, by contrast, numerous government agencies now publish different casualty information on the Web, while also trying to cater to cable television's voracious appetite for breaking 24/7 news. TV is also eager to personalize issues. Rather than dealing in cold statistics, it wants to show names, faces, and families.

This growing personalization of casualty coverage has been an important counter to the traditional focus on hard figures. In earlier wars the national casualty debate tended to revolve around numbers: the likely number of losses if the United States should go to war, the total number of dead at any point in time, whether the number of non-battle deaths or lightly wounded should be included in the official statistics. Beneath the various statistics, however, lay real human tragedies, from gory combat deaths to bereft and grieving relatives whose lives will never again be the same. To its credit, the modern media rarely neglects this human dimension, but its more emotive coverage has clearly contributed to another major change: the public's growing sensitivity to casualties.

This new type of media coverage has not been the only cause of such sensitivity. Political leaders have increasingly engaged in public displays of grief, consoling relatives, and thereby drawing attention to specific deaths. Political scientists, in trying to ascertain whether the home front is casualty tolerant, have framed opinion polls around the question of how many deaths the public will stomach—polls that are then endlessly repeated in the echo chamber of modern 24/7 news. In all these various forums, a common assumption is that public attitudes have also changed because of one major historical event: Vietnam. After America's first defeat a "Vietnam syndrome" emerged that, until the so-called War on Terror, made presidents think twice about sending troops into combat lest domestic support collapse as soon as American boys began to die. Even after 9/11 Vietnam has still loomed large, as columnists and analysts have looked for patterns between the public's tolerance for casualties then and now.

Although particularly powerful, the Vietnam syndrome is by no means unique. Earlier wars also generated their own casualty-related hangovers. Some proved hard to shake: after World War I, for instance, the sense that American troops should "never again" be sent to slaughter in faraway lands endured for more than twenty years. Others proved more fleeting: the bloodiness of Tarawa in 1943, for example, loomed large when the United States went to war in Korea less than a decade later, but has since faded. How such historical memories have shaped and sharpened political debates therefore needs to be kept in mind when exploring the ways the public has reacted to casualty news at different points in time.

So does the American government's ability to learn. Although it now faces far tougher challenges than a century ago, the military has acquired enormous experience in dealing with this delicate problem. In 1917 it had few precedents on which to draw. Indeed, although the Civil War had been enormously costly, in that period the federal government played no systematic role in notifying either the press or families about the large loss of life. Instead, individual generals kept careful lists of active soldiers, together with the numbers of dead and wounded, but only to ascertain the strength of their army for the battles ahead. Neither they nor the military establishment in Washington deemed they had a duty to notify the next of kin of the fallen, let alone the public. In fact, Civil War officers lacked even a reliable method of establishing precisely who had become casualties on the battlefield. Soldiers who wished to be remembered were left to their own devices. Often this meant simply writing their names on slips of paper and pinning them to their uniforms. Once the battle was over, it was up to individual officers or regimental chaplains to send letters to the families of the fallen, but this devolution made reporting an even more haphazard affair. Sometimes such missives never arrived. On other occasions they were pre-empted by the deceased's name appearing in the newspaper or on the notice board in a town square. Frequently, it took weeks or months for any information to filter back home, either by letter or by stories in the press.[11]

Only at the turn of the twentieth century did a wave of bureaucratization give the military a chance to develop clear and centralized procedures. In Europe the great powers were already in the process of developing more elaborate staff structures to deal with personnel, intelligence, operations, logistics, and the like. Soon after the Spanish-American War of 1898 the U.S. Army followed suit, not only creating its own general staff but also establishing staff and line colleges to generate new ideas and inculcate them into a fresh cadre of officers.[12] Although still meager in comparison to what was happening in most European powers, these initiatives at least provided the War Department with the capacity to think about its responsibility to the relatives of citizen soldiers. They also enabled it to start grappling with the practical problems associated with collecting, collating, and publishing casualty information in a timely and accurate fashion.

The most important upshot of all these changes came in 1913, when the general staff decided to introduce ID tags (or dog tags), the key prerequisite for correctly identifying the fallen soldiers on the battlefield.[13] The timing was significant. This was still the height of the progressive era. The vast majority of Americans remained preoccupied with reforming their own country, which had undergone such tremendous changes after decades of mass immigration and rapid industrialization. No one seriously thought that the dog tag would have much impact on U.S. society in the coming years. Certainly, few predicted that a European conflagration would erupt a year later. Even fewer guessed that the United States would ultimately intervene in this bloody conflict, let alone later wage war in North Africa, Italy, Western Europe, the Pacific, Korea, Vietnam, the Persian Gulf, and Afghanistan.

But in fact the dog tag—along with the condolence letter, the list of casualty names in local newspapers, the cumulative totals announced by top civilian military leaders, and the oft-censored stories of grim battlefield deaths—would soon become all too familiar aspects of American life. Indeed, during the ensuing bloody century, the brutal and depressing message that began with a dog tag being ripped from a fallen soldier, sailor, or airman would spark a series of controversies that shaped how the nation viewed both war and its own place in the world. This book tells that story.

1

Censorship and the First Casualty Controversy

World War I, 1917–1918

President Woodrow Wilson was in subdued and somber mood on April 2, 1917. Just five months before, he had narrowly won reelection as the man who had kept the United States out of World War I. Rejoice, Democratic Party slogans had proclaimed, "You are working—not fighting! Alive and happy;—not cannon fodder!"[1] Soon after, Wilson made a concerted effort to broker a peace settlement between the two sets of belligerents. His policy had been underpinned by a simple calculation. Modern war, he believed, had no redeeming features. It was nothing more than a mass slaughter, as armies burrowed into impressive defensive systems, based around the trench and made almost impregnable by barbed wire, machine guns, and an immense array of artillery. Since 1914 Wilson had been desperate to keep the United States out of such a fight, but now, as the German government launched an unrestricted submarine campaign, which resulted in the sinking of three American ships, he was reversing course. Reluctantly, he would ask Congress for a declaration of war against Germany.

Wilson left the White House at 8:20 in the evening. A warm drizzle fell as he made the short journey to Capitol Hill surrounded by a cavalry guard. After taking a moment to compose himself, Wilson strode into the House of Representatives chamber to a tumultuous reception. Unfolding his speech, he made the case for war, stressing that Germany's recent actions had left him little choice. The response was powerful and passionate. Legislators stood, cheering and waving small American flags—much to Wilson's intense mystification. "My message tonight was a message of death for our young men," he remarked on returning to the White House. "How strange it seems to applaud that."[2]

Despite these congressional cheers, Wilson worried that the rest of the country was unprepared for the heartache ahead. The United States, after all, had no track record of intervening in distant Old World conflicts. Worse, his own progressive base hated the prospect of militarism and war, while Irish Americans and German Americans were leery of aiding the British cause. Wilson's government therefore had a tough task on its hands. It would have to work hard to prepare the home front for the large number of American battlefield deaths that were bound to come, offering its own spin on why such sacrifices were necessary.

The Wilson administration would also have to work hard to create an American army almost from scratch. While the War Department had developed a general staff with the capacity to plan, regulate, and systematize a whole range of military tasks, the U.S. military still had a long way to go if it was to come close to matching the battle-hardened European powers. When the United States declared war, the general staff in Washington consisted of just twenty officers.[3] A month later, when the first contingent of the new American army set sail for Europe, its commander, Gen. John J. Pershing, was supported by only 190 officers, and he faced the unenviable task of trying to ship over hundreds of thousands of draftees, training these raw recruits in the most basic of tasks, and ultimately trying to turn them into a cohesive fighting force.

At its various layers, then, the U.S. military was suddenly engaged in a crash course of training, learning, and drafting new guidelines, procedures, and structures. As with any new enterprise on this scale, teething troubles abounded. Initially the military, working from scratch, acted clumsily when announcing casualty lists. As a result, politicians and the press were inadvertently presented with a clear opportunity to complain about delays and restrictions—complaints that sometimes were little more than thinly veiled allegations that the government was hiding the true scale of the war's human cost.

Significantly, though, when American forces finally went into combat in large numbers, these criticisms were muted. The big American battle of this war—the fight at the Meuse-Argonne—dwarfed any engagement the United States had ever fought before, even such bloody Civil War battles as Shiloh, Antietam, or Gettysburg. Indeed, the losses on the Meuse-Argonne were truly staggering. In just three weeks the American Expeditionary Force (AEF) suffered 122,000 American casualties, of which more than 26,000 were killed in action.[4] Yet initially, the press reported this massive death toll in a way that had no real impact on popular support for the war. Only after the armistice did the public's aversion to modern warfare reappear, this time with a vengeance, casting a long shadow over the 1920s and 1930s.

Casualties and the Long Road to the Trenches, 1914–17

Before its belated entry in 1917 the United States witnessed World War I vicariously, and with a growing sense of horror at the size of the tragedy unfolding across Europe.[5] The bloodshed on the Western Front was certainly appalling, especially in the big attritional battles of 1916. Over a period of months thousands of men were chewed up by artillery as they tried to shelter in their trenches or were mowed down by machine guns the minute they went over the top. At Verdun, where the fighting lasted most of the year, the French suffered about 377,000 casualties to the Germans' 337,000. On the Somme, where the Allies sustained their attack from July to November, the British lost 420,000 men and the French 194,000, while subsequent estimates placed German casualties at about half a million.[6]

All the belligerents had obvious incentives to control the dissemination of such staggering losses. In the hands of their foes, they feared, accurate and timely casualty information would provide key intelligence about army strength and the success of particular engagements. If the full horror was known on the home front, they further fretted, then perhaps morale might sag alarmingly. Each of the belligerents therefore clamped down hard on war news. Both the British and French armies allowed only a small number of correspondents at their headquarters, and they placed them under close military supervision. In the British sector, these accredited reporters were subjected to restrictive rules that permitted no mention of units or places. French censorship was even more onerous, proscribing a long list of subjects, from news that might engender excessive optimism to stories that suggested the high command had made mistakes. On the other side of the hill, the German army followed suit, ruling that all war news gathered by individual papers had to be cleared with the respective local military commands, which were rarely known for their openness.[7]

With such tight control over the channels of communication, the military commands worked hard to influence the extent to which the outside world could witness the true horrors of war. The French and Germans were the most restrictive. After August 1914, when its parliament passed a strict censorship law, the French government's position on casualty totals was uncompromising. It prohibited the publication of all "lists of killed, wounded, and taken prisoner."[8] The German state adopted a similar stance, its censors likewise suppressing all casualty lists.[9] Meanwhile, British authorities, although generally less heavy-handed, were also wary about what the press could publish. Throughout the war they never announced cumulative totals, even in face of opposition allegations that this policy misled the public and gave the Germans a chance to claim huge British losses.[10]

Ultimately, however, the censors were unable to completely conceal the scale of the unfolding carnage. For one thing, the sheer size of the tragedy was impossible to hide, as whole communities reeled under the incessant casualty telegrams that grimly revealed the loss of yet more husbands, sons, and brothers. For another, governments recognized the need to commemorate those who had made the ultimate sacrifice—a calculation that prompted the British government to permit newspapers to publish daily casualty names of all ranks, which for some of the bloodier engagements took up two whole pages.[11] Propagandists, moreover, either through inattention or design, also allowed certain graphic casualty images to seep into the public domain. In France, for instance, they permitted the illustrated press to print gruesome pictures of corpses in the trenches or no man's land, while in Britain they even made a movie titled *The Battle of the Somme*. Shown on both sides of the Atlantic, this film provided audiences with particularly jarring images of the battlefield dead. According to one content analysis, 13 percent of the film was devoted to the dead and the wounded.[12]

The American correspondents who visited the front added more depth and color to this depressing picture. They were an enterprising bunch: well respected, highly paid, and generally heedless of the dangers.[13] Despite facing stringent Allied controls, they worked hard to give the American public a feel for what the war was like, which often meant stressing the unprecedented carnage. Richard Harding Davis was a case in point. The dean of American war correspondents, Davis made frequent references to the human tragedy in his war dispatches, wiring home reports of healthy soldiers who were soon broken by shells and bullets, or descriptions of the battlefields at Arras and Verdun that were like "an endless grave." "In Flanders," Davis wrote at the start of 1916, "death hides in a trench of mud like an open grave. In the forest of the Vosges it lurks in a nest of moss, fern, and clean sweet-smelling pine."[14]

Such stories inevitably influenced the U.S. domestic debate, especially during the heated election year of 1916 when most Americans remained determined to stay out of the war. The public's overwhelming commitment to neutrality had numerous causes. There were those who wanted to concentrate on domestic reform, or whose ethnic ties made them leery of supporting the British cause, or who retained an overpowering sense of detachment from the distant Old World. What united most, however, was a growing revulsion at modern warfare's sheer human cost. According to one editorial assessment, no less than nine-tenths of the public opposed "sending American troops to fight in Europe" where all that awaited them was the prospect of a grisly death. William Jennings Bryan, until recently Wilson's secretary of state, spoke for many when he observed that "Across the seas our brothers' hands are stained in brothers' blood. The world has run mad." Socialist leaders were even more graphic. "The six million men whose corpses are now rotting upon the battlefields of Europe were mostly working men," they declared. "If the United States is drawn into war, it will be American workers whose lives will be sacrificed."[15]

In the spring of 1917, in the wake of civilian casualties caused by Germany's unrestricted U-boat campaign, Wilson finally asked Congress for a formal declaration of war. But he remained deeply disinclined to send American boys into the meat grinder of the Western Front, initially hoping that he could get away with just providing money and material to Britain and France.[16] Other senior politicians shared his lack of enthusiasm. A week after Wilson's war address, when one War Department official told the Senate Finance Committee that we "may need to have an army in France," the chairman was incredulous. "Good lord!" he declared. "You're not going to send soldiers over there, are you?"[17]

Such reluctance, however, soon clashed with the reality of the Allies' needs. At the beginning of May the British and French sent high-ranking military missions to Washington. Both emphasized the plight of their own armies after almost three years of grueling warfare. They therefore called on the United States to send as many troops as possible to bolster their publics' morale. Within days, War Secretary Newton Baker agreed to send one division as soon as possible. By the end of the month, this commitment had burgeoned into a promise to dispatch an American Expeditionary Force (AEF) totaling upwards of half a million men to be commanded by General Pershing.[18]

These troops would come from the new selective service law that the administration had just passed through Congress. To enact this controversial piece of legislation, a number of officials had loudly beaten the patriotic drum. They then intensified the rhythm at the start of June, in a successful effort to register ten million men aged between twenty-one and thirty, keeping up the pace throughout the summer to make sure that the local boards filled their first quota of 687,000 draftees.[19]

The creation of this large army soon generated its own momentum. "Our own country," Baker informed the still doubtful Wilson, "will not be willing to continue here a long drawn out process of training with the ultimate intention of doing the fighting on a large scale at some time later." It was vital, Baker believed, to get the AEF to Europe as soon as possible. Until the fall of 1917 Wilson remained unenthusiastic, but Baker and his advisers continued to press him strongly. They warned Wilson not to listen to armchair strategists who pedaled peripheral strategic visions. They also reminded him that U.S. troops were, "in some sense, pledged for use on the Western Front in cooperation with British and French forces there." With Wilson recognizing that a presence on the battlefield would translate into power at a peace conference, his opposition gradually crumbled.[20]

The problem was the likely public reaction to high casualties. Throughout the summer and fall the American debate remained fixated on the huge losses in Europe. While peace activists inevitably cited these as a reason for the United States to remain aloof, hawks totted up the large lists on both sides to demonstrate that Germany would soon be bled into submission. As journalists tried to estimate the overall casualty toll, the result was truly horrifying. As the *Washington Times* reported in November 1917, more than three years into the war, almost ten million had been killed and a further 23.5 million injured.[21]

Senior officials fretted that such stories could easily undermine the public's fragile morale. With American troops getting ready to depart for Europe, they were particularly eager to dampen talk of prospective U.S. casualties. A telling moment came when the War Department privately debated the wisdom of establishing training centers for the troops who would replace those killed or wounded in action. It was a question that required estimating the likely losses when U.S. troops finally went into the line, and the figures were far from reassuring. In fact, Baker warned his officials that the whole plan, if it leaked out, would be a major propaganda disaster. He therefore stepped in to scupper the idea. "The country at the outset," he explained to the army Chief of Staff, "would have been shocked to discover how large we thought the losses were likely to be."[22]

Casualties and Censorship, 1917–18

The first American troops departed for Europe in June 1917, starting what would prove to be a massive, but inevitably slow, process. By October, when the United States had been at war for almost six months, only 65,000 doughboys—as the GIs of this era were soon dubbed—had made it to France. By Christmas this figure edged up to 129,000, and by the following May it reached 650,000. Not until the summer of 1918, however, did the AEF have sufficient forces to make a major difference on the battlefield.[23]

These doughboys were raw and inexperienced. Pershing, who was a stickler for discipline, therefore set about establishing an intensive training routine. Throughout eastern France he created schools to teach staff officers, artillerymen, quartermasters, chaplains, and cooks. He also sent off many officers to receive lessons from experienced British or French instructors, albeit tempered by qualms about exposing his men to what he considered the excessive caution of the Allied way of war. In fact, Pershing hoped to instill in his army a more dynamic—and American—style of fighting. He wanted to move away from the defensive-mindedness imposed by the trench and an excessive reliance on artillery. His aim was to break out into the open where the unique American proficiency with the rifle would come into its own. Across France, while officers were exposed to these ideas, their men were slowly socialized into the military world by daily drills during one of the coldest winters in memory. It was an endless cycle of nine-to-five days of marching, parading, cleaning, skirmishing, and shooting in subzero temperatures.[24]

Ideally, the AEF's training regimen would have had many months to transform these raw recruits into hardened soldiers. But time was one thing the Allies lacked in the winter of 1917/18, for the war was going far too badly. To the northwest of the new American training camps, in the rain-drenched Flanders fields, Britain's Passchendaele campaign was reaching its inglorious conclusion, at the staggering cost of 110,000 casualties during the month of October, all for the sake of advancing just a few extra miles. To the southeast the Italians suffered a major defeat at Caporetto, while much farther to the east the new Russian government, in power only since the tsar had abdicated in February, was itself overthrown in early November when the Bolsheviks seized power in Petrograd and prepared to withdraw Russia from the war.[25]

With the outlook so bleak, the British and French looked for the United States to make an immediate battlefield contribution. Recognizing that the AEF was still focused on basic organizational and training tasks, the two Allies pushed for individual American units to be amalgamated into the more battle-hardened French and British armies, where they could begin to fight much sooner. It was an initiative that Pershing, desperate to retain the core identity of the U.S. Army, viewed with horror. But he did make one impor-tant concession: he would permit the First Division to enter a quiet section of the front, under the auspices of French command, to give it a modicum of combat experience.[26]

On the night of October 21, selected units from the First Division got their first taste of life in the trenches. The plan was for each regiment to spend just ten days at the front, essentially in training rather than pure combat. Their time would be spent acclimatizing to the demanding conditions, the proximity of the enemy, and the risks of sniper fire and artillery barrages. Many men were eager for action: to be the first American to go on a raid, fire a shell, or kill the enemy. But the Germans had different ideas. As soon as they got wind that Americans were in the line, German commanders decided to test their mettle. On the night of November 2–3, in a whirlwind fifteen-minute attack, a Bavarian assault com-pany captured eleven and killed three doughboys—the first American casualties of the war.[27]

This was a harbinger of what was to come, especially once American troops went into the line under their own commanders early in the new year. The First Division again led the way, taking over a section of the front on one side of the Saint Mihiel salient—where the German position projected into the Allied line—in the middle of January. During the next two weeks, when the French remained tactically in charge, the doughboys maintained the norms already established in this quiet sector of the front, doing nothing to annoy the Germans and force them into a major retaliation. But when Gen. Robert L. Bullard took over and ordered his men "to stir up Germans," U.S. troops immediately displayed real exuberance for combat. The basic figures were telling. During February the doughboys lobbed an average of one thousand shells a day at the enemy, a figure that more than tripled the next month. Yet, predictably, this increased activity came at a cost. The German response, although not as intense as the U.S. effort, was brutal. During March the Germans fired more than forty thousand shells into American lines. One enemy attack included seven tons of phosgene, which killed eight and forced the evacuation of seventy-seven soldiers who had breathed in the toxic fumes. During its first months in the line the First Division suffered, in total, 549 losses.[28]

With these first casualties, the military immediately faced a series of practical problems. For a start it had to take enormous care to make sure that the correct family was notified—and this inevitably meant some delay in readying total figures for publication. Bodies had to be recovered and identified. In Washington the War Department had to telegraph the next of kin the dreadful news. Only then could the Committee on Public Information (CPI) release lists of the dead and wounded, taking great pains to provide the name and address of the dead soldier, along with the name of the nearest relative, "so that relations of other soldiers bearing the same name will not be unduly worried."[29]

Over the winter of 1917/18, the AEF also recognized that it had to be extra sensitive in order to spare families the gruesome details of trench fighting. The AEF censorship office considered gas attacks to be particularly nasty. A new form of warfare, gas had taken combat away from its masculine roots where, according to tradition, virtues of "valor, resourcefulness, endurance, and 'grit'" decided the day. More to the point, it induced particularly horrific suffering, with victims "gargling from froth-corrupted lungs," in the war poet Wilfred Owen's vivid phrase.[30] In the wake of the first German gas attacks on American troops, AEF censors carefully scoured correspondents' copy, drawing attention to any language "designed to cause unnecessary apprehension and pain on the part of friends and relatives of our soldiers in France."[31]

Standard trench raids had their grisly side, too. In their first assault against the doughboys, German troops tricked two of their victims into thinking that they were American soldiers. The next day the third dead man was discovered with his throat slit from ear to ear, his chest sliced open, and no less than twelve bayonet wounds. As rumors about the attack started to swirl around the AEF, many thought that this last action was perfect evidence of yet another German atrocity.[32]

Over the past three years alleged German savagery in Belgium or the Eastern Front had become a staple of Allied propaganda, with stories appearing of "Hun" soldiers cutting off children's hands, bayoneting babies, and generally engaging in "wild orgies of blood debauchery."[33] Since the American entrance into the war, many individuals and organizations within the rapidly expanding Wilson administration—especially the propagandists in the CPI and the war bond sellers in the Treasury Department—had recycled such material. Their motive was simple. They thought that teaching the public to hate all things German was the easiest way to rally popular opinion.[34] It was a view shared by many soldiers in France. The AEF's censors certainly had no love for the German enemy, believed that its army had committed all sorts of savagery in Belgium, and were keenly aware that "atrocities of any sort committed by the Boche [as Germans were often unkindly labeled at the time] are very powerful weapons for us."[35]

Still, they were dubious about using this particular story. Some AEF censors were motivated by an ingrained legalism: a desire to sanction atrocity stories based only on "information which would pass in any court," perhaps even a war crimes court after the war was won. The censors' dominant motive, though, was a powerful concern for relatives. At a time when only three American soldiers had been killed, the victims' families would clearly recognize that this story was about their own loved ones, even if no names were printed. More broadly, the censorship office fretted that the families of all sons in the rapidly growing AEF would despair if they thought such a nasty fate was in store for their own next of kin.

The censors therefore clamped down hard. When one *New York Herald* correspondent described how German raiders had cut the throat of a captured U.S. sentry, comparing this deed to the brutality of the Filipino "savages" that America had fought at the turn of the century, the censors quickly spiked the story. In its place, they passed only anodyne descriptions of men who had "died bravely in hand-to-hand fighting with the enemy."[36]

Relatives were just one priority, however. Pershing's command was also determined to deny the German enemy any useful intelligence. This was not a calculation unique to World War I. The military, faced with hazardous life and death decisions, always wants tight control over any information that might imperil the troops. But at this particular moment on the Western Front, the AEF's instinct was especially restrictive.

In part this was simply a reflection of the top man's wishes. General "Black Jack" Pershing never had much time for reporters, who in turn tended to view him as dour and taciturn: a tight-lipped commander whose press conferences were rare and memorable sound bites still rarer.[37] On arriving in France, Pershing's major media initiative was to persuade Frederick A. Palmer, one of America's leading war correspondents, to take over as the AEF's chief press officer and censor. It soon proved a thankless task, not least because Palmer faced weeks of grueling toil, working out guidelines, recruiting censors, and liaising with Allies. Still, with a skeleton staff of just a few untrained volunteers, he managed to sketch out the basic framework of the U.S. military's first comprehensive system of media relations.[38]

Palmer's most important decision was to accredit a small number of correspondents who lived with the AEF's press headquarters in the field. They all had to post a $2,000 bond for good behavior with the War Department, which would be forfeited if they broke the new censorship guidelines. Although theoretically free to travel in the immediate army zone, they also had to provide the press office with details of their movements for the next day, while those planning longer tours had to have a press officer as a chaperone.

In establishing this new system Palmer was heavily indebted to the British and French, who had pioneered the establishment of press camps and the use of accreditation on the Western Front. Like his new wartime partners, Palmer was hopeful that the correspondents stationed at his press camp would acquire an affinity with, and an understanding of, the military's approach to the war. In modern parlance, he was aiming to "embed" them, albeit only with the higher echelons of command. His hope was that these accredited reporters would come to understand the value of being extra cautious and the need for stringent restrictions on information in a war zone.[39]

Unfortunately, Palmer initially lacked trained officers who could establish a close rapport with these reporters. Indeed, his first censors, like almost all of the AEF, were a green bunch, chosen on the basis of availability rather than exposure to newspaper reporting. Acutely aware of this inexperience, Palmer soon ordered a clampdown. To stop his novice censors passing copy that would endanger the troops, he instructed them to err on the side of caution, suppressing anything that might conceivably be considered a security breach.[40]

The problem was trying to decide precisely what this meant in practice. When it came to American losses, Baker instructed that "no effort could be made by the War Department to interfere with the publication of casualties, as was the case in France," for the simple reason that the American public "demanded" basic lists of dead and wounded. Still, there were plenty of details that were not that important to the public but which might be "helpful" to the enemy, and these clearly had to be withheld.[41] It took time, however, for the inexperienced censors to judge precisely what could—and could not—be safely published. The result was a creeping sense of uncertainty over casualty information, which led to the first major home-front controversy.

One difficulty was the need to "camouflage" casualty announcements so as to mislead the enemy about the results of specific engagements. Here the AEF's new partners, worried about "sensational American journalism," offered their counsel.[42] The French pointed out that if the U.S. military published full casualty lists as soon as they were ready, the Germans might calculate the success of a certain raid or artillery attack. The British, having long recognized this danger, staggered publication of their own casualty lists "in such a way as to absolutely prevent the published lists being connected with any particular operation." In early March 1918, when the AEF released the numbers, though not the details, of the dead and wounded in a German gas attack, the French command implored the AEF to follow this British example. Its current practice, the French complained, "seriously harm[ed] not only the American troops in the [French] sector but also all the troops at the front by revealing to the Germans the result of all their gas attacks."[43]

Pershing was immediately receptive to this advice. In early March, at a time when more and more U.S. troops were going into the line, his subordinates informed reporters that they would begin to "camouflage" casualty announcements forthwith. The censors, instead of announcing that, say, five hundred had been killed in a particular battle, would release a hundred names a day at various intervals.[44] At the same time Pershing also asked Washington to stop publishing the addresses of the killed and wounded, lest the enemy use these to piece together the identity of regionally generated units.[45] The War Department readily complied on the principle that the field commander knows best. But the CPI, which had hitherto worked with the Associated Press (AP) to circulate lists, refused to have anything to do with this particular initiative. Aware that smaller newspapers only wanted to print the names from their own area, the CPI balked at releasing casualty lists they would deem worthless. George Creel, the CPI boss, even made his opposition public, issuing a terse statement that "correspondents, editors, and the public should apply in future directly to the War Department for all information concerning casualties."[46]

For the next four weeks the War Department struggled to fill the hole left by the CPI's refusal to touch these truncated lists.[47] Then in early April, in the wake of a massive change in the battlefield situation, the military suddenly announced its most controversial action: a complete suspension of all casualty lists.

The backdrop to this stunning suppression was the Ludendorff Offensive. On March 21 the Germans began their last major attack of the war, unleashing seventy-one divisions that made substantial gains against a weakened part of the British line. In a little under two weeks German troops ripped a forty-mile gap in the front, penetrated another forty miles, and inflicted more than two-hundred thousand casualties on the British. Although Ludendorff failed to make a decisive strategic breakthrough, he achieved a major tactical victory. He also continued to press, launching blows against the British in the Ypres sector in April and against the French along the Chemin des Dames ridge in late May.[48]

As luck would have it, Baker was in France when the Ludendorff Offensive began. The Allied mood was tense as the German attack gathered pace. A wrong move and the war might be lost. At times the battlefield situation appeared so bleak that senior generals issued "backs to the wall" proclamations to their troops. Clearly everything had to be done to safeguard the security of the troops, so Pershing made a suggestion to his visiting boss: his AEF headquarters should now release all military information. The War Department, not knowing what might hazard the troops, should halt its own press releases. Baker immediately agreed. On April 2 he wired the War Department with instructions to ban any official inside the United States from issuing public information on the activities of the AEF in France. The result was stark. With Pershing's press office providing no detailed information of American losses, the media faced an effective suspension of basic casualty news, at a time when the great German offensive was in full flow.[49]

The First Casualty Controversy, 1918

These restrictions, in hindsight, were clearly the result of a series of vexing practical problems. The military had many audiences to satisfy. It also lacked both a tried-and-tested script and an experienced director to guide its actions. Like any novice it made a series of mistakes, although these stemmed largely from honest oversights rather than sinister machinations. Baker's order was the most obvious example. It was issued in the heat of the moment, at a time when Allied armies were forced into one of the longest retreats of the war. It was also interpreted far more restrictively than Baker ever intended.

At the time, however, few informed observers were willing to give the military the benefit of such a detached perspective. Journalists and politicians understandably tended to view these casualty restrictions as an outrage. They were, for a start, introduced hastily. The press was neither warned nor consulted. Instead the government offered only defensive explanations why it was necessary to withhold such newsworthy information at such a crucial time.

Nor were these explanations always believed. After all, Palmer's censorship office had often proclaimed that the families' feelings were such a high priority that no stories could be written detailing German savagery at the front. Now, however, Pershing had introduced restrictions that seemed likely to trouble many of these families. The initial decision to withhold addresses was a good example. As the *New York Times* pointed out, while this initiative might deny important information to the enemy, it would also "bring distress to the fathers, mothers, or the other kin of all J. B. Smiths in the expeditionary forces, except the nearest of kin of the particular J. B. Smith reported killed, who would have had the news of their sorrow telegraphed to them by the adjutant general of the army."[50]

As the congressional mailbag started to fill with similar complaints, Republicans glimpsed a chance for political advantage. Adopting the mantle of the families' friend, they introduced a series of congressional resolutions calling on the War Department to explain and then overturn its stupid restriction; some even questioned the military's use of security as a justification. "I can see no reason," declared Sen. John W. Weeks (R-MA) in a typical comment, "why it will furnish the Kaiser with any particular information to know that Frank Kelly of Omaha or Frank Kelly of New York was the Frank Kelly killed." The "military information reason," Weeks insisted, was "a flimsy pretext for concealment. It is a case of being arbitrary without the slightest warrant."[51]

As this parting barb suggested, the AEF's attempts to restrict the publication of casualty details raised deeper fears. Was the government trying to conceal the true nature of battlefield reverses in France? Was it using censorship not for legitimate reasons of military security but for more political motives: to cover up mistakes, incompetence, or even defeats?

Such suspicions predated the growing furor over casualties. During the winter of 1917/18, as Palmer's censorship office moved to clamp down hard on all war reporting, its oft-thwarted accredited correspondents had retaliated by creating the War Publicity League. According to its manifesto, the league was founded by the "best newspapermen" from the quality dailies, men like Wythe Williams of the *New York Times* and Herbert Corey whose analytical articles were syndicated across the country. By the turn of the year these journalists had become so exasperated with the AEF's censorship regime that they issued a stinging attack on its excessive stringency. "Censorship should cover real and not imaginary secrets," they declared in a series of public statements. "Honest constructive criticism should be allowed. No political censorship should exist."[52]

When Pershing continued to prove deaf to these pleas, the media's outraged response was predictable. A newspaper like the stately *New York Times* was not normally a major troublemaker. In 1918 it was neither vehemently opposed to the Wilson administration nor a major critic of the war effort. But it was increasingly irritated with Pershing's media policies, which had already seen Williams, its accredited correspondent, expelled for publishing a stinging assault on censorship in *Collier's* magazine.[53] And Pershing's casualty restrictions were the final straw. "To suppress legitimate news," the *Times* editorialized on April 4, "and to hide or withhold losses, denying relatives even the names of those who fall in battle, would be to foster apathy about the cause for which America is fighting, to provoke sedition among enemy aliens, and to encourage pacifists to renew their agitation for a negotiated peace. There is one thing that the most patriotic Americans will not stand—an arbitrary and stupid censorship."[54]

The *New York Times* was not an isolated voice. Numerous other newspapers, senior Republican leaders, and Creel's CPI all agreed that Pershing's casualty restrictions were worse than stupid; they were also bad propaganda. According to these voices, the public was tough enough to handle the realities of war. Moreover, they argued, the government had a duty to educate Americans about the true nature of the German beast. If it failed in this task—if, to be precise, it refused to publicize who this brutal enemy had killed, and how—then the home-front support was bound to fade away.[55]

This was not a hypothetical fear. In the spring of 1918, popular morale did seem to be sagging, as demonstrated by the public's appetite for war bonds. Six months earlier, the first two Liberty Loans had been a tremendous success, demonstrating widespread enthusiasm among the citizenry, who clearly wanted to play a tangible role in the war effort. The second loan drive yielded particularly impressive results. "More than nine million subscriptions were received," commented Treasury Secretary William G. McAdoo, "against four million for the first loan." But disillusion soon set in. During the first months of 1918 these bonds started selling below par. This was a clear sign that enthusiasm for the war was waning, especially as McAdoo estimated that the country was, in purely financial terms, nowhere near saturation point.[56]

Many censorship critics concluded that this ebbing support was partly due to the military's efforts to hide the true cost of the fighting. But this was by no means the only factor. In any war, faced with an information vacuum, the press and public tend to speculate, pedaling rumors that invariably err on the side of exaggeration. In the spring of 1918, with the war's outcome hanging precariously in the balance, rumor was particularly rife. At the very start of the Ludendorff Offensive word spread that one Allied army—it was not clear which one—had suffered 250,000 casualties.[57] Amid such slaughter how many Americans had died? A hundred? A thousand? More? No one knew, but those who had an opinion rarely underestimated. And their inflated guesses, which spread rapidly, became yet another charge in the growing indictment list against Pershing's command. "Rumor has many tongues," observed the *New York Times*, adding that the government only had itself to blame for the current bout of speculation. Had the AEF officers devised a sensible media policy, the *Times* explained, they might well have prevented such damaging scuttlebutt. As it was, "a great deal of sorrow would result from this [its current] method of publishing casualties."[58]

Instituting Improvements, 1918

This concerted criticism quickly concentrated the official mind. Within a week Baker issued an important exception to his blanket ban on information being released from Washington. Bowing to intense media pressure, he allowed the War Department to publish casualty figures once again. Then a month later

Pershing reversed course on the publication of addresses in these casualty lists. Faced with a personal intervention from Wilson, he reverted to his earlier, more open, policy—much to the media's relief. "It is hoped," noted the *New York Times*, "that the controversy over casualty lists will clear the air and point the way to an intelligent publicity in the conduct of the war."[59]

This hope was well placed. During the spring and early summer the AEF, learning rapidly from its earlier mistakes, undertook a major effort to improve its media relations. It was greatly helped by the influx of new officers, especially after an ailing Palmer left the press office to become Pershing's roving investigator. His successor was soon able to draw on the know-how of more experienced hands, men like Mark Watson, formerly a reporter on the *Baltimore Sun*, Gerald Morgan, who had covered both the Russo-Japanese War and the big battles of 1914, and Guy Viskniskki, who had recently launched the army's own newspaper, the *Stars and Stripes*. Six months earlier Palmer had instructed his novice censors to err on the side of caution. Now these experienced media hands were more confident about what could safely be passed and more sensitive to reporters' overall needs.[60]

They were also quick to learn from the United States' wartime partners, especially the British. In the past year, the British press office had introduced numerous changes. It now briefed correspondents ahead of engagements so that their copy was informed by the broader strategic context. It also issued more detailed communiqués, including the county names of regiments.[61] Above all, the AEF censors were attracted to the British pooling system, which made sure that reporters were no longer in constant fear of being scooped by a rival who was at another, more newsworthy, part of the long front.[62]

Still, the British model had its limits. The American newspaper industry was much more scattered and diverse than its London-based counterpart. The twenty-five hundred U.S. dailies and more than sixteen thousand weeklies mostly catered to a small, local market.[63] Moreover, their readers, AEF censors concluded, were not satisfied with impersonal narrative; they wanted intimate, human-interest stories.[64] The AEF therefore had to devise new routines to cater to basic American needs. During the spring it accredited more correspondents, while easing the restrictions on visiting correspondents. It also liberalized censorship rules, so that the press could now refer to individual soldiers by name whenever this "materially and obviously" helped the story.[65]

That the AEF was increasingly strung out across a large section of the Western Front soon prompted other changes. By the summer of 1918 more American troops were arriving in France and being sent to the trenches. Some units went to the British sector, while others were fighting with the French, and still others were being concentrated in the new American First Army established on August 10. As the press office recognized, lone correspondents now found it impossible to cover the whole American battlefield experience. Introducing a British-style pooling system was one solution, allowing reporters who went off in different directions to share their findings. An even more groundbreaking idea was to deploy AEF press officers at corps level. These officers could then gather news of the war's big picture, write up their findings as twice-daily press releases, and disseminate them to war correspondents for incorporation into their own dispatches. With big battles looming, this initiative would save the time of busy staff officers, who were often bombarded with similar calls from numerous correspondents. The AEF recognized that some correspondents might recoil at officers doing an important part of their job, but it hoped most could be won over, not least because they would now have more freedom "to watch the larger aspects of the operations and . . . more time to prepare their copy."[66]

These general innovations inevitably impacted on casualty reporting. The more media-savvy officers in AEF censorship office were desperate to distance themselves from the storm caused by Pershing's earlier casualty restrictions. Despite the continued practical difficulties, they worked hard to prepare timely and informative lists for publication. They also moved to loosen up certain casualty guidelines. From that spring, correspondents were allowed to identify dead soldiers in their dispatches, with two provisos: they had to hold their stories for twenty-four hours after the next of kin had been notified, and "some definite good end, such as offering examples of heroism," had to "be served by printing them."[67]

The accredited correspondents were pleased. Most had a keen sense of their domestic audience. They believed that many readers "knew nothing and cared less about strategy or tactics." What they wanted was news about the average fighting man. Often, therefore, reporters "specialized in 'name stuff'": the enormously popular human-interest stories about individual heroes. Now finally, American war correspondents could write such stories about doughboys who had made the ultimate sacrifice for their country.[68]

These improvements did not entirely eradicate tension between the military and media. One new clash erupted in the middle of July when the AEF participated in a vital battle that stopped the final thrust of the Ludendorff Offensive and gave the Allies the initiative for the first time that year. The American units thrown into action alongside the French and British discovered to their cost that the Germans still possessed local air supremacy, deadly machine gunners, and skillfully directed artillery. In the face of the enemy's dogged defense, the doughboys were able to edge slowly forward, but their losses were high. By July 20 the First Division alone had lost 8,365 men, of whom 1,252 were dead—a mauling so bad that it had to be pulled out of the line.[69]

The scale of these new battles soon posed a practical headache. With so many American troops fighting under British and French command, the problem of gathering accurate casualty figures was immense. Nine days into the battle Pershing's command was still unable to furnish Washington with a list of recently dead and wounded—much to the growing irritation of the media and Congress. When Baker testified before Congress on July 26, he was forced to concede to an audience of skeptical legislators that the death rate Pershing had reported so far was a mere "eight per thousand," which some newspapers reported sarcastically as "the lowest rate in the world's history." Baker hastened to explain that the AEF was desperately trying to update this number, but it took time to get accurate figures from all the British, French, and American hospitals along the front.

Once again, however, speculation and distortion quickly filled the gap. The United Press (UP) was the central culprit on this occasion. In a dispatch avidly picked up by the *Washington Times*, it claimed that Pershing had estimated the Aisne-Marne death toll at no less than twelve thousand men—a large number that, as Baker hurried to proclaim, "grossly misinformed the country" and "needlessly distressed" relatives. According to the War Department, this twelve thousand figure was the sum total of all American casualties before the current Marne battle. The *Washington Times* had either been incompetent in not understanding what this amount related to or irresponsible in passing it off as recent losses.

Trying hard to reassert a measure of control over the public debate, Baker promised reporters that he would prod Pershing to provide a timely list of recent victims. "The publication in the United States of small casualty lists coincident with statements of severe fighting," the army Chief of Staff wired the AEF commander on July 30, "has created a feeling of distrust toward the War Department, and there is a general belief we are concealing casualties." Although Pershing privately smarted at the tone of this missive, he soon released more accurate lists. These contained 716 killed and wounded. They were followed by thousands of new names over the next couple of weeks. The War Department tried hard to put a positive gloss on such figures. They were the first "toll of victory in the Marne-Aisne Offensive," according to one of its spokesmen. With the battlefield fighting intensifying, leading legislators also united behind the military men. To the War Department's relief, Congress concluded that the *Washington Times* had indeed been guilty of misrepresentation.[70]

Still, it was another dispiriting controversy. Despite all the military's efforts to improve and innovate, once again a series of practical problems at the front, together with the determination of at least one media outlet to fill an information vacuum, had resulted in a flurry of stories exaggerating the human cost of the war. Yet this episode should not be overplayed. During the summer the general process remained one of progress, which was vital because the AEF was finally poised to enter the war in earnest. In September, it would launch two offensives, at Saint Mihiel and then the Meuse-Argonne, which would be both bloody and grim.

The Murderous Meuse-Argonne, 1918

Saint Mihiel was Pershing's battle. He had long eyed this salient as the perfect place for AEF operations. If all went according to plan, he hoped to push U.S. troops as far as the German fortress at Metz and the iron mines at Briey. By September 12, with more than a half-million troops in place, he was ready. That day, despite the constant rain, which dampened morale and hampered movement, these forces drove forward. Soon, they had captured no less than 450 guns and sixteen thousand prisoners, and all for the loss of just seven thousand of their own men. By the bloody standards of the Western Front, it was an astonishing achievement, but it was also misleading. On September 10 German forces had already received orders to evacuate the salient. The American attack caught some parts of their front without artillery and ammunition, while in other areas the Germans were happy to concede the ground they were planning to give up anyway. As one joke described it, Saint Mihiel was the battle "where the Americans relieved the Germans."[71]

By stark contrast no one coined jokes about the Meuse-Argonne Offensive, which began barely two weeks later. Under pressure from the British and French, who saw Saint Mihiel as a strategic dead end and wanted a concerted Allied attack to exploit growing German weakness, on September 16 Pershing broke off his battle. With Col. George C. Marshall playing a leading role, Pershing then set

Figure 1.1 The government title for this picture was "Streams of Americans in olive drab pouring into the Saint Mihiel salient, pressing the German retreat." Passed by the censor, this was the type of battlefield image the military wanted to project. National Archives 111-SC-1-20903.

about the enormous task of moving hundreds of thousands of men to the new sector almost sixty miles away, using the cover of darkness to deceive the enemy.

As the rain continued to pour, confusion and chaos inevitably set in. By a herculean feat most troops were in position for the start of the attack on September 26. But some had only just made it in time, while many were already tired, even exhausted, by the long trek to their new positions. The terrain only added to their problems. In the east, the Meuse River was impossible to ford. In the west, the Argonne Forest was scarred with deep ravines and prone to dense fogs. The center looked more promising, but here the AEF would have to concentrate its attack in a narrow funnel-like area, which jutted sharply up to the high ground held by the enemy. About the only saving grace was the fact that the German defenders had been weakened by a combination of years of grueling warfare, particularly the recent failure of Ludendorff Offensive, and the rapidly spreading influenza pandemic. But this soon proved scant consolation given the enemy's skillful exploitation of its geographic advantages to create an impressive defensive system bristling with barbed wire, concrete gun emplacements, and three major elaborate strong points. It was a position that Pershing's "open warfare doctrine"—his emphasis on dashing infantry attacks with rifles rather than relying on artillery and the trench—was particularly ill-suited to confront, especially since many of his troops were still learning their trade.

The result was predictable. Insufficient artillery fire support at key points left the American attackers dangerously exposed. Inadequately trained troops tended to bunch together and became easy prey for German machine gunners. To make matters worse, communication and liaison between different units swiftly broke down, which in turn compounded the problem that many divisions had been given overly optimistic, even open-ended, objectives. Perhaps the worst moment came in the Argonne Forest, where the Germans counterattacked the Thirty-fifth (Kansas-Missouri) Division, sparking a panic that swiftly turned into a rout, despite the best efforts of officers like Col. Harry S. Truman, who commanded an artillery battery. Elsewhere, Pershing's men made only limited gains, and nowhere did they penetrate German defenses before September 30, when Pershing called a halt to regroup.

When the attack resumed on October 4 the situation was largely unchanged. The AEF faced another bloody setback on the first day. Almost a week later the combined might of a million men had still been unable to penetrate the Germans' major defensive positions. Only after October 12, when Pershing split his forces into two new armies, led by Bullard and Hunter Liggett, respectively, did the situation start to improve. In early November, with the rain easing, the supply situation less chaotic, and the enemy weakening, the AEF finally started to sweep forward. At last, it breached the German defensive lines and pushed on more than ten miles toward the key town of Sedan astride Germany's east-west railway line.[72]

The cost had been huge. One division lost five thousand men from a German artillery barrage even before it made it to the front line. Another attacked with twelve thousand men, of whom only two thousand returned. In late September alone, the AEF lost, in total, 45,000 men—a figure that was close to some of the worst slaughter at places like Verdun and the Somme. And this was just the first phase of the operation. By October the AEF's medical branch reported that base hospitals were 107.9 percent full. By the end of the offensive, overall casualties had shot up to 122,000, with more than 26,000 killed in action.[73]

Such massive losses seemed likely to have a profound impact on the home front. In private, even the AEF press office was prepared to concede that "there was no glamour to this advance. It was merely a mixture of death, desolation, and drudgery. It held, to the outside observer, few high spots of outstanding heroism, for naturally the progress was at times slow and of a routine character."[74] With the U.S. media publishing increasingly long casualty lists, culminating in 1,453 names in a single day toward the end of October, the slaughter on the Meuse-Argonne seemed likely to have a calamitous effect on popular morale.[75]

A somewhat perverse decision by army Chief of Staff Peyton March threatened to make matters worse. In the middle of October the War Department

Figure 1.2 By contrast, the censor did *not* pass this picture showing American, French, and German graves. National Archives 111-SC-1-23431.

finally received an overdue list of fifteen thousand slightly wounded men. These injuries had been sustained over the past few months, but the AEF had only just gotten around to confirming and then compiling them in publishable form. The problem was how to make them public. The CPI, worried about the impact of suddenly revealing so many names in the press, recommended their publication in a separate pamphlet with a clear explanation. March refused, however. The army had already been burned by allegations that it had been trying to sugarcoat or conceal bad news, and March insisted that this new batch of figures be handled in the usual way. As a result, in the second half of October the public was suddenly faced with an unprecedented list of names in its daily newspapers—the large number victims of the ongoing battle as well as those fifteen thousand who had picked up minor wounds over the summer—and all with just the barest of explanations from the War Department.[76]

Significantly, however, these immense casualty lists struck the home front with a dull muted thud, not an earth-shattering crash. The reasons are instructive. The AEF's improved press office played a major role. Its recent reforms, especially its "very explicit" background briefings and highly "readable" corps-level press releases, "set the pitch" for correspondents' dispatches, by encouraging them to place these battles in their larger context. They also encouraged reporters to emphasize the major obstacles—in terms of terrain, weather, and German defenses—that American troops were struggling against.[77]

Reporters could have rebelled, as they had the previous winter, charging that the military was effectively trying to cover up a major disaster. Crucially, though, the twenty-five accredited correspondents who reported on the Meuse-Argonne campaign had become embedded into the military system, fulfilling Palmer's initial hopes. Indeed, after a year in close day-to-day contact with the AEF, they had become a tame bunch ready to echo the military line and engage in self-censorship. Their handling of the ill-starred Thirty-fifth Division was the perfect illustration. "There was," one of them remarked later, "enthusiastic silence about this. No correspondent wrote, no censor passed, a word." Likewise, although reporters were fully briefed on the demoralizing halt to operations on September 30, none attempted to send home copy that could have been encased beneath sensationalist headlines like YANKS' BIG DRIVE FAILS, OUR BOYS SUFFER BLOODY REPULSE, HEAVY LOSSES. They had now become team players, labeled "helpful" even by Pershing's HQ.[78]

Relying on these stories, newspapers from across the geographic and political spectrum framed the Meuse-Argonne in a way that deadened the impact of the battle's more disastrous episodes. Each day, moreover, news of this big battle competed for space alongside two other significant developments. One was the major Allied offensive along the remainder of the Western Front. In the years since the end of World War I, American historians have been apt to overplay the contribution of their own army to the German defeat in 1918. At the time, newspapers never fell into this trap. All were acutely aware that the British and French were making major strides toward an impending Allied victory. According to the Scripps chain, for instance, the American push in the Meuse-Argonne was just one of fifteen "crowbars" that the Allies were stabbing "deep into vital places in the enemy lines," with the British in the north proving particularly effective at "forcing [the] Huns to quit Belgium." The *New York Herald* similarly boasted coverage that contained stories from every part of the long front—coverage that crucially emphasized that the "Hun defenses . . . , on which he put four years of work and considered impregnable, [were] slowly crumbling under the assaults of British, French, American, and Belgian troops."[79]

Not everyone applauded this cosmopolitanism. At least one American war correspondent, resentful that his copy was not getting the page-one billing he thought it deserved, complained that "news of the Meuse-Argonne seemed buried."[80] For this reporter, editorial calculations back home were undoubtedly frustrating. Yet given the huge American losses, the fact that the press was directing the public's attention toward other, more successful battles, was undoubtedly a major boon during September and October 1918, especially since these victories were fuelling another major story that increasingly dominated the headlines: Germany's decision to sue for an armistice.

After weeks of public haggling over the terms, the decisive moment came on November 9 with Kaiser Wilhelm II's abdication. News of this German revolution, which saw the emergence of a new German republic, seemed to confirm that the United States had achieved one of its central war aims. "Thanks," as one commentator put it, "to Woodrow Wilson." Wilson, after all, had been firm in telling Berlin that he "could not trust the word of those who had hitherto been the masters of German policy." Since the middle of October his public position had been clear: the United States would only accept an armistice from a new democratic government in Germany.[81] Now that this objective had been attained, Wilson was not slow to claim complete vindication. "Everything for which America fought has been accomplished," he declared on November 11, 1918, the day the guns finally fell silent. "It will now be our fortunate duty to assist by example, by sober, friendly counsel, and by material aid in the establishment of just democracy throughout the world."[82]

The Western Front Syndrome, 1919–39

By the time of the armistice, then, the fallen doughboys appeared to have died for a victorious cause. Their sacrifice would also give Wilson the chance at the upcoming Versailles Conference to insure that the world moved forward, to a

new era of international politics where disputes would be resolved through discussion and mediation, not force. If these were indeed the last ever battlefield
dead, then perhaps the cost had not been too exorbitant.

The exact cost remained to be calculated, however. Although the War Department had released large casualty lists throughout the Meuse-Argonne campaign,
within weeks of the armistice Baker and March were hauled before the Senate
Military Affairs Committee to face another grilling on this sensitive issue. The
legislators explained that they were now receiving letters from their constituents
complaining that the military had grossly underreported recent casualties.
Under intense questioning the War Department bosses conceded that only
forty-two thousand of the sixty thousand deaths in France had as yet appeared in
published casualty lists. Baker and March defended this discrepancy by pointing
to all the familiar practical problems, from identifying bodies on the battlefield
to liaising with the British and French, but the senators were skeptical. They had
heard all these excuses before. While prepared to give Baker the benefit of the
doubt when the battles had still been raging, their patience had worn thin.
Republican legislators, emboldened by their recent victory in the midterm elections, were particularly eager to depict these new delays as evidence of gross
incompetence. They also hinted that perhaps something much more sinister
might be at work.[83]

Two months later, their Republicans colleagues in the House of Representatives got the opportunity to fuel the glowing embers of suspicion, after Henry
J. Allen, the recently elected Republican governor of Kansas, made an incendiary speech. Allen had been with the ill-fated Thirty-fifth Division in the
Argonne when it had broken down in the face of stiff German resistance.
Returning home to assume his new office, Allen immediately began to speak
out about the conditions that had "caused the Thirty-fifth Division to suffer
needlessly large casualties." Not that these losses had been accurately reported.
Allen claimed that the Red Cross, for whom he had worked during much of his
time in France, had developed a highly efficient system to "send accurate and
speedy casualty reports" back home. But the War Department, he charged, had
refused to use this Red Cross service "when casualty lists began to grow large,"
because, as one senior officer had told him, such prompt reports "would put
the army in a bad light."[84]

Allen's testimony on Capitol Hill did more than lambast the "pettifogging"
War Department for using every trick to minimize casualties. It also revived a
recently dormant aspect of the public debate: the notion that war is hell. While
the Meuse-Argonne battle was actually being fought, the AEF's censors, working
closely with its embedded accredited correspondents, had presented a deliberately detached and often antiseptic picture of battlefield conditions. The home
front, as a result, had received few stories of the horrific nature of trench warfare,

of blood and guts, mangled limbs, and bloated corpses. Once the censorship had ended, however, the field was open for all those who had witnessed these conditions to deliver speeches, write memoirs, and inspire writers. Governor Allen was in the vanguard of this trend. Gathering together testimony from survivors, he read out countless accounts of doughboys going into battle without proper equipment, or being "mowed down" by their own artillery, or sustaining wounds that were not treated in time. "Imagine the plight of our wounded," one recently returned captain had written to Allen:

> There were 800 at the advanced dressing station; 1,400 more at the triage, just back of the fighting lines. Some were legless; others armless; many with sides torn out by shrapnel. All, practically, were in direst pain. It was bitter cold. The mud was knee-deep. A half sleet, half rain was beating mercilessly. And for thirty-six hours those 2,400 [*sic*] men were compelled to lie there in the mud, unsheltered. We had neither litters on which to lay them or blankets to wrap around them. That was not all. Although winter practically had set in the men had not been issued with heavy clothing.[85]

In the weeks after Allen's explosive testimony, the military top brass launched a concerted effort to respond to these damaging allegations. The Thirty-fifth Division's commanding officer insisted that his losses had actually been "marvelously low." Senior AEF officers, meanwhile, conducted studies of American losses sustained under U.S. and French generals. They reached the conclusion that, for the most part, divisions were "better handled, had less killed, and gained more important results under American command."[86]

Still, the controversy would not die down. Recognizing the enormous damage it could do to his reputation, Pershing moved to mobilize powerful supporters in the press, asking them to go on record in support of the AEF's massive achievements. Perhaps the most prominent was Charles Grasty, a highly experienced war correspondent, who attacked the congressional investigation into the Thirty-fifth Division's collapse on the grounds that it was "endless, fatuous, and disillusioning. The record in gross of the American army," Grasty declared in early 1919, "has been incomparable. The efficient service rendered by it was indisputably necessary to the winning of the war. . . . The fundamental conditions of organizing, supplying, training and fighting a great army," he concluded, "involve mistakes and losses that are inherent in the thing itself. . . . War is waste by its very nature. No man can ever see a battlefield or men in action without carrying away a heavy heart at the wanton destruction of it all."[87]

Grasty's remarks were meant to be helpful, but their tenor pointed to an obvious problem. The war had indeed resulted in a massive loss of human life.

Few firsthand observers had remained unmoved by the appalling destruction they had witnessed all along the front. In the postarmistice environment anyone wishing to write or talk about their experiences no longer faced the censors' blue pencil—or any military intelligence incentive to withhold key details. As a result the American popular discourse inevitably began to focus on the grimmer aspect of the fighting. Even the AEF's supporters were tempted down this route. Many of the first postwar articles and books were written by officers, censors, and correspondents. Although their narratives tended to emphasize the heroic nature of the doughboy experience—their courage, indomitable spirit, and ultimate victory—they could hardly avoid discussing the gruesome nature of what even Palmer described as "the most terrible of all wars." Before long, moreover, these sympathetic memoirists were superseded by John Dos Passos, E. E. Cummings, William March, and other disillusioned writers who were not shy about trying to "expose the war" in all its bloody horror. They also attacked the generals who had ruthlessly sent thousands to their death and "then tried to hide the truth about their demise."[88]

Such antiwar writings struck the public with greater force because of a growing disillusionment with the political goals for which the doughboys had apparently fought and died. By the summer of 1919 Wilson's elaborate promises about the war's noble aims were clearly foundering against the messy compromises negotiated at the Versailles Conference. Progressives, in particular, thought the treaty's terms far too harsh—"enough to chill the bones of the world," as one of them put it. Wilson retaliated by pointing to his central achievement: a League of Nations. This new organization, he declared in a speech at an AEF cemetery in France, "is the covenant of governments that these men shall not have died in vain."

Back home a significant minority was unconvinced that the League should be the central monument to the war dead. In the Senate, which had to ratify the treaty, skeptics were particularly active. Wilson refused to compromise, though. Instead, in a nationwide speaking campaign, he sought to turn the public against his congressional critics. Exhausted by the effort, he suffered a massive stroke. Unwilling to accept the "reservations" suggested by his political foes, he watched helplessly as the Senate voted down the treaty. Even some of Wilson's erstwhile supporters now turned his language against him. They argued that the failure of his liberal internationalist agenda meant that the dead had indeed died in vain.[89]

Soon after the armistice, then, the dominant view about casualties was transformed. According to the new conventional wisdom, the human cost of the war had been far too high—in fact probably far higher than the government, which had often been accused of fiddling the figures, had been prepared to admit. These lives, moreover, had been squandered for a set of grandiose war aims that had never been achieved. They had also been sustained in combat conditions that were truly appalling. Small wonder that a sense of "never again" permeated American attitudes toward overseas intervention for the next twenty years.

Americans certainly did not forget their war dead. During the 1920s thousands mourned at the Tomb of the Unknown Soldier, applauded efforts to create massive monuments near the sites of the French battlefields, and cheered on the Gold Star Mothers, who finally got Congress to fund widows' trips to France to visit their husbands' graves.[90] Mindful of the war's huge human toll, they also joined peace movements, supported diplomatic efforts to ban war, and endorsed congressional investigations into arms manufacturers, those infamous "merchants of death" who benefited financially from the human tragedy of war. In 1936, at a time when Adolf Hitler was rearming in Germany, Benito Mussolini had conquered Abyssinia, and Japan had made its first inroads in China, the dominant public mood was revealed by one of the very first straw opinion polls. This found that 95 percent of Americans adamantly opposed to staying out of any future conflict.[91]

Thus the central impact of the World War I casualty controversy came not when the climactic battles still raged. During the fall of 1918 censorship was too tight, the correspondents too tame, and the battles over too swiftly for the casualty debate to do any real damage to the public's support for this war effort. Over time, however, the situation changed. Politicians questioned how the casualties were reported, numerous writers focused on the more grisly aspects of Western Front conditions, and the noble aims for which so many doughboys were supposed to have died came to naught. In this new environment, the memory of the war dead began to exert a powerful hold on public opinion, and by extension U.S. foreign policy.

This was a crucial development because the armistice of 1918 proved to be just that: a mere ceasefire in what some historians have dubbed a thirty-year war. By the late 1930s both Europe and Asia were again plunging headlong toward an even bloodier conflagration that Americans wished to avoid. Franklin D. Roosevelt, the president after 1933, had served as Wilson's assistant secretary of the navy during World War I. He now summed up the prevailing mood when recalling a visit to the Western Front: "the blood running from the wounded," the "men coughing out their gassed lungs," "the dead in the mud," and "two hundred limping, exhausted men come out of line—the survivors of a regiment of one thousand that went forward forty-eight hours before." "I have seen war," Roosevelt declared in 1936. "I hate war." Hence, in seven simple words one of America's greatest presidential publicists embodied the sense of "never again" that was the main consequence of America's first modern casualty controversy.[92]

2

Bad News in the "Good War"

World War II, 1941–1943

In a nation so haunted during the 1920s and 1930s by the Western Front casualties, World War II ultimately became a surprisingly popular conflict for the United States. In fact, it is widely remembered as the "good war" fought by the "greatest generation"—a war so different to the awful trench slaughter that preceded it, not to mention the "bad" conflict in Vietnam that came after.

The reasons for this war's domestic appeal are not difficult to fathom. Pearl Harbor immediately cemented a sense of national unity. After December 7, 1941, the "date that will live in infamy," as Roosevelt immediately dubbed it, few Americans denied that their Axis enemies were the very embodiment of evil: the perpetrators of unprovoked attacks and unprecedented atrocities. Nor, as the fight back began, could many doubt that the American war effort was a tremendous success story. On the battlefield the military enjoyed a string of impressive victories from the low point of the summer of 1942 to the unconditional surrender of Germany and Japan in the spring and summer of 1945. At home Roosevelt's efforts to make the United States "the arsenal of democracy" also brought the country out of its decade-long economic slump, as war orders flooded in to many sectors of the economy. "War is hell," historian Mark H. Leff has observed. "But for millions of Americans on the booming home front, World War II was also a hell of a war."[1]

Yet it is important to remember that even during this good war the public received its fair share of bad news. There were the all too numerous cases of casualties sustained by "friendly fire"; the moments of battlefield stalemate, such as the protracted Italian campaign during the grueling winter of 1943/44; the periods of anxiety waiting for the risky invasion of Europe before D-Day in June 1944; and above all, the stiff reverses at Kasserine Pass, in the skies over Germany, or during the opening stages of the Battle of the Bulge. Back home the worst news of all was undoubtedly the dreaded condolence letter, received by the relatives of nearly three-hundred thousand military personnel who fell fighting the Axis.

Despite the pro-war consensus forged by Pearl Harbor, the Roosevelt admin-istration had good reason to fear the domestic impact of all this bad news. Before the Japanese attack the country had been fundamentally divided about the wisdom of sending another generation of American troops overseas, largely because of lingering memories of the earlier carnage on the Western Front. For much of the war, Roosevelt and his senior advisers still fretted that the post–Pearl Harbor unity was fragile: Would the public stoically accept the large losses needed to defeat the Axis? Especially when casualties accompanied defeats, set-backs, or chaotic mess-ups, would the result be a bout of deep defeatism, leading to calls for some form of negotiated peace? Or perhaps, conversely, the public was too distant from the war, too ignorant of the issues at stake, and, crucially, too complacent about the large sacrifices needed to defeat the Axis.

Ultimately none of these fears were fully justified, but even during the long years of the good war casualty reporting sparked a series of major controversies. Some stemmed from the need to respond to these perceived public opinion problems, which prodded certain officials toward the treacherous territory of trying to connect casualty reporting to the government's broader propaganda objectives. Others were related to the unprecedented nature of the fighting, which presented a new set of practical problems that had not been part of the earlier World War I experience. This, after all, was a truly global conflict, with the military strung out across various theaters, which made compiling figures much more difficult. The United States was increasingly entangled with Allies, which meant that coordination with the British and Dominion governments was essential. Its leaders also faced new forms of warfare, especially air power, which created its own set of new headaches. This chapter explores these prob-lems during the period of defeat and preliminary offensives between 1941 and 1943; chapter 3 takes up the victorious campaigns in Europe and Asia during 1944 and 1945.

Casualties and the Tortuous Path to War, 1939–41

At first glance the United States' tortuous path to war in 1941 appears uncannily similar to the events between 1914 and 1917. Indeed, just like Wilson a genera-tion before, Roosevelt's first instinct when the new European war erupted in September 1939 was to assert American neutrality, largely because he was acutely aware that the public, as in 1914, was determined to stay out of this new bout of Old World slaughter. Like Wilson, Roosevelt then found neutrality impossible to maintain. After more than two years, and prodded by a major act of aggression, he therefore took the United States to war on the side of Britain and against the Germans, Japanese, and Italians.

Yet on close inspection the differences between the two presidents were marked. In stark contrast to Wilson, who had generally shared the antiwar neutralism of most of his compatriots, Roosevelt was always far more certain about the issues at stake. From an early date he thought that Hitler was a "madman." In the wake of the führer's aggressive blustering during the Munich crisis in 1938, FDR became firmly convinced that the Nazi leader could not be appeased. He therefore began, secretly at first, to align himself with Britain and France. When war erupted in September 1939 he moved to make sure that these two countries would have access to American materials on a cash-and-carry basis. After the fall of France in June 1940, when an embattled Britain increasingly lacked either the cash to pay for American largesse or the shipping to carry it across the Atlantic, Roosevelt moved into the breach. While lend-lease provided weapons, the U.S. Navy helped to convoy them to their British destination.

In Asia too Roosevelt was far from neutral. His response to the outbreak of the Sino-Japanese war in 1937 was to talk publicly of the need to "quarantine" aggressors. Initially this thinly veiled attack on Japan was merely a presidential effort to find a "new concept for preserving peace," and Roosevelt was not yet ready to consider anything so bold as trade sanctions. But as Japan's war in China became ever more brutal, he began to flex America's considerable economic muscle, starting with the extension of loans to China in December 1938 and ending with the Japanese oil embargo in August 1941. The latter was a fateful decision that ultimately pushed the Japanese toward the even more fateful move to seize regions like the oil-rich Dutch East Indies, covering their new conquests by trying to destroy the American fleet at Pearl Harbor.[2]

In a country still haunted by the memory of the vast Western Front casualties, Roosevelt's early moves were deeply controversial. Throughout the 1930s isolationism remained the dominant creed. Most Americans believed their country was protected from the wars unfolding in Europe and Asia by the impregnable Atlantic and Pacific Oceans. Convinced by numerous books and a major congressional investigation that scheming British propagandists and profit-seeking capitalists had dragged the United States into war in 1917, they were eager to avoid anything that would drag them into another fight.

World War I was thus uppermost in the American mind when another European conflict began in September 1939. Newspapers from across the political spectrum immediately rekindled memories of the earlier bloodshed, when millions of lives had been expended in attritional battles that had scarcely moved the front line forward. Some even ran interviews with veterans who emphasized that the United States should have nothing to do with this new bout of Old

World slaughter. Others printed cartoons of "a pro-war activist being haunted by a skeletal World War I doughboy."[3]

With the Western Front syndrome looming so large, few Americans were prepared for the abrupt change in the nature of warfare that came in May–June 1940, when Hitler's stunning blitzkrieg rapidly defeated France. Within the space of just six weeks, the European balance of power was completely overturned—and with it the strong American faith in its own invulnerability.[4] Small wonder that polls soon detected a major weakening of some of the key isolationist tenets, including a sharp increase in those believing they would be personally affected by the war and a major spike in popular support for sending military aid to Britain.[5]

Still, hardcore isolationists were by no means defeated. Instead, they now began to organize in earnest. During the fall of 1940 America First, their major mouthpiece, expanded so rapidly that it soon boasted more than eight-hundred thousand members in 450 chapters. It also began to churn out publicity material aggressively calling on the United States to stay out of a war that was none of its business. Isolationists certainly did not think their country should fight alongside a British Empire that was perhaps no better than Nazi Germany. Nor did they think that Americans should be tricked into war by a president whose bid for an unprecedented third term in 1940 was proof of his dictatorial tendencies.[6]

The election campaign of 1940, fought at a time when British survival hung in the balance, also gave the isolationists hope. By inclination the two candidates were interventionists, but significantly they both ran campaigns that reflected, and in turn deepened, the nation's strong antiwar consensus. Wendell Willkie was the more vigorous and vehement. As he barnstormed across the country, the Republican candidate claimed that a vote for Roosevelt would be a vote for placing another American generation on troopships bound for another European slaughter. Thrown on the defensive, and slipping in the polls, Roosevelt retaliated with a bald promise. In public he had long proclaimed his hatred of war. Now with election day looming, Roosevelt sought to reassure the electorate that he would not mire the United States in another European bloodbath. "Your boys," he told a large audience in Boston on October 30, "are not going to be sent into any foreign wars."[7]

In the aftermath of Roosevelt's election victory, American opinion remained remarkably stable. For the next thirteen months a clear and consistent majority continued to support all aid to Britain, even at the risk of war. But an even larger number was still firmly opposed to the United States' full and formal involvement in the fighting. The fear of large American casualties was undoubtedly a major reason behind this widespread determination not to send another AEF to Europe—a fear that Roosevelt's stark campaign promise had clearly reinforced. Beyond this simple calculation, casualties had surprisingly little impact on the ongoing tussle throughout 1941 between Roosevelt and the isolationists, even though both sides had very real hopes and fears about exploiting different casualty controversies for their own ends.

Roosevelt's principal concern was simple enough. While he moved swiftly after his reelection to strengthen the American commitment to Britain, unveiling his lend-lease proposal in December, he knew that the isolationists would try to tag him as a warmonger. He was therefore extremely careful to sell lend-lease as a war-avoidance measure. "The people of Europe who are defending themselves do not ask us to do their fighting," he told millions of Americans glued to their radio sets at the end of 1940:

> They ask us for the implements of war, the planes, the tanks, the guns, the freighters which will enable them to fight for their liberty and for our security. . . . There is no demand for sending an American Expeditionary Force outside our own borders. There is no intention by any member of your Government to send such a force. You can, therefore, nail any talk about sending armies to Europe as deliberate untruth. Our national policy is not directed toward war. Its sole purpose is to keep war away from our country and our people.[8]

Isolationists, however, utterly distrusted anything that emanated from Roosevelt's lips. In their eyes lend-lease was simply a transparent ploy to give the president the unprecedented power to "wage undeclared wars for anybody, anywhere in the world." As the Senate hearings got underway, the invective on both sides reached a crescendo. On January 12, 1941, Sen. Burton K. Wheeler (D-MT) told a large radio audience that lend-lease "will plough under every fourth American boy"—a remark that so infuriated Roosevelt that he told reporters it was "the most dastardly, unpatriotic thing that has ever been said. Quote me on that."[9]

Wheeler's attempt to frame the debate around massive prospective casualties has often been noted by historians. Less well known, however, is the postscript that unfolded two weeks later when Henry L. Stimson appeared in Congress to testify in favor of lend-lease. The venerable Stimson was a veteran Republican who had held senior cabinet posts in two previous Republican administrations. Roosevelt had recruited him to head the war department after the fall of France, in an effort give his government a bipartisan complexion. Now Stimson intended to use his allotted time on the Hill on January 29 to demonstrate how lend-lease would bring more order to the United States' military mobilization, but the isolationists soon ambushed him.

That day numerous newspapers carried an AP story detailing a new dog tag that every soldier would have to wear. A few months earlier, it reported, the War

Department had placed an order for four million of these tags, which contained a novel system for storing and retrieving vital information about each soldier that would hopefully speed up the whole process of casualty identification. At the time, the military had considered this order a routine affair, on a par with purchases of mess kits, razors, and underwear. In the context of the lend-lease debate, however, the AP revelation suddenly became explosive.[10]

When he arrived on Capitol Hill, Stimson immediately faced barbed questions about these "death tags." Isolationist senators emphasized that four million was an exorbitant number. Congress, after all, had not authorized an army anywhere near this size. Was the Roosevelt administration secretly planning for a large military force it would soon send to Europe? Or perhaps this story was even more sinister. As isolationist senators were quick to ask: What about other rumors that the president had recently asked the Red Cross to prepare four million surgical dressings by the spring. Was the government actually planning for casualties at this level?

Nonplussed by this aggressive line of questioning, Stimson's initial response was to try a feeble joke. The new tags, he quipped, were "mere pieces of paper" that soldiers would probably roll into cigarettes the minute they were sent to the rear. Isolationists failed to see the funny side. "The placing of a government order for four-and-a-half million identification tags to be placed on disabled or wounded men," declared Sen. Wayland Brooks (R-IL), "clarifies the government's plans and intentions more forcibly than any or all the evidence that will be obtained by questioning witnesses." Brooks, who had been wounded seven times during World War I, then launched into a long disquisition about the carnage he had personally witnessed on the Western Front. But it was his colleague, Sen. Hiram Johnson (R-CA), who asked perhaps the most germane question: "How many coffins have been ordered?"[11] At a time when the War Department was worried by "lurid" rumors "that the army had purchased 1.5 million coffins for immediate delivery," this was a question that Stimson desperately wanted to quash before the debate careened totally out of control.[12]

Ultimately, however, the lend-lease debate rarely strayed too far from the narrow parameters set by the administration, and in March Congress finally passed Roosevelt's bill by healthy margins.[13] For isolationists this outcome was a disaster, mostly because they distrusted the motives behind the legislation but partly because their allegations about massive prospective casualties had not found much resonance.

Why did this argument fail to resonate? Stimson's own congressional performance offers one clue. Although briefly caught off balance by the "death tag" allegations, the veteran war secretary personified the government's strengths: steady, serious, and above all a symbol of bipartisanship. Crucially, other leading moderate Republicans also endorsed Stimson's testimony. Willkie was the most conspicuous. The ex-candidate now dismissed his previous jibes at the president as mere campaign rhetoric. He then launched into a stinging attack on the isolationist case. "If the Republican Party . . . makes a blind opposition to this bill," Willkie declared, "and allows itself to be presented to the American people as the isolationist party, it will never again gain control of the American government." Reluctantly agreeing with this logic, even many Republican skeptics decided to rally behind lend-lease, especially after its passage was assured.[14]

These Republicans were not merely being public spirited. They also recognized that the isolationist attacks on lend-lease did not have all that much traction outside the capital. The claims about the likelihood of millions of American casualties were a case in point. They probably reinforced the fears of those already committed to the isolationist cause—and they were certainly reiterated endlessly by isolationist newspapers like the *Chicago Tribune*. But they patently failed to convince the majority of Americans who were already firmly committed to providing Britain with all possible support. This at least was the conclusion of an important opinion poll by George Gallup.

In May 1941 Gallup conducted an intriguing survey to ascertain if "the opinion of those American families in which there are sons and brothers, or husbands, of draft age—families which would be called on to make the most direct sacrifices if the nation got into war"—were any different from the rest of the nation. If the isolationists' talk about government plans to purchase millions of coffins, death tags, and surgical dressings had stuck, then such families, recoiling from the prospect of losing their loved ones, might well be far more isolationist. Significantly, they were nothing of the sort. Gallup found little difference between this "special group" and the broader public. In both categories, more than 60 percent thought the United States should help Britain even at the risk of getting dragged into the fighting.[15]

This persistent support for the British cause was partly a reflection of the public's deep-seated fear of Nazi Germany. It also stemmed from a growing sympathy for those British civilians who were suffering under the blitz launched by the Luftwaffe during the winter of 1940/41, as German air power obliterated large chunks of cities like London, Coventry, and Plymouth.

The blitz was a radio story. It was relayed back to the United States by a new breed of journalist, men like Edward Murrow and Eric Sevareid, whose familiar voices dissected each day's raid in chilling detail, recounting their own experiences of living in a city where any building, any person, could suddenly become a casualty of a German bomb.[16] Yet ultimately it was also a story whose impact on American opinion was distinctly limited, much to the surprise of those who remembered the public's emotional response to civilian casualties in 1916 and 1917.

Before the outbreak of the European war isolationists had certainly dreaded the prospect of a public so disturbed by such news that it would demand direct American intervention. The "one condition" that would push the United States directly in the fighting, Herbert Hoover had fretted in February 1939, would be "if wholesale attacks were made upon women and children by deliberate destruction of cities from the air." Significantly what the former president had found so troubling, the current incumbent had welcomed as a possible way of rallying the country. As Roosevelt had remarked to King George VI during his royal visit in the summer of 1939, "If London was bombed USA would come in."[17]

In reality, the public, while sympathizing with Britain's plight, never became emotional enough about civilian casualties to demand direct U.S. involvement in the war. Indeed, during 1940 and 1941 most Americans were surprisingly inured to the death and destruction unleashed by the Nazi war machine. This was most strikingly true in the Atlantic, where the U.S. Navy gradually began fighting German U-boats in order to guarantee that lend-lease material arrived safely in Britain. Even when American ships were hit, the public scarcely reacted. Alan Barth, a Treasury official whose opinion surveys reached the Oval Office, summed up the mood after the unprovoked sinking of the American merchant ship *Robin Moor* in June 1941. Barth concluded that the public now "expected" such incidents. "They arouse apprehension," he observed, "but not indignation. The press, and presumably the public too, asks about each of them only whether it is the particular 'incident' which will touch off the shooting. It was freely predicted a few years ago," Barth continued,

> that American indignation would be beyond control if great cities and civilian populations were indiscriminately bombed. Yet the air attacks on London have evoked little more than pious regrets and philosophical reflections on the military potency of the airplane. Through a long process of insulation . . . American sensibilities have become calloused to the acceptance of horrors. The public has been reduced to a condition of moral and emotional anesthesia.[18]

It would, in fact, take a far bigger incident—and a large loss of American life—before this anesthetic finally wore off. The Battle of the Atlantic, which the U.S. Navy was gradually fighting with greater vigor during the summer and fall, would not suffice, despite Roosevelt's depiction of German U-boat attacks as an integral part of the Nazi effort "toward creating a permanent world system based on force, on terror, and on murder."[19] When Hitler then decided to turn east in June 1941, launching 121 divisions against the Soviet Union, this Nazi threat seemed briefly to recede, although the German blitzkrieg was soon making great

Figure 2.1 The Japanese attack on Pearl Harbor transformed the American debate on casualties. National Archives 80G 19948.

strides toward Moscow. But it was in the Pacific, not Europe, that the transformative event came. In the wake of the American oil embargo the Japanese leaders faced a stark choice: they could either retreat from China, giving up their vision of an East Asian new order, or they could push forward, conquering more territory, including oil-rich areas like the Dutch East Indies.

On December 7 Japan struck. Its surprise attack on Pearl Harbor sank or damaged eighteen U.S. naval vessels, destroyed 180 aircraft, and killed 2,403 men while wounding another 1,178. Within hours American isolationism was dead. Within days Roosevelt successfully got Congress to declare war on Japan, while Hitler and Mussolini obligingly stood by their Axis ally and declared war on the United States. From now on the public debate over casualties would unfold in a very different context.

Reporting Casualties at a Time of Defeat, 1941–42

As well as slaying isolationism, the sudden Japanese attack was the first American censorship problem of this new world war, and the military's knee-jerk reaction was highly revealing. Determined to prevent the Japanese from acquiring hard evidence about the success of their operation, and worried about the impact on domestic morale if they were too honest, military leaders clamped down hard. The navy immediately stopped all radio-telephone transmissions from Hawaii, even cutting off a UP news alert halfway through, while the army censored the mail. The government's first communiqué was also suitably sketchy, only confirming the loss of an "old battleship and destroyer" and insisting that the Japanese had come off worse. When newspapers like the *New York Times* got hold of the hard facts that suggested a much bigger disaster, the Navy Department quickly prevailed on them not to publish.[20]

The result was eerily familiar. In the absence of hard official information, the press and public were quick to speculate about the extent of the losses. The War Department was immediately inundated with anxious inquiries from relatives of soldiers dotted across the globe who fretted that their loved ones had been injured or killed.[21] In the next few days rumors then abounded that the scale of the disaster was much bigger than the government was prepared to admit. In New York City a "whispering campaign" was soon under way "to the effect that 1,500 bodies had arrived without coffins from Hawaii"—an "utterly false" campaign, the War Department briskly pointed out, not only in terms of the numbers of victims but also because the U.S. military always "accords its honored dead the honor and dignities rightfully due the defenders of our Nation."[22] But the speculation did not end. "One of the biggest yells about Pearl Harbor, when it is aired," claimed Walter Winchell, the popular broadcaster, on January 5, "will be the revelation that the shortage of medical supplies there necessitated an over amount of amputations among the casualties."[23]

Scurrying to respond to this damaging scuttlebutt, Roosevelt adopted a calming tone at his weekly press conference. The army and navy, he reassured reporters, would release all relevant military information, as long as it was accurate and did not give aid and comfort to the enemy. In the middle of December, Navy Secretary Frank Knox, another Republican recruited to give the administration a bipartisan complexion, then toured Hawaii and returned to offer his own soothing impressions. Although Knox was still vague about details, most newspapers applauded his candid willingness to admit that the navy had been caught unaware. "The losses which he documented," according to one administration media survey, "were less than had been feared. And, while there was some tendency to wonder about the damage undisclosed by the Knox catalogue, the emphasis in news stories and in editorial comment was placed mainly on the heroism of American sailors and officers."[24]

It was not until February 23 that the government offered any hard facts about Pearl Harbor. That evening, in a fireside chat that drew a staggering audience of 78 percent of all American households, Roosevelt himself revealed the true extent of American deaths on Hawaii, adding for good measure an attack on all the recent speculation. "You and I," he declared,

> have the utmost contempt for Americans who, since Pearl Harbor, have whispered or announced "off the record" that there was no longer any Pacific Fleet—that the fleet was all sunk or destroyed on December 7— that more than a thousand of our planes were destroyed on the ground. They have suggested slyly that the Government has withheld the truth about casualties—that eleven or twelve thousand men were killed at Pearl Harbor instead of the figures as officially announced. They have even served the enemy propagandists by spreading the incredible story that shiploads of bodies of our honored American dead were about to arrive in New York Harbor to be put into a common grave.[25]

In launching this public attack Roosevelt was, to some extent, still fighting old battles. His principal target remained the small number of isolationists who had yet to repent—politicians like Wheeler who had been telling reporters, "off the record, that 'we no longer have a Pacific fleet,'" while also claiming "a casualty list of twelve thousand" that was the fault of "lend-lease aid sent to Britain." Yet Roosevelt also had a deeper purpose in mind: to deter mainstream newspapers from turning to Axis sources—something that happened with surprising frequency.[26]

Media bosses, for their part, were obviously well aware of the risks of publishing enemy figures. In their view, repeating what the Germans or Japanese were saying was a desperate last resort, especially at a time when the most famous of these propagandists was Joseph Goebbels, the blackest practitioner of this dark art. They continued to opt for this last resort, however, because of the paucity of news coming from their own government. They also bristled at Roosevelt's attack, which they considered well wide of the mark. The more pertinent question, they thought, was why their own government remained so reluctant to provide them with hard information.

The answer stemmed partly from the disaster unfolding in the Pacific, where Pearl Harbor was merely the prelude. In the next few weeks the Japanese rapidly overran Guam, Wake Island, and Hong Kong. In February Britain's vital base at Singapore fell, followed by the loss of Java and Rangoon in March. Two months later the Philippines finally surrendered after much bitter fighting, and the surviving U.S. troops were herded off on the horrific Bataan death march.[27]

The nature of these defeats made it extremely difficult for the government to provide the press and public with war news in general and casualty details in particular. For one thing, the sheer geographic scale of the Pacific theater— which stretched from China in the north to the shores of Australia in the south, from India's borders in the west to the American base at Midway in the east—created enormous logistical problems that complicated, hampered, and above all delayed the flow of accurate information.

Even more salient was the basic fact that Japan was on the offensive throughout this vast region. It controlled the battlefield. While the U.S. military could tabulate how many men had failed to return from abandoned islands like the Philippines, only the Japanese had a firm sense of how many were dead, wounded, or captured. Inevitably, therefore, official American figures were tentative—and swollen with huge numbers of MIA whose fate was unclear.[28]

In the Pacific, moreover, the navy was the principal American actor in the unfolding drama, first as the victim at Pearl Harbor and then as the avenger in two close-run battles in the Coral Sea and at Midway during May and June. This was highly significant because the navy's restrictive approach to releasing information was notorious. Admiral Ernest King, its chief, set the tone. A tough, abrasive character, King was described even by one of his own family members as the "most even-tempered man in the navy. He is always in a rage." In the first months of the war King's legendary ire was often reserved for reporters who attempted to publish anything he deemed could help the enemy—so much so that, as one in-joke put it, his "idea of war information was that there should be just *one* communiqué. Some morning we would announce that the war was won and that we had won it."[29]

Yet there was always much more to the navy's reluctance to divulge hard information than its boss's uncompromising personality. Back in 1917 senior admirals had been much more hawkish about censoring information than even the hard-nosed Pershing. They had been especially fearful that if German U-boats got a sense of when, where, and how many American ships were about to sail, then they would have a massive advantage in the deadly game of hide-and-seek on the high seas.

If anything, security during the perilous months of 1942 was even more vital. The Pacific fleet had already been mauled at Pearl Harbor. Its battered remnant now faced the risky task of trying to prevent further Japanese advances. As battles like Pearl Harbor and Midway demonstrated, modern technology meant that the two sides invariably engaged each another at such long distances that neither side had a clear sense of how many losses they had inflicted on the other. Small wonder that King and his Pacific commanders were as determined as their World War I counterparts not to give out any information that might give the enemy any sort of edge.[30]

The upshot was a highly restrictive casualty reporting policy. In mid-December 1941 an AP investigation found that the army and navy had no plans to announce official lists of wounded or dead, "except probably in case of major figures." Roosevelt, it added, while "not specifically object[ing] to local publication of local casualties obtained from next of kin," hoped that newspapers would desist from publishing casualty statewide lists. The situation scarcely improved in the new year. The White House persisted with its preference for having casualty lists published only in local newspapers. The two services were also at loggerheads over a system for announcing cumulative casualty totals. By the summer the bureaucratic snarl-up was so bad that the government had still to release any "overall national figures."[31]

The press and public were outraged. According to a *Fortune* survey, newspaper support for the administration's foreign policy dipped below 50 percent only on two occasions between July 1941 and July 1942, first with the fall of Java in March 1942 and then because of "disapproval over news suppression" a month later. Editorial writers, another media analyst concluded in the middle of April, were particularly upset "at the navy's belated announcement of [the] sinking of aircraft tender *Langley*, naval tanker *Pecco*, and destroyer *Peary*" in the Java battle, and the absence of information about "our losses generally."[32]

The populace echoed these sentiments. Before Roosevelt's February fireside chat, 57.8 percent of those surveyed thought "that some important portion of the story about Pearl Harbor [was] still being held back, while 59.5 percent [felt] that important news from the Philippines remains undisclosed." Afterwards, officials monitoring the popular mood continued to record complaints "that the government deliberately withheld bad news." They also discovered that such public complaints were "directed especially toward the prohibition against the publication of news about casualties or maritime losses."[33]

It was in this context that the media, rather than heed Roosevelt's warnings about the perils of reiterating Axis propaganda, continued to print enemy figures, with alarming results. In the first months after Pearl Harbor media surveys still detected "a marked disposition on the part of the American press and radio" to use official German news agency sources, which in turn "conveyed to the public the impression that losses far greater than those officially admitted by the United States were sustained in the Pacific." In March the situation was particularly bad. In private, officials complained about the "gratuitous repetition of the Axis 'line' by [the] American news media." In their view the AP was the main culprit, especially after it printed Japanese claims that ninety-three thousand Dutch and five thousand British and American troops had surrendered on Java.[34]

As the military's restrictive policy persisted into the summer of 1942, the public's frustration grew. Opinion polls revealed that almost one-third of Americans were highly dissatisfied with the amount of war news they got in their newspapers and on the radio. "Individuals who wanted more information about 'the progress of the war,'" reported one official public opinion expert, "were hungry not only for news of how U.S. troops are faring in different parts of the world, but also for analyses of the probable length of the war and the prospects for victory. They were insistent that the treatment be frank. They wanted the complete war picture—in the words of one respondent, 'Full discussion of all facts—good, bad, or indifferent.'"[35] It was a hunger that the government would soon try to satiate, but first its military leaders had to decide how to take the war to the enemy.

Roosevelt, Casualties, and American Strategy, 1941–43

Roosevelt was deeply disturbed by these casualty controversies. While many Americans griped about the overly sanitized nature of the war news, he often fretted that the public remained casualty sensitive. He even suspected that there was an upper limit, albeit fairly vague, beyond which the nation would not go in sacrificing its young men, whatever the cause.

Before Pearl Harbor, of course, this limit had basically been zero: the public had wanted no troops, and hence no casualties, overseas. In this constraining environment Roosevelt had sought to use lend-lease to make the United States the "arsenal of democracy." In his mind the United States' rapidly expanding, mass-producing, and un-bombed economy could churn out thousands of ships, tanks, trucks, and jeeps for the British and later the Soviet Allies, who would use them to do the actual fighting. But it could also do much more: it could innovate, developing a new generation of weapons that would outperform anything the Axis, with its far smaller economic base, could come up with. Roosevelt, as the historian David Reynolds points out, had a vision of "technowar"—a vision of bombers obviating the need for large land armies, or, more broadly, of "massive firepower applied with the intent of minimizing American casualties."[36]

For Roosevelt, Pearl Harbor did nothing to alter the low-casualty appeal of technowar. Throughout the war he would continue to champion the use of airpower over Germany and Japan, which reached its apogee in 1945 with his ultimate technowar project: the atomic bomb. Significantly, Roosevelt also remained leery about using the term "AEF," given the encrusted layers of political controversy that had accumulated around it since 1918. Increasingly too, he was sensitive to the mounting congressional opposition to a large army—opposition that united farm bloc legislators who feared an exodus of farm hands into the military, liberals who fretted about condemning the United States to an excessively militaristic future, and those who simply continued to echo the logic behind Roosevelt's own "arsenal of democracy" concept.[37]

Still, despite all these underlying qualms and complexities, Roosevelt did recognize that Pearl Harbor had removed the public's basic hostility toward sending U.S. troops overseas. Indeed, if Americans had been unwilling to endure any casualties before the Japanese attack, afterwards the limit of their toleration became much higher. In this new permissive environment, Roosevelt became a convert to land power. During the first months of 1942 he moved to increase the army's size, endorsing the War Department's plan to have a force of 3.6 million by the end of 1942, a figure that would more than double for the following year. Crucially, even though Japan was still very much on the offensive, he was also eager to get U.S. ground forces fighting the much stronger German enemy as soon as possible.[38]

Roosevelt was tugged in this direction by alliance politics. With the United States in the war, both the British and the Soviets pushed for some sort of second front, albeit with a crucial difference in emphasis. While Joseph Stalin demanded an immediate invasion of France, Winston Churchill much preferred to probe Germany's supposedly "soft underbelly" in the Mediterranean. Roosevelt quickly agreed with Churchill that a cross-channel invasion was too risky. Anglo-American forces simply lacked the numbers, the air supremacy, and, in the U.S. case, the experience, to launch a successful invasion of France anytime soon. North Africa was a far safer alternative. But even Operation Torch—the codename for the North African invasion planned for November 1942—would test the new U.S. Army to the fullest.[39]

Operation Torch certainly presented immense problems. In Virginia, chaos reigned before the largest invasion force ever to leave American shores finally departed. In "naughty Norfolk," raucous GIs were determined to make the most of their last days of leave. On docksides, the muddled packing of vital equipment created major problems for the future. Once on the high seas, all the ships safely evaded the potent German U-boat menace, but off the North African coast they had to disgorge their men at various locations hundreds of miles apart. The unpredictable November weather added extra anxieties, especially the high Atlantic surf that threatened to complicate the western landings. But the biggest danger of all was the threat of a hostile reception from French forces in Morocco and Algeria, who were commanded by leaders of a Vichy regime allied to the Germans.

Despite these enormous risks, the Torch gamble initially succeeded. Gen. Dwight D. Eisenhower, in his first taste of high-level politics, cut a controversial deal with the Vichy leadership in North Africa, which kept French troops relatively quiescent. Then, in surprisingly cold temperatures compounded by a chilling rain and cloying mud, Eisenhower's troops slogged slowly eastward toward their destination in Tunisia. On arrival, they found a major challenge. Tunisia had become an Axis stronghold, reinforced by a hundred thousand German and Italian troops, many of them veterans. In the middle of February the most fearsome of these enemy units, Erwin Rommel's Afrika Korps, struck at poorly positioned units of the U.S. II Corps at Kasserine Pass. The outcome was an American debacle: an "uncoordinated withdrawal," in the euphemistic description of one officer, which left a vital region in German hands, threatened a major strategic reverse in the whole theater, and resulted in about five thousand American casualties.[40]

Yet unlike the 1942 defeats in the Pacific, the Kasserine setback failed to spark a major home-front controversy about war news and casualty reporting. The military instead handled it in a much smoother fashion, partly because it had enjoyed a year's breathing space since Pearl Harbor, and partly because it had used this precious time to analyze the lessons from previous battles, not just in 1942 but also in 1918.

Learning—and Other Improvements, 1942–43

At this stage of the war, in fact, the U.S. military should have been well placed to handle casualty reporting, for it had already been through the birth pangs associated with establishing a brand new system. In the censorship realm, it was actually something of a wizened veteran who knew all about the pitfalls and opportunities ahead.

During the disastrous first few months after Pearl Harbor, most officers had made policy on the hoof, their restrictive instincts heightened by a real fear that security lapses would doubtless be punished by yet another defeat at the hands of the marauding Japanese. Increasingly, however, as senior generals developed offensive plans, their PR specialists delved back into the past. They were helped by the military's institutions of learning. During the 1920s and 1930s, the Army War College had run courses on censorship with the help of some of the men involved in the successes of 1918. Relying heavily on this institutional memory, the new generation of officers dusted off old systems and implemented what had worked so well before.[41]

On censorship this translated into a new set of guidelines that resurrected the main elements of Palmer's earlier system of press accreditation. Harking back to the Western Front, war correspondents would be granted eating, traveling, and accommodation facilities at the rank of a commissioned officer. In return they would have to pledge to submit their copy to military censors, who would check to see if it included any of the thirteen proscribed topics, from the names of units to the exaggeration of allied activities.[42] As 1918 had also demonstrated, these censors would have to try to be as liberal as possible. In fact, a crucial lesson from the Western Front was the need to construct a smooth relationship with reporters, which meant occasionally relaxing the censorship rules—a lesson that was only sharpened by the constant griping from press and public about excessive restrictions throughout 1942.[43]

Similarly, when it came to casualty reporting, the army vividly recalled all its earlier problems trying to balance the competing demands of families, intelligence officers, and the press. Desperate to prevent a repeat of the unseemly quarrels of 1918, the War Department allowed the press to publish the addresses of all casualties. It also permitted reporters to print the individual names of dead or wounded heroes in their human-interest accounts of the fighting, taking care to extend these fairly liberal guidelines to the new medium of radio, which was where most Americans now got their war news.[44]

While such initiatives were largely a throwback to the past, the military also had to innovate and evolve, for the simple reason that a number of things had changed since World War I. One of the biggest differences was the size of the military bureaucracy. In contrast to the shoestring operation of 1917, by the time of Torch the War Department had been expanding rapidly for almost two-and-a-half years, so rapidly that in the summer of 1941 Roosevelt had given the go-ahead for a massive new construction project. This was the Pentagon, the world's largest office building, which would relocate twenty-four thousand army employees currently scattered across seventeen different buildings into a single structure that contained no less than 3.6 million net square feet of office space.[45]

The large stately rooms inhabited by the new Pentagon's top brass, with impressive vistas overlooking Washington's grand monuments, opened for business exactly a week after the Torch landings. With everyone under the same roof, the army hoped for improved coordination. To this end, senior officers had already been working hard to get their burgeoning bureaucracy toeing the same public line. In the summer of 1942, they had greatly beefed up the Bureau of Public Relations (BPR), headed by Gen. Alexander D. Surles, giving it enhanced authority to stop individual units from releasing unnecessary, exaggerated, or even misleading stories to boost their own profile.[46]

When it came to casualty announcements, the BPR had to liaise with a bewildering array of bureaucratic players. There was the Casualty Section of the Adjutant General's office, which had ultimate responsibility for getting all the facts straight; the Army Service Forces (ASF), which coordinated casualty reports from various battlefronts; the medical section, which treated the wounded in a range of hospitals from the frontline to the United States; and the Dependency Board, which established who should receive relatives' entitlements when soldiers were killed or grievously injured.[47] As the war progressed, these multiple bureaucratic layers could sometimes cause headaches, particularly when casualty information seeped into the public domain via congressional committees whose remit coincided with different components of the Pentagon's sprawling bureaucracy.[48] Yet ultimately, the fact that the army had such a massive support staff did allow it to develop a number of important practical changes.

One early initiative was to enhance communication between wounded soldiers and their relatives. Soon after Pearl Harbor, those family members who received telegrams about a wounded relative "were invited to send a five-word message of cheer to Washington to be transmitted by radio to the casualty." In return, the military wrote progress letters to the next of kin. As the ASF pointed out, this was a massive task undertaking that "required the writing of several thousands of letters per day after a great many casualties had occurred and fifty to one hundred thousand were hospitalized for battle wounds."[49]

Casualties on this scale naturally created big problems. Accuracy was vital, for no one wanted to notify the wrong relatives. So was speed, since no one desired a repeat of vicious public inquests of 1918. As well as the bureaucratization of the whole process, this time the army had another major strength: new technology that promised to remove errors and holdups.

In the first months after Pearl Harbor, overseas armies continued to rely on the radio or cable to relay casualty information back to Washington. At a time of retreat and defeat, though, radio transmission resulted in too many errors. According to one estimate, more than one-quarter of the names and serial numbers sent from various theaters to the capital failed to correspond to War Department records. Determined to release only correct information, the army initially established a special identification unit charged with sifting through all the evidence to piece together the identity of the casualties. Then technology came to its rescue in the guise of a new punch-card system. Where possible these cards, which contained the soldier's details, were compiled in the theater within eight days of the casualty being sustained. They were then flown to Washington, where they "were immediately run through IBM tabulators to automatically produce casualty reports." As the ASF proudly pointed out, these new tabulators could now process about eight hundred casualty reports per hour, "a number which formerly took the efforts of sixteen people working an entire day to transcribe." They also dramatically reduced the number of mistakes in transmitting names and details from distant commands back home to the United States.[50]

If this was technowar applied to its most gruesome aspect, the payoffs promised to be high. In particular, although delays and confusion would never be entirely eliminated, most newspapers were likely to endorse the army's efforts to hasten its casualty reporting operation, especially after January 1943 when the War and Navy departments "relaxed rules on publication of military casualties and advised editors that national roundups would be permitted henceforth."[51] The media would also doubtless applaud the greater bureaucratic support mechanisms that were now in place, in case the new technology did not perform as billed. For those who thought that this grisly task needed a human touch, rather than just impersonal machines or faceless bureaucrats, the army made sure that all casualty totals were released by Stimson, the very dignified, very experienced, and very Republican secretary of war.

Candor—and Its Consequences, 1943

Kasserine turned out to be the first major test of this system. In North Africa, army censors were quick to give reporters a fairly wide degree of latitude to send home stories that, far from covering up the debacle, painted the setback in fairly stark terms. Ernie Pyle, fast becoming the nation's most influential and revered war correspondent, set the tone. Having established a close relationship with officers at all levels, Pyle cabled out copy that made no effort to hide what had happened. The battles culminating in the reverse at Kasserine Pass, Pyle declared in his widely syndicated column, were a "damned humiliation" that ended in a "complete melee."[52]

In Washington, the War Department was similarly downbeat. On February 12 Stimson tried hard to prepare the public for a spate of likely bad news, using his weekly press conference to warn the country to "get set for heavy American casualties, 'perhaps in the very near future.'" When the details were duly reported, the press and radio, as one government survey recorded, spent most of their time analyzing the causes of the defeat. Many believed "that the Germans were superior in numbers and equipment or that American troops were lacking in battle experience." But many also echoed Stimson's warning "that we should neither exaggerate nor underestimate the losses we had suffered."[53]

This effort to prime and prepare the public was quite different from what had happened in 1918 or 1942, when the army's knee-jerk reaction had been toward suppression—an instinct based partly on a sense that the public was too casualty-shy to handle the truth. Now basic common sense prodded the army in a very different direction. After all, previous crackdowns had largely been counterproductive. Often, they had resulted in a massive public inquest that had tended to exaggerate the extent of American losses. No officer wanted a rerun, but Stimson also had a subtler reason for adopting a different PR strategy. By 1943 he was increasingly concerned that much of the nation viewed the army as a separate entity. There was, Stimson insisted in one speech, "a growing disposition on the part of our people to set apart the army and the navy from civilian life," to view them "as a disconnected task force which has been selected to perform a difficult, unpleasant, and dangerous job." Stimson believed that this chasm could be narrowed only by truthful information about conditions at the front. As soon as home-front Americans became aware of just how difficult life was for the average GI, they might also shed another worrying trait: a complacent conviction that the war could easily be won.[54]

Stimson was not alone in fretting about complacency. From the very start of the war many officials had complained that most Americans were "much too disposed to think that the war is about over," which in turn lowered "the general sense of urgency" and led to "opposition to government calls for sacrifice."[55] In the spring of 1943, as the combined American and British army recovered from Kasserine and moved toward victory in North Africa, this official fear grew. It then reached a pitch in the summer and fall of 1943 with the Anglo-American invasions of Sicily and Italy. Both campaigns, to be sure, were tough and costly. In Sicily sixty thousand Germans held off half a million allied troops for more than a month before successfully evacuating. In Italy many of these same Germans came close to driving back the Salerno landings into the sea. Yet what the U.S. public tended to see was its own army firmly on the offensive in Europe. The most telling moment came in July, when Mussolini's Fascist regime collapsed in the wake of the allied advance. Gripped by a spasm of euphoria, many Americans reached the simple conclusion that the Axis alliance had fatally cracked. According to a string of polls, almost 60 percent of the public now thought Germany would be defeated within a year, a figure that had jumped 20 percent in just a few months.[56]

As a number of officials recognized, a bold and graphic use of American casualties could clearly jolt the public out of its complacent sense that the war was a breeze. They disagreed, however, about how far it was safe to go. In Washington, Roosevelt's civilian propaganda bureau, the Office of War Information (OWI), wanted to push to the outer limits. Throughout 1943 OWI officials complained constantly about attempts to sanitize the war, especially when it came to visual images. With the military in charge, one grumbled, the home front invariably received an antiseptic version of the war in which "soldiers fight, . . . some of them get badly hurt and ride smiling in aerial ambulances, but . . . none of them get badly shot or spill any blood." Elmer Davis, the OWI chief, fully agreed. In his view, this misguided Hollywood approach to propaganda only intensified the public's persistent overconfidence. In July, his first response was to make a concerted effort "to have national casualty lists more widely carried by newspapers throughout the country." More controversially, he also lobbied for the release of more graphic footage of Americans fighting and dying on the battlefield.[57]

To some extent Davis was pushing at an open door, as military leaders were also fully aware of the perils of suppression. Initially, however, the Pentagon did not take kindly to Davis's intervention in its sphere. Since the OWI's creation in the summer of 1942, the army and navy had always viewed the propaganda bureau with suspicion. In their opinion it was an excessively liberal organization, which was essentially clueless about the vital need to protect military secrets. As a result, they often joined forces to keep it well away from the task of providing war news.[58]

On the specific matter of publicizing more realistic battlefield information, a number of officers in both services had substantive reservations. It was one thing to make the public aware of setbacks and losses, they argued. It was quite another to open up totally and start ramming the war's grisly nature down the public's throats. During the Kasserine battle, Surles had already kept a sharp eye open for excessively gloom-laden press dispatches. His motive was revealing. He thought that such stories damaged the morale of the still-green army, worried the relatives of men in North Africa, and generated a popular sense that the army was not up to its task. During the spring and summer, the War Department adopted a similar attitude when keeping its "Chamber of Horrors" under wraps. This was an archive consisting of hundreds of photographs of dead and mutilated GIs, deemed far too explicit ever to see the light of day.[59]

Inside the administration, however, opinions were shifting decisively in the OWI's favor. The persistence of popular complacency was one cause. Another was Davis's threat to resign unless he was given more input in the release of war news. With Stimson and Army Chief of Staff Marshall both convinced that the public needed a greater sense of reality about the war, the scene was set for a major policy change. In the fall of 1943 Roosevelt directed the army to be much more open with the public. The War Department thereupon released one photograph that showed the body of a dead American paratrooper and another that "featured a close-up view of the leg of a soldier whose foot had been shot away." Marshall, meanwhile, wrote to subordinates in the field urging them to send him pictures for publication that would "vividly portray the dangers, horrors, and grimness of war."[60] At a time when big photo magazines like *Life* were at the height of their influence, reaching into millions of homes each week, this new policy promised to have a big impact.[61]

While the army tried to locate realistic images of the fighting, on November 20 the navy was suddenly presented with the perfect opportunity to underline the bloody nature of modern war. That day, the marines attacked Tarawa. Against fierce Japanese resistance, they lost one thousand dead and two thousand wounded, and all for sake of only a meager prize: a tiny island of less than three square miles.

Despite its size, Tarawa was significant for a variety of reasons. The operation demonstrated that the United States had sufficient resources to begin a concerted naval-based offensive against Japan. The actual invasion was a harbinger of what was to come, as many more islands were stormed on the long journey to Tokyo.[62] And domestically, the bloodiness of the battle presented a perfect opportunity for officials to sharpen their "war-is-hell" message.

Navy Secretary Knox was certainly in no mood to sugarcoat the news. "You can't capture a well-defended island fortress without heavy losses," he explained to reporters on November 26. "It was bitter, hard fighting. The first waves of troops had to take a lot of punishment."[63] Within days, the marines took up this cue, labeling Tarawa the costliest battle in their history. Weeks later, the navy was still underlining this theme, issuing graphic news releases on mass burials, with "as many as twenty-five or thirty" American bodies being placed in single graves "over which both Catholic and Protestant services were read."[64] Even more eye-catching was a training movie, *With the Marines at Tarawa*, which Roosevelt allowed to go into general release in March 1944. Based on graphic combat footage, it included film of wounded marines on stretchers and casualty-identification teams at work on the beach. "These are the marine dead," intoned the narrator toward the end, over pictures of prostrate bodies lying on the sand and bobbing in the shallow sea. "This is the price we have to pay for a war we didn't want. And before it's over, there will be more dead on other battlefields."[65]

These images certainly grabbed the nation's attention, but with dangerous consequences. In private, the navy believed the battle had been worth the cost. Tarawa's seizure, senior officers concluded, not only provided a valuable air base for the next phase of operations but also demonstrated that U.S. amphibian operations could prevail against a strongly defended coastline.[66] As the media

Figure 2.2 The government did nothing to hide the scale of losses at Tarawa. The official caption to this picture read: "Sprawled bodies on the beach of Tarawa testifying to the ferocity of the struggle on this stretch of sand." National Archives 80G 57405.

inquest began, however, some saw the battle very differently. On the radio Drew Pearson, the muckraking commentator, told his large audience that both the purpose and cost of the invasion were questionable. The *Chicago Tribune* agreed, adding mischievously that there ought to be a public investigation. The "severity of the casualties," the *Tribune* thundered, suggested that "evidence should be developed to determine whether better planning and conduct of the plan might not have avoided some of them."[67]

Knox soon worried that the navy had overdone things. He therefore instructed Frank E. Mason to respond to this media criticism. An NBC vice president who had recently been recruited to burnish the navy's image, Mason's first move was to call Walter Kiplinger, the influential editorial writer. Mason wanted Kiplinger to write a major piece that would stem the "terrific criticism" that was building up, but this soon proved to be a hazardous move.

Knowing little about the battle, Kiplinger began by working the Washington beat, calling a range of officials, politicians, and journalists. A few days later he reported to Mason that he had compiled "a very dirty story." "Tarawa," he discovered, "was a very bad blunder—the loss of life may have been three thousand instead of the one thousand published." Even worse, he added ominously, "the operation was undertaken on orders from someone higher up (no names mentioned at all) maybe the White House in order to make a showing for political reasons."[68]

Mason was dumbfounded. With yet another casualty initiative threatening to rebound disastrously, he swiftly prevailed on Kiplinger to write his story "cautiously." In the next few weeks the navy then resorted to more orthodox methods. The most important was its release of a more precise Tarawa toll, which significantly was much lower than the number included in the first communiqués.[69]

Nonetheless, the damage had been done. Tarawa's bloodiness stuck in the public mind. The navy's faltering PR efforts also became an object lesson in the perils of being too bold and graphic about combat losses, although it was a lesson that at least one senior White House figure failed to learn—with even more alarming results.

The Roosevelt administration's most controversial effort to use casualties as part of its anti-complacency message came against the backdrop of an increasingly complex military situation in Europe.

By December 1943 the fighting in Italy had bogged down. In wake of the allied invasion, Hitler had poured German troops into the region, occupying the northern half of the Italian peninsula, establishing strong defensive positions, and even restoring Mussolini to power. Throughout the winter allied forces continued to slug away at the German defenses, but little progress was made. More to the point, casualties looked set to spike rapidly, and not just because of the deadly Italian fighting. In November the first Big Three meeting took place at Tehran. With Stalin pushing for a decision, Roosevelt and Churchill finally agreed to mount an invasion of northern France in the new year, setting D-Day for some time in the spring. Dubbed Operation Overlord, this invasion would be enormously risky given the German army's continued fighting qualities, not to mention the bad weather and rough seas that often churned the English Channel. And allied casualties were bound to be heavy.[70]

In this foreboding context, James F. Byrnes, the chief White House domestic policy adviser, sought to tie together all the strands of the government's unfolding casualty strategy into one neat package. On December 22 he led a group of White House reporters to a quiet room in the Mayflower Hotel. Radiating festive good cheer, Byrnes plied them with oysters and drink, before launching into a "not for attribution" briefing session in which, according to one participant "he said quite flatly that in the next three months there would be more than three times the war casualties there have been up to the present." On returning to the White House press room the three wire-service correspondents looked up the current number of reported casualties, which totaled 131,000, and did some rapid math. Worrying less about accuracy and more about placing their copy with as many newspapers as possible, they dispatched separate stories to the effect that a "high government official" was predicting losses of half a million American fighting men in the next ninety days.[71]

It was news that, as one reporter aptly put it, "hit Washington, and undoubtedly the country, like a punch in the kidneys." From across the political spectrum reporters, columnists, and editors were, to put it mildly, distinctly unimpressed with this clumsy effort at openness. As an OWI survey pointed out, Byrnes's comment "evoked strongly emotional, antagonistic editorial comment. It was viewed as untactful, brutal, unnecessary, stupid, in execrable taste and as a shocking blunder, contributing to general confusion and domestic wrangling."[72]

In part, this intensely adverse reaction was simply due to Byrnes's ham-handed statement and the wire service reporters' "cleverly phrased" copy. As the army angrily pointed out, Byrnes had no reason for his ninety-day timeline, for no operations were planned during this period that could possibly result in such losses. But neither had the wire service reporters covered themselves in professional glory. On the contrary, they had clearly acted in a somewhat artful way by giving the impression in their first stories that Byrnes was forecasting 500,000, and not "just" 390,000, casualties.

Deeply alarmed by how badly his briefing had boomeranged, Byrnes tried hard to limit the damage. He immediately instructed his press agent to call those correspondents who had attended the Mayflower session to demand that they "tone down their stories." "There were matters of security involved," the press officer duly implored. "Byrnes hadn't intended they should go so far, and in short for heaven's sake temper it with mercy." Coming from such a senior official at such a turbulent moment of the war, these desperate pleas had an impact. In the next few days most newspapers printed the more accurate estimate of 390,000 casualties. Many also did their best to avoid "scarehead" page-one leads.[73]

Even this more muted story caused enormous popular outrage, most of all because of its timing. While the administration was still fretting about complacency, a large chunk of the nation was now reeling from the recent news of Tarawa.

Seen in this context, Byrnes had clearly gone too far. Any wartime government is engaged in a delicate balancing act between openness and suppression. At this point in time, officials were seeking to drive home the realities of war in order to dampen overconfidence. More specifically, Byrnes was eager to manage expectations so that a big burst of casualties did not hit the home front too hard. But in the media's eyes, he had tipped the balance excessively in the direction of doom and gloom. An editorial in the *Philadelphia Inquirer* put it particularly colorfully: "Our leaders, in their outgivings," it declared, "ought to guard not only against hip-hip-hooray over-optimism, but against dire and awful forebodings. Super-gloom is almost as bad for the war effort as super-joy"—especially since such super-gloom seemed likely to engender angst amongst the many families with sons, brothers, or husbands overseas.[74]

Indeed, when it came to linking casualties and propaganda, a number of senior officials seemed strangely tone deaf to this family connection. Byrnes was the most blatant offender, but Stimson had also patently ignored it when worrying that the public saw the army as a distinct entity—a worry that underpinned his own particular preoccupation with complacency. As a backlash developed, some in the press hastened to point out that Stimson's analysis was well wide of the mark. If anything, these critics insisted, Americans were overly attached to, and concerned by, the fate of their *civilian* army, which consisted, after all, mostly of draftees. As one editorial writer put it, many U.S. families felt they simply had "loaned" their boys to "the army for its big job." In other words, they were expecting them back at the end of the fighting, and did not take kindly to insensitive predictions that a large number would soon be killed or wounded.[75]

Although the administration's casualty utterances were often clumsy, the public clearly craved realistic news from the battlefield, including vivid stories about the dead. At the end of 1943 Pyle wrote a particularly moving piece about Cap. Henry T. Waskow, a young officer whose "sincerity and gentleness ... made people want to be guided by him." After Waskow had been killed in action, his was one of five bodies brought down an Italian mountain. "They came lying belly-down across the wooden packsaddles, their heads hanging down on one side, their stiffened legs sticking out awkwardly from the other, bobbing up and down as the mules walked." When they reached the bottom, Pyle reported, one GI reached down and took the captain's hand, and he sat there for a full five minutes holding the dead hand in his own and looking intently into the dead face. And he never uttered a sound all the time he sat there. Finally he put the hand down. He reached over and gently straightened the points of the captain's shirt collar, and then sort of rearranged the tattered edges of the uniform around the wound, and then he got up and walked away down the road in the moonlight, all alone.[76]

The public response was overwhelming. The *Washington Daily News*, Pyle's editor noted proudly, "devoted its entire first page to the column—not even a headline, just solid text." Within hours, the paper sold out. In the next few days, radio commentators read Pyle's moving story on air, while editorial writers discussed its deeper meanings. Some concluded that it signified the enlisted men's reverence for their commanders, while the *Washington Post* declared that the soldiers leaning over the captain's body had "silently dedicated themselves to fiercer opposition to oppression."[77] Clearly what the story did *not* do, though, was create a spasm of doubt about the need to fight. Pyle might have brought a vivid story of death into many American houses, but like the government's attempts to be candid about casualties, he had not cracked the sturdy façade of domestic unity.

The military certainly had little trouble getting young men to accept the grim reality of a short-term "loan" from civilian life. Far from it: throughout the war the draft worked remarkably smoothly, peacefully registering 49 million men, selecting 19 million, and inducting 10 million.[78] During the anxious winter of 1943/44, the selective service system faced surprisingly few problems, even in the midst of extravagant predictions of big casualties. In fact, the high point of "draft delinquency," as it was phrased in this war, had come earlier, at the start of 1943 when new FBI investigations had exceeded 12,500 a month. From December 1943 to March 1944, this figure edged inexorably downward, from 8,264 to 5,715. In short, the prospect of fighting nasty battles in Europe or the Pacific was not encouraging the vast majority of American boys to shirk their duty.[79]

Nor, at first glance, were the majority of Americans concerned enough by all the casualty stories to change their basic attitude to the war. True, on the extreme fringes groups like Peace Now or the National Council for the Prevention of War were now more visible and vocal. But the mainstream attitude toward them was highly revealing. While the media viciously assailed Peace Now as a pro-Axis stooge, Congress launched an investigation into its "un-American" views.

Bristling at this un-American tag, peace groups pointed out that their views had been squarely within the mainstream just three short years before. Back then, hardly anyone had advocated sending American troops to fight in Europe. With D-Day in the offing, peace campaigners tried desperately to revive this key isolationist tenet. "A peace offensive should be made before the order to attack is given," they declared. "It is wrong to continue the slaughter of thousands of young Americans until we have made an honest attempt to adjust grievances and come to terms with all our adversaries."[80]

After two years of hard fighting, few mainstream voices were willing to endorse anything that smacked of a deal with the Axis regimes. Still, beneath the surface unity, ripples of unease were gradually starting to appear. No one doubted that the new year would be climactic—that a series of campaigns in Europe and the Pacific would take the Allies ever closer to Berlin, Rome, and Tokyo but probably at a high cost in human life. In private, even tough former military men like Knox wondered whether the country had "the guts to stay with it to the finish." Key media voices gave him little grounds for confidence. Some favored an intensive new propaganda effort to weaken the enemy's resolve. According to radio commentators like MBS's Sam Balter and NBC's Morgan Beatty, qualifying the American call for unconditional surrender would counter growing Axis propaganda claims that an allied victory would mean extinction. Only by offering assurances of fair postwar treatment, agreed the *Washington Times-Herald*, could the United States weaken the enemy's will to undertake desperate last-ditch fights in Italy, Asia, and above all northern France.[81]

While some opinion makers wanted to qualify unconditional surrender, many more Americans were suddenly attracted to the idea of a negotiated peace in Europe, with one crucial condition: only if the German army first overthrew Hitler. By the spring of 1944 more than 40 percent favored such a course, a figure that was noticeably higher than at any other time of the war, including even the nervy months of setback and defeat during 1942.[82]

Although the government's gloomy predictions about future American casualties were not solely responsible for such polling figures, this shift in the public mood still raised profound questions. Was this the time to be candid about casualties? Could the public really take bad news? Perhaps it might be safer to finesse the figures, or at the very least make a tactical retreat from publishing the goriest details. Some officers fighting the European ground war certainly started to think this way, but they were by no means the only ones. Similar questions were being asked by those waging the U.S. air war over Germany, a battle that was also going badly during the long, hard winter of 1943/44.

The Air War, 1942–44

The allied bombing campaign had been launched with high expectations. From the outset air commanders had viewed their trade not merely as a way of avoiding the enormous casualties that had resulted from ground-war operations. They were also convinced that they could win this new war on their own—that a strategic bombing campaign could destroy the enemy's economic ability to carry on the fight.

Although Roosevelt, a technowar enthusiast, was always attracted to these notions, it was not until Operation Torch and the subsequent Mediterranean campaign that the American air force got a real boost. With their armies still a long way from the German frontier, Roosevelt and Churchill saw air power as the best method of striking directly at the enemy. Both leaders therefore sanctioned a round-the-clock bombing campaign against German cities. While the British would send over their planes at night, the Americans would bomb by day—and the Germans would get no respite until the war was won.[83]

At first glance, the bombing campaign seemed a happy compromise between two increasingly fractious Allies, but in reality it did little except mask their deep differences. The Americans, for their part, remained leery of the hit-and-miss quality that characterized Britain's policy of literally groping in the dark. Equipped with Nordern bombsights, and with their Flying Fortresses and B-24 Liberators flying in a tight defensive formation, U.S. air leaders like Henry Arnold, Carl Spaatz, and Ira Eaker were convinced that they could precision bomb key German industrial targets in daylight without suffering disabling losses. The British were skeptical. As they knew from painful experience, German defenses were impressive. American bombers would have to make long journeys over enemy airspace, fully exposed to the twin dangers of ground flak and Luftwaffe fighters. "God knows, I hope you can do it," the British bombing chief told Eaker in 1942, "but I don't think you can. Come and join us at night. Together we'll lick them."[84]

The confident and cocky U.S. Air Force, however, had too much at stake in this campaign to listen to such naysayers. The size of its enterprise was truly staggering. By the end of 1943 the Americans had four thousand planes and 185,000 men stationed in Britain. A year later the air force would account for 31 percent of the entire army strength, with more men under colors than Pershing had commanded at any stage during World War I.[85]

Yet to Arnold, Spaatz, and Eaker this last fact was itself jarring, for they had no desire to remain a mere adjunct of the army. They wanted independence. In headier moments they even hoped to become the most important of the three military services, a goal that could be achieved only by making their daylight raids work. With the hard-driving Arnold at the helm—a man who pushed himself to four heart attacks during the war—these air commanders would press on regardless of the cost to demonstrate that air power could be decisive on its own.

They would also work hard to burnish the air force's public image. As one senior American journalist observed, Eaker's Eighth Air Force "was a high-octane outfit. It was run by ambitious men and backed by an ambitious command in Washington. It had set up a large public-relations staff—men from newspaper, publicity firms, advertising agencies—and made use of Hollywood celebrities." It was never shy about seeking headlines and was always on the lookout for opportunities to get war correspondents covering its bombing raids, moviemakers filming its stalwart crews, and veterans proselytizing about its successes.[86]

Still, even for these high-powered PR operators the daylight bombing campaign was an enormously tough sell. One potential problem was so-called collateral damage. By the summer of 1943, as the U.S. and British air forces began pounding Germany by day and night, civilian casualties inevitably rose. One particularly appalling moment came on July 22–23, when a sustained attack on Hamburg left more than 40,000 dead.

Civilian casualties on this scale belied the air force's claim that it was "accurately and scientifically" destroying only targets "of military or production importance in a strict order of priority."[87] They also raised possible questions about whether the Allied air raids were any better than the German attacks on London that both the U.S. government and American reporters had so roundly condemned in 1940. The Roosevelt administration was therefore eager to reassure the public that it was not engaged in "the indiscriminate bombing of the civilian population of enemy countries."[88] Arnold went on record claiming that terror bombing was "abhorrent to our humanity, our sense of decency." Roosevelt's denials were even clearer. The United States was "not bombing tenements for the sheer sadistic pleasure of killing, as the Nazis did," the president claimed in a September fireside chat. "We are striking devastating blows at carefully selected, clearly identified strategic objectives—factories, shipyards, munitions dumps, transportation facilities, which make it possible for the Nazis to wage war."[89]

The media, for its part, was inclined to believe such claims. It was also generally willing to celebrate, rather than condemn, the fact that the Allies were now taking the war to Germany's heartland. In the immediate aftermath of the Hamburg raid, for instance, more than a hundred editorials urged a more intensive bombing campaign against Germany, in the belief that "salvation of allies may lie in all-out air attacks."[90] A number of commentators even pointed out "with obvious satisfaction that the raids were greater than any ever made on England by the *Luftwaffe*."[91]

That the American air force raided Germany in daylight gave a certain credence to this congratulatory self-assurance. When it came to American losses, however, daylight raids soon created a much larger PR problem, for the simple reason that British misgivings proved prescient: without fighter escorts over German air space, American bombers were easy prey. By the fall of 1943 the Luftwaffe was shooting so many out of the sky that less than a quarter of air crew members could expect to complete their tour of twenty-five missions. Two-thirds would either die or be captured bailing out over enemy territory, while a further 17 percent would sustain serious wounds, suffer a mental breakdown, or become the victim of an accident over Britain.[92] The situation was so bad that privately even Eaker fretted that "our official supporters at the highest levels, and our supporting public, may not be able to stand our losses in combat." And this was before the disastrous Schweinfurt raid of October 1943.[93]

Schweinfurt marked the culmination of an intensive three-month effort to savage German industry. Like numerous other raids since August, it was conceived as an illustration of U.S. air theory in action: a daylight raid deep into German territory that targeted a crucial ball-bearing plant whose destruction would deal a massive blow to the Nazi war machine. Unfortunately, however, Schweinfurt actually turned into a graphic illustration of the bombing campaign's deep flaws, as German fighters equipped with deadly new rockets decimated the Flying Fortresses. So bad was the slaughter that it capped what became known as "Black Week"—a deeply demoralizing seven-day period when the air force lost 148 Fortresses, sixty of them in the raid on Schweinfurt alone.[94]

Covering up a disaster of this magnitude was no easy task. While the Eaker's dynamic publicists were already well versed in emphasizing German losses, rather than their own, they seemed taken aback by the scale of the Schweinfurt reverse. Worse, for all the Eighth Air Force's emphasis on the glossy side of PR, the size of these losses brutally exposed its lack of a practical and systematic system for reporting American air casualties.

This is not to say that air force public-relations officers did not make every effort to play down what had happened. After the Schweinfurt raid their first official communiqué was suitably brief and vague, containing just fifty-one words and offering only the sparest account of sixty bombers failing to return. But the air force's own penchant for publicity-seeking now backfired, for having invited reporters to observe the return of the surviving planes, air force censors at the scattered American bases were unable to coordinate a clear and uniform line. As a result, the correspondents wired back a number of interview accounts with survivors, telling graphic tales of the hellish conditions in the air.

As the extent of U.S. losses began to sink in, the focus shifted to Washington. In the next few days Roosevelt, Stimson, and Arnold all chimed in, releasing separate statements about the numbers of bombs dropped and crew members lost, and the damage done to the enemy. But it took days for the government to reveal the positive news that enough planes had gotten through to put the target out of action. It then took another couple of weeks before officials finally divulged that the Germans had come off worse in the sky, losing 186 planes, 120 more than the Americans.

The end result, the air force believed, was far worse than a cover-up: it had been a public-relations disaster of the first order. Uncertain how to act, the government had let the story spill out in dribs and drabs. Consequently, as one internal media survey noted, the American people initially "took a pretty hard slap—the loss of sixty-two planes and 593 men—for about sixteen hours" before they were given the first official justification for the attack. Thereafter the remainder of the story, because it was released belatedly over a period of days, tended to get "lost well inside the paper." "Delay," one official concluded, "weakened the impact the story should have had on the reader"—or, rather, delay insured that the public debate essentially concentrated on the appalling American losses.[95]

The air force was clearly chastened by the whole experience, and in the wake of Schweinfurt it decided to overhaul its entire casualty-reporting system. Arnold, the chief, was at the forefront. "Valuable information," he argued, "is being given to the enemy by the immediate announcement in theaters of action of our combat losses." Worse, he lamented, was "the emphasis in the American press on Army Air Force losses," which "obscures the most important aspect of air operations—the damage done to enemy targets." Arnold's proposed solution was to centralize and streamline the process, so that only two types of information would ever reach the public domain. "Operational" press releases would be given to correspondents soon after a raid. They would emphasize the target and its importance to the German war effort, but only use the words "light," "moderate," or "heavy" to describe U.S. casualties. "Summary" press releases, by contrast, would be released monthly, but they would give more details and would place bomb tonnage, target destruction, and American losses in a broader perspective.[96]

Underpinning Arnold's suggestion was a strong desire to regain the PR initiative, which was so vital if the air force was to become a separate service. Unfortunately for Arnold, the air force still remained part of the army—and the army responded to his proposal with a scorn born of years of experience trying, and failing, to gloss over its own losses. The BPR's opposition was typical of this skepticism. Any "refusal to make public the number of American planes lost on missions," Surles firmly believed, "will result in [a] general belief on the part of the American public that the army is attempting to conceal its losses. This will have a detrimental effect on the information policy of the army by raising doubts concerning its accuracy and honesty."[97]

Previous efforts to bury bad news had invariably raised the specter of giving away valuable intelligence to the enemy, and Arnold was also keen to push this familiar line. Yet the bombing campaign, which had been sold as such a new type of war, was indeed novel in a way that made it much more difficult to cover up casualties. Unlike the land and naval spheres, where the enemy could glean valuable intelligence from overly hasty or indiscreet newspaper stories, in the air war the German Gestapo invariably knew more than the Americans. As the War Department's intelligence chief noted, it was quite pointless to use censorship to conceal plane losses from the Nazis for the simple reason that "practically all of the planes lost will fall in enemy territory and the wrecks may be counted."[98]

Stymied by these arguments, Arnold had to settle for a new style of communiqué, which simply shifted the emphasis away from American casualties and toward the effect of bombing. "Our own losses," the new policy guidance declared, "should be presented in the perspective of damage to targets—attainment of objective—instead of in ratio to enemy aircraft destroyed."[99]

This shift in emphasis was important because U.S. air casualties remained high. March was a particularly grim month, with the loss of 409 Eighth Air Force planes. Yet soon after, the allied air campaign began to win in all areas. As early as February, in the so-called "Big Week," the Allies dropped more than ten thousand tons of bombs on Germany, which was about the same amount that the Eighth Air Force had dropped in its entire first year. With the welcome arrival of long-distance fighter planes, they also began inflicting such huge losses on the Luftwaffe that the balance of the air war tipped decisively in the Allies' favor. In June, when the Allies finally launched their long-awaited invasion in Northern France, German air power was stretched so thin that the Luftwaffe could launch only about 250 defensive sorties, a derisory number that proved utterly inadequate against the largest invasion force ever assembled.[100]

Still, despite the hopes and expectations of air power proponents, this air victory was merely a prelude. The European war would have to be won on land, in a long hard slog through Western Europe to the heart of Germany that would turn the next months into the bloodiest of the war. For many Americans, a lot more bad news was on the way, even though the "good war" now looked certain to end in victory.

3

The Price of Victory

World War II, 1944–1945

Although the Allies dominated the skies over Western Europe, Overlord remained a tremendously risky operation. The unpredictable weather along the British coast might easily nullify this newly won air superiority, while also turning the English Channel into an uncrossable barrier for the British and American navies. Once the attack was launched the Allies needed to gain a foothold on the five carefully chosen beaches along the Normandy coast. They then had to construct makeshift ports through which to pour sufficient men and materiel to beat back German counterattacks. Even when the Allies pushed inland, they still faced a fight in tricky *bocage* terrain, where high hedgerows gave the Germans the perfect opportunity to erect a stubborn defense, perhaps re-creating the bloody stalemate that had emerged in France during the previous war.

Before it was launched, then, Overlord was an operation that demanded the strictest secrecy. If word leaked out about the details of the attack—and the Germans could prepare a concerted hostile reception for the Allied landing party—then few senior officials doubted that a disaster of the first magnitude was in the offing. Churchill, never an enthusiast for a cross-channel offensive, was the most prominent of these security-obsessed worriers. When Eisenhower assumed supreme command of the operation in January 1944, the British prime minister almost immediately sent him a firm missive stressing the need to halt all press speculation about the timing or location of the proposed landing.[1]

Eisenhower was more than happy to oblige. He even sent home one general in disgrace after the hapless man divulged sensitive information about the invasion plan at a cocktail party. By the late spring, as D-Day moved ever closer, Eisenhower stopped civilians from entering sensitive areas along the south coast of England, before confining more and more soldiers to camp so that they could not blurt out sensitive information to the friends they had made during the endless months of training.[2]

Yet if Overlord required the utmost secrecy before the event, as soon as D-Day was given the green light almost every officer inside Eisenhower's Supreme Headquarters Allies Expeditionary Force (SHAEF) believed it essential to relax these onerous restrictions. The lessons learned both in 1917–18 and 1942–43 certainly pointed in this direction. Overlord was bound to be *the* news story of the war. Many media outlets had already sent their star reporters over to Britain so that they would be on hand to cover it. Most newspapers were also planning special D-Day editions that they hoped would be so full of timely facts, strategic overviews, and eyewitness accounts that their readers would purchase copies in record numbers. The major radio networks were intending to suspend their normal programming on the fateful day, replacing it with wall-to-wall coverage from Washington, New York, London, and the invasion fleet.[3]

If all these news providers were denied meaningful material from their own side, SHAEF knew only too well where their editors would turn. "The allied publics are keyed up to expect a great volume of dramatic news as soon as the 'second front' opens," observed one public relations specialist in April. "If adequate news is not available from official allied sources, the [home front media] will certainly make immediate use of news from enemy and neutral sources together with comment and speculation based thereon."[4]

Rather than create a potentially disastrous information vacuum, Eisenhower and his top publicity officers were more than happy to work with the 180 American war correspondents who were now accredited to their command. As Brig. Gen. T. Jefferson Davis, SHAEF's PR chief, commented at a major publicity meeting on April 24, most of these reporters were "men of tremendous responsibility." His boss agreed. "At my first press conference as supreme commander," Eisenhower noted two weeks later, "I told the war correspondents that once they were accredited to my headquarters I considered them quasi-staff officers. . . . They should be allowed to talk freely with officers and enlisted personnel and to see the machinery of war in operation in order to visualize and transmit to the public the conditions under which the men from their countries are waging war against the enemy."[5]

Of course these reporters would also be subject to clear rules about what they could and could not publish, which Eisenhower's censors had collated together in one big "bible." Nothing in SHAEF's proscribed list was particularly novel, especially since the censors—well aware of the problems associated with overzealous restrictions in the past—were eager to include "the statement of principle that 'the minimum of information will be withheld from the public consistent with security.'" The reporters, for their part, were a highly experienced bunch; many were also fully domesticated in the ways of the military, knowing perfectly well what they could get away with. Consequently SHAEF's censorship office did not anticipate many battles over controversial copy. They recognized that most correspondents, having already internalized the censorship code, could be trusted to stay away from such sensitive matters as the strength and location of Allied forces, the new equipment and tactics being employed, and above all "what our casualties are, either in number or by percentage."[6]

Operation Overlord

Shortly after dawn on June 6 the long, tense wait finally came to an end, as the first American troops waded ashore on two separate beaches, code-named Utah and Omaha. On Utah everything proceeded surprisingly smoothly. With relatively calm seas and an effective naval bombardment, American troops cleared the beaches within an hour and were soon pushing inland to link up with the airborne divisions that had parachuted earlier in the night to capture key bridges and road junctions.

On Omaha the situation was quite different. The navy's opening salvo, as well as a short, intense bombing raid, mostly missed their intended targets and so failed to stifle the German defenders. The sea's large swell, along with confusing currents, then played havoc with the landing craft: some were pushed off course, others disgorged their overladen men in deep water, and most were reeking badly of vomit by the time their seasick soldiers, debilitated by their rough journey, clambered out toward the beach. Faced with German machine guns, artillery, and sniper fire, the first beleaguered GIs had to make an almost suicidal rush for cover, before trying to get their own water-soaked weapons functioning. Soon the beach "was just one big mass of junk, of men and materials," an officer recalled later. Burned-out equipment was strewn everywhere. Waxlike corpses were washed in on the tide to lie beside the hundreds more men who had been riddled with bullets or blown apart by artillery and mines.

Nevertheless, even on bloody Omaha the Americans prevailed. Increasingly accurate naval fire from boats positioned perilously close to the shoreline silenced some of the German guns. Crucially a number of brave leaders in the experienced First Division rounded up groups of men crouched in the sand, with exhortations like that shouted by Colonel George Taylor: "Two kinds of people are staying on this beach, the dead and those who are going to die—now let's get the hell out of here." Thus emboldened, soldiers started to crawl inland, easing the bottleneck on the beach and making room for the next wave of men and machines to come ashore.

The cost was high: approximately two thousand dead, wounded, and missing, including at least one company in which almost half its members were killed without inflicting any significant damage on the enemy. Having witnessed such carnage, the survivors were often shocked and dazed. They simply assumed, wrote the official historian Forrest C. Pogue after interviewing many of them, that "everyone else had been killed or captured."[7]

This dazed assumption of a wholesale D-Day slaughter could be extremely dangerous if it became an unstoppable rumor, especially as the Omaha landings had initially failed to achieve their original objectives. Although the losses here had been bad, the Overlord operation as a whole soon proved to be a clear success. Within days, as more and more troops and supplies poured onto the Normandy beaches, the Allies' precarious grip was slowly but surely tightened. It came at a relatively small cost—certainly not the "futile slaughter" of some pre-invasion predictions, which had gloomily estimated 70 percent losses for some airborne units, or two in three casualties for regiments in the first assault waves. The 101st Airborne, for instance, which had the perilous task of a night-time drop to the west of the Utah landings to secure key roads and bridges, suffered 1,240 casualties on D-Day, including 182 killed and 501 missing—much smaller than anyone had feared before the event.[8]

For the commander of the U.S. First Army this tension between lurid rumors appearing in print and the reality of establishing the beachhead at a relatively low cost pointed in one direction: the need to reveal precise casualty figures as soon as possible. This commander was Gen. Omar N. Bradley, who had a very personal stake in getting accurate casualty figures into the public domain as soon as possible. Prior to the invasion, as he toured Britain trying to boost GI morale, Bradley had constantly tried to reassure anxious GIs that rumors "about tremendous losses" were "tommyrot." "Some of you won't come back," he had told his men, "but it'll be very few." To Bradley's horror, a *Stars and Stripes* reporter had picked up these private comments, and they had soon found their way into numerous newspapers back home, accompanied by a bewildering array of semi-official estimates, educated guesses, and sheer speculation that put possible invasion losses at anywhere up to half a million men.[9]

With Allied forces safely ashore, such extravagant predictions had indeed turned out to be "tommyrot," and Bradley felt a justifiable sense of vindication. But he was also concerned that the real story was not making it to the folks back home. In the immediate aftermath, the enormous welter of news coverage about the landings lacked a clear, single narrative about casualties. Worse, in the absence of official figures, media speculation was starting to create a sense of big losses.[10]

On June 16 Bradley, determined both to set the record straight and to reassure an anxious populace, held his first press conference on French soil. Almost immediately he announced that U.S. invasion casualties to date were just 3,283 dead and 12,600 wounded. These figures, he explained, though high, "fell far below anticipated losses," and this ought to "reassure the American people after having been exposed to so many exaggerated losses before D-Day."[11]

In both the Pentagon and SHAEF some senior officials welcomed this candid release. Marshall, who firmly believed that "there is not today a more vitally important feature of our public relations than the prompt and efficient handling of casualty reports," was generally in favor of getting accurate figures into the public domain as soon as possible. Walter Bedell Smith, Eisenhower's fearsome Chief of Staff, likewise saw a distinct upside in Bradley's press conference. As he told a meeting of senior SHAEF PR officers on June 21, Bradley's comments had demolished the enemy's "grossly exaggerated [stories of] the slaughter on the beaches." They had also confirmed that the army had nothing to conceal, since "present casualties were only approximately 33 1/3rd percent of pre-invasion estimates."[12]

Such relaxed responses were by no means typical. Civilian officials in the White House and War Department, both of whom had been vying for the chance to provide these first—surprisingly low—figures to the public, felt cheated out of a great PR coup. To make matters worse Bradley had failed to mention how many troops were listed as "missing," complicating the task of providing accurate future casualty releases that differentiated between the various categories.[13] What had happened? Immediately undertaking an investigation, SHAEF discovered, to its horror, that despite intensive pre-invasion planning in so many areas, Bradley's press statement had revealed a startling omission: no one had devised a "directive designating the authority to approve the release of casualty statistics to the press."[14]

It was an omission that proved particularly embarrassing in the wake of highly irritated responses from the British and Canadian Allies, whose divisions had landed to the east of the Americans on D-Day, on the Gold, Juno, and Sword beaches. Behind closed doors British generals were particularly angered that the Americans had stolen the headlines, although they professed to be concerned principally about security. As they complained to Eisenhower, Bradley's premature release had provided the Germans with hard evidence to piece together Allied strength, which would make the hard slog to take key objectives like Saint Lô and Caen even harder.

As British and Canadian officials contemplated how to prevent a recurrence, they mostly reached the same conclusion. What was needed, they believed, was a clear and coherent system that provided the public with casualty figures on a frequent and regular basis, say toward the end of each month; the Allies could then release agreed-upon figures at the same time.[15] A number of American officials also saw the wisdom in this course. In their view frequent and regular lists would insure that the public, already fed a daily diet of the names of local casualties in their small hometown newspapers, would have a broader idea of the cost of the war. Congress, moreover, would be denied the opportunity to accuse the military of concealing botched affairs, as it had in 1918. And newspapers would be unable to print the sensationalist headlines that were certain to accompany the big increases revealed in rare announcements.[16]

Yet, as the campaign in Europe progressed, the U.S. military found it surprisingly difficult to implement such a clear and coherent policy for announcing total losses. This was partly because the War Department preferred to release figures on an irregular basis so that the enemy could not gauge the success of particular engagements.[17] Crucially, it also stemmed from a simple and familiar reason: the sheer difficulty of gathering accurate numbers from the battlefield.

The first weeks after the invasion were a particularly chaotic time. While units frequently became disorganized during and after the contested landings, officers were often so preoccupied with desperate fights against stiff German resistance that they simply lacked the time to complete the relevant paperwork. In July, when the adjutant general of the U.S. First Army inspected the Seventy-Ninth Division's casualty reporting methods he discovered that "not one casualty report" had been passed from this division up to corps level, even though the division estimated it had suffered more than five thousand losses in heavy fighting on the Cotentin peninsula. Still the reason was understandable. Troops at all levels were suddenly faced with the enormous pressures of combat, and the relevant officers were totally unschooled in both the importance and techniques of this grisly task.[18]

During July, as the allied position solidified, reinforcements arrived, and officers gathered experience, senior American commanders worked hard to rectify the problem. But they now faced the grim fact that losses were mounting alarmingly—about one hundred thousand casualties during July alone, as U.S. forces tried to establish positions from which to break out of Normandy. Indeed, this was one of the bloodiest and most frustrating periods of the European campaign. The tenacious German defense was one reason. Another was the difficulties created by the *bocage* hedgerows, which helped to confine the growing number of Allied troops to an ever more claustrophobic Normandy bridgehead, where space was at a premium and the need to break out became ever more desperate.[19]

Then suddenly the nature of the fighting changed. On July 25 Bradley launched Operation Cobra, his concerted effort to break through German defenses. Although the German response was initially fierce, by late afternoon on July 26 American forces were finally through the enemy's defenses. Soon they were sweeping across the French countryside with astonishing rapidity, making August one of the war's most successful months. By August 19 they joined up with the British and Canadians, having trapped somewhere between twenty-five thousand and fifty thousand German troops in the Falaise pocket. With George Patton's Third Army quickly generating the greatest speed, by August 25 they had liberated Paris and seemed poised to sweep through Belgium, the Nether-lands, and Germany.[20]

These were heady days, which seemed to herald the impending end of the European war, but they also created very real difficulties for prompt and precise casualty reporting. In August, after Bradley had assumed overall control as head of the U.S. Twelfth Army Group, Gen. Courtney Hodges, Bradley's successor at First Army, sent a message to his corps and division commanders stressing that the old excuses were no longer applicable. "Those unavoidable delays occasioned by the nature of the initial amphibious operations are behind us," he declared. "Every effort must now be made to insure continuous and prompt reporting. Special pick-up and messenger service must be provided; personnel concerned must be skilled and adequate; every available source of casualty information must be checked rapidly and carefully."[21]

Yet even now it was difficult to translate such strictures into meaningful action, largely because of the rapid, and somewhat chaotic, nature of the advance. As one army investigation concluded, "because of the extremely fluid operational picture" Patton's Third Army provided no "reliable daily casualty estimates" in the first two weeks of August. "Communications and the flow of administrative infor-mation were meager, for all priorities went to operations." With many French roads very narrow and gasoline for the thirsty tanks at a premium, some units even instituted a strict one-way traffic policy, which further complicated the compilation of accurate information. For a time, Gen. Clarence R. Huebner, commander of the First Division, would not even permit ambulances to return to the coast, insisting instead that "casualties would have to be cared for as best they could along the route of advance."[22]

To make reporting even more problematic, the rapid advance meant that various armies and their divisions sometimes lost contact with one another. When this happened, officers in charge of compiling overall totals were unable to meet their counterparts lower down the chain of command to resolve dis-crepancies or query potential errors. Instead, as one complained in the military lingo of the day, they had to make "synthetic adjustments on some of these reports [which] will serve only to 'snowball' the figures into something not even approximating the true situation and, when we are called upon to submit figures for release, we will have nothing with which we will be justified in releasing."[23]

Because of all these difficulties, the Pentagon found it tough to compile timely and accurate lists. As late as June 30 Stimson could still only announce figures that "did not include casualties in France" for the simple reason that the relatives of D-Day losses had yet to be informed.[24] Thereafter he released just three sets of figures from the European theater in the next six months, announcing totals of 115,665 on August 5, 174,780 on October 19, and 257,624 on December 18 (adding that only 3 percent were mortal wounds in August, while the KIA figures for October and December were 29,842 and 44,143, respectively).[25] In the same period, Stimson made more effort to announce the nation's cumulative losses in all theaters since Pearl Harbor. But even these disclosures were decidedly uneven, with big gaps between announcements; they also consistently underreported the total.

While the military's release of overall casualty totals was, because of a series of practical and security reasons, both irregular and laggardly, its handling of specific details was characterized by a careful consideration for appearances.

Losses from friendly fire were an especially vivid example of this trait. Such casualties were often a product of one of the major characteristics of the current war: joint interservice operations. Whenever the army tried to liaise with the air force and navy to insure close support for its ground forces, the potential for miscommunication or misunderstanding grew.[26]

One particularly costly mistake had already occurred in July 1943 during the invasion of Sicily. After these initial landings had gained a foothold on the island, the army decided to drop 2,300 airborne troops from the Eighty-second Division around Gela to reinforce its bridgehead. But the navy never received

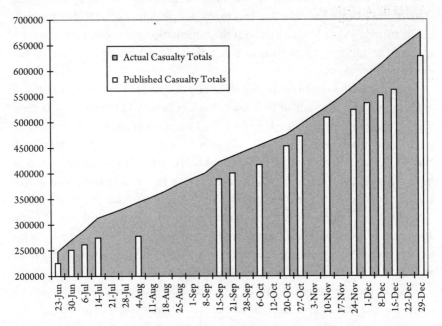

Graph 3.1 U.S. Combat Casualties, Actual and Announced, June–December 1944.
Source: Published totals compiled from what appeared in the *New York Times*; actual figures from U.S. Army, Adjutant General's Office, *Army Battle* Casualties.

word that such an operation was in the offing—a disastrous turn of events because its gunners were already nervy after two days of Luftwaffe attacks. The result was predictable. As the first of the 144 friendly planes passed over the Allied invasion ships, navy gunners opened fire. Soon tracers were tearing into faltering planes and falling parachutists alike, downing twenty-three of the former and killing 410 of the latter.[27]

Afterward, the military made every effort to understand what had happened in order to prevent a repeat, but mistakes still occurred. In Normandy the worst came in late July, during Operation Cobra, when Bradley called in the heavy bombers to help him pierce the Germans' stubborn defense line, and the "heavies" proceeded to drop almost 3,500 tons of bombs on enemy positions. Bradley had hoped to protect his own troops from this awesome bombing display by preventing planes from flying directly over Allied lines and limiting the size of the bombs, but the air force thought both suggestions impractical. On the day of the raid, a mixture of cloud, enemy antiaircraft fire, and the ineffectiveness of ground markers resulted in a fatal human error: bombs from thirty-five heavy and forty-two medium planes were dropped directly on U.S. forces, killing 111 and wounding 490.[28]

Divulging such casualties to the public was clearly a tricky business, but by this stage of the war the army knew full well that it had to avoid a clumsy crackdown that tried to hush up the matter completely. In these joint operations it was always the case that too many people knew what had happened, and someone was bound to blurt out the information at an awkward moment, leaving the military to explain not just the original blunders but also the subsequent cover-up.

This, at least, had been the lesson taught by the Sicily case, when it had taken eight months for the facts to be known. Back in July 1943 the censors had initially gone into overdrive, seeking to ban all mention of the highly embarrassing friendly-fire losses. This was a risky move, for as one correspondent noted, the "story was all over [the] ETO [European Theater of Operations]—and as high officers, couriers, and others poured back in a steady stream to Washington, it spread over the Pentagon Building. Every reporter knew it."[29] In the face of such an open secret, it was perhaps surprising that it took until March 1944 before word of it finally appeared in the press—and only then because a lowly sergeant working for *Stars and Stripes* divulged the details in a speech at San Francisco's Commonwealth Club. The media, which had long been screaming for permission to print, immediately called on the Pentagon to come clean. With little choice, Stimson duly obliged, but his grudging concession did nothing to stop the probing questions. Reporters still wanted to know why the Pentagon had decided to keep the whole matter secret for so long. Clearly they suspected that the military was using censorship not for reasons of legitimate security but to prevent the public from learning about avoidable mistakes.[30]

As media criticism reached a crescendo, Marshall issued a stern command to his censors. "War Department information policies are being subjected to damaging attacks by the press," he observed at the beginning of April 1944, "under the general accusation that the army is concealing mistakes and blunders under the guise of military security. . . . Unless security reasons are obvious, consideration should be given to the prompt publication of loss and damage due to accident or misfortune except where that information would be useful to the enemy."[31]

In dealing with the Cobra incident, then, the army had a clear policy direction from Marshall that pointed toward openness. This was important because in the heat of the moment the censors' temptation was inevitably to downplay such a costly mistake. In the case of the Cobra casualties, the censors also had a perfect security excuse to gag the press completely, for the friendly bombs had tragically reaped an illustrious victim: Gen. Lesley J. McNair.

As a leading player in shaping the U.S. Army since 1942, McNair's death had obvious news value. As far as the public knew, however, McNair was not in France at all. Rather, as part of an elaborate deception plan to convince the Germans that another invasion was in the offing, he was meant to be in Britain as "commander" of a fictitious army group. Not wanting this particular angle to get out, the censors went into overdrive to make sure that McNair's death and hastily arranged funeral were totally hushed up. Yet significantly they did not use this episode as an excuse to institute a complete embargo. Instead, within days SHAEF permitted correspondents to report the broader story of what had happened when the air force erred.[32] It even allowed some journalists to record the army's "unmistakable" anger at the air force's performance, although such stories were carefully counterbalanced by the air force's rejoinder that most bombs had found their intended target and that overall the operation had successfully disrupted German defenses.[33]

In fact, both services found it much easier to be candid about this particular incident because, for all the friendly-fire victims, the outcome was a clear Allied victory that paved the way for the stunning escape from the Normandy stalemate. According to *Time*, before the attack Bradley had told the war correspondents that if he had "three hours of good flying weather any forenoon . . . he would break out of Normandy." When the Cobra air barrage vindicated this promise, reporters naturally framed their copy around this dimension of the story; some even went as far as to describe the resulting phase of open warfare as "a twentieth-century version of the winning of the American West, with roaming bands of Germans marked for extermination."[34] As for the unfortunate U.S. victims of friendly fire, on July 26 a military spokesman pointed out that even though the heavies had dropped so many bombs, "the number of American casualties from our bombing was much less than was thought the day before."[35]

If the military's management of friendly-fire losses was marked by a careful discretion, its handling of the wounded was typified by a well-thought-through blend of publicity and control.

Before D-Day, SHAEF's medical section had prepared meticulously for the large numbers of likely flesh wounds. It had stockpiled huge quantities of plasma and penicillin so that medics could help wounded GIs anywhere in the combat zone, including the beaches. It had planned field surgeries just behind the front line so that life-saving operations could be performed on the most seriously wounded soldiers. At least for the dangerous first day or two, it had readied landing craft and hospital carriers close to the beaches to transport the thousands of expected casualties back to ports in the south coast of England. Within days, air strips would also be established close to the landing beaches so that many of these soldiers could be transported back across the Channel by plane, accompanied by nurses trained to administer plasma. The hope was that men wounded in the morning would be on the operating table of a British general hospital within ten hours.[36]

With so many resources dedicated to saving as many lives as possible, SHAEF naturally wanted to emphasize this particular medical success story as it unfolded. "So well organized is the routine for handling American casualties," Gen. Norman T. Kirk, the surgeon general, told reporters soon after D-Day, "that 80 to 90 percent of the men wounded in the invasion of Normandy received medical care within ten minutes of being hit." "Veritable miracles" were being performed by doctors, he continued. "The thing that's saving lives is surgery—surgery—surgery—plus plenty of blood plasma, penicillin, and the sulfa drugs and the fact that the whole set-up was so well planned in advance."[37]

For SHAEF publicists, however, it was one thing to crow about the large number of successful recoveries from flesh wounds; it was quite another even to mention the growing number of GIs whose problems were psychological. As the official historian has pointed out, during the Normandy campaign such casualties grew alarmingly. Within weeks, they "totaled an additional 25 to 30 percent of the number of men physically wounded," prompting each division to make "informal provision for treating combat fatigue cases, usually at the regimental collecting stations, and several divisional neuropsychiatrists established exhaustion centers." In the First Army the peak of such cases came in August when "almost 17 percent of all hospital admissions were for combat exhaustion."[38]

The cause was clear enough. For the average GI, none of the extensive training regimens undertaken before D-Day were adequate preparation for the dreadful

Figure 3.1 Having planned meticulously for dealing with the soldiers WIA on D-Day, SHAEF was eager to publicize their treatment. These wounded men were destined for hospitals in Britain. National Archives USCG 26-G-2413.

shock of combat—the days without sleep, the long monotonous hours waiting for something to happen, and then the short, sharp periods of intense fear and abject horror as modern weaponry destroyed comrades, machines, and familiar landmarks. During the bloody battles to escape the hated *bocage*, a growing number of men soon displayed the classical symptoms of combat exhaustion. These were described by the army's chief neuropsychiatrist as dejection and dirtiness, a depressed facial expression sometimes marked by tears, trembling, or jerky hands, and "varying degrees of confusion, perhaps to the extent of being mute or staring into space."[39]

Herein lay the problem: these symptoms were not an aspect of war that the army was eager to share with the folks back home. So in stark contrast to the controlled publicity surrounding flesh wounds, which even extended to scheduled hospital visits for accredited correspondents, the army suppressed news of "neuropsychiatric casualties." Except for the percentage of those who had made a full recovery, it prohibited the release of all statistics on this sensitive matter. It also refused to permit the publication of "names or identifiable photographs."[40]

This rigid censorship was clearly designed, in part, to protect the men who were suffering in this way. But the army, fretful that the public was less understanding, perhaps even more squeamish, about this consequence of combat, wanted to spare the public any details, lest this damage home-front morale.[41] Nor was the army eager for these particular wounds to show up in the overall totals. "Sick and non-battle casualties," it insisted from the start of the campaign, "are *not* included in the casualty figures." With combat fatigue usually classified under sickness—rather than under the many categories of flesh wound—the growing numbers of such victims were often discreetly omitted from the casualty totals.[42]

Casualties and the 1944 Election

That the army was so careful about what it released—not to mention its inability to promptly reveal the true scale of Operation Overlord losses—was important because the home front was far from quiescent during the summer of 1944.

The invasion itself generated a marked sense of anxiety. In states like Illinois, Indiana, Michigan, and Wisconsin, the days after June 6 witnessed an extensive number of prayer meetings, while schools, offices, and war plants all recessed for religious services—actions that, as one reporter observed, "attest [to] the people's awareness of the cost of the invasion in American casualties."[43] In subsequent weeks the success of the landings, and above all the stunning victories of August, helped to calm the public mood. Then the political calendar almost immediately ratcheted up the excitement levels again, for 1944 was a presidential election year—the first time Americans had voted for their commander in chief while at war since 1864.

With the benefit of hindsight, it is tempting to view this wartime election as a moment of surprising bipartisan unity. The Republican Party, after all, was much more docile than in most other twentieth-century wars, determined to position itself as a "loyal" opposition that would do nothing to undermine the final push

toward victory. Since Pearl Harbor many of its leaders had worked hard to eliminate any hint of isolationism. With election day approaching, the Republican
nominee, Thomas E. Dewey, even treated the issue of American membership of
a world organization—the issue that had so poisoned politics in the aftermath
of World War I—"as a non-partisan subject which must be kept entirely out
of politics."[44]

Yet hindsight tends to smooth over the harsh edges of partisan conflict. The
passage of time has a habit of turning issues, which used to be deeply controversial, into quaint anachronisms that become difficult to take too seriously. More
to the point, no one at the time knew the outcome of the political struggle, and
some participants were prepared to do desperate things to come out on top,
especially when the prize was as big as the White House—and, for Republicans
in 1944, the rival was as hated as Roosevelt and his statist New Deal.

Four years before, such desperation had prodded the then-GOP candidate to
argue that a vote for Roosevelt would be a vote to send thousands of Americans
to their deaths in Europe. In the context of Overlord, this argument appeared
remarkably prophetic. But now they were dressed up as post-isolationists,
few Republicans wanted to dredge up this unfashionable aspect of their past.
Instead, Dewey harked back only to what he dubbed Roosevelt's ponderous and
pusillanimous pre–Pearl Harbor mobilization effort—an argument that shrewd
campaigners could still connect to the nation's growing casualty list, albeit safely
clothed in a suitably new internationalist garb.[45]

Clare Booth Luce (R-CT), the combative and controversial congresswomen
who was married to the proprietor of *Time* and *Life*, led the way. At the Republican
Convention in June, Luce launched an impassioned assault on what she dubbed
Roosevelt's mismanagement of foreign affairs, using the fate of "GI Jim" to give her
claims added resonance. "His young bones bleach on the tropical roads of Bataan,"
Luce told both the party faithful and a large radio audience:

> A white cross marks his narrow grave on some Pacific island. His dust
> dulls the crimson of the roses that bloom in the ruins of an Italian village.
> The deserts of Africa, the jungles of Burma, the rice fields of China, the
> plains of Assam, the jagged hills of Attu, the cold depths of the seven
> seas, the very snows of the Arctic, are the richer for mingling with the
> mortal part of him. Today his blood flecks the foam of the waves that fall
> on the Normandy beaches. He drops again and again amid the thunder
> of shells, while silently down on the tragic soil of France the white apple
> blossoms drift over him.

Why had so many GI Jims succumbed to this fate? For Luce, their deaths had not
been inevitable. They could have been "averted" by "more skillful and determined

leadership" during the 1930s, or, at least, more "truthful and fearless leadership" that would have mobilized the nation more speedily when it became clear that only force could halt Axis aggression.[46]

By so directly and prominently basing her attack on casualties, Luce was clearly treading on treacherous ground. Most obviously her references to the past conveniently ignored the earlier isolationist mood, which had been embraced by many of her party colleagues and which had forced Roosevelt to maneuver so slowly against the Axis before Pearl Harbor. These were awkward facts that some mainstream newspapers emphasized when they criticized Luce's "insinuation" that Roosevelt was culpable for all these casualties. Even more awkwardly Luce's speech came at the time that the Pentagon was sending the first casualty telegrams to D-Day victims' next of kin. Luce was therefore exposed to the damaging charge that her emotive reference to battlefield losses were both tactless and tasteless, a clumsy effort to use relatives' misery for political gain.[47]

Nor, in purely political terms, did Luce's speech seem particularly adroit, since drawing attention to the war played directly to the president's main strength. Even before Overlord's success, numerous polls had consistently placed Roosevelt as the nation's favorite to deal with international issues, including the war. In contrast, despite the president's reform record during the Depression, Republicans were moving into a clear lead on domestic matters, as the public tired of the strikes, the rationing, and the taxes that had scarred the home front in recent years.

Dewey's emergence as the clear GOP frontrunner did nothing to alter this basic dynamic. Between May and July a series of polls found that the war was so important to Roosevelt's appeal that if it was over by election day Americans would favor the Republican candidate by a margin of 55 to 35 percent. In contrast if Americans were still fighting overseas, the president would win by a comfortable ten-point margin, 51 to 41 percent. When asked what they considered Roosevelt's main strengths, almost 70 percent responded that "he shows great courage in carrying on the war," while only just over 20 percent felt that he had played "politics too much during the war."[48]

With such strong levels of support persisting into the campaigning season, the Democrats could initially adopt a decidedly relaxed attitude toward Republican efforts to exploit the casualty issue. In fact, Roosevelt was more than happy to speak about his war record, even if this meant directly alluding to the growing death toll in Europe. As he told the nation in a revealing fireside chat on 12 June:

> I think from the standpoint of the enemy we have achieved the impossible. We have broken through their supposedly impregnable wall in northern France. But the assault has been costly in men and costly in materials. Some of our landings were desperate adventures; but from

advices received so far, the losses were lower than our commanders had estimated would occur. We have established a firm foothold. We are now prepared to meet the inevitable counterattacks of the Germans— with power and with confidence. And we all pray that we will have far more, soon, than a firm foothold.[49]

As Roosevelt emphasized, military success was not confined to northern France. Japan was firmly on the defensive too. This was a crucial, because Roosevelt's one war-related vulnerability was the oft-heard refrain that he had prioritized Europe at the expense of the Pacific. In July he sought to demolish this charge once and for all. Instead of staying in the country for the Democratic Convention, he undertook the long trip to Hawaii, where he met MacArthur, Admiral Chester Nimitz, and others who "seem[ed] to feel a little neglected for to them the Pacific operations seem at least as important as those in Normandy."[50]

MacArthur clearly posed the biggest political danger, since he had close connections with the Republican Right and had recently been touted as a GOP presidential candidate. On arriving in Pearl Harbor, the canny president was therefore particularly solicitous toward the egotistical general, especially on the vexed question of Pacific strategy. Back in 1942 MacArthur, having been ordered off the Philippines to organize Allied defenses from Australia, had publicly vowed to return. Now, two years later, the two men probably reached an implicit agreement. Roosevelt would throw his weight behind a strategy focused on recapturing the Philippines (rather than aiming for Formosa first, as some senior officials were advocating). For his part, MacArthur would effectively boost Roosevelt's reelection chances by issuing press releases that "would portray great battlefield successes stemming from increased Washington support."[51]

By October MacArthur was poised to return. With the pugnacious Adm. William F. Halsey attacking Leyte, where in a confused naval battle he effectively ended the threat posed by the Japanese navy, MacArthur's troops landed on two major beachheads. Although Japan's initial resistance was light, these forces were soon engaged in a fierce fight as they tried to push inland—a fight so fierce that MacArthur had to postpone his planned invasion of Luzon to the new year.[52]

Despite the delay and the cost, Roosevelt recognized that the invasion of Leyte was fraught with political symbolism. In a specially convened press conference the day MacArthur's men touched Philippine soil, he declared triumphantly: "We promised to return; we have returned." A week later, in a major election address, Roosevelt then used the navy's massive success at Leyte Gulf to counteract another GOP argument: that he had failed to prepare the country for war. As he happily pointed out, "the ships of Admiral Halsey's powerful Third Fleet that helped to give the Japanese navy the worst licking in its history" had all been built on his watch. "And speaking of the glorious operations in the

Philippines," he concluded exultantly, "I wonder—whatever became of the suggestion made a few weeks ago, that I had failed for political reasons to send enough forces or supplies to General MacArthur?"[53]

If the Philippines' campaign presented the perfect opportunity to emphasize that the United States was making great strides against the Japanese, the other prong of America's "dual-axis" Pacific attack—some 1,500 miles away in the great expanse of the Central Pacific—highlighted the administration's confidence that it was relatively invulnerable on the casualty issue.

In the summer of 1944 the United States' fiercest battle in the Central Pacific was for the island of Saipan in the Marianas, the capture of which would provide the new long-range American bombers with an important new base to attack Japan's home islands. In an echo of Tarawa, once again the toll was very high. With the Japanese determined to make the attackers pay a high a cost, the Americans suffered more than fourteen thousand casualties in a grisly fight that lasted almost a month.[54]

For the war correspondents who covered Saipan, the battle was not only grim and bloody; it was also unglamorous in a purely professional sense. Particularly galling was the apparent hypocrisy of their own bosses back in the United States, who often claimed that the Pacific War was of paramount importance but then buried eyewitness accounts of it on their inside pages. As Keith Wheeler, the war correspondent who covered Saipan for the *Chicago Tribune*, complained in late July, this major fight had been given the "brush off" by most editors, who placed it a "very bad fourth," way behind the Normandy invasion, the developing air war against Japan, and the Republican National Convention. Saipan, Wheeler observed in a public letter, "was a bloodier battlefield than Tarawa. It seems to me that it is the duty of an informed American press to educate the people to the implications of this war in the Pacific."[55]

What was particularly revealing about this indictment was the absence of a usual suspect. Wheeler, while railing against his own profession, curiously omitted any criticism of the U.S. Navy, which had a well-earned reputation for excessive censorship. This omission was no oversight. In recent months the navy, which was increasingly involved in a PR battle with the army and air force to raise its domestic profile, had worked hard to develop swifter transpacific communications. This enabled the reporters who landed at Saipan to cable back more than seventy-five thousand words from the forward area. When scouring what these correspondents had written, naval censorship remained fierce, especially when reporters attempted "to interpret, to speculate or prognosticate." Yet, revealingly, the navy's blue censorship pencils remained unused whenever correspondents talked about the "bloody battle, bitter fighting, fierce resistance."[56] The navy's own communiqués also emphasized that "the land campaign for

Saipan was severe" with "heavy" losses on both sides, while conceding that "many of our casualties were incurred in the first days of the fighting, in the desperate battle which raged along the beaches."[57]

When it came to putting a precise number on these losses, the navy moved much faster than the army had been able to do in Normandy. As early as July 12, just three days after the battle had finished, James Forrestal, the new navy secretary, revealed that the conquest of Saipan had resulted in more than 15,000 U.S. casualties, of which 2,359 were killed, 11,481 were wounded, and 1,213 missing. The public, added the marine commandant, would have to become hardened to such figures, for they "indicated [the] growing severity of the opposition to be expected in the war with Japan."[58]

Significantly, most Americans applauded the government's candor. Unlike two years before, when the administration had been buffeted by constant complaints about excessive censorship, in the summer of 1944 more than 60 percent thought the government was "giving the public as much information as it should about the war." This high figure was doubtless a testament to the fact that Americans were happily reading stories about great victories in both Europe and the Pacific. These victories, in turn, suggested that the large losses had not been in vain. They also appeared to make Roosevelt's political position more unassailable than ever.[59]

In any election campaign, a week or two can prove a very long time. And in September, as the fortunes of war started to shift, Dewey was suddenly presented with an opportunity to grasp the initiative on both the war and the casualty issue.

Ironically, this opening stemmed largely from the success of Allied arms in Europe. In late August, the possibility that the war might suddenly end exposed the lack of bureaucratic agreement on policy for postwar Germany. Henry Morgenthau, the treasury secretary, stepped clumsily into this policy breach. He encouraged Roosevelt to endorse a tough peace that included depriving Germany of an industrial base to build the weapons of war.[60] Unfortunately for Roosevelt, in late September word of this Morgenthau plan for German "pastoralization" leaked to the press, creating a sensation. Compounding Roosevelt's misfortune, this press leak coincided with a sudden stiffening of German battlefield resistance in the Netherlands. Around Arnhem, the Allies even suffered a major reverse. Although Operation Market-Garden was principally a British enterprise, two American airborne divisions sustained about 3,500 casualties.[61]

In retrospect this Allied setback was clearly the result of an overly optimistic plan to capture too many bridges, together with the chance presence of crack panzer divisions in key landing zones.[62] At the time, however, politicians and the press from both ends of the spectrum reached a very different conclusion, linking the bloody fate of Market-Garden to the Morgenthau plan press leak.[63]

Dewey certainly hurried to claim that the plan had enabled the Nazis "to terrify the Germans into fanatical resistance," with disastrous results for U.S. troops. "On the basis of the Treasury Department's ill-conceived proposals," Dewey declared in October and again in early November,

> the German people were told that a program of destruction was in order for them if they surrender. Almost overnight the morale of the German people seemed wholly changed. Now they are fighting with the frenzy of despair. We are paying in blood for our failure to have ready an intelligent program for dealing with invaded Germany.[64]

Put another way, not only had Roosevelt's mismanagement before Pearl Harbor caused needless deaths, as Luce had insisted back in June, but his continued incompetence also remained a bane for "GI Jim" who had to deal with the costly consequences of his amateurish meddling on Europe's increasingly bloody battlefields.

As election day approached, Roosevelt and the Democrats were clearly rattled. At the beginning of September one aide had reported that "Roosevelt leads Dewey in the public's estimate of his ability to handle: (1) peace making; (2) winning the war."[65] The following month Dewey's skillful attack made the president vulnerable on both scores. Polls even suggested that the race was tightening, with Roosevelt losing ground in such pivotal states as New York and Pennsylvania.[66]

Roosevelt's response was to distance himself from the Morgenthau plan. "Every story that has come out," he indignantly told reporters in his weekly press conference following the leak, "is essentially untrue in the basic facts."[67] Although many reporters swallowed this artful piece of presidential patter, Roosevelt found dealing with the burgeoning casualty list a far trickier matter. In the face of Republican claims that government policy had caused unnecessary deaths, the White House could not simply withhold news of the Market-Garden losses, for such a politically inspired cover-up could easily be exposed, and this itself might be electorally fatal.[68]

Nor, for that matter, did the White House have any real control over what was released and when. The War Department had long controlled casualty announcements. When Morgenthau asked Stimson to refute Dewey by stating that his pastoralization plan "had absolutely no effect on the course of the war," Stimson refused. He told Morgenthau that he was "entirely opposed to allowing the army to enter last-day politics." Instead, Stimson made one of his four European casualty pronouncements on October 20, just two weeks before the country voted, which revealed that almost 175,000 Americans had died on French soil.[69]

Still, there were limits even to Stimson's detachment from the fray. As the campaign became increasingly bitter, he was careful not to inflame the casualty issue.

He even delayed an important initiative until after the nation had voted. This was an improved accounting system, which enabled the military to publish a more up-to-date picture of losses. As Stimson explained two days *after* the election, this "bookkeeping change over" added about twenty thousand new casualties to the toll, taking the cumulative total above the landmark half a million figure.[70]

This delay was probably responsible for a potentially damaging rumor that began to spread in the first days of November. With the race continuing to tighten, a partisan-fueled whispering campaign went into overdrive, spreading all manner of damaging accusations, half-truths, and plain untruths to try to scare the undecided voters in key states. Democratic campaign chiefs were already fretful that the Republican attack dogs were taking this dark art to new heights. They therefore paid immediate attention when on November 2 the White House press office received word that canvassers in New York were picking up a "whispering rumor that casualty lists are being withheld [by the government] until after [the] election."[71]

Roosevelt's response was immediate. The very same evening he used a national radio address to launch a spirited rebuttal. "This campaign," he declared, "has been marred by even more than the usual crop of whisperings and rumorings." Rather than answer all these "hysterical, last-minute accusations," which "are trumped up in an attempt to panic the people on election day," he was proud to stand on his record—albeit with the technowar, casualty-saving ethos very much to the fore. "In winning this war," Roosevelt told his large audience, "there is just one sure way to guarantee the minimum of casualties—by seeing to it that, in every action, we have overwhelming material superiority."[72]

By election day these efforts to defuse the casualty issue had worked. Sufficient Americans voted for the commander in chief who had led them to the verge of victory to reelect him for an unprecedented fourth term. Roosevelt, though, was not in any sort of physical shape to enjoy his win. By November he was visibly suffering from the illness that would kill him within half a year. Heading off for a long vacation to recuperate, he left his subordinates in Washington to grapple with the consequences of two very different types of battle in the European theater: attrition along the German frontier, followed by the stunning Wehrmacht counterattack in the Ardennes—battles that would take the debate over casualties into interesting, if sometimes familiar, territory.[73]

Huertgen Forest and the Bulge

As allied forces reached Germany's borders, enemy resistance began to stiffen noticeably. To the north of the American sector, Hodges' First Army faced one of the most formidable sections of the German defense line, as well as the city of

Aachen, which provided the enemy with a chance to nullify U.S. mobility by launching a series of vicious street fights. During the first three weeks of October, the First Army's battle to capture Aachen—the first German city to come under direct Allied ground assault—was so bloody and brutal that it left two divisions "depleted and exhausted."[74] But it was on their southeastern flank, in the Huertgen Forest, that Hodges' men faced perhaps their stiffest fight.

Huertgen in 1944 immediately rekindled memories of the Argonne in 1918: a dense, damp, and dark forest, where rocky ridges and steep hills inevitably favored the defender. Like Pershing earlier, U.S. commanders, fearful of leaving their flank exposed, decided to push into this inhospitable terrain, with costly results. The Ninth Division, which began its assault in mid-October, rapidly lost 4,500 men. The Twenty-eighth Division, which took over in early November, fared even worse, suffering more than six thousand losses. By the time the forest was finally cleared, twenty-four thousand American troops had been killed, wounded, or listed as missing in this dismal campaign, while another nine thousand suffered from non-battle ailments—cold, flu, trench foot, and fatigue.[75]

Losses at these levels, coming after the hard slog in Normandy and the recent setback in the Netherlands, inevitably placed enormous pressure on the American manpower pool. Before Overlord, Marshall had made a calculated gamble. Brushing aside Stimson's fear that the army needed more men to be certain of prevailing against the tough German enemy, Marshall had pegged the overall size of the army to ninety divisions. Suddenly this seemed too small. With every division in the line occupying about twenty kilometers (nearly twelve-and-a-half miles) most officers thought their men were too thin on the ground. They also had trouble getting replacements. By the end of October Eisenhower's command had thirty thousand replacement riflemen on hand, an improvement on recent months but still well below the army's preferred safety margin given the high casualty rates among this type of soldier.[76]

Technowar was, of course, meant to alleviate such manpower problems; the army, rather than relying on overwhelming numbers of infantrymen, was supposed to be able to crush the enemy with mass-produced weapons.[77] By the fall of 1944, however, it was not only soldiers who were at a premium. Equipment was lacking too. The shell shortage, in particular, was so bad that some commanders had to institute rationing or even resort to expedients such as trying to use captured German ammunition.[78]

Overstretched supply lines were clearly the root cause of these shortages. As Allied troops advanced farther from the few functioning ports, their elongated supply lines became so taut that they threatened to snap, making it increasingly difficult to get the necessary war materiel to the correct part of the front.[79] Back in Washington, though, a number of officials believed the shell shortage stemmed from another problem: a slackening off on war production caused by constant news of battlefield success.

In August, with the Allies on the offensive everywhere, the media's war coverage had inevitably been tinged with triumphalism. But, in October, when the Allied advance slowed down, the Pentagon thought that SHAEF's censors were still too willing to allow correspondents to paint an optimistic picture of the war. "Maximum American support of the war effort," it warned SHAEF's press office, "will probably not be best solved by over-emphasis on success."[80] Taking this advice to heart, SHAEF soon started to give a clear new direction to war correspondents. "The weightiest argument that could be advanced for increased production of all types of ammunition by the American war industry," a SHAEF-based reporter for the *New York Times* revealingly argued at the beginning of December, "is the total number of casualties suffered by the four American armies participating in the present offensive on the western front."[81]

This argument would be even weightier if accompanied by timely and accurate casualty lists. As it was, the current time lag in casualty reporting, as one U.S. officer openly complained, gave the American public the false and dangerous impression that "only Germans have been killed and wounded."[82] What could be done? As Gen. Frank A. Allen, Eisenhower's new press chief, fully recognized, it was impractical to speed up the whole reporting process at a time when so many units were already overworked. So he tried to find more innovative solutions. Early in December Allen hit on the idea of publicizing in percentage form the casualties of one particular division since D-Day. After talking it through with reporters, he concluded that only by announcing such hard figures could he get the press to paint a "realistic picture" of the battles unfolding on Germany's borders, without at the same time providing valuable intelligence to the enemy.[83]

While this idea was under discussion, Allen's briefers tried to fill the gap as best they could. "Advances are being made at a cost of considerable, and at times severe, casualties," they now stressed, adding the careful caveat that "the role of the attacker is always more costly than that of the defender," particularly when the defender could sit behind established positions as impressive as the Siegfried Line (known in Germany as the West Wall).[84]

Still, emphasizing casualties to downplay complacency was a dangerous game, and a story by Wes Gallagher threatened to ruin it entirely. Gallagher, known widely as "the bellwether of American correspondents," spent late November with the Ninth Army. Talking to officers and GIs, he found that they did not blame their complacent compatriots for the worsening frontline conditions. Instead, their constant complaints about the "shortages of ammunition and tires," targeted a very different culprit. "The situation on the western front," these soldiers apparently informed Gallagher, "is due to short-sighted and optimistic planning in Washington which led to heavy commitments to the Pacific theater along with general cuts in munitions and men in the belief that the war would be over this year."[85]

This was a damning indictment, which directly undercut Roosevelt's laudatory campaign rhetoric about continued production achievements. It also gave congressional Republicans, licking their wounds from a fourth straight presidential election defeat, an opportunity to exploit. Their ranking member on the House Military Affairs Committee, J. Parnell Thomas (R-NY), grasped it with alacrity. The shell shortages were "affecting the progress of the war, the casualty rate, and soldier morale," Thomas charged. A full-scale congressional inquiry, he added menacingly, ought to be launched at once.[86]

With this threat hanging over their heads, Pentagon officials immediately embarked on their own internal investigation. As well as trying to ascertain the precise situation on replacements and ammunition stocks, they swiftly got SHAEF to concede that the "Gallagher story [was] not based on facts." "We know of no responsible officer," Eisenhower's press office insisted, "who has stated [that the] situation is due to optimistic planning in [the] War Department." So far, so predictable: few military men were prepared to ruin their careers by admitting they had bad-mouthed their superiors to a newspaperman. But even if the story was indeed a fabrication, this still begged an important question: Why had the censors passed it in the first place? Perhaps the recent relaxation in the name of revealing reality had gone too far. Perhaps it was time to be more rigorous.[87] Such were the thoughts already circulating around SHAEF headquarters in mid-December when all of a sudden the Allies suffered their biggest reverse of the European campaign.

The Battle of the Bulge was Hitler's last gamble. In mid-September, with Allied troops approaching Germany's borders, he unveiled a daring plan. He would cobble together three armies and then throw them against the Allies in a desperate attempt to relive his greatest victory. Back in 1940 Hitler's Wehrmacht had scythed through thin lines of unsuspecting French troops in the apparently impenetrable Ardennes, paving the way for the dazzling success that had almost won him the war. Now his troops would use the cover of ice, fog, and snow to push through the same terrain, with the goal of destroying twenty-five to thirty Allied divisions, recapturing the vital port at Antwerp, and inflicting such a heavy defeat on his western adversaries that they would sue for peace.[88]

As in 1940, Hitler certainly caught the Allies by surprise. He also struck at a relatively unguarded portion of the front, for U.S. forces were already depleted by the Huertgen battles, while Bradley had gambled that the German army was on its last legs and the Ardennes was the last place for it to make a sudden revival. The result was a series of big, if uneven, German gains, especially around the towns of Saint-Vith and Wilz.[89]

For Eisenhower, this sudden and surprising turn of events offered a major test. Meeting with senior officers at Verdun on December 19, he swiftly developed a response. First he would hold the "shoulders" to the north and south of German attack in order to "direct its force into the center." Then he would to try to insure that the Germans in the center did not make it beyond the Meuse River. Finally, he would redirect Allied armies to the north and south of the developing German bulge so that they were in a position to counterattack and hopefully encircle the enemy. It would take time, however, for the various ingredients of this policy to blend together. In the meantime the Allied situation looked quite bleak, especially for those units, such as the 101st Airborne, which had been hurriedly sent into action. Rapidly surrounded, these troops faced a major battle in plunging temperatures to cling on to the vital road junction at Bastogne.[90]

Reeling from the German attack, on December 16 SHAEF instituted a total news "blackout." As the fighting was so "fluid," a briefing officer explained, the high command wanted "to give no additional information to the enemy." Reporters were incensed. One of the biggest news stories of the war was unfolding, and the military was denying them the opportunity to get their copy on page one. Correspondents also doubted SHAEF's military security rationale, especially when faced with restrictions they deemed petty in the extreme, and on December 19 their tempers quickly boiled over. George Lyon, the OWI representative at SHAEF, who had been editor of the *Buffalo Times* and *PM* before the war, charged that the army's policy was "stupid." "You complain about complacency," added Joe Evans of *Newsweek*, "but when there's bad news you won't release it."[91]

The worst news of all was the large numbers of likely casualties. As *Time* observed, "the size of the military defeat would be measured some day in American soldiers killed, wounded, captured." What the press wanted to know was how soon this day would come. As always, correspondents demanded haste, but on this occasion the army's casualty reporting was tardier than usual. With some Allied units surrounded and cutoff by the marauding Wehrmacht, the need to deny sensitive information to the enemy was particularly acute. Everywhere the situation was so confusing that any official announcement was bound to be little more than guesswork. Rather than worry relatives with a misleading release, SHAEF fell back on a well-worn tactic: it adopted a position of studied silence.[92]

Yet newspapers were desperate to print something. In the absence of official figures, they inevitably turned to enemy sources. Even mainstream newspapers were tempted into this practice. As the *New York Times* reported at the turn of the year, German broadcasts were proclaiming "that 140,000 Americans had been lost on the Western Front in December."[93]

This was a massive total, but was it true? After more than a decade of exposure to Nazi propaganda, many Americans had acquired a deep and healthy skepticism of anything that emanated from Berlin. At this particular moment, however, Nazi information was all they had to go on—indeed, as war correspondents were quick to stress, SHAEF's blackout had effectively given the Nazis "a clear field for exaggeration." Small wonder that the public's innate skepticism was often pushed to one side, to be replaced with a spasm of angst during one of the least festive of all holiday seasons.[94]

Congress was one revealing indicator of the fretful new mood. On Capitol Hill the daily mailbag was suddenly inundated with missives from "worried parents asking for news of their boys fighting on foreign fronts, and particularly those in action around Bastogne and the Belgian bulge." Opinion polls detected a similar anxiety. In the third week of December a State Department survey found that only 49 percent thought that the president was taking good care of the country's interests, down from 65 percent just after D-Day and 53 percent at the time of the election. These hard figures were reinforced by findings from the OWI's correspondence panels, an early form of focus group that tried to give a degree of depth to the bald figures revealed in opinion polls, which reported a "general spirit of discouragement, dejection, and disillusionment" across the country.[95]

Although such dejection did not translate into a widespread desire for peace at any price, the Allied reverse—and particularly the prospect of more than one hundred thousand fresh casualties, if the headlines were to be believed—clearly exerted some impact on support for the war. At the start of 1945 an official media survey found that those "who wanted elaboration of the unconditional surrender formula included representatives of almost all shades of political opinion." On the right the usual isolationist suspects like Wheeler had long attacked this policy as "brutal" and "asinine." Now, liberals like Cecil Brown and the Union for Democratic Action also mouthed the anti-unconditional-surrender line, as did moderate newspapers such as the *Des Moines Register* and the *Richmond Times-Dispatch*. In a troubling repeat of the previous winter, when speculation about massive new casualties had boosted support for negotiations, the distorted news from the Ardennes was also partly responsible for a new spike in those willing to discuss peace terms with the German army if it overthrew Hitler. This rose to 36 percent (up from 27 percent in October), with only 57 percent rejecting such a move out of hand (down from 66 percent in October).[96]

At SHAEF press headquarters in Paris, Allen soon became so "disturbed" by these consequences of the blackout that he instituted a series of changes. He began by relaxing the news embargo a little, allowing some copy through after a thirty-six hour hold "to make sure that the enemy will not reap benefit from the information."[97] Then as Allied forces slowly regained the initiative, opened the roads to Bastogne, and "smoothed" out the Bulge, his censors became more liberal. Just before Christmas they started to pass dispatches based on interviews with the bedraggled survivors of the initial German thrust. A week later, having come to recognize that one of the correspondents' biggest bugbears was the inability to name specific units, they also eased this restriction. All of a sudden journalists could make the first "announcement of units on whom had fallen some [of the] heaviest brunt of fighting." As correspondents hastened to report, one was the "First Infantry, Brooklyn and the nation's pride in two world wars." Another was "the veteran Eighty-second Airborne Division, whose cocky lads gave their lives halting Panzer tanks with bazookas."[98]

When it came to precise numbers, however, SHAEF remained cagey. On December 23 its briefing officer, in a revealing quadruple negative, awkwardly informed reporters that he now saw "no reason why we should not say our losses have not been inconsiderable." But, he added, the same old practical constraints still prevented the publication of harder numbers. "One does not know positively what our losses are," he concluded, "because you always, in a case like this, get stragglers who come in from unexpected places. . . . I would not like to commit myself to a figure."[99]

In fact the War Department was not in a position to commit to precise figures until the new year. Then on January 15 Stimson divulged the happy news that the cost had been much lower than the enemy had tried to claim. According to preliminary data, Stimson revealed, the U.S. Army had sustained "slightly less" than forty thousand casualties in the Ardennes sector since December 15, of which eighteen thousand were missing (and most of these were presumed to be prisoners of war). With German losses much higher—Stimson's estimate was about ninety thousand—top military leaders now began to insist that the Bulge was a major victory. Stimson even went as far as claiming that it would probably "hasten the end of the war."[100]

That the actual casualty figures were much lower than initial media reports further underlined the negative consequences of the blackout. It was scarcely surprising, therefore, that early in the new year, as the military continued to lick its wounds, SHAEF's command looked for ways to prevent a recurrence.[101] In Washington, too, officials were eager to improve their publicity efforts. Historians have often pointed to the State Department's concerted new efforts to drum up domestic support for an internationalist postwar agenda.[102] Less familiar, however, was the surprising resurrection of an almost-dead agency: the Office of War Information.

The Bloody Denouement, 1945

By common consent the OWI had not been a success. From its earliest days it had suffered from lukewarm presidential patronage, for Roosevelt had been determined to remain the propagandist-in-chief. Denied the power to issue news releases, the OWI had swiftly become a loser in the bureaucratic dogfights that had scarred wartime Washington. All too often it had been overpowered and outfought by the established military and diplomatic bureaucracies who had viewed it as an excessively liberal organization. Although dependent on congressional funds, it had also foolishly angered a powerful bipartisan coalition of Republicans and southern Democrats. The payback came in August 1943, when this congressional coalition duly combined to slash the OWI's funding.[103]

Most accounts of the OWI take this as a fitting place to end their discussion of its domestic record. Yet the OWI was not quite dead. With the support of its erstwhile adversaries in the Pentagon, in the middle of March 1945 it suddenly found a major new domestic task: sending out the first combined list of army and navy casualty names to newspapers across the country.[104]

The wire services had previously undertaken this tough task. In February, as the sheer volume of names threatened to overwhelm their communications' network, they suddenly told the military that they could no longer perform the job.[105] As the Pacific War reached a bloody crescendo—with more than one hundred thousand casualties during the successive invasions of Luzon, Iwo Jima, and Okinawa—the navy rapidly recognized that it lacked the personnel to take over. It therefore agreed with a reluctant army to divest this distasteful and time-consuming task to the OWI: the collating of thousands of names, the checking for mistakes, the type-setting of on average twelve thousand lines a day six days a week, and the mailing out of almost three thousand packages to newspapers every single day.[106]

In March, the OWI sent out the first-ever combined list of all casualty names. It also liaised with newspapers to ascertain precisely how they wanted to receive this information. It worked with the Government Printing Office to discover the most cost-effective way of producing documents that comprised of up to ninety pages a day. It broke down the casualty lists into eighteen regions, so that they could be targeted at newspapers and radio stations whose audiences were overwhelmingly concerned only with local losses. And it tried to reduce the time lag between when the next of kin was notified and when the name appeared in the newspaper, which currently was an unacceptable couple of weeks.[107]

An obvious danger existed in making this operation too efficient: newspapers would suddenly be filled with a huge number of names of dead, wounded, and missing. This was precisely what happened. Just two weeks into the new regime the OWI announced its first red-letter day: its published list, which contained 14,664 names, "was the biggest since the war began." As OWI officials hastened to explain, this large number was only partly a product of the big casualties recently suffered at Iwo Jima. It was also inflated by the new sense of urgency the OWI had brought to the task, which enabled it to eliminate "a backlog of some 200,000 casualties which had piled up in the Army Public Relations Bureau."[108]

* * *

While these OWI lists provided a grim punctuation to the daily media coverage of the war's final campaigns, the reporters operating at the front filled in the details with more colorful prose, telling the story of a deadly fight that was mutating into an ever more aggressive, gruesome, and bloody enterprise as U.S. forces inched slowly toward Japan's major home islands.

Certainly the long campaign in the Philippines and the invasions of Iwo Jima and Okinawa were all covered in great detail, and not just because the intensely PR-conscious MacArthur was determined to have his revenge fight in the Philippines well publicized. By 1945, as the European war approached its end, the media also began to show an unprecedented interest in the Pacific. Over the winter some of journalism's biggest names, including Ernie Pyle of the *Washington Daily News* and Homer Bigart of the *New York Herald Tribune*, even switched theaters, although they tended to find the transition quite hard. "Things over here are so different," Pyle observed privately in February, "—the distances, and the climate and the whole psychological approach—that I still haven't got the feel for it yet. Also censorship is much different, due to a different type of security necessity, and I'm afraid I may be frustrated quite a bit in trying to give the average guy's picture of the war."[109]

Figure 3.2 A group of American correspondents about to embark on a ship for the Okinawa invasion. Ernie Pyle (*fifth from left*, seated) would be killed on the island. National Archives 80G 321043.

These interlopers' concerns soon receded when they discovered that the Pacific censors were initially determined to have their bloody battles reported as fully as possible. The Luzon landings in January were a case in point. MacArthur's PR officers provided the sixty reporters who covered the start of this grueling eight-month fight with a floating press headquarters on three small ships moored just offshore. This contained a high-speed radio teleprinter, which enabled them to wire out more than 170,000 words in the first week of the operation alone. The navy was not to be outdone. A month later, it laid on equally impressive facilities for the big-name journalists who gathered to report on the Iwo Jima invasion. Navy publicity officers even established laboratory and transmission facilities on Guam, where censors were on hand to develop and pass photographs of the landings, some of which made it back to the United States within eighteen hours of the start of the attack.[110]

Significantly the army and navy censors made little effort to sugarcoat all the news that soon flooded out of this theater. The story of Luzon, the *New York Herald Tribune* was able to announce in mid-February, was characterized by "a slow, brutal, [and] costly advance in jungle scrub."[111] Iwo Jima was just as bad. "Seldom," observed John Beaufort who covered the battle for the *Christian Science Monitor*, "have casualties been mentioned so early in a communiqué in the Central Pacific amphibious campaign"—a deeply disturbing inclusion since it was obvious that "marine losses in the first twenty-four hours of fighting undoubtedly were heavy." "For this desolate heap of volcanic cinders," wrote Bigart in a far more graphic dispatch in early March, "the marines have paid in blood, and more casualties will be counted before the island is secured."[112]

The Okinawa invasion, by contrast, was initially something of a cakewalk, as the Japanese generally failed to contest the American landings, and correspondents reported the unusual sight of medics "sitting among their sacks of bandages and plasma and stretchers with nothing to do." This easy opening quickly proved to be tragically misleading, for the GIs soon encountered an impressive Japanese defensive system burrowed deep into tunnels and caves. The fighting, as one historian points out, then "degenerated into a series of desperate rushes against prepared defenses—the results of which very closely resembled the horrors of the worst of trench warfare in World War I." On April 17, Pyle became a casualty of this desperate struggle, gunned down by a sniper, leaving other correspondents to report it in gory detail. Some revealed that the battle had "settled down to a slow, slogging battle of attrition," with even small objectives like a "craggy knoll" only being captured after "three days of grim and costly fighting." Others recorded that "American casualties are mounting sharply on this island as all hope of a cheap and quick American contest evaporates."[113]

This evaporation of hope was not confined to the Okinawa fight. As stories of this vicious battle filled U.S. newspapers and were underscored by the mounting casualty figures, attention inevitably turned to the likely cost of compelling Japan to surrender. "As our military and naval leaders have predicted all along," wrote the war correspondent Harold Smith on Okinawa in the wake of a week of big losses, "the closer we get to the Japanese main islands the more fierce and effective becomes the fanatical resistance of the enemy infantrymen." Some of Smith's colleagues were even prepared to speculate about the likely human cost of this resistance with concrete numbers. The most prominent was Kyle Palmer of the *Los Angeles Times* who returned from the Pacific in May convinced that the public had to be prepared for a tough, long fight. To drive home this point, Palmer quickly began insisting that "between 500,000 and one million more American fighting men would probably die before the war's end"—a truly staggering figure that was widely circulated and discussed during the ensuing crucial weeks.[114]

With this mounting public speculation as their backdrop, by June senior military officials privately agreed that Japan would have to be invaded in an operation that was bound to add if not a million then perhaps upwards of one hundred thousand new names to the already lengthening casualty roll.

This decision was not uncontested. The navy had long advocated bringing Japan to its knees by a blockade. The air force, dropping incendiary bombs to enormous destructive effect, still hoped to use its campaign to demonstrate the decisiveness of air power. But, with Marshall leading the way, the army success-fully pushed for a full-scale invasion. The sheer ferocity and tenacity of the Japanese defense of islands like Tarawa, Saipan, Iwo Jima, and Okinawa—which had often seen a Japanese fatality rate above 90 percent as most soldiers refused to surrender—was itself used as a clinching argument. After all, an enemy that was willing to sustain such losses was hardly likely to sue for peace without being coerced by a massive land campaign, such as the one that had recently swept across Germany.[115]

Would the American public accept massive losses to its own forces? The bottom line was a clear yes. In recent months the OWI's entrance onto the casu-alty scene had seen unprecedented numbers of names appear in the daily press. In March the media made much of the fact that the published death toll exceeded that of the Civil War. Three months later newspapers heralded the grim news that the total cumulative figure had passed the million mark. But not once had there been any suggestion that domestic support for the war against Japan was about to collapse in any way.[116]

Thoughts of compromise were certainly unlikely while Pearl Harbor remained such a vivid memory. Nor was the nature of the Pacific War conducive to letting Japan off the hook. Indeed, although the government had censored the most gruesome stories of Japanese atrocities, including reports of cannibalism, the brutal and bloody Pacific fighting had placed Americans in an unforgiving frame of mind.[117] As the OWI discovered in an exhaustive media survey conducted over the winter, the dominant view in news stories was that the Japanese were "dirty fighters, suicidal in battle," while only eight out of fifty-seven editorials that described the enemy failed to use terms like "vicious, cruel, barbaric." "Americans had to learn to hate Germans," editorialized *Life* magazine in May, "but hating Japs comes natural—as natural as fighting Indians once was." With levels of instinctive animosity so high, it was scarcely surprising that three-quarters of the country remained fully behind the policy of unconditional surrender—a figure that approached 90 percent in some regions.[118]

Still, the impact of heavy new casualties on the home front could not be entirely discounted. The brutal battles on Iwo Jima and Okinawa had clearly exerted a "sobering" effect on the public mood. Many prominent voices had also been highly critical of the way that the military had allowed these battles to turn into costly attritional struggles.[119] For its part, the military was concerned enough about the possible home-front reaction to mounting losses that it felt the need to tinker with its censorship policy.

The navy was in the vanguard. As the Pacific fighting intensified, it clamped down so hard that it threatened to end the war as it had begun: embroiled in a major spat with the media over covering up casualties. In the summer of 1945 Japanese kamikaze missions took a particularly heavy toll of the naval task force that was supporting the Okinawa invasion, sinking or damaging 334 vessels during a three-month period. This was not news the navy was anxious to share with the public. Naval censors claimed that they did not want the Japanese to discover from the American press the extent of damage their kamikazes were inflicting. War correspondents, however, began to suspect a more sinister motive. The navy, complained William H. Lawrence of the *New York Times*, had a policy "of doing things in a way best calculated to bury the bad news by over-whelming amounts of good." In the summer Lawrence even suspected that naval censors were holding two of his stories—including a major exclusive about over-all naval losses in the Okinawa fight—until a much bigger story came along to prevent this scoop from grabbing a front-page lead.[120]

Nor did the navy have a monopoly on such casualty concerns. In the White House Harry Truman, who had unexpectedly become president in April after Roosevelt's death, was equally sensitive. His own war experience cast a long shadow. Truman had fought with the ill-fated Thirty-fifth Division in 1918, a memory that remained vivid.[121] As the Joint Chiefs of Staff (JCS) developed their plans for an attack on Kyushu, he asked for "an estimate of the losses killed and wounded that will result from an invasion of Japan proper." His intention, Truman explained, was "to make his decision on the campaign with the purpose of economizing to the maximum extent possible in the loss of American lives."

The new president's request immediately provoked a flurry of bureaucratic activity, which resulted in a bewildering array of estimates. But at the crucial meeting on June 18 Marshall, rather than divulging specific projections, simply fudged the whole issue. He began by insisting that the Pacific War experience had been "so diverse as to casualties" that it would be "wrong to give any estimate in number." He then launched a diversionary lecture on the task of wartime leadership. "It is a grim fact," Marshall reminded his inexperienced commander in chief, "that there is not an easy, bloodless way to victory in war and it is the thankless task of the leaders to maintain their firm outward front which holds the resolution of their subordinates." Faced with Marshall's forceful presentation, Truman predictably endorsed the Kyushu invasion plan, but he clearly had qualms. As he told his senior military advisers, he "hoped there was a possibility of preventing an Okinawa from one end of Japan to the other."[122]

Just over a month later, the possibility of avoiding a larger Okinawa did exist. On July 16 an atomic bomb—the apogee of America's technowar strategy—was successfully tested in the New Mexico desert. Truman suddenly had the capability to end the war short of a full-scale invasion, and he had no doubt that this weapon had to be deployed.

Truman's calculations have been hotly contested.[123] Some of his senior advisers were mindful of the diplomatic benefits that might accrue if the United States deployed their powerful new weapon, especially in dealing with the increasingly difficult Soviet ally. For Truman, though, the paramount consideration was to end the fighting—and the dying—as soon as possible. True, dropping the bomb would undoubtedly result in large numbers of civilian casualties. But Truman was less concerned about this prospect and, as the historian Barton Bernstein argues, engaged "in what can only be interpreted as self-deception" about the large number of likely Japanese losses.[124] On the size of American casualties in any invasion of Japan, the record is particularly contentious. After the war Truman and other senior officials, eager to justify their decision, would greatly inflate the number of American lives they thought had been saved by dropping the bomb, throwing out figures of up to a million men.[125] At the time, however, Truman was confident that he was doing the correct thing. In the face of the recent mounting losses, which had hit the home front with greater force given the OWI's efficiency in getting them into the public domain, he wanted to use all the military power in the American arsenal to end the war and bring U.S. troops safely back home.[126]

When Japan sued for peace soon after two bombs were dropped on Hiroshima and Nagasaki, most Americans were duly thankful that these lives had been saved. "Those who lived," declared *Time* on August 20, "had one immediate comfort: they who had stormed scores of Pacific beaches under fire felt sure that the bloodiest invasion of all would be called off; men destined to occupy Japan would walk ashore down gangways, instead of fighting in the shallows and on the sands." It was a view that Truman echoed when he delivered a national radio address to mark the end of the fighting. "Our first thoughts," he told his compatriots,

> go out to those of our loved ones who have been killed or maimed in this terrible war. On land and sea and in the air, American men and women have given their lives so that this day of ultimate victory might come and assure the survival of a civilized world. No victory can make good their loss. We think of those whom death in this war has hurt, taking from them fathers, husbands, sons, brothers, and sisters whom they loved. No victory can bring back the faces they longed to see. Only the knowledge that the victory, which these sacrifices have made possible, will be wisely used, can give them any comfort. It is our responsibility—ours, the living—to see to it that this victory shall be a monument worthy of the dead who died to win it.[127]

That such a total victory had long been in the offing helped to insure that World War II did not become as controversial as America's other wars. But this so-called good war was still never an easy sell. Ironically, the likelihood of victory was part of the problem, for it resulted in periodic bouts of public complacency— a worrying disposition to think the war would soon be over and that sustained sacrifices would unnecessary. In response the Roosevelt administration made a concerted effort to blend casualties into its overall propaganda message, underlining the bloodiness of battles like Tarawa and even issuing alarming projections about future losses. But it was a dangerous rhetorical strategy, especially at a time when actual casualties were so high.

The 960,000 casualties suffered to defeat Germany, Italy, and Japan, of which almost 300,000 were fatalities, dwarfed American losses in any other twentieth-century war. Most came in the final year, when Roosevelt was running for an unprecedented fourth term and the public could easily have started suffering from war weariness. These losses were also sustained in battles on land, sea, and air, which threw up a range of new problems, from the navy's initial determination to suppress all casualty news to the air force's preoccupation with burnishing its reputation. Interservice operations generated additional headaches, not least the friendly-fire incidents on Sicily and just before the Normandy breakout. Although battlefield setbacks were rare, the army's news blackout during the Battle of the Bulge not only appeared hypocritical in the wake of its earlier efforts to undermine complacency but also prompted news organizations to speculate or even turn to inflated German claims about American losses.

Faced with all these problems, the U.S. government learned important lessons. Over the course of the war the navy became more open and publicity-conscious, the air force decided not to bury its bad news, and the services ultimately delegated the publication of combined lists to the OWI, which proved highly efficient at getting this information into the public domain. Senior officials also used the growing casualty toll to mobilize the home front behind the war effort. Roosevelt led the way, stressing publicly that the cost in American life was bringing the day of victory over an evil enemy ever closer. Truman then followed suit. In 1945 he called for a peace worthy of the dead in 1945. A year later he revealed a plan to find and repatriate the remains of those bodies not yet recovered, as part of the nation's "deep and everlasting appreciation of the heroic efforts" of those who had made the "supreme sacrifice" in a noble cause.

The result was a poignant blend of sorrow, remembrance, and patriotism. In October 1947, when the first 6,200 coffins arrived from Europe, almost half a million people gathered to watch the military procession that accompanied a solitary casket along New York's Fifth Avenue. Inside the coffin was an unnamed Medal of Honor recipient, who had fallen during the Battle of the Bulge and was meant to represent all the returning dead. The simple symbolism was certainly powerful. As a crowd of 150,000 assembled for a service in Central Park, some wept openly, while others could hardly bear to look. One woman screamed "'There's my boy, there's my boy,'" as she stared at the coffin, shaking with emotion."[128]

As this moving moment demonstrated, for those left bereft, the "good war" created deep scars that the cause, however noble, would never erase. But even for those who had not directly suffered a personal loss, the war's legacy soon belied the rosy outcome that total victory had promised. Indeed, rather than a serene period of international cooperation, Americans faced a cold war as the grand alliance cracked and the United States vied with the Soviet Union for ideological, economic, technological, and territorial supremacy. It was a vicious struggle that would be waged at the cost of countless lives, thousands of them American, as U.S. presidents intervened against the communist threat to protect allies in South Korea and South Vietnam. A new era of so-called limited war was about to dawn.

4

Partisanship and the Police Action

The Korean War, 1950–1953

At the midpoint of the twentieth century, returning American casualties were not always treated with the same moving dignity accorded to those bodies repatriated in October 1947. The advent of television was one culprit. During the early months of the Korean War, a new CBS entertainment show, *Truth or Consequences*, flew home a wounded GI. On a live broadcast the show's presenter paraded the soldier in front of his stunned mother, whose "anguish and relief" was plain for all to see. Some viewers were appalled. "Television reached a new low in taste last night," complained the *New York Times*. "It was an intensely private moment," the *Times* added, "which no outsider had the right to share."[1]

At the time, this TV intrusion into such a sensitive subject was both novel and uncharacteristic. Throughout the Korean War casualty debates invariably followed a familiar pattern, with politicians and the press disputing the total number of dead and wounded, rather than dwelling on the private anguish of individual relatives. In fact, these years would witness the most intensely partisan challenges to official casualty statistics—challenges that ultimately became so damaging the Truman administration was forced to rethink how it packaged casualty information.

But Korea also marked the start of a new era. Limited war was one reason, since this threw up a variety of new problems. For one thing, the limited nature of the fighting emboldened many competing voices in the polity to offer only limited support. For another, the absence of a major attack on the American homeland gave these critics an obvious opening to challenge the righteousness of the cause—and, by implication, the necessity for many American boys to make the ultimate sacrifice. In addition, when the fighting dragged on as diplomats sought a negotiated solution, these critics were further encouraged to pose the damning question of whether American boys should ever be asked to "die for a tie."

While all these problems would plague both the Korean and Vietnam wars, CBS's clumsy attempt to turn nameless numbers into specific victims offered the starkest glimpse into the future, albeit one that was only dimly visible in the summer of 1950 as the United States once again went to war.

Bitter Summer, 1950

Sunday, June 25, 1950, was a quiet, hot day in Washington. Most top officials were out of town, seeking rest after a hectic few months of debating Cold War strategy and pressing for domestic reform. They immediately hurried back to the capital when word came through of a dire new crisis. The massed ranks of the North Korean army had crossed the thirty-eighth parallel and were heading directly for Seoul.

The North Korean goal was simple. At the end of World War II the Korean peninsula had been artificially divided along the thirty-eighth parallel, as Washington and Moscow agreed to share occupation responsibilities. In the intervening years these two occupation zones had hardened into two competing regimes, the communist North ruled by Kim Il Sung and the U.S.-sponsored South led by Syngman Rhee. Both craved unity, but in 1949 and early 1950 Kim had been the more insistent, repeatedly lobbying Joseph Stalin to let him conquer the South.

The Soviet leader was initially reluctant to give the green light. Unlike the United States' earlier twentieth-century adversaries, Stalin much preferred low-risk, high-gain initiatives, not this sort of military adventurism that threatened war with the American superpower.[2] Then in early 1950 Stalin changed his mind. In the wake of Mao Zedong's victory in the Chinese Civil War, he was increasingly convinced that the correlation of forces was tipping in favor of the communist cause. He also concluded that the North Koreans could wrap up another communist victory so quickly that the Americans would not have time to intervene. In the spring of 1950 Stalin therefore gave Kim the go-ahead. He also provided North Korea with vital—if camouflaged—military support, which enabled Kim to assemble almost ninety thousand well-armed troops into seven divisions. By the end of June these soldiers were poised to plunge south across the thirty-eighth parallel, launching the first major hot war of the Cold War era.[3]

On that tense June Sunday, as the North Korean invasion gathered pace, Truman's first move was to fly back to Washington from Missouri to take direct control of the U.S. response. Decisive by nature, he immediately concluded that Stalin was behind the invasion. He also decided that the United States had to respond. With many other countries sharing this view, Truman was able to mobilize the United Nations behind a resolution "to repel the armed attack and to restore international peace and security in the area." With the State Department reassuringly concluding that Stalin "did not intend to bring about a general war," Truman could also contemplate a military intervention without risking World War III. Crucially too he had four of the United States' ten divisions close at hand, occupying Japan under the leadership of Gen. Douglas MacArthur, from where they could be rapidly sent to defend South Korea.[4]

Driven by these considerations, Truman led his foreign-policy team through a week of momentous decisions. On the first day of the crisis he agreed to provide South Korea with military supplies. On the second day he ordered U.S. planes to attack the North Korean invader, while also placing the Seventh Fleet in the Taiwan Straits. On the fifth day he directed the first troops from Japan to facilitate the evacuation of Americans from the peninsula. Then on the sixth day he made the momentous decision to send U.S. ground troops into combat to defend South Korea—before heading off, on the seventh day, for a well-earned rest.[5]

Unlike the United States' slow path into the two world wars, this rapid flurry of activity unfolded without any great debate about prospective casualties. The national mind-set, after all, was quite different from that of 1941 or 1917. Isolationism had already been destroyed by a combination of Pearl Harbor, Hiroshima, and the onset of the Cold War. A steely resolve, rather than a desire to remain aloof, prevailed in most sections of society. "Surprise and concern," recorded one official public opinion specialist on June 26, "are prominent in initial reaction to the Korean invasion, but commentators show little sign of alarm or fright at the war. The invasion is generally viewed as Soviet inspired, and those commentating lay greatest stress on the need for united and determined action on the part of the nations of the West to meet this challenge of communist aggression."[6]

Although Truman's decision to intervene was not dictated by this resolute and hawkish popular mood, he was able to bask in the almost universal public applause. "The president has acted—and spoken—with a magnificent courage and terse decision," declared the *New York Herald Tribune*. "The exhilarating lead provided by President Truman," agreed the *Washington Post*, "responds, in our view, to the deepest instincts of the American people." "Young Americans are now gambling their lives in battle," proclaimed Eric Sevareid on CBS. "The American people and the American Congress are overwhelmingly behind them and the decision to take the gamble. Those are the dominant facts of our immediate situation."[7]

In both Washington and the Far East this first hot war of the Cold War era would be waged by the World War II generation. In the Pentagon. Omar Bradley, now chairman of the JCS, had been the senior commander of American forces during the campaign across Western Europe, while Lawton Collins, the army chief, had been a corps commander under Eisenhower. In the Far East, Douglas MacArthur, the new United Nations (UN) commander, had spearheaded the army's campaign against Japan, while Walton Walker, who headed the Eighth Army in Korea, had fought the Germans as a corps commander. Lower down, too, many division-level officers as well as their support staffs had been heavily involved in fighting in Europe or the Pacific just five short years before.

While this experience would soon prove vital in many areas, in the chaotic first days it gave the U.S. military an important head start in dealing with the practical problems surrounding casualty reporting. MacArthur certainly wasted little time. On July 4, as his first units prepared to face the North Koreans, he instructed qualified personnel "to assist local commands in improving [their casualty] reporting technique."[8] In the next few weeks, as GIs entered the fight, these qualified men were put to work. At each layer of the military command— from individual regiments up to MacArthur's own headquarters in Tokyo— they made sure that every one of the growing number of casualty figures was "checked, rechecked, and double checked to guarantee its authenticity." In the Pentagon, the Casualty Section of the Adjutant General's office then used Western Union to dispatch telegrams confirming the deaths. Once the telegram company had informed the Pentagon that the grim delivery had been made, the Pentagon then released the name to the press.[9]

Acutely aware of the media complaints in previous wars, the U.S. military was at pains to make this publication process as swift and orderly as possible. During the first month, when total figures were still quite small, the Pentagon grouped all the casualties into one list, arranged alphabetically, which newspapers could publish the minute they received it.[10] Then from August 1, as the numbers mounted, the Casualty Section broke the list down by states, "for the convenience of newspapers and radio stations" who invariably catered to a small local market. Working with the Office of Public Information (OPI), it then mailed these out about sixty hours ahead of their release time, to insure that all newspapers could publish at the same time.[11]

This system, the Pentagon was quick to point out, was similar to the tried-and-tested methods devised during the two world wars, but with some significant enhancements, which promised to reduce the delays that had scarred earlier efforts. One change was related to the simple fact that the three services had been unified in 1947. As a result the military released just a single list, containing losses in the army, navy, marines, and air force. Another improvement stemmed from the existence of new technologies. Whereas in World War II the army had sent machine record cards from theater headquarters to the War Department, MacArthur's command now used electrical messaging to relay the same information, which cut down the transmission time dramatically. As the adjutant general observed, this service was "a far cry from the days of the Civil War" when relatives and the public had received the information in haphazard fashion from newspapers, town square message boards, and letters from chaplains and officers. But the army even thought that utilizing all possible speed, it could improve on its record during the two world wars.[12]

This, at least, was the plan. In war, however, many of the best-laid plans are discarded the minute they collide with the brutal reality of the battlefield. And Korean casualty reporting soon proved no different, largely because the early fighting was both so fluid and so discouraging.

The first American troops arrived in Korea on July 1, convinced that their task would be "short and easy." While the South Korean army had rapidly crumbled under the unexpected North Korean onslaught, the incoming GIs were supremely confident that they could rapidly stem the tide. As one of them put it, "as soon as those gooks see an American uniform they'll run like hell."[13]

Such cocky overconfidence quickly proved tragically misplaced. MacArthur's unfolding plan was to use three divisions from the Eighth Army in Japan to fight a rearguard action down the Korean peninsula. This would buy him time to gather reinforcements for a daring amphibious counterstroke, but at first MacArthur looked set to lose this race against the clock. The reasons were simple enough. The first units to arrive at the front were too small to make a difference. Because of severe budget cuts since the end of World War II, they often lacked serviceable equipment. Training levels were also poor. Tasked with an occupation role since 1945, most Eighth Army GIs had received limited practice with live ammunition, hardly any experience with weapons like anti-tank rockets, and no coordinated exercises above battalion level. Just as bad, in recent months their turnover rate had been far too high, with manpower reductions and home reassignments making the Eighth Army effectively "a force of strangers."[14]

The American army that entered the Korean War was thus a curious blend of the experienced and the unprepared. Within months the fierce Korean crucible would forge these underequipped "strangers" into a formidable fighting force, but at first they inevitably found the going extremely tough. Some wilted in the intense heat of a Korean summer, as temperatures soared above 110ºF. Others struggled with forced marches through unfamiliar, often mountainous terrain. Many became victims in the short, sharp clashes with some of the North Korean Army's best divisions. Forced back to the Pusan perimeter on the southern tip of the Korean peninsula, they soon sustained substantial casualties: 6,003 during the month of July alone, of which 1,884 were killed, 2,695 wounded, 523 missing, and 901 captured.[15]

These early setbacks made accurate casualty reporting extremely difficult. In the aftermath of any defeat the enemy invariably controls the battlefield, making it hard to recover bodies. In these particular defeats, outnumbered and disorientated GIs were often encircled by North Korean forces in short and vicious encounters; suddenly cut off, they had to make long, dispiriting marches through hostile territory before they renewed contact with their unit command. As a result the army's first estimates of losses were often inflated by large numbers of MIAs who could, within days or weeks, be accounted for. This created a major problem. The military's new improvements pointed in the direction of speed, but the practical matter of fighting the war often entailed countless delays.[16]

In a spirit of openness and cooperation—and acutely aware of the perils of suppression—the Pentagon's first instinct was to try to explain this difficult situation to potential critics. At the end of July, with U.S. forces still retreating, army officials met with senior media figures to justify the current delay in releasing figures. "The front is too confused now to make any real estimate," they informed a senior *Time* correspondent. For the time being the Pentagon asked the magazine to refrain from publishing weekly casualty "box scores," as it had during the last war. At this stage of the fighting, the military warned, such figures "would be meaningless, and certainly inaccurate." Although somewhat skeptical, *Time* took the obvious path for any self-respecting, patriotic, and communist-hating media outlet: it accepted the military's judgment. With U.S. forces still taking a beating, *Time* deferred using box scores for a few weeks until the frontline was "considerably shorter, tighter, and better organized."[17]

In Korea, meanwhile, MacArthur adopted a very different approach. Rather than explain, he tried to spin. MacArthur had already compiled a long record of PR overreach. During World War II his communiqués had often lauded his own military genius; on occasion they had even announced victories before they had actually been won. Now MacArthur again hoped to dominate media coverage with his own communiqués and briefings, which were rarely neutral. Most contained a clear slant, invariably stressing successes and downplaying disasters—particularly when it came to mentioning casualties.[18]

One MacArthur tactic was to announce American losses alongside a bigger enemy toll in an effort to emphasize that U.S. sacrifices had not been in vain.[19] Another was to minimize the number of U.S. casualties in big battles, even disastrous ones. On July 19, for instance, as the Kum River line crumbled and the fall of the key city of Taejon loomed, MacArthur's communiqué was relentlessly upbeat. "Our hold upon the southern part of Korea represents a secure base," he told reporters. "Our casualties, despite overwhelming odds, have been relatively light. Our strength will continue to increase while that of the enemy will relatively decrease."[20]

As the military hastened to add, casualties had been so light largely because of the sterling work of the U.S. medical teams. As this was one of the few success stories of the first weeks of the war, the military naturally encouraged correspondents to follow these medical units around in Korea. It was then delighted when reporters like Marguerite Higgins of the *New York Herald Tribune* duly reported that "the speed with which the wounded were tended and evacuated was one of the most remarkable performances this correspondent has seen in the Korean War."[21] Back home, Defense Department officials also worked hard to shift the media's attention in this direction. Because of air evacuation, exemplary cooperation between the services, and the very latest treatments, Pentagon spokesmen repeatedly stressed, "the death rate in military hospitals from battle wounds has been the lowest of any similar military campaign in our nation's history."[22]

The M*A*S*II image of the Korean War—which due to the long-running 1970s TV comedy show remains the dominant one in American popular culture—was thus born at a very early stage, the product of a particular propaganda urge to mute the public's response to casualties. Along with other efforts to minimize the costs, however, it did not really work. Rather than accept the military's efforts to soften the blow, other opinion makers in the American polity challenged official figures. In the process they often served to magnify the growing popular conviction that Korea was a particularly bloody war.

In one sense this challenge was surprising. In the first weeks of the war the rally-'round-the flag instinct was particularly strong—as *Time*'s willingness to postpone publication of its casualty box scores vividly demonstrated. The anticommunist Red scare, which had been building for the past few years, also gathered momentum. News organizations, filmmakers, teachers, professors, and union leaders all felt compelled to comply with the dominant anticommunist mood. If not, they were likely to be hounded, investigated, fired, or even imprisoned.

Yet this Red-scare-induced conformity soon proved of little help to Truman, for the simple reason that it was intertwined with an intensely partisan mood on Capitol Hill. Republicans, desperate to win back the White House after their fifth straight defeat in 1948, were looking for any stick to beat the administration. Before Korea, their nationalist leaders had even tacitly endorsed the controversial claims of Sen. Joseph McCarthy (R-WI), the most notorious Red baiter. Quietly, and somewhat nervously, senators like Robert Taft (R-OH) and Kenneth S. Wherry (R-NE) applauded McCarthy's attempts to indict figures connected with the last two Democratic administrations. They also believed that McCarthy's emphasis on locating U.S. officials responsible for "losing" China to communism would help to build bridges to their internationalist colleagues. These were centrist legislators who had concluded that the Truman administration had been too soft on Asian communism.[23]

With the outbreak of the Korean War, this claim that Truman had neglected Asia had an obvious appeal. It certainly helped to unite the two wings of the

Republican Party, particularly when the home front was overwhelmed with dark stories from American war correspondents at the front—stories that, crucially, were written in a censor-free environment.

This lack of battlefield censorship was MacArthur's decision. It stemmed from a variety of calculations: the practical (a lack of trained censors); the political (an awareness that the media generally disliked censorship); and the novel (the notion that such a controversial measure might not be necessary in a new type of limited war against a North Korean foe who could be rapidly beaten). Above all MacArthur seemed driven by a curiously naïve faith that he could control what reporters wrote about. In his view, if reporters failed to regurgitate the official line, he would impugn their loyalty or threaten to expel them from the theater altogether.[24]

These war correspondents were not cowed by such threats. Many of the two hundred or so who rushed to Korea were battle-hardened veterans who had already compiled impressive records covering World War II. Traveling to the front, and observing the initial string of demoralizing defeats at first hand, they cabled home dispatches that clearly undermined MacArthur's rose-tinted communiqués. Some wrote personal accounts describing what it was like to be stuck with outnumbered and undertrained troops who had been encircled by the enemy and then suffered large losses. Others tried to give a more precise estimate of the human cost, suggesting that about 15 to 20 percent of the American troops who had fought in the first battles had become casualties. Higgins even scored a notable scoop for the *New York Herald Tribune* when she produced an eyewitness account of the first infantryman killed in the war, felled by machine-gun fire as he was taking aim with his bazooka.[25]

By far the most common story, though, was one centered on interviews with dispirited and disillusioned GIs, whose ground-level view of the war was, as *Newsweek* pointed out, so very different from the official version. "Maybe an army spokesman in the Pentagon was right in declaring that 'it is not hopeless like Bataan' and there is 'no Dunkirk in sight,'" *Newsweek* noted skeptically in one of its first roundups of the war:

> Maybe it wasn't "a catastrophe" or "a rout" or "a slaughter." But for the GIs who last week were trading space—and blood—to gain time against North Korean "gooks," it wasn't a picnic. They exercised their inalienable right to gripe to front-line reporters, whatever Gen. Douglas MacArthur's GHQ might think.

A sample of their statements was revealing. "It was a slaughterhouse," declared a junior officer from San Jose, California. "They mounted machine guns on hills above us and swept us clean." "I don't claim to understand the grand strategy of this thing," said another from Godley, Texas, "but I will never again lead men into a situation like that one. Our orders were to hold at all cost. We did, but the cost was awful high as far as I'm concerned."[26]

In New York and Washington, anti-administration partisans inevitably picked up on these stories, adding their own twist. WHY ARE WE TAKING A BEATING? asked Luce's *Life* magazine toward the end of July, alongside a graphic photograph of a dead GI "face down on a Korean roadside." The answer, *Life* concluded, was simple: Truman had wasted American tax dollars on expensive liberal projects at home but had neglected the nation's defenses. Republicans agreed. "The whole burden of redeeming the blunders in blood," declared Harold Stassen, "is thrust upon American armed forces by a short-sighted, socialistically inclined national administration."[27]

But exactly how much blood had been spilled? On this crucial question the military's attempt to be candid (rather than its effort to slant or spin the figures) suddenly interacted with these harrowing stories from the front to add yet another ominous twist to Korea's first casualty controversy.

During July and August, with the battlefield situation remaining fairly fluid, the Pentagon struggled to release timely totals. Fifteen days was the normal length of time before names and numbers appeared in the press. This long lag continued to annoy editors, who saw casualty totals as a firm frame around which to construct their coverage of the fighting. It also riled Congress, which was already restless at Truman's refusal to ask for a formal declaration of war. Acutely aware that legislators felt they were being ignored or bypassed, the Pentagon hastened to brief key congressional committees on all aspects of the war. On casualties, military officials decided to follow the precedent established in World War II. They would provide the relevant committees with "unconfirmed flash figures" in closed-door sessions, so that legislators would have a current sense of what was happening at the front.[28]

Yet in the partisan environment of 1950s Washington, such briefings quickly backfired. The influential Senate Appropriations Committee, which contained a number of leading nationalists, was particularly skeptical. In August, Styles Bridges (R-NH), the committee's ranking Republican, spotted a large discrepancy between the relatively high "flash" figures he and his colleagues had received in secret session and the still-small official numbers the Pentagon had so far released to the press. In public Bridges professed to being appalled. The administration had "concealed" the war's human cost, he declared, and Americans would be shocked when officials finally divulged "the whole truth" about the real losses.[29]

The media was especially eager to fan these flames. Drew Pearson, who reached millions of Americans through his syndicated column and radio show, quickly latched on to Bridges's allegations. "The army is holding back the true casualty lists in Korea," Pearson claimed, which were perhaps as much as 75 percent higher than what had been announced. Bert Andrews of the Republican-leaning *New York Herald Tribune* then amplified this charge, pointing to a paragraph that had been "buried in a dispatch from Tokyo" by the war correspondent Keyes Beech. "The greatest source of anger and frustration here is Washington's apparent refusal to recognize the Korean War as a first-class war," Beech had written. "It may not be a first-class war in any conventional sense. But Americans are going to be in for a rude shock when they see the casualty figures." If this was a hint by Beech that the military had been glossing over the true state of affairs, then Andrews had absolutely no doubt who he would believe. "Newspaper reporters who know Mr. Beach's [sic] reputation as an accurate reporter," Andrews declared, "are aware that he was saying between the lines that he knew what the casualties were, and that the shock when the true number was announced would be 'rude' indeed."[30]

In Washington, the Pentagon moved swiftly to counter these cover-up allegations. The figures provided to the Appropriations Committee, it insisted, were unconfirmed figures. Yes, they had been included in a secret briefing, but only as a courtesy to keep committee members informed—and the briefing officers had clearly stressed that these totals were not accurate enough for general release. On August 7 the Pentagon then issued its first official total, announcing casualties of 2,616, of which 153 were killed in action. The delay, a spokesman explained, was "not because the army is hiding anything but because of the mechanics of handling casualty notifications in a dignified and considerate way."[31]

In Tokyo, MacArthur was equally quick to retaliate. Just weeks into the war, his whole attempt to dominate media coverage without censorship seemed to be in tatters. At the front correspondents roamed freely—and then, equally freely, sent home stories of harrowing experiences that were published to great acclaim. MacArthur was particularly upset with the correspondents' emphasis on the enormous human cost of the war. "Losses sustained by American forces in Korea have been greatly exaggerated in press reports at the front," he announced in a July communiqué. "Reports of warfare are, at any time, grisly and repulsive and reflect the emotional strain normal to those unaccustomed to the sights and sounds of battle. Exaggerated stories obtained from individuals wounded or mentally shocked have given a completely distorted and misrepresentative picture to the public." To support his claims MacArthur mentioned the case of a so-called Lost Battalion. Media reports had depicted it as "close to annihilation," MacArthur complained, whereas in reality "its actual losses amounted to only two killed, seven wounded, and twelve missing."[32]

The media's response was revealing. Many news organizations, rather than recoil at MacArthur's riposte, sought to target him instead. War correspondents were particularly angry. Those who had witnessed battles firsthand often responded that, while they reported the ugly truth, MacArthur and his minions shamelessly sugarcoated the news. As well as covering up snafus and obscuring defeats, they charged, MacArthur sought to bury losses. Crucially their editors often agreed. Many bristled at MacArthur's claims that their reporters were sensationalist or disloyal; above all they were not about to abandon correspondents whose stories were selling copy.[33]

While editors had a strong interest to defend their journalists' stories, Republicans had an even stronger incentive to place the blame closer to home. Nationalist Republicans focused on Secretary of State Dean Acheson. "The blood of our boys in Korea is on his shoulders," charged Wherry, "and no one else."[34] Internationalist Republicans, meanwhile, considered Louis Johnson, the controversial defense secretary, a better culprit. As the public face of recent military cuts, Johnson was certainly vulnerable. And Truman, already exasperated with Johnson's erratic behavior, decided to make him the scapegoat. On September 12 Johnson was fired.[35]

Just three days later this first Korean casualty controversy, which had gained momentum in the context of battlefield defeat, slowed in the wake of MacArthur's stunningly successful counterattack at Inchon. It was a victory made possible by the arrival of reinforcements from the United States, as well as by MacArthur's decision to launch a daring amphibious landing. But it was a victory that did little to dampen Republican barbs.

Indeed, as the midterm elections neared, Republicans continued to claim that Truman had left the United States dangerously unprepared for this new crisis, with the result that American boys were still paying with their lives. "Republicans believe the principal issue of this campaign," declared the GOP chairman in the middle of October, "is the incompetence of the party in power to achieve peace or provide an adequate national defense. This incompetence was demonstrated by the Korean War and its background. It was admitted by the firing of Louis Johnson as secretary of defense. It has cost the American people more than twenty thousand casualties, untold suffering, heartache, and sacrifices."[36]

A few weeks later this claim seemed likely to resonate when the fortunes of war underwent yet another dramatic change. Just days before the election, Communist China entered the war, albeit in a puzzling and brief flurry of activity. In retrospect Mao's motives were clear: he was both fearful of the American march into North Korea and eager to demonstrate that the new China was a major Asian player. Yet Mao's generals initially had sufficient strength for only a short series of attacks, although these were fierce enough. The most ferocious was launched at Unsan on November 1, when Chinese forces used a combination of surprise and the cover of darkness to inflict a major reverse on the Americans. In one eight-hundred-strong battalion only two hundred GIs escaped, before their Chinese attackers suddenly disappeared again, fading into the depths of North

Korea's mountains. "It was a massacre Indian-style," one shaken officer told reporters soon after, "like the one that hit Custer at the Little Big Horn."[37]

With Republicans seizing on such stories to sharpen their attack on Truman's "blinded, blundering, bewildering Far East policy," Democrats were worried. Behind closed doors the manager of their congressional campaign committee even speculated that voters would turn decisively against Truman and his party on the basis that they were "incapable of bringing off a clean-cut, effective, and not-too-bloody victory" in Korea.[38]

As a matter of fact, the Democratic vote held up quite well. The appearance of Chinese troops was too fleeting to wreak too much electoral havoc. Instead, like most midterms, local issues tended to predominate, giving Republicans a major fillip in key states like California, Illinois, Maryland, and Ohio but not providing them with sufficient momentum to take overall control of Congress. Nonetheless, Republicans were buoyant. They had made major inroads into a Democratic majority that had with one two-year exception dominated Congress for the past two decades. Poring over the returns, their leaders reached a straightforward conclusion: aggressive partisan assaults worked. It was a conclusion that many Republicans would bear in mind in the long run-up to the 1952 presidential campaign, especially as the Korean War was about to enter a more violent phase, with Chinese troops poised to enter the fight in earnest.[39]

Crisis Winter, 1950–51

Cocooned for the much of the time in his quiet office in Tokyo's Dai Ichi Building, MacArthur was unperturbed by the first appearance of Chinese troops in northern Korea. Even in mid-November he remained confident. In MacArthur's firm opinion, Chinese soldiers were no match for American firepower. Dividing his command into two prongs, Eighth Army in the west and X Corps in the east, he therefore pushed ahead with plans for a final "end the war offensive." MacArthur's intention was to drive all the way to the Chinese border, heedless not just of the mountain range separating his two forces but also the impending harsh winter conditions in which temperatures would plunge below minus 30°F.

In fact, MacArthur was walking straight into a trap, which the Chinese sprang at the end of November. Two days after Thanksgiving almost 400,000 "volunteer" Chinese troops suddenly scythed through the two prongs of the UN's own offensive. In western Korea the Second Division was the worst hit of all Eighth Army units. Forced into harrowing retreat from Kunu-ri, it ran headlong into a strong Chinese roadblock and was ambushed in a bloody, one-sided fight. The Second Division's grim rearguard action did at least help to cover the withdrawal of the other units in the west. But Walker was stunned. Dubious that the Eighth Army could contain the enemy in northern Korea, he soon ordered his men to beat a hasty retreat more than one hundred miles back toward the thirty-eighth parallel.[40]

On the east of the peninsula, meanwhile, the situation was equally fraught. In late November, strung-out units of X Corps were surrounded by about sixty thousand Chinese troops and faced the prospect of fighting their way back almost eighty miles to safety across icy terrain to the safe haven of Hungnam. With impressive discipline most duly escaped. After evacuation by sea, they were then redeployed in southern Korea, arriving just in time to bolster the Eighth Army's precarious defensive position below Seoul.[41]

Although such a massive defeat was impossible to disguise, MacArthur certainly tried hard to dress it up in a favorable light. The "end-the-war offensive," Tokyo declared throughout December, far from walking blindly into a massive Chinese ambush, had "probably saved our forces from a trap which might well have destroyed them." The UN forces, MacArthur's public information officers explained in a string of press handouts, were withdrawing in an orderly fashion, with ground troops simply "trading space for time." The air force, they added, was also imposing high casualties on the Chinese aggressors, far higher than those being sustained by American forces.[42]

When it came to divulging the precise number of U.S. losses, however, MacArthur and the Pentagon remained reticent. Both were naturally keen to blunt the home-front impact of this massive defeat, but this was by no means their only consideration. They were also driven by familiar practical problems. Because the retreat was often chaotic, it took time to reach an accurate accounting. With China holding the initiative, senior officials were desperate to deny it sensitive information. The result was a major time lag. Although the Pentagon continued to release monthly numbers, these were roughly six weeks behind events on the battlefield. The figures therefore looked suspicious. Until now, reported casualties had risen rapidly: 6,886 by the end of August, 20,756 by the end of September, 27,610 by the end of October, and 31,028 by the end of November. Despite the massive reverse inflicted by the Chinese, however, reported totals only rose to 33,878 by mid-December and 40,176 by the turn of the year—still high, but not as much as those sustained in the summer defeats.[43]

The reaction was equally predictable. With the United States effectively at war with China—a war it appeared to be losing—Korea was suddenly an even bigger story. American news organizations already had three hundred correspondents in the Far East, many of them claiming large salaries and hefty expenses. With MacArthur's command providing little hard information, most editors naturally

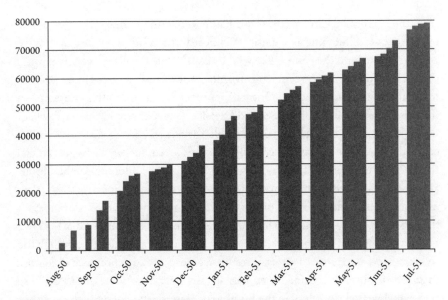

Graph 4.1 Published Combat Casualties, August 1950–July 1951. Source: *New York Times*. Note these are the published totals of all casualties (KIA, WIA, MIA, and POW) of all three services.

looked to their own reporters to tell a story that the military seemed bent on either hiding or obscuring.

In Korea many of these scoop-seeking war correspondents were caught up in the cold and chaotic march back down the Korean peninsula. In the west Homer Bigart of the *New York Herald Tribune*, who was with the imperiled Second Division, described the result as "slaughter. Many wounded had to be left behind. It was as ghastly a night as the veteran troops had ever spent." In the east Fred Sparks of the *Chicago Daily News*, who was with X Corps during its retreat from the Chosin Reservoir in the eastern part of the peninsula, believed this grue-some episode would be "irrevocably etched in the mind—and the conscience—of the American people. The etching will show frostbitten boys slipping, falling, and dying—but fighting, though facing a vastly greater foe, dragging out their dead and wounded, by hand, by jeep, by oxcart."[44]

As well as providing these dramatic firsthand accounts, many reporters tried to piece together the death toll of defeat. One obvious problem was the large number of surrounded troops, which meant the MIA figure was initially very high. MacArthur's command clearly expected that many would return, which was one reason for its sluggishness in providing totals. Some war corre-spondents effectively challenged this assumption, however, sending home grim eyewitness accounts that suggested that many MIAs would be lost forever. For example, Charles Moore reported in early December that the survivors from the harrowing Chosin Reservoir battle were telling gruesome tales. Some even recounted watching as "fanatical Chinese burned wounded prisoners alive and danced around the flames 'like wild Indians' while the GIs scream in pain."[45]

Washington correspondents, meanwhile, probed their sources in an attempt to establish the precise cost. One AP reporter found that after the Kunu-ri debacle no less "a third of the Second Division [had] entered the casualty list," while "other units have taken considerable casualties." In the east the marines seemed to have fared particularly badly. In early December one Pentagon official told a *Time* reporter—off the record—that the Chinese intervention had probably inflicted about seven thousand casualties on the marines (including an estimated four thousand cases of frostbite). This massive figure was not lost on the headline writers.[46] In mid-December, the *Washington Post* blared that MARINE LOSSES HEAVIER THAN TARAWA. The connected story explained that though the military had yet to release figures of confirmed dead, it had announced that more than four thousand wounded men had already been flown out of the Chinese trap, which was almost double the number of wounded at Tarawa, "the costliest single Marine action in World War II."[47]

This assertion said more about the popular memory of the last war than the reality of this new one. True, Tarawa had been a nasty fight in which a thousand Americans had died and another two thousand had been wounded. But it had not been the marines' costliest action—Iwo Jima had taken that dubious distinction.[48] Tarawa had, however, been the first major bloodbath. It had also stuck in the popular mind, partly because of its precedence and partly because it had coincided with some ham-handed official attempts to drive home the grisly nature of war. It therefore remained a byword for a bloody battle, which made the *Washington Post's* reference particularly inflammatory.

Desperate to confirm these early reports of massive casualties, some journalists were highly innovative. On December 6 one *Time* correspondent wired his editor with an interesting snippet of information. "You might be interested in the fact," he wrote,

> that the Defense Department asked the Red Cross this week to double its blood collections during December. As of now, the Red Cross is collecting over ninety thousand pints of blood a month, for the armed forces and civilian hospitals. This month, the Red Cross and other cooperating blood banks have been told to increase collections by nearly 100 percent.

The implication was unmistakable: this massive increment in blood supplies suggested that U.S. troops had sustained truly staggering losses.[49]

* * *

In both Washington and Tokyo senior military officers were appalled by the tenor of such stories. Clifton B. Cates, the marine commandant, was particularly proud of the way his men had fought their way back to Hungnam. But, he complained, their heroic exploits had been totally obscured by "highly exaggerated" newspaper accounts of a bloody reverse.[50] MacArthur wholeheartedly agreed. "Sensational and exaggerated stories concerning number of casualties sustained and references to units being decimated are having detrimental effect on UN effort," MacArthur insisted in one communiqué. Such "unofficial, persistent, and speculative casualty reports from the Korean Theater," he added in another, "continue the artificial nuance of 'disaster' that has been given to UN military operations."[51]

By the end of December MacArthur had had enough. He was so riled by press reporting that he decided to issue his own set of figures. In a clear swipe at media speculation and exaggeration, MacArthur noted acidly that actual casualties since China's intervention had "not even approximated the battle losses in certain comparable operations of World War II."[52] MacArthur clearly had the Battle of the Bulge in mind—another sudden enemy offensive launched in freezing temperatures. He was not wrong: U.S. losses in Korea would prove to be far fewer than those sustained in December 1944 (just thousands now compared to tens of thousand then). Significantly, though, these totals were far less important than the way that casualties were refracted through the distorting prism of media reporting and partisan debate—a refraction that varied in subtle ways to what had happened six years before.

In both battles the military faced major practical difficulties that prevented the release of timely casualty figures. While the resulting information vacuums were then filled with inflated media claims, there was a crucial difference. In 1944 the press had often turned to the enemy, reporting that the Germans had made claims of 140,000 U.S. losses. In 1950 the source was closer to home. This time, casualty stories were spiced up with a variety of semi-official estimates and off-the-record briefings, which actually proved far more troubling. During World War II newspapers had naturally treated enemy claims with great care, repeating them, yes, but often burying such controversially sourced stories on their inside pages. Now, however, many press stories were based on American information, albeit informal or speculative, which editors gave far more prominence.

Unlike SHAEF in 1944, MacArthur tried desperately to set the record straight. Six years before Eisenhower had remained shrewdly above the fray, never once breaking with established precedent to take the task away from Stimson's Pentagon. MacArthur, by contrast, had little time for this established hierarchy. Always imbued with an innate superiority complex, he played on the fact that many staffers at the White House and Pentagon had been, at one time or another, his direct subordinates.[53] Nor was he ever shy about issuing press statements to protect or burnish his image, although this time he dramatically overreached. By December 1950 MacArthur was already a far less credible voice than the Pentagon. As the crisis developed, his constant attempts to shift the blame for defeat were then so transparent—and not a little incoherent—that many observers wondered openly if his use of casualties was simply another brazen attempt at data massaging. As the *New York Herald Tribune* pointedly declared that month, "On the record of the last three weeks, it is impossible to put any confidence in such figures; and it is becoming increasingly difficult to put confidence in the military capacity of a headquarters which has so gravely compounded blunder by confusion of facts and intelligence."[54]

To some extent this jaundiced media view of military information had distinct echoes in the barbs directed at SHAEF in December 1944. Now, though, a lot more journalists were on hand to complain about MacArthur's mendacity—about twice the number that had been in Paris at the end of World War II, according to one contemporary observer.[55] Crucially, these Korean War correspondents were still free to report without the threat of censorship. This freedom clearly helped to magnify the perception of Korea's bloodiness. Although the news blackout during World War II had created a brief eruption of media protest, it had at least prevented the publication of grim stories of battlefield death and defeat. Now the American public was being bombarded with numerous stories that emphasized what one correspondent dubbed the "Chinese communist death snare in the 'frozen hell'" of North Korea.[56]

On Capitol Hill, Republicans avidly exploited such stories. Taft was in the vanguard. Already planning to run for president in 1952, Taft immediately began focusing on the war's human and financial cost. When asked by one reporter what he would have done if he had been president in June 1950, Taft's reply was categorical: "I would have stayed out." When asked by another "What would you do now?" his response was particularly revealing. "I think I would get out and fall back to a defensible position in Japan and Formosa. I certainly would if I thought there was danger by staying of losing any considerable number of men."[57]

In early January, with defeat still looming in Korea, this partisan emphasis on casualties interacted threateningly with a heated debate about the UN's (in)action on Korea. Nationalists had long argued that the UN flag under which MacArthur fought was little more than a symbol. In their jaundiced view, Americans did all the fighting (and often the dying), while so-called allies simply talked. Early in the new year headline writers gave this claim a major boost. WE HAVE LOST MORE MEN THAN REST OF UN [HAS] SENT, boomed one. Underneath, the figures revealed the unequally shared burden: more than 50,000 Americans dead, wounded, or missing, compared to just "44,000 soldiers from all other UN armies in the fight."[58]

Figure 4.1 Bodies of UN forces at Koto-ri, December 1950. While an uncensored media magnified the cost of the Chinese intervention, the military refused to allow publication of graphic photographic images such as this one. National Archives 127-GK-2345.

Such headlines could not have come at a worse time. Throughout January the UN was engaged in a protracted debate over whether to indict China as an aggressor in Korea. In the General Assembly, America's allies were reluctant to pursue this course. They were convinced that such a resolution would give the reckless MacArthur a mandate to use military force against China—which in turn would spark World War III. In both Congress and the media, however, the matter was viewed quite differently. At a time when so many Americans were dying under the UN banner, the UN's failure to vote on an aggressor resolution was seen nothing short of spineless appeasement. "Our losses in Korea are probably approaching 65–70,000," proclaimed Sen. George D. Aiken (R-VT) in a typical comment, "and the UN still continues its debate." Perhaps, Aiken added in a note of bitter sarcasm, this was because the UN believed that "all of our boys in Korea are expendable."[59]

Across the country, as politicians and the press continued to stress the high level of casualties, support for the war started to dip. The most visible sign of a change in the popular mood came on January 21, 1951. That day Gallup published a poll revealing that 66 percent of Americans wanted to "pull our troops out of Korea as fast as possible." Although this single result was undoubtedly driven by numerous factors—above all the overall military setback currently being suffered by U.S. and UN forces—the casualty controversy undoubtedly played a role. For one thing, Gallup's interviews were conducted during the first weeks of January, at precisely the time that inflated casualty reports were widespread in the media.[60] For another, those groups in American society who were in some way vulnerable to appearing in future casualty statistics now clearly had grave doubts about the wisdom of fighting in Korea.[61]

University students were one such group. During the first weeks of 1951 universities reported a wave of panic enlistments. Suddenly thousands of college students were dropping out and volunteering for military service. Their motive was clear. If they volunteered now, they could pick what service to enter. If they waited until they were drafted at the end of their studies, the military would instruct them where to go. Significantly most students opted for the air force or the navy, which seemed a far safer option given that so many army casualties were currently being reported in Korea. By January 19 the situation was so bad that, to end the panic, the Pentagon changed the draft law. From now on, students could complete their studies in their summer and then choose what service to apply for.[62]

Even with this hasty change, the draft still faced major problems. For most of the Korean War, to be sure, it operated in a remarkably smooth fashion. Unlike the Vietnam era there were no protests about unfairness, let alone efforts to dodge military service or burn draft cards. In fact, selective service was remarkably successful, delivering 5.5 percent more men than requested during the first year of the war. It was also widely popular. A series of opinion polls found that about 60 percent favored the current system, and in June 1951 Congress approved its extension with wide bipartisan support.[63] But there was one highly significant exception. During January 1951, in the wake of exaggerated casualty reports, the FBI suddenly faced the job of tracking down 2,200 new cases of Selective Service Act violations. According to one account, in some parts of the country the growing number of "draft delinquents" who failed to respond to their selective-service call-up was now much higher than compared to a similar period of World War II.[64]

In this frenzied atmosphere, official statements sometimes served to heighten, rather than dampen, the impression of a full-scale disaster. On one occasion, for example, the army announced that that thousands of national guardsmen might soon be sent into the combat zone because casualties had been so high and army training centers had not been able to produce sufficient men.[65] Another time the ongoing rivalry between the army and the marines resulted in a spate of press stories about the hapless Second Division suffering another bloody reverse during the long, cold Korean winter.

This particular story began on the night of February 12, when a group of marines discovered the bodies of men from the Second Division, who had been killed by a Chinese attack. These marines immediately dubbed the area "Massacre Valley." An AP reporter then latched on to this nickname, using it in a story suggesting that upwards of two thousand men had been killed. Appalled, the army launched an investigation, which eventually resulted in the AP publishing a detailed apology for its "deceptively written story." But this retraction came too late. As one senior officer complained, the idea of a "massacre" stuck in the public mind, while "the correction was never given the circulation the original story had gotten."[66]

Although it was another dispiriting episode, a senior Eighth Army press adviser viewed it as an opportunity to change. James T. Quirk, a man with hands-on newspaper experience treading the Philadelphia beat, conceded that "In my original anxiety to protect the reputation of the Second Division I made the mistake of giving out no information." This was a misguided reticence, he realized, that allowed unscrupulous reporters to hit the newsstands with their own exaggerated version of events. The time had come to learn and improve. "Sooner or later we have to admit our losses as well as tell of our successes," Quirk concluded. "We waited too long. If the necessity should arise again, I hope that I shall be able to handle it more intelligently."[67]

"Die For a Tie," 1951–52

During 1951 and 1952 the military would indeed handle casualty publicity more intelligently. An important reason was Quirk's boss. At the very end of 1950 Matthew Ridgway arrived on the scene, initially to command Eighth Army after Walton Walker was killed in a car crash.

Ridgway inherited a bleak situation. After the long retreat of December, many senior commanders thought that Eighth Army would have to skedaddle from Korea altogether. In January, when the Chinese then launched the third phase of their great offensive, Ridgway had little choice but to evacuate Seoul and pull his army back in another series of retreats to avoid encirclement. But he soon began to institute significant tactical changes. He insisted that Eighth Army units maintain close contact with one another, so that they were neither isolated when attacked nor vulnerable when probing enemy positions. He also encouraged U.S. soldiers to get off the roads and into the hills, so that they could attack Chinese troops who were wilting at the end of a long and tenuous communications network.

During January and February these changes helped Ridgway stem the communist tide. He then launched two limited offensives of his own, Operations Killer and Ripper, which, in a major reversal of fortunes, led to the recapture of Seoul in the middle of March.[68] Still, Ridgway's problems were by no means over. Although the danger of defeat had passed, the Truman administration saw no realistic prospect of evicting the large Chinese army from the Korean peninsula. As a result it changed the war's goal. As an official source put it, from now on "the objective was an end to the fighting and a return to the status quo; the mission of the Eighth Army was to inflict enough attrition on the foe to induce him to settle on these terms."[69]

On close inspection, this deceptively simple formula generated at least three casualty-related problems that would continue to plague the government. One was the home front's squeamishness. Would the public accept a war fought with death as the main goal? As the speculation, rumor, and exaggeration of the winter demonstrated, Americans were likely to recoil from any hint that their own forces were coming off worse in this brutal new contest. Would they also stomach a war fought with the expressed aim of inflicting "maximum loss" on the enemy at "minimum cost" to the UN?

The Pentagon was unsure. In February it nervously protested Ridgway's use of Operation Killer to designate a limited offensive, worried that it "struck an unpleasant note as far as public relations was concerned." But Ridgway was unrepentant. "I am by nature opposed to any effort to 'sell' war to people," he explained, "as an only mildly unpleasant business that requires very little in the way of blood."[70] In making this case to his superiors, Ridgway was in a strong position for the simple reason that his offensive was effective. Soon the Pentagon came around; it even began issuing candid briefings to reporters based on an early version of the "body count." As one general publicly conceded in March, the new goal was "not how much ground you can cover but how many of these people you can kill." Here, the Pentagon was keen to admit, Ridgway was enjoying a spectacular success: tens of thousands of casualties on the U.S. side, compared with hundreds of thousands of losses for the Chinese.[71]

While the prospect of public squeamishness was effectively brushed aside, a second problem became acute. This was the difficulty of sustaining support for a stalemate war. Korea was already a conflict lacking in officially forged sound bites. Unlike its two predecessors, it was a war neither "to make the world safe for democracy" nor to implement the "four freedoms." For a brief period after Inchon it had become a crusade to turn the whole Korean peninsula into a beacon of democracy. But with the Chinese intervention even this goal had contracted to merely returning to the prewar status quo. It was scarcely a rousing rally cry. In fact as correspondents started to report, it had prompted soldiers to coin one of the war's few enduring sound bites. Increasingly men at the front were now complaining that they were not fighting to win but being asked to "die for a tie."[72]

If this charge was not damaging enough, a number of major voices claimed that the conflict did not have to end in a tie. MacArthur was by far the most prominent. In March he tried Truman's patience with a series of statements suggesting that

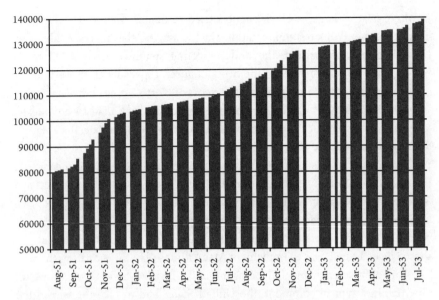

Graph 4.2 Published Combat Casualties, August 1950–July 1951. Source: *New York Times*. Note these are the published totals of all casualties (KIA, WIA, MIA, and POW) of all services.

victory could be achieved by escalating the war. A month later Truman finally sacked him for persistent insubordination. In response MacArthur returned home and immediately embarked on a major speaking tour. At the heart of his case, which got its most extensive airing at a special congressional hearing in May, was the mounting human toll. Our losses, MacArthur stressed numerous times,

> are approaching 65,000. This conflict in Korea has already lasted almost
> as long as General Eisenhower's decisive campaign which brought the
> European War to an end. And yet the only program that I have been able
> to hear is that we shall indecisively go on resisting aggression, whatever
> that may mean. And if you do, you are going to have thousands and
> thousands of American lives that will fall, and in my own opinion events
> will finally catch up with you, so that you will have to stop it in some way;
> and then the great question is—Where does the responsibility for that
> blood rest? This I am quite sure—It is not going to rest on my shoulders.[73]

As Republicans were quick to point out, MacArthur's challenge was under-pinned by a basic pessimism that the United States could ever win a drawn-out attrition fight against the Chinese. In this view Mao's manpower pool was just too big. But the more partisan Republicans went even farther. In an effort to demonstrate that the difference between friendly and enemy casualties was nowhere near as large as official figures tried to depict, they also revived the claim that the Truman administration was massaging the figures. Only now, these Republicans insisted, the underreporting stemmed from a failure to include non-battle casualties in the overall figures, especially all those soldiers and marines who had succumbed to the rigors of North Korea's bitter winter.

Having asked the Pentagon for a precise breakdown, nationalist Republicans knew full well that including non-battle casualties would inflate the total by about sixty thousand.[74] Senator Harry Cain (R-WA) was the most persistent public advocate of this higher figure. As Cain repeatedly stressed, it meant that the stalemated Korean "police action" had been more costly than the decisive European campaign of 1944–45.[75] Taft agreed. Honing his presidential bid, Taft claimed that the United States was sustaining a thousand casualties a week in what had become a "useless and expensive waste." The only alternative, many of these voices agreed, was to implement MacArthur's plan for escalating the war. To stop our "sons dying and being injured," insisted Sen. Owen Brewster (R-ME), in a typical comment, the United States had to take the war to the source of the problem. It needed to send its airplanes over the Chinese border to destroy "the mobilization bases, concentration centers, and the material which is pouring over the Yalu."[76]

As Brewster spoke, however, the fortunes of war were already dealing a blow to this Republican assault on Truman's war policy. In May the Eighth Army, now commanded by Gen. James Van Fleet, confirmed its skill as an attrition force. Although the Chinese launched their massive Easter Offensive in two waves, the Eighth Army held its ground. As its public information officers stressed, it also inflicted vast numbers of casualties on the enemy, at a ratio of 1:36 in the UN's favor.[77]

These large battles were the prelude to the war stabilizing along a frontline that was, for the most part, just north of the thirty-eighth parallel. For the next two years the fighting along this line would prove extremely bloody; in fact, the United States would sustain 45 percent of its overall battlefield losses during this long period.[78] This fighting would also be largely static. Each day both sides sent out patrols. From time to time, they also launched limited offensives. For the next two years, however, neither the Americans nor the Chinese sought a knock-out blow to win the war.

As the fighting stabilized, the focus shifted to the armistice talks, which began in the summer of 1951. Although these talks created hopes that the killing might soon be over, they also raised a third problem: How much blood should be spilled while the diplomats were haggling over increasingly esoteric details? On the fundamentals, Van Fleet agreed with Ridgway, who had taken over from MacArthur as the UN commander in April. Both men deeply distrusted the communists, and they were in no doubt that maintaining "unrelenting pressure" was the only way to force this perfidious enemy to make concessions at the bargaining table.

Beyond these generalities, the two men soon clashed over key aspects of the war. Van Fleet was more aggressive. On the one hand, he feared that if the Eighth Army became too defensive-minded, its soldiers would be gripped by a desire not to be the "last man killed," and its combat readiness would collapse accordingly. On the other hand, Van Fleet believed his own force was far superior to the enemy's. Especially in the immediate aftermath of China's failed Easter Offensive, he was convinced that the Eighth Army had sufficient firepower and mobility to launch an effective amphibious counterattack that would push the front-line northwards, to the Korean "neck."[79]

In short, Van Fleet believed that an aggressive posture would ultimately save lives. As well as weakening the enemy and disrupting its plans to kill American troops, it would strengthen his own force's morale and effectiveness. Ridgway increasingly disagreed. With the truce talks underway, he became, as the historian Allan R. Millett observed, "a strategic pessimist" who "doubted that Korea was worth the bones of one more GI rifleman." In November 1951, as the negotiations shifted to Panmunjom and began to progress, Ridgway instructed Van Fleet to adopt a posture of "active defense." This was a far more cautious policy that translated into an order to make "every effort . . . to prevent unnecessary casualties."[80]

On at least two occasions these differences spilled into the public domain, fueling the continuing debate over whether the administration's limited-war strategy was costing or saving lives. As early as July 1951, two Pentagon briefing officers told an astonished press corps that senior officials had stopped Van Fleet from pushing into North Korea, even though he had the Chinese "hanging from the ropes." As an internal investigation discovered, this spectacular blunder only fueled nationalist Republican claims that Truman's limited-war strategy was prolonging the contest and adding to the casualty lists.[81] A more damaging revelation then came in the spring of 1953, when Van Fleet returned home after completing his Korean tour of duty. In a pale imitation of MacArthur two years earlier, Van Fleet went before Congress to attack the Truman administration for not letting him win the war. Van Fleet claimed that he faced constant ammunition shortages and that the truce talks had provided the enemy with a respite to strengthen its positions. Truman's limited-war policy, he complained, gave "the enemy all the initiative. He can save up his ammunition and his strength and strike when and where he feels like it."[82]

"Forgotten Heroes," 1951–52

As these claims multiplied, the government hit back hard. In Washington, the senior Pentagon brass responded to both MacArthur and Van Fleet with a fiercely united front. Senior officers were eager to point out that these two commanders were proposing an escalation of the war, which could well result in massive new casualties. But this was not their only retort.

The government's 1951 effort was particularly impressive in both detail and scope. Throughout the MacArthur hearings, senior military officials lined up to demolish the sacked general's allegation that this war was much bloodier than Eisenhower's successful sweep across Europe in 1944–45. As the Pentagon's number crunchers pointed out, whereas back then the "battle casualties of the first six American divisions engaged in Europe averaged three percent a week of strength," now the army's Korean casualties "averaged nine-tenths of one percent a week since June 1950." And this figure, the Pentagon's publicists added, meant that contrary to the claims of MacArthur and his allies, World War II losses had in fact been three times greater than the current Korean conflict, which were actually "very low."[83]

Nor, as senior officers hastened to add, did the Republican effort to include non-battle casualties make any sense. Quietly forgetting that as recently as February 1951 the military had itself announced an important set of cold weather losses (which had totaled 2,620 by the middle of December rising to 5,300 by the middle of January), the army brass now did its level best to remove all such figures from the public debate.[84] As Lawton Collins, the army chief, told senators in the MacArthur hearings, "of all the non-battle casualties, so-called, in the Far East Command, including both Japan and Korea, 90.4 percent have been returned to duty in the Far East." In any case, he added, the term "non-battle casualties" was a complete misnomer. These men were simply the "sick and injured," he insisted, and it was "sheer doggerel" to think of them as anything else.[85]

In launching this vigorous counterattack the Truman administration had a significant ally in the mainstream media, which was already deeply suspicious of MacArthur. Here, after all, was a commander who just months before had vehemently attacked any reporter who had tried to expose the human cost of the war. He had also accused the media of giving an "artificial nuance of 'disaster'" to the fighting. Now that MacArthur had lost his command, however, he was shameless about emphasizing the war's bloodiness to make his own political points. And his rank hypocrisy left many reporters so unimpressed that it colored their skeptical reporting of his casualty claims.[86]

In Korea, meanwhile, war correspondents faced a much-changed environment. As the battlefield gradually stabilized, media interest in the day-to-day fighting rapidly weakened. By the second half of 1951, those correspondents with the prestige to pick their own beat realized that Korea was no longer the place to grab a page-one scoop. They therefore began departing in droves, leaving their editors to replace them with unattributed wire-service overviews, which lacked the bite of earlier dispatches.[87]

Figure 4.2 Casualties were an important subtext of the Truman-MacArthur controversy over whether to escalate the war with China. This Herblock cartoon from May 1951 emphasized that the cost of such a war would be extortionate. A 1951 Herblock Cartoon, © The Herb Block Foundation.

The reporters that remained, moreover, faced a new set of challenges. With the fighting taking place along a relatively static line, the military was increasingly able to control journalists' access to the front, something that had rarely been possible during the fluid battles at the start of the war. More importantly, in the wake of the Chinese intervention Eighth Army commanders concluded that their troops were in so much danger that formal censorship was now vital.[88] This was a crucial decision. For the first time in Korea, the military was finally in a position to delete unsubstantiated claims about overall casualty figures. It could also tone down reports that vividly detailed the bloodiness of particular battles—as the big battles between August and October 1951 amply demonstrated.

These battles were part of Van Fleet's ongoing attempt to maintain "unrelenting pressure" on the enemy, but they came at a cost. In attacking a series of sophisticated North Korean and Chinese defenses, U.S. forces suffered horribly: about twenty-two thousand killed and wounded for positions that GIs ominously dubbed "Bloody Ridge" and "Heartbreak Ridge." For the troops caught up in the carnage, conditions were just as appalling as anything that had been encountered at earlier stages of the war. "Minutes seemed like hours, hours like days, and days like one long, terrible, dusty, blood-swirled nightmare," recorded the Second Division's historian in an apt description.[89]

Significantly, though, little of this brutal reality was now conveyed back to the home front. The army began by instituting a clamp-down, allowing reporters to mention the battles only after the first partial victory had been won. Even then, the story was carefully orchestrated. Correspondents were permitted merely to report that the United States and the UN had launched a series of "limited objective attacks," whose aim was to wrest key areas from the enemy "with a minimum of casualties to UN troops." And crucially, the censors also made sure that the "Bloody Ridge" label was used *not* to describe the awful conditions faced by UN forces but to depict the terrible suffering of enemy troops, whose "positions had been shattered by a tremendous torrent of artillery—390,000 rounds."[90]

With the military sanitizing news of this stalemate war, public support began steadily to climb from the depths of January 1951. Back then, in the aftermath of constant news speculation about casualties, no less than two-thirds of Americans had advocated an immediate withdrawal. Exactly a year later, the mood had shifted to one of unenthusiastic tolerance. In the media, as one official survey recorded, most editorialists and commentators were convinced that "the present situation, though unsatisfactory, is better than an extension of the war, for which the U.S. may not be adequately equipped." According to the polls, a majority of Americans agreed. At the beginning of 1952, for instance, 63 percent believed that the continued war in Korea was at "least some help" in preventing the current world situation from getting any worse. In addition, 56 percent of those polled thought the United States was right to have intervened in Korea in the first place, while only 16 percent were in favor of "pulling our troops out of Korea."[91]

These surprisingly robust levels of popular support were not the only consequence of the more sanitized coverage of the war. A darker result was that those still fighting now felt a growing sense of neglect. "Korea just didn't seem to exist," complained one naval officer home on leave. The soldiers and marines on the frontline, agreed James Michener in a *Saturday Evening Post* article, had become "forgotten heroes." In October 1951, when the *U.S. News & World Report* framed a story around 2,200 American casualties that week, it ran with an eye-catching headline. Korea, it proclaimed, was already "The 'Forgotten' War."[92]

Korea as the "forgotten war" is one of the hoariest of clichés. Although the term was coined as early as 1951, even then it was not strictly true because the government had in fact made some effort to keep the fighting before the public eye.

Part of this effort revolved around the administration's blood campaign. By the fall of 1951, U.S. reserves of dried human blood plasma were severely depleted. Although medics needed 300,000 pints per month to guarantee sufficient reserves to treat Korean casualties, the figures for June and July were only fifty thousand and thirty-six thousand pints, respectively. To make up this enormous shortfall, senior figures like Marshall, Bradley, and Ridgway implored citizens to donate at Red Cross centers. At numerous manufacturing plants management and labor joined hands to encourage employees to boost the output in blood-donor programs.[93] Ridgway's public information officers even encouraged media outlets to emphasize this dimension of the war. In October, for instance, the Scripps Howard newspaper chain sent one of its journalists to witness citizens giving blood in San Francisco. This reporter then followed this particular shipment of blood all the way from the West Coast to a field hospital in Korea—a stunt that, as his proud editor reported, not only boosted circulation but also helped to insure that "donors at the blood bank more than doubled."[94]

Across the country these efforts proved such a success that by November 1951 the Pentagon's target of seventy thousand pints per week was being regularly exceeded. When it came to depicting the war, though, the central message of this blood campaign was hardly uplifting. "Korea," the Pentagon repeatedly stressed in its literature, "is one of America's costliest wars in numbers of casualties compared to forces engaged in fighting"—a fact that made the blood drive essential. The only upside was that the military could again focus public attention on its successful medical teams. Although this was a costly war, military ads stressed repeatedly, overall death rates were far lower than in previous conflicts. "Out of every one hundred wounded American servicemen who reach the most forward hospitals in Korea," asserted one poster, "ninety-seven are being saved." The reason was clear: "Medical authorities credit this splendid record almost entirely to the prompt use of plasma and whole blood."[95]

After spending the last months of 1951 rebuilding the military's blood supplies, the Truman administration devoted the early part of 1952 searching for an issue that would reenergize public enthusiasm for the stalemated war. Ultimately senior officials latched on to the idea of voluntary repatriation. At the Panmunjom truce talks U.S. negotiators insisted that they would only hand back those communist prisoners of war who wanted to return home. It was an issue, Truman believed, that would appeal to the American impulse to fight for a positive, humanitarian goal, for the simple reason that many POWs would inevitably prefer the freedoms of the West to the prospect of being sent straight to a gulag in the East. In May 1952 Truman therefore headed a concerted PR campaign that tried to redefine the war. No longer were American troops fighting in Korea to unite the peninsula or kill Chinese troops. They were now engaged in a moral crusade waged on behalf of America's traditional respect for human rights.[96]

Although opinion polls suggested that a majority of Americans supported this new objective, Truman faced two obvious problems. One was the enemy's categorical rejection of voluntary repatriation, which meant that the war would continue into the 1952 election campaign. The other was that as the fighting dragged on, so those American prisoners still languishing in communist prison camps became yet another group of "forgotten heroes."[97]

For Truman, neglecting these Americans was a risky business. At the very start of the truce talks a powerful group of Republicans had put the administration on notice that it considered the immediate release of U.S. prisoners "a primary condition."[98] When Truman then decided to focus on the fate of communist POWs, one senior State Department publicist noted the dangers. We "could be accused of sacrificing the moral obligation of any government to rescue its own prisoners," he shrewdly observed, "in order to help some Chinese and North Koreans who are not political defectors but prisoners of war who were once shooting at us and who surrendered to save their own skins."[99]

It was a prescient warning. By the summer of 1952 grassroots pressure was gradually starting to build. Veterans' organizations were now pushing the administration to prioritize U.S. POWs. Meanwhile a petition drive gathered 75,000 signatures from small towns in "virtually every state of the union," urging officials to take "immediate action . . . to obtain release of the American prisoners of war held by the communists. We feel that you have a duty to the citizens of the United States," the petitioners implored Truman and Acheson, "which transcends your personal concept of obligation to the Korean prisoners who state they do not want to be returned to the Korean reds."[100]

Casualties and the 1952 Election

Against this backdrop, the Democrats entered the 1952 election in an uncertain mood. On the one hand, the Truman administration had vigorously rebutted the MacArthur challenge. The military had also masked some of the more vivid media coverage of the fighting. Partly as a result, officials had seen opinion polls on Korea rise back to a respectable level of support. With Truman not running for reelection, the Democrats turned to Adlai Stevenson, a fresh candidate who was not directly tainted with managing the war. But Stevenson was up against a formidable opponent. In their yearning to win back the White House after five straight losses Republicans nominated Eisenhower—a war hero with a centrist, essentially nonpartisan reputation.

In discussing Korean War casualties, Eisenhower initially lived up to his non-partisan billing. His approach to non-battle casualties was especially revealing. Throughout 1951 and 1952, nationalist Republicans continued to inflate the official figure by adding those victims of frostbite or other non-combat ailments. Eisenhower, by contrast, stuck closely to the official Defense Department figures, which by now were edging up to 117,000. He was similarly restrained when discussing whether the war was worthwhile. Whereas the Republican Right tended to mention big losses in the same breath as the need to get out of Korea altogether, Eisenhower generally accepted that the war was necessary, and emphasized casualties only in the context of the administration's failure to deter communist aggression before June 1950.

Yet Eisenhower was not prepared to depoliticize the war's death toll entirely. On the stump he often referred to Truman's and Acheson's prewar mistakes, which, he maintained, were chiefly responsible for such a large loss of American life. He also pointed to the large casualty lists when criticizing the administration for lacking a plan to bring the war to any sort of conclusion. "Tonight," Eisenhower reminded Ohioans just weeks before election day "—while the life of a nation at peace goes on at home—the casualty lists in Korea grow. . . . This is the shadow that escapes the camera's eye. This is the shadow that haunts the hopes of all of us."[101]

Unlike Republican nationalists, Eisenhower gained a significant amount of traction with these casualty charges. In part this was because he was a more temperate and trusted voice, but a sudden flare-up in the fighting also helped. In October the Chinese launched an assault on White Horse Mountain, in the center of the allied line.[102] Although the military censors again worked hard to sterilize the story, the gist of what happened soon seeped back to the United States. While South Korean troops bore the brunt of the fighting and dying, the American media focused largely on U.S. losses. The coverage in *Time* magazine was typical: BLOODSHED IN THE HILLS or THEN HE WAS DEAD, boomed its headlines.[103] In a story published the day before the country voted, *Time* described what was happening:

> In Korea last week there was more dogged, costly, back & forth fighting for Triangle Hill, Sniper Ridge, Iron Horse Mountain. Temperatures dipped below freezing as another wretched winter approached, and this time, with no peace in sight, warm clothing and boots had been distributed

early and efficiently. U.S. casualties were sharply up. Latest Defense
Department figures listed 122,117 (an increase of 963 in one week). They
include 21,377 battle deaths, 88,128 wounded, 10,793 missing, 1,819
known captured.[104]

As a result of all these developments Eisenhower's constant claims about casualties clearly helped to spark the second dip in popular support for the war. Back
in January only 33 percent had viewed Korea as one of the gravest issues facing
the country. In October, this figure suddenly shot up to 52 percent. That same
month another poll also found that 56 percent of the population now thought
that "the war in Korea was *not* worth fighting"—a level of disillusionment not
recorded since January 1951.[105]

Eisenhower's emphasis on U.S. casualties was not the only reason behind this
dip, but it certainly played a key role. During the campaign Samuel Lubell, the
writer and noted political pollster, conducted numerous grassroots interviews with
American voters, and he was in no doubt that Eisenhower's use of the American
death toll was important. Parents whose sons have been drafted, Lubell wrote,
"were bitterly resentful of the [Truman] administration." Although Stevenson
tried to change the basic narrative of the campaign by shifting the emphasis to the
strength of the economy, even this initiative backfired. As Lubell put it, "surprising
numbers of voters came to resent the prevailing prosperity as being 'bought by the
lives of boys in Korea.' The feeling was general that the Korean War was all that
stood in the way of an economic recession. From accepting that belief, many per-
sons moved on emotionally to where they felt something immoral and guilt-laden
in the 'you've never had it better' argument of the Democrats."[106] Put another way,
in 1952 the controversy over the current human cost of the war for once trumped
the electorate's normal focus on bread-and-butter domestic issues.

The Democrats, for their part, were certainly worried that this new casualty
controversy was destroying their chances at the polls. Small wonder. Since the
start of the war the politicians and the press had combined forces to depict
Korea as a particularly bloody war. Now, with this perception threatening
to undermine Democratic chances in the only poll that mattered, Truman
decided to respond. Just weeks before the election the White House undertook
a desperate—and revealing—gambit to "do something about the huge casualties reported every week by the Department of Defense." As one reporter
discovered, the White House was eager for the Pentagon "to get over to the
public the point that the 122,000 casualties mentioned by Republican orators
were not all dead; forever lost, and that the majority of the wounded had been
returned to duty."[107]

As in 1944, the Pentagon was not enthusiastic about getting drawn into the
maelstrom of a presidential campaign. Not until after the election, in fact, did the

Pentagon make the kind of concerted PR effort that the White House had called for. On November 13 the army surgeon general issued a public plea to the press to correct the public misperception that "much of the flower of American manhood is going down the drain." Two weeks later the Pentagon then abolished its practice of referring to men killed, wounded, or missing as "casualties." The new policy, it explained, was designed "to correct an apparent widespread and popularly accepted impression that 'casualty' means 'fatality.'" If we can convince the home front that the total of 125,000 casualties "does not represent a dead loss," added the surgeon general, "then we have gone a long way toward taking some of the bugaboo out of this particular controversy."[108]

Before election day, however, the Pentagon made only a few token efforts. On October 8 the military's public information office added a brief explanatory note to its regular casualty list, emphasizing that the overall total included wounded and missing, not just killed. A few days later an official spokesman on a Pentagon-sponsored television show emphasized that "all casualties were not actually lost—that many returned to duty." Finally on October 24 the Defense Department instructed the marines to copy the army's more restrictive policy on wounded casualties. As a result, both services now excluded from their lists anyone who had just been treated at a frontline aid station before immediately returning to duty—a measure that one Pentagon source estimated would reduce reported marine casualty totals by as much as 30 percent.[109]

Although these measures helped to build on the success of the earlier blood campaign, they were, in electoral terms, a case of too little, too late. They certainly did little to halt Eisenhower's growing momentum, which became unstoppable when he proclaimed in the last days of the campaign that, if elected, he would go to Korea. With many Americans interpreting this pledge as a sign that Eisenhower could bring this bloody war to a swift conclusion, the Republicans swept the elections for the first time since 1928. Eisenhower took the White House with just over 55 percent of the vote.[110]

The Korean Syndrome

Despite his forceful pledge to visit Korea, Eisenhower had few clear ideas about how to bring the war to an end. He was also buffeted by conflicting domestic and alliance pressures. An object of suspicion on the right of his own party, Eisenhower could not ignore the Republican nationalists who dismissed negotiation and advocated victory. Inclined toward "Koreanizing" the fighting, Eisenhower knew full well that Rhee was vehemently hostile to any armistice that resulted in the division of his country. He also recognized that the United States' other allies were desperate to end the war as soon as possible. Nor was the American home front uniformly hawkish. On the contrary, as Eisenhower's own campaign had revealed, the population was best described as intensely war weary. In a series of meetings in the spring of 1953, the Pentagon's top officers underlined this point. The public, they insisted, would not support the high levels of casualties that would come with an escalation of the war.[111]

While Eisenhower deliberated, the situation suddenly changed. On March 5 Stalin died. Within weeks the Chinese proved willing to reach a deal on voluntary repatriation. After much haggling over details, both sides signed an armistice on July 27, and the fighting finally came to an end.

Inside the United States there was no rejoicing. Eisenhower set the tone. In a brief and somber speech, he reminded compatriots that "the cost of repelling aggression has been high. In thousands of homes it has been incalculable. It has been paid in terms of tragedy. With special feelings of sorrow," he added, "we think of those who were called upon to lay down their lives in that far-off land to prove once again that only courage and sacrifice can keep freedom alive upon the earth."[112]

Apart from this short presidential tribute, there was no rush to commemorate the war, its survivors, or even its dead. In Arlington Cemetery, the grave markers were initially instructed not to write "Korean War," and only after a protest did they add "Korea"—though still without the "war." But at least Arlington gave Korea a mention. Across the Potomac the war would not get its own memorial for more than forty years. It was as if the country was gripped by a bout of willful amnesia. As the historian Charles S. Young has observed, "It was like a terminally ill relative whose family had lived with the loss so long the actual moment of death was anticlimactic. The trial could now be put behind them."[113]

Yet not everyone could forget so easily. Democrats winced when they remembered how Korea had spawned years of right-wing Republican attacks, eroded Truman's popularity, and ultimately unraveled Roosevelt's dominant election-winning coalition. Republican nationalists, for their part, took the opposite view. They continued to rekindle the charge that Truman's limited-war strategy had wasted tens of thousands of lives for nothing more than a tawdry stalemate.

Still, it was in the center of the political spectrum that Korea's dominant legacy was initially entrenched. Here Eisenhower and his internationalist supporters reached a simple conclusion. They believed that the American people would not support another protracted Asian ground war. Instead, the United States would have to revert to technowar.[114] In Eisenhower's Cold War strategy this translated into building up the American nuclear arsenal. With the ability to threaten "massive retaliation," his aim was to deter the communists from launching another Korean-style invasion, although he also contemplated reviving a new version of Roosevelt's 1940–41 strategy of aid, short of war. In 1954, for instance, when the Vietnamese communists threatened to overrun

French forces at Dien Bien Phu, John Foster Dulles, Eisenhower's secretary of state, suggested letting local and regional troops do the fighting, while the United States extended air and naval support, money, and supplies. In Congress Democratic leaders fully agreed. There must be "no more Koreas," insisted Sen. Lyndon B. Johnson (D-TX), "with the United States furnishing 90 percent of the manpower."[115]

It was a lesson that Johnson would have been well advised to recall a decade later when he was president. But memories of the Korean War, like the fighting itself, had a messy, confused, and indecisive quality. Although Democrats were haunted by the war's unpopularity in the 1952 election, they were equally troubled by the constant Republican jibes that they were too soft on Asian communism. The Korean syndrome therefore placed them in a bind. They could either insist on no more Koreas and risk right-wing attacks, or they could fight another hot war in Asia and risk retribution at the voting booth. It was a conundrum that would have to be solved, one way or another, when Democratic presidents faced the Vietnam problem a decade later.

5

Vietnam

The Escalating War, 1961–1968

By the 1960s the U.S. military was no longer the puny poor relation it had been at the turn of the twentieth century. If World War II had created a cadre of high-profile generals whose reputations still shone brightly, the Cold War had given the military a centrality in the American state that it had never before achieved. Architecturally, the result was striking. Across the Potomac River from the massive Pentagon structure, Washington bristled with new buildings to house the burgeoning national-security bureaucracy—so much so that one leading historian has dubbed the city as, "at heart, a military headquarters."[1]

The pace of change left even Eisenhower bewildered. "Our military organization today bears little relation to that known by any of my predecessors in peacetime," he observed in January 1961, "or indeed by the fighting men of World War II or Korea." But the outgoing general-president was far from comforted. In his farewell TV address Eisenhower famously cautioned his compatriots that this new "military-industrial complex" posed a grave danger to the health of the Republic, warning that it must not be allowed to acquire "unwarranted influence . . . in the councils of government."[2]

In a narrow sense Eisenhower's warning soon appeared overstated. Although his successor, John F. Kennedy, came to office pledged to increase spending on conventional forces, the young liberal Democrat never developed a close relationship with the Pentagon's military bureaucracy. In fact, Kennedy considered the military's advice staid and stale. He much preferred to listen to Robert McNamara, the hyperactive business executive he recruited to head the Defense Department. McNamara in turn looked to his "whiz kids": the management number crunchers he brought to town and who promised to make military accountancy more efficient. Within months, rather than exerting "unwarranted influence," senior Pentagon officers were complaining of being ignored and bypassed, as the cool Kennedy and brusque McNamara brushed aside their suggestions during a string of Cold War crises.[3]

Still, Eisenhower was not entirely wrong. The military establishment that emerged to wage the long-term fight against communism was far more lavishly funded than its cash-starved peacetime predecessors. It had developed rules, procedures, and guidelines for most types of situations, often based on intensive study of recent conflicts. Its officer corps was highly professional and intensely ambitious. Throughout the ranks, it was infused with a can-do spirit even when faced with an unconventional guerrilla war in Vietnam against a foe that had already defeated the French.[4]

Casualty reporting was a case in point. When the United States massively escalated its Vietnam commitment in the summer of 1965, the military drew not only on a growing institutional memory forged in earlier conflicts but also on lessons learned between 1961 and 1964, when politicians and the press had heavily criticized it for trying to conceal the extent of initial American involvement. By 1965 military information officers had honed their systems, while promising to pursue a new policy of "maximum candor."[5] They had also devised a method for publicizing casualties, which promised to be more regular, more detailed, and more accurate than anything attempted before, albeit with due consideration to family sensibilities and the dictates of military security.

Yet this structure, which seemed so impressive on paper, quickly ran in trouble as soon as the Vietnam fighting bogged down into a bloody stalemate. The reason was simple: during the mid-1960s the rules of the game suddenly shifted. In Vietnam the military devised a system designed to counteract criticism, which, if previous wars were a guide, would come principally from politicians and the press. This time, however, domestic debates would spill onto the streets, in numerous protests charging that the Vietnam War was immoral, illegal, and, in casualty terms, an unfair burden on particular sections of society.

The resulting controversies were so intense that they threatened the fragile domestic consensus behind the Vietnam War, making it politically costly for any White House occupant to consider expanding U.S. involvement after 1968. But Vietnam also had a longer legacy, particularly in the way that it undercut the prestigious position the military had carved out for itself in the early Cold War era.

Casualties and the Long Path to Escalation, 1961–65

To American political leaders of the 1960s the unfolding crisis in Vietnam seemed like an unsettling case of déjà vu. They had been here before, they fretted—in Korea, a war that none of them had forgotten.

The surface parallels between the two conflicts certainly seemed close. Once again the United States was coming to the rescue of a beleaguered southern ally against the designs of a northern communist aggressor. Once again the stakes also appeared high, for if the communists won American credibility would be destroyed with three separate audiences: with allies who would conclude that Washington could not be trusted; with the Soviet Union and China, who would be emboldened to expand elsewhere; and with political opponents at home, who would charge that Democratic softness to Asian communism was to blame for a major Cold War defeat.

Yet Korea contained a restraining lesson too. As Democrats painfully remembered from 1952, the public was likely to punish any party that mired the nation in a long and costly Asian ground war. The Democratic presidents of the 1960s therefore faced a difficult dilemma. They needed to contain communism in order to demonstrate their resolve, but they also wanted to avoid the domestic uproar that would ensue if they sent large numbers of American boys to fight and die in another Korea.

Until 1964 the Kennedy and Johnson administrations could at least take solace in the fact that they were not yet faced with a clear choice between losing an ally or deploying a large number of U.S. troops. Unlike the clear-cut case of aggression in Korea, the United States faced a gradually developing insurgency in Vietnam. In the 1950s Eisenhower had tried to bolster the South Vietnam regime, principally by providing large amounts of military aid.[6] In the early 1960s, though, this Saigon ally was clearly in trouble: beset by political fragility and military weakness, the South Vietnamese government could barely control Buddhist protests in the cities, let alone the growing communist threat in the countryside. Still, the situation was not yet desperate enough to require a massive infusion of American military power.

Kennedy's response was therefore relatively restrained. During the course of his presidency Kennedy sent sixteen thousand military advisers to South Vietnam, but he was reluctant to do more. In November 1961 he explicitly ruled out deploying six thousand to eight thousand troops to Vietnam in a logistical and combat role, telling his advisers that he would not be able to justify such a decision to the American people. Two years later, just before his assassination, Kennedy remained convinced that war in Vietnam would be a tough sell. In public he even pledged to bring home a thousand U.S. military advisers by the end of 1963 (reducing the total to fifteen thousand), while contemplating a complete withdrawal after the 1964 election.[7]

Johnson, on assuming the presidency, was equally tentative. Eager to fulfill Kennedy's legacy—which, to his mind, meant preventing the loss of South Vietnam—Johnson was equally determined to achieve this aim with the men Kennedy had already deployed. "I just can't believe that we can't take fifteen thousand advisers and two hundred thousand people [i.e., South Vietnamese troops]," he told his national security adviser in March 1964, "and maintain the status quo for six months"—just long enough, in other words, to get him safely elected as president in his own right. When that same month the JCS mooted sending ground troops, Johnson was blunt. "We haven't got any Congress that will go with us," he explained, "and we haven't got any mothers that will go with us in the war. I've got to win the election . . . and then you can make a decision."[8]

Driven by this firm conviction that the home front was not yet ready to accept another Asian war, both the Kennedy and Johnson administrations devoted enormous attention to downplaying American actions inside Vietnam. It was not an easy task. In reality the U.S. military advisers were soon dragged directly into the fight, using "all means at their disposal" when faced with ambushes in the countryside and bombs in the cities. Against this backdrop, minimizing American involvement inevitably translated into a policy of concealment and misrepresentation. In Saigon it meant trying to stop correspondents from being "transported to military activities of the type that are likely to result in undesirable stories." At home it meant instructing returning advisers to say they had "not [been] in combat status" when many had clearly been in combat situations.[9]

Such mendacity rapidly backfired for reasons that would continue to plague the government. Vietnam was not a conventional war with a clear frontline. It was a guerrilla fight being waged throughout the countryside. As a result the military found it impossible to restrict media access to the fighting. Moreover, the ambitious and hardworking correspondents who worked the Saigon beat soon constructed numerous relationships with advisers in the field. These advisers often viewed the war in a more depressing light to their superiors in Saigon, and they did not take kindly to the clumsy attempts to stop them from speaking out.[10]

Among American advisers in South Vietnam, air force personnel were perhaps the most aggrieved by the fact that they were effectively fighting an unknown war. Unlike army advisers, who could chat with correspondents when making their regular excursions from Saigon into the countryside, many pilots were holed up at the Bien Hoa airfield. Here, security soon became incredibly tight. After one correspondent took photographs that showed "blond, Western faces in the pilot's seat," air force commanders even banned all correspondents from the base. The air chief hastened to reassure reporters that they were not missing much, since the American job was only to train South Vietnamese pilots, not to fight. "The role of U.S. forces in South Vietnam," agreed the Pentagon, "is still only to support and train the South Vietnamese."[11]

The problem was that such statements were simply untrue. As early as January 1962, U.S. pilots were flying more than two hundred combat sorties a month, a figure that rose to a thousand within a year. When they started to suffer casualties, their sense of grievance grew. Some complained openly about the lack of official recognition of their sacrifices; the fact that wounded pilots were not awarded a Purple Heart particularly rankled. Others found a way to advertise their gripes, despite a lack of access to reporters: they mailed home candid letters to family members, which soon seeped into the public domain.[12]

In March 1964, the *Indianapolis News* published undoubtedly the most famous of these letters, written by Captain Edwin G. Shank, Jr., an air force officer who had recently died in action. Before his death, Shank had made numerous complaints in his frequent letters home—about the poor state of equipment, about the South Vietnamese ally, and above all about his actual job. The publication of these letters caused a major stir. Within days *U.S. News & World Report* gave the letters a national audience, devoting no less than four pages to them. "I don't know what the U.S. is doing in Vietnam," Shank had written just before his death in perhaps his most eye-catching indictment. "They tell you people we're just in a training situation and they try to run us as a training base. But we're at war, we are doing the flying and fighting. We are losing. Morale is very bad."[13]

Within weeks the Republican Party eagerly picked up on this story. In Congress the GOP rank and file already suspected a Democratic cover-up on a grand scale. Some were even declaring wildly that "thousands of American military personnel may have been casualties in Vietnam."[14] In April 1964, Charles A. Halleck (R-IL), the Republican leader in the House, seized on the Shank letters and decided to use them as the centerpiece of his weekly press conference with Everett M. Dirksen (R-IL), the GOP leader in the Senate.

This "Ev and Charlie Show," as reporters dubbed it, was a major fixture in the Washington landscape at the time, providing the Republican leadership with a chance to push its own policy agenda and challenge the Democratic administration.[15] As luck would have it, Halleck was the Shank family's congressman. He was also perturbed by a recent *Chicago Sun-Times* story detailing mounting U.S. losses in Vietnam since the beginning of the year. With the full support of his colleagues on the Hill, Halleck used the Shank letters to tell assembled reporters that the Johnson administration was concealing Vietnam's grim reality from the public. "If we are going to war," Halleck declared, "let us prepare the American people for it." "Let's have the whole brutal business out on the table," agreed Dirksen, "and let the American people see it for what it is."[16]

With the presidential election just six months away, Johnson had absolutely no desire to give the public a glimpse of the grim brutality of war. His unfolding campaign strategy was to focus on his great domestic agenda. Vietnam, he was convinced, contained only danger—the chance for opponents to accuse him either of losing a country to communism or of muddling into another Korea. In private, Johnson therefore pursued his path of postponing a decision until after the election. In public he was bland in the extreme. "I think that our position there," he told reporters on the same day as the Halleck-Dirksen challenge, "is somewhat like it was ten years ago, in 1954, when the then-President Eisenhower wrote the then-President of South Vietnam and said: 'We want to help you help yourselves.'"[17]

Republicans immediately bristled at Johnson's claim that the American commitment was no different than what Eisenhower had contemplated. In mid-May they were able to keep their claims of a cover-up afloat by ballast from a surprising source. In a Saigon speech designed to pay tribute to the American role in Vietnam, Nguyen Khanh, the South Vietnamese premier, made a major slip. "More than three hundred American heroes," he claimed, "have given their lives to this land." At a time when the Pentagon's public casualty list showed only 131 U.S. personnel killed in action, official spokesmen were reportedly "mystified" by Khanh's statement.[18] But other voices clamored to claim that the government had finally been caught out. Some family members of the fallen even took out a full-page ad in the *Washington Star*, listing all the Americans who had so far died in action and adding a barbed disclaimer. "This list was not complete," they charged. "Many more Americans have been killed by communist bullets in Vietnam than has been reported by the Department of Defense."[19]

To Barry Goldwater, who emerged as the surprise Republican nominee in the summer, these developments seemed like a godsend. As he campaigned, Goldwater was quick to read out the Shank letters to his audiences; in the fall he even appeared alongside Shank's widow in a television ad. In his speeches Goldwater also used casualties to sharpen the GOP claim of administration deception. Vietnam, he claimed on one occasion, was "'soaked with American blood,' a casualty of Johnson's secretive, indecisive, and dishonest policy." "American sons and grandsons are being killed by bullets and communist bombs," he insisted another time. "And we have yet to hear a word of truth about why they're dying."[20]

Ultimately Goldwater was never able to make much headway with this or any other issue. Partly he was the victim of his own unbending posture, especially his disastrous acceptance speech at the Republican Convention, which indelibly stained his candidacy. Indeed, after speaking angrily about the need for "extremism in defense of liberty," Goldwater never shook the image that he was a dangerous throwback to the old right-wingers of the McCarthy era.[21]

After September Goldwater's canny opponent ruthlessly exposed these intrinsic weaknesses. On the campaign trail Johnson had few scruples. His ethos was simple: he would say or do whatever was necessary to get reelected in as big a landslide as possible. On Vietnam, Johnson continued to minimize American involvement.[22] He also stressed that it was Goldwater, not himself, who wanted to escalate the U.S. commitment at the cost of "significantly higher casualties." "We are trying as best we can *not* to enlarge that war," Johnson insisted a month before the election, "not to get the United States tied down in a land war in Asia, and not for American boys starting to do the fighting that Asian boys ought to be doing to protect themselves." Our whole policy, he added in another major speech, was "very cautious and careful."[23]

Ultimately Johnson's campaign was a stunning success. At first he had a few tricky moments, especially when the main television networks began to frame Vietnam around the steadily growing number of American deaths, but even these TV shows turned out have very little sting. A CBS special was typical. Aired in April, and given the ominous title *Vietnam: The Deadly Decision*, it ended on a decidedly upbeat note. "We are fighting here," declared the veteran war correspondent, Peter Kalischer, "a cheap war. In the crucial arithmetic of wars, we have lost something like—I won't say lost—we have suffered about 750 casualties in the last two-and-a-half years. 53,000 Americans died in Korea."[24]

With major media organizations doing little to follow up Republican claims of a casualty cover-up, Johnson's effort to play down U.S. involvement found a ready audience. As a string of polls revealed, most Americans simply did not care too much about Vietnam. According to one Harris survey, 63 percent said they paid "little or no attention to events in South East Asia."[25]

Johnson, Casualties, and American Strategy, 1965

In 1965, with his landslide safely won, Johnson fixed his gaze on Vietnam. It was not a pretty sight. While Saigon was wracked by political instability, in the countryside the insurgents that the Americans called the Viet Cong (VC) were pushing the South Vietnamese army to the edge of destruction. The Saigon government, concluded William Westmoreland, head of the Military Advisory Command Vietnam (MACV), in June, "cannot stand up . . . to this kind of pressure without reinforcement." These reinforcements would have to come from the United States.[26]

Johnson agonized before finally agreeing to escalate. He was a reluctant warrior partly because he wanted to use his mandate to pursue domestic reform. He also hated the thought of sending young American boys to their deaths in Vietnam: "It just makes chills run up my back," he once told a confidant.[27] Equally chilling was the old nagging fear that the public would just not accept large casualties in another Korea-style fight. In July 1965, when one adviser suggested that a Gallup poll showed the "people are basically behind our commitment," Johnson's retort was revealing. "If you make a commitment to jump off a building," he explained, "and you find out how high it is, you may withdraw the commitment."[28]

To advisers who opposed taking this risky plunge, the president's preoccupation with prospective casualties seemed to provide a perfect opening. George Ball was the most outspoken. In one crucial White House meeting, Ball came armed with a chart showing the "correlation between Korean [War] casualties and public opinion." As casualties increase," he warned, "pressure to strike at [the] jugular of the NVN [North Vietnamese] will become very great." Conversely, of course, as losses mounted, the public might rapidly tire of the whole grim business of war, which was another reason to withdraw as gracefully as possible.[29]

Yet, with the election out of the way, Johnson increasingly brushed aside all thoughts of this Korean syndrome. He let Ball have his say largely because he wanted to go through the motions of listening to all viewpoints. As the situation inside Vietnam worsened, Johnson's mind was increasingly made up: he would not countenance losing South Vietnam. To sweeten the bitter prospect of having to fight, Johnson listened to advisers like McGeorge Bundy, his national security adviser, who thought, on balance, that war would probably be "cheap." As Bundy put it, if Saigon fell, the cost Johnson's own reputation at home and America's wider reputation in the world would be exorbitant. In contrast, the cost of escalation, though "real," would be tolerable.[30]

What promised to make this cost so bearable was McNamara's strategy for waging the war. By 1965 McNamara had sold Johnson on the idea of applying "graduated pressure." By carefully calibrating the use of force, McNamara hoped to persuade the communist leaders in Hanoi to come to the negotiating table. The start of the bombing campaign in March was to be the first sign of American resolve. The next was Johnson's July decision to authorize 175,000 combat troops. McNamara was confident that as soon as Hanoi had a chance to digest these signals, it would realize that the United States would never let South Vietnam fall. The communist leaders would then pursue the only sane and rational course: rather than face a destructive and unwinnable war with the American superpower, they would call off the insurgency and negotiate an acceptable settlement.[31]

Such a strategy would not be without pain. Graduated pressure was predicated on sustaining American casualties. As one of McNamara's key advisers suggested, the best way to communicate U.S. resolve was for American troops to "get bloodied"; only then would the "world [recognize the] lengths to which [the] United States will go to fulfill its commitments."[32] Hopefully, though, the pain would be limited: just four hundred casualties between now and October, insisted McNamara in a June meeting with the president. And perhaps Hanoi might be willing to come to terms by then. McNamara was certainly optimistic that the United States stood "a good chance of achieving an acceptable outcome within a reasonable period of time."[33]

Most senior military officers were deeply skeptical, however, of McNamara's optimism and the strategy behind it. In the firm opinion of both the JCS and the MACV, signaling was doomed to fail, especially since it placed excessive constraints on bombing targets and troop numbers. Rather than seeking to persuade, the military men thought that force had to coerce. Their aim, put simply, was victory, not a negotiated peace, and they realized that victory would not be cheap: more than half a million troops on the ground for more than five years, according to one JCS study, which would inevitably lead to much higher casualties than McNamara was suggesting to Johnson.

Crucially, though, neither the Joint Chiefs nor the president probed this gloomier scenario in any great detail. The military men prioritized getting troops into action to save South Vietnam. Since they were divided among themselves on strategy and faced a president clearly skittish about high casualties, they scrupulously avoided any discussion of how best to use these troops, let alone the likely cost. Johnson, for his part, was a willing accomplice in this conspiracy of silence. Always ill at ease around the brass, he invited the JCS to only one staged meeting before his fateful July decision to expand the American commitment. Eager to avoid a potentially bruising bureaucratic battle on the eve of war, he generally kept policy discussions focused firmly on Westmoreland's specific short-term troop requests.[34]

Significantly, the administration's public stance would be very different. Whereas its private policy debates revolved around detailed discussions of troop levels together with a careful avoidance of prospective losses, in public officials did the exact opposite. While Johnson was loath to talk about troop numbers, his officials paradoxically began handing out incredibly full and prompt casualty figures.

In the summer of 1965, Johnson was determined to go to war quietly. In public, as the historian Brian VanDeMark points out, "he deliberately obscured the magnitude" of the new troop commitment, while also denying that it meant a policy change. Doubtless this was partly out of habit: Johnson had been disguising the extent of American activity in Vietnam for so long that it was almost second nature. But he was also driven by more substantive considerations. Johnson was determined to protect his domestic agenda, which might easily encounter congressional hostility if legislators thought a long and costly war was in the offing. But he also worried about waging a strategy of graduated pressure under the full glare of public scrutiny. As McNamara revealingly concluded, it was better instead to go to war "in cold blood," speaking softly so as to avoid "arousing the public ire" and precipitating domestic demands for a dangerous escalation.[35]

Historians have often emphasized these two motives. Less well known, however, is a far more prosaic calculation. Like Wilson, Roosevelt, and Truman in earlier wars, Johnson was determined to keep troop movements secret from the enemy. He probably believed that Hanoi's appreciation of American resolve would be all the greater if large numbers of U.S. troops suddenly appeared on the battlefield. He certainly did not want to give North Vietnam a chance to prepare a hostile reception. If we "explain with candor what we are doing to the American people," Johnson pointed out, "we help the NVN get their requests fulfilled by China and Russia," with potentially fatal consequences for incoming GIs. It was far safer, his senior officials therefore concluded, to play the new troops deployments in a "low key."[36]

Still, what was necessary to protect American troops was also potentially dangerous for Johnson's domestic reputation. "We can't allow the country to wake up one morning and find heavy casualties," Ball warned in July. "We need to be damned serious with the American public."[37] Once again, however, Ball's prescient concerns were brushed aside, with deeply damaging results. While Johnson cloaked the American troop commitment in secrecy, a mixture of number-crunching capabilities, tempting incentives, and fears of a media backlash prodded his military men to prepare the most timely, detailed, and comprehensive casualty lists of any American war.

McNamara obsession with statistics helped to create the capability. Since 1961 his Pentagon had instituted all manner of numerical devices to measure efficiency, cost effectiveness, and, increasingly, progress in Vietnam. McNamara's mania for math was indeed so notorious that he had once rejected a policy paper with the brusque question: "Where is your data? Give me something I can put in the computer. Don't give me your poetry."[38]

McNamara would never fault Westmoreland on this score, even though the statistics the MACV commander soon generated were to support a very different strategy to that championed by his Pentagon boss. Westmoreland shared the Joint Chiefs' deep distaste for graduated response and bristled at the constraints it placed on fighting the war. Once he had more than one hundred thousand men at his disposal—not to mention little guidance from Johnson on how they should be used—he had a considerable leeway to devise his own strategy.[39]

Westmoreland's basic concept was simple. He would send out patrols, reinforced by the mobility provided by helicopters, to seek out the VC insurgents. American forces would then use their overwhelming firepower to kill the communists in such large numbers that the "crossover point" would be reached. This was the crucial moment when enemy casualties would exceed the number of men the communists could infiltrate into the country. When this happened, Westmoreland was confident that the VC would collapse and the war would be won.

Westmoreland's "search and destroy" concept was based, in essence, on attrition: killing the communist troops of the VC and People's Army of North Vietnam (PAVN) in such large numbers that they could no longer sustain the insurgency. As such, it was a way of war peculiarly dependent on number crunching. And soon Westmoreland's command was spewing out all manner of data for

McNamara's "whiz kids" to enter into their computers in a desperate attempt to gauge what was happening on the battlefield. Most importantly, to calculate how soon the crossover point would be reached, Westmoreland needed to know precisely how many enemy troops had been located in a particular engagement, how many had escaped, and above all how many had been killed. Because his war of attrition was based on making sure that a lot more enemy troops were killed than friendly soldiers, Westmoreland's command also closely monitored the so-called kill ratio, the difference between losses on both sides.[40]

Westmoreland's determination to quantify the fighting would soon become notorious, not least because it was difficult for soldiers in the heat of an intensive firefight to compute the precise number of enemy casualties. Communist troops also prided themselves on taking their killed and wounded off the battlefield, leaving U.S. officers to make estimates. These Americans had little motivation to underestimate. On the contrary, with promotion tied to battlefield success— and with success determined by the number of communists killed—their inclination was always toward erring on the side of exaggeration.[41]

Westmoreland's fetish for figures also had another consequence: his command had a much clearer sense of friendly casualties. Westmoreland was certainly better informed than his counterparts in previous wars. Unlike in Normandy in 1944, for instance, Westmoreland's officers were hardly in a position to claim that they were too busy fighting for geographical objectives to compile figures— for in Vietnam winning was gauged by casualties, not territory. Nor for that matter could Westmoreland's officers use the excuse of their Korean War predecessors who had found it difficult to piece together timely lists when so many troops were encircled in big battles—for in Vietnam American patrols were more likely to be caught up in short, sharp engagements in which the enemy soon melted away.[42]

In short, then, the MACV invariably had access to prompt casualty reports from units in the field. Crucially, moreover, despite Johnson's continued desire to minimize the extent of the American involvement, Westmoreland's command also faced both an obvious incentive and growing pressure to reveal such figures to the press and public.

The incentive stemmed from the importance of statistics in the military culture of the day. With McNamara at the helm, figures were not only a way of measuring progress but also gave a veneer of rationality and scientific precision to military actions. As James William Gibson has argued, body counts, kill ratios, and the like "presented Vietnam as a war managed by rational men basing their decisions on scientific knowledge. Statistics helped make war-managers appear legitimate to the American public."[43] As early as October 1965, McNamara, desperate to get some good press for the war, was already speaking openly about the number of enemy killed in recent weeks, providing percentage comparisons with previous years—and encouraging, in the process, the media to frame their stories in a similar vein. A few weeks later Westmoreland adopted exactly the same course, prefacing his background briefing with the revealing statement: "statistics are about the best indexes we have for measuring the level of activity in the conflict."[44]

While this calculation prodded the MACV to reveal detailed data, the legacy of its earlier media relations made it much harder to contemplate concealing casualties. By the time the United States finally intervened on a massive scale, Washington's repeated efforts to mask, misrepresent, and muzzle had generated a mood of profound media distrust. In 1964 the Pentagon had responded by recruiting Barry Zorthian to become the MACV public affairs chief. On paper his job was simply to coordinate the official message and respond to inaccurate press reports, but Zorthian also tried to bring a new ethos to press relations. "Since the truth was seldom as bad as hearsay," he believed, "getting it into the open where it could awaken the American public seemed the correct thing to do."[45]

In 1965, as Washington took the fateful decision to escalate, the MACV's inclination to openness was initially tempered by the temptation of formal censorship. With Johnson still desperate to keep a lid on war news, Zorthian and his team discussed the feasibility of a censorship regime on three separate occasions, but each time they concluded that the obstacles were far too great. Like MacArthur's command in 1950, they believed they lacked sufficient trained personnel. Unlike MacArthur's command in 1951, though, they faced no "Chinese intervention moment," which would justify a policy reversal. July 1965 provided an obvious opportunity, but Johnson was determined to go to war quietly. In the absence of a dramatic and demonstrable new threat, MACV publicists were in no doubt that the sudden introduction of censorship would produce howls of protest from an already skeptical media. War correspondents, in particular, would doubtless view it as an even more invidious method of concealing Vietnam's grim reality.[46]

Still, some "fixed set of ground rules" were required not only to stop the publication of sensitive information but also to placate correspondents who continued to complain of "outright obstructionism by various [official] spokesmen."[47] In July, therefore, Zorthian briefed the Saigon press corps on an informal new set of guidelines. Official communiqués and press briefings, he explained, would avoid specific casualty totals for particular battles. They would merely use the terms "light," "moderate," or "heavy," so that the communists could not precisely piece together the cost of any single engagement. Beyond this proscription, though, reporters would be relatively free. "I certainly would not deny any correspondent the right," Zorthian explained, "if he's on an operation, to say that he saw a casualty or he saw a man die, providing he doesn't give close to the statistical rundown."[48]

Even this "statistical rundown" would not remain secret for long. As soon as casualty totals were no longer of value to the enemy, the MACV and Pentagon would include them in their weekly press releases. The MACV handout was particularly impressive. On a single page it contained no less than four boxes detailing the number of actions involving friendly forces; the number of VC–inspired incidents; the amount of naval activity; and finally personnel losses, broken down into the KIA, WIA, MIA of the United States, South Vietnamese, and Viet Cong.[49] In Washington, meanwhile, the Pentagon issued its own weekly cumulative list of all U.S. casualties since 1961, which, if anything, was even more comprehensive. For one thing the Pentagon included both battle and non-battle losses, in order to avoid a repeat of the Republican-inspired charges of a cover-up that had scarred the Korean War debate. For another its wounded totals contained everyone who received a Purple Heart, even those whose condition was not serious enough to be hospitalized, another notable and liberal break from some past practice.[50]

Although this impressive statistical bombardment meant that no one could reasonably accuse the government of covering up losses, problems were still bound to ensue. After all, if lists were too prompt and accurate they could easily have the opposite impact: they would make the public acutely aware of the high human cost. Such lists were also likely to hit the home front all the harder because of Johnson's low-key way of going to war.

In the summer and fall of 1965 the public had scarcely been told that they were now in a big Asian conflict. As Walter Lippmann, the dean of American columnists, observed in September, Johnson had "managed to obtain the assent of most of the country to . . . a sporadic low-grade war carried on chiefly by a professional American army. There is no immediate prospect of big battles with big casualties."[51] But what if the fighting turned out very differently? How would the public react if they suddenly found that the war would not be on a small scale? Given the president's failure to level with the home front over the scale of what was in store, the first detailed casualty lists threatened to be momentous, suddenly underscoring the new scale of America's undertaking. And these lists were not long in coming.

Trust, Taxis, and Television—Ia Drang, 1965

On November 24 the MACV public information office issued a terse press release. "Action west of Plei Me began [on] 14 November," it stated,

> when elements of the First Cavalry initiated a S&D [search and destroy] operation along the Ia Drang River. An enemy attack on a company-size unit in a LZ [landing zone] initiated a week-long battle. The First Cavalry

Division elements and supporting arms killed 1429 VC, captured 20 and 855 weapons at the end of the period. Friendly casualties were moderate.[52]

This press release typified how the U.S. military wanted the home front to view the Vietnam fighting. It was factual and anodyne. It offered a straightforward narrative that depicted a success story without the gore. It gave, in short, the impression of a textbook battle in which communists were killed or captured while American boys suffered only moderate losses.

At one level the MACV undoubtedly believed its own success story. Ia Drang had certainly been a stern test for the army's new concept of airmobile combat, which the First Cavalry, as its commanding officer declared, had apparently passed "with flying colors." Tactically these airmobile troops had used their massive firepower to inflict such high casualties that "the better part" of three PAVN regiments had been destroyed. As a result, the United States now had the strategic advantage in this key region, for the enemy was no longer in a position to push to the sea and cut South Vietnam in two. Small wonder that Westmoreland soon told reporters that Ia Drang was an "unprecedented victory." The enemy had "fled the scene," he added, after sustaining much heavier casualties than the American and South Vietnamese troops.

Yet on close inspection, Ia Drang had been a much messier fight. It had actually been a series of battles, beginning more than a month earlier when the communists laid siege to a special forces camp at Plei Me. After this siege had been lifted, units of the First Cavalry began pushing west into the mountains to try and locate the PAVN. On November 14 they succeeded too well. Troops under the command of Lieutenant Colonel Harold G. Moore suddenly found that their Landing Zone, dubbed X-ray, was smack in the middle of a large enemy force. After three days of sustained PAVN attacks these men stood their ground and, with the help of hastily flown-in reinforcements and savage air attacks, were able to force back the enemy. The PAVN, though, was not beaten. On November 17, as one battalion of Moore's force withdrew to another Landing Zone, called Albany, it too was ambushed, with disastrous results: 151 killed, 121 wounded, and 5 missing, which out of a total force of 400 amounted to almost 40 percent KIA.

Although this Albany ambush was clearly a bloody setback, Westmoreland's public talk of a major victory was not entirely disingenuous. Details of the LZ Albany fight were slow to make their way up the chain of command, so that the first official statements were issued before the MACV had grasped the full story. Like any senior commander, Westmoreland also tended to take a broader strategic overview, which was indeed rosier than the final fiasco. Still, even when all the facts became known Westmoreland and his subordinates remained reluctant to dwell on the LZ Albany reverse. Westmoreland himself was simply relieved that this first brush with the enemy had gone much better than Kasserine in 1943 or the battles to Pusan in 1950. Those in command of airmobile units, meanwhile, feared that this new concept of warfare might never recover from news of a disastrous first outing. So while Westmoreland talked about victory, his press office painted a rosy, if antiseptic, picture of success. And it was left to the correspondents to write about the ambush in grim and graphic detail—with ruinous consequences for media trust in Westmoreland's command.[53]

As Moore recalled, soon after the battle "the wires were burning up with reports of the heaviest American casualties to date; hints of an army cover-up of a disastrous ambush; reports that the American forces were withdrawing— some accounts said 'retreating'—from the valley."[54] Coverage in the *New York Times* was typical. BATTALION OF G.I.'S BATTERED IN TRAP; CASUALTIES HIGH, its headline blared on November 19. Neil Sheehan, the *Times* correspondent who had been to X-ray in the midst of the battle, had no doubt that the airmobile troops had won their inaugural fight. But Sheehan had also witnessed some horrific scenes, both here and at Albany, and his dispatch recounted "large numbers of American dead and wounded [who] lay scattered ... among trees, brush, and patches of elephant grass."[55]

Like other correspondents, Sheehan tried to reconcile what he had seen with the military's description of "moderate" casualties. His own approach was to observe pointedly that the MACV's judgment of "light," "moderate," or "heavy" was frequently at odds with the correspondents' own conclusions. Other observers were much blunter. As the AP concluded in a widely used dispatch, American losses might have been moderate relative to the "total troop commitment," but some of the small units engaged in the heaviest fighting "took huge losses."[56]

The military was appalled. Pentagon briefing officers immediately lashed out at what they considered the media's overemphasis on American losses. Such coverage, Westmoreland angrily agreed, was "distorting the picture at home and lowering the morale of the people who are emotionally concerned (wives)."[57]

Despite these angry outbursts, the media was actually treading a well-worn path. In the past, whenever the government had failed to provide hard figures, media speculation had invariably inflated the human cost. What was different about this battle was the military's response. The MACV provided precise figures much faster. Rather than the month or two gap of past wars, Westmoreland's command waited just days before confirming that the Ia Drang battles had taken eighty-six American lives in one week and another 240 the next.[58] During the Battle of the Bulge and China's intervention in Korea, the extensive time lag had been partly due to the large numbers of units involved in the fighting. This, in turn, had spread the anguish across the nation, as numerous communities had spent an anxious Christmas waiting for word about relatives at the front. Now, it was a single town that experienced the bleakest of Thanksgivings.

Columbus, Georgia, was the town in pain. It was here that the First Cavalry had been stationed before heading to Vietnam. And it was here that the closest relatives remained, fretful and anxious, their suffering greatly exacerbated by the Pentagon's unpreparedness for handling such a large numbers of deaths.

The Pentagon was not insensitive to these families. On the contrary, it was currently in the process of introducing two new initiatives. First, it would dispatch casualty-notification teams of trained men and chaplains who would personally deliver the awful news, before staying "to comfort a young widow or elderly parents until friends and relatives could arrive." Then the Pentagon would send out its "casualty assistance" or "survivor officers" who would keep in close touch with the next of kin to "help them filling out forms, offer legal advice, and assist them in dealing with government agencies."[59]

With the war in its infancy, however, the Pentagon had not yet fully developed either capability. Instead, it continued to use Western Union to dispatch the brutal telegrams. This proved contentious, for in Columbus, Georgia, Western Union was equally unprepared. Faced with a sudden spurt of telegrams to deliver, it decided to use yellow taxis to get the message speedily to the next of kin—much to the disgust of the entire community. Soon stories were circulating of relatives hiding whenever a yellow taxi appeared, in the vain hope of escaping the bad news. The First Cavalry commander's wife was so appalled that she protested publicly about "the heartless taxicab telegrams." Inevitably, the press also picked up on such comments, fueling the outrage and forcing the army to into a defensive apology.[60]

Television latched on to Columbus's tragedy too. ABC was first off the mark. In a show titled *Next of Kin*, it described in detail "how the wives and children of American fighting men in Vietnam spent their Thanksgiving holiday amid reports of mounting casualties at the front."[61]

It was a telling moment. Here was one of the first TV shows on America's first big battle, and it contained very little footage of Vietnam combat. As such, it belied the well-worn myth that television cultivated distaste and dissent by beaming images of death and destruction into the nation's living rooms. The truth, both in this battle and the war more generally, was much less striking: fewer than one hundred out of more than nine thousand television reports contained "actual combat close up, with casualties," according to one analyst.[62] The reasons were clear. In Ia Drang, as in other battles, TV correspondents had to work hard to get footage of the fighting. Cameras were cumbersome. It needed three men to cart around gear that weighed as much as fifty pounds, with cables, batteries, and sound equipment adding to their load. Although television reporters—like their print counterparts—gained professional kudos only when they experienced real combat, their network bosses were generally leery of airing anything too graphic. Audiences might complain. Worse, so might the government with its precious licenses and advertisers with their equally precious revenue.[63]

Television still had the ability to cause trouble, however. In covering Ia Drang, the networks had little fighting footage, but they could easily send their cameras down to Columbus to cover the anguish of the First Cavalry's families; ABC led the way, and in its wake came CBS with a far more elaborate affair.

The CBS news special was made with "direct assistance" from the Pentagon, which enabled it to show a few, generally bland, battlefield scenes. CBS reporters were also on hand to interview soldiers who had just survived the battle, and who provided moving comments about watching helplessly as their "buddies" were hit.[64] Again, though, the most emotive passage revolved around events in Columbus. On the screen, viewers watched a simple pictorial narrative: first the happy scenes of the First Cavalry departing for Vietnam to the rousing sounds of a military band; then the searing images of coffins being unloaded from aircraft, somber military funerals, and tearful relatives. Over it all came Walter Cronkite's slowly delivered and solemn message: "Their lives," he intoned, "the price of victory in the Battle of the Ia Drang Valley."

For Cronkite, this casualty angle had a particularly important purpose: he could use it to tell the American public that the nation was in a big war—something the administration had been eager to play down until now. "Just six days ago," Cronkite reminded his massive living-room audience, looking evenly into the camera,

> the people of America were jolted by an announcement. Our casualties in Vietnam in a single week had exceeded the average weekly rate of dead and wounded in the Korean War. Two hundred and forty Americans killed, 470 wounded. If the American public had not known until then, they know now: the United States is indeed at war—a full-dress war against a formidable enemy.[65]

Thus Cronkite—who just over two years later in the midst of the Tet Offensive would famously pave the way for the gradual U.S. withdrawal by broadcasting that the war could not be won—was using the shock of the Ia Drang casualties to tell the Americans that they were in a fight akin to the Korean War. In the absence of a keynote presidential address, it was perhaps the closest the country would come to a high-profile declaration of hostilities.

Johnson's later reaction to Cronkite's 1968 Tet broadcast has passed into lore: "If I've lost Cronkite," he is reputed to have remarked, "I've lost Middle America."[66] Now, recuperating from a gall bladder operation at his Texas ranch, Johnson appeared equally rattled. In a filmed press conference Bill Moyers, his press secretary, even spoke openly about Johnson's reaction to the recent losses. "I do not know of any situation which concerns the president more," Moyers told the nation, "and I do not know of any matter that causes him deeper personal anguish, or any matter over which he grieves more than the loss of American lives in Vietnam.... I remember very well," he added,

> the spontaneous and extemporaneous remarks the president made to the marine veterans of Vietnam on that day he departed Bethesda Naval Hospital. I think he said something like: "Every time I make a decision that involves the sending of more of your buddies into war, I do with a heavy heart." That feeling is not one that is turned on or off, no matter whether the casualty list is two or two hundred. . . . He watches the situation every day and even when it is not a matter of big bold black headlines, weighs the loss of every life very great indeed.[67]

This was a stunning statement. Johnson was not the first president to talk publicly about casualties, but he was certainly the first to try to feel the nation's pain. When Wilson and Roosevelt had periodically spoken of losses, they had done so to highlight the sacrifices being made to win the war and create a new world order. In 1943 Roosevelt had made one brief public appearance at a recently established military cemetery in North Africa, but this had been an exception.[68] More typical was a visit Truman made to the Walter Reed Hospital in September 1950. Not only were no reporters present, but the White House press secretary revealed that Truman had asked only about the care the men were receiving—he had not actually visited the ward.[69]

Moyers's press conference admission therefore marked a departure in presidential responses to combat casualties. Significantly, moreover, it also represented a sharp turnaround in Johnson's own public posture to the Vietnam War. No longer was he trying to minimize what was happening. Like the rest of his administration, he was talking publicly about this deeply distressing aspect of the war. As one aide explained, the White House was keen on "presenting the president as one who is concerned over the heavy responsibility of sending American men across the seas to fight." Clearly Johnson was also motivated by a deep sense of personal anguish. "I never sleep well at night," he remarked privately, "when I know that an action in Vietnam may cost an American lad his life."[70]

In the wake of Ia Drang other officials were equally troubled. The battle was a particularly bitter blow to McNamara. The once hyperconfident defense secretary was suddenly racked with "gnawing doubts" about the whole concept of graduated pressure. North Vietnam, he feared, intended to match any American escalation man for man. With Westmoreland calling for 410,000 troops in 1966, American casualties were soon likely to hit a thousand a month, with no end in sight. Searching desperately for a way out of this bloody abyss, McNamara lobbied vigorously for a bombing pause, with the hope that this might give Hanoi a chance to consider a negotiated settlement.[71]

Johnson was not enthusiastic. He fretted that a bombing pause might itself kill more Americans, by giving the enemy a chance to recuperate, rebuild, and come back stronger. But he was also troubled by the domestic eruption over the Ia Drang casualties, and so to placate the doubters he went along with McNamara's "gamble." In public, he even depicted the bombing pause as an imaginative bid for peace.[72]

In the new year the Pentagon then launched a major media blitz. Its objective was straightforward: to place the casualty lists in some sort of historical perspective. Some officials pointed to the continued improvements in medical treatment. American servicemen, they stressed, were at a hospital within thirty-five minutes of sustaining a wound anywhere in Vietnam—a major achievement that helped to confirm that only 1 percent of WIA were dying, down from 4.5 percent in World War II and 2.4 percent in Korea. Harking back to the Roosevelt era, other officials stressed that the high-tech, low-casualty emphasis of the American war effort was now even more pronounced. "We are using in Vietnam what we have more of than anything else, money," McNamara emphasized, "instead of that which we value so highly, lives. Never has any army in history had such equipment and firepower. In short, we are substituting dollars for lives."[73]

The Rules of the Game Change, 1966–67

Had Vietnam been like any other war the United States fought in the twentieth century, then Johnson's spirited reply to this first casualty controversy might well have stilled the home front. The president certainly had grounds for optimism. Just before Ia Drang, pro-war demonstrations in New York had attracted more than twenty thousand participants, dwarfing the much smaller antiwar protest of a few weeks before. Many key groups, moreover, had strong reasons if not to support the war enthusiastically then at least to keep their qualms quiet. Black leaders, for instance, had an incentive to stand by a president who had passed so much civil rights legislation. Liberal Democrats, likewise, felt the strong pull of party loyalty to a president who was doing his best to implement domestic reform. Even the youth—especially those American boys who would be drafted to fight and possibly die—appeared to accept the war. "On campus after campus," noted *Newsweek* in the spring of 1966, "student bodies still vote overwhelming support for the war."[74]

According to an array of opinion polls, the bombing pause had apparently worked its magic on the majority of the country. When Johnson announced a resumption of the air campaign in early 1966, 63 percent approved of his handling of the war, while 66 percent believed he had done everything possible to make peace. Strikingly, no less than 73 percent thought he was correct to resume the bombings. As the Harris survey concluded in February, "There is 'consensus' in the country today on one point about the Vietnam War: the American people long for a honorable end to hostilities, but by two to one they believe we have to stay and see it through."[75]

On Capitol Hill, by contrast, the surface signs were more troubling. In early 1966, Sen. William Fulbright (D-AR) used the Senate Foreign Relations Committee to grill senior officials and spokesmen about the war.[76] On the other side of the aisle, Republicans, still smarting from their mauling in the 1964 campaign, seemed primed to extract a measure of revenge on a president who had repeatedly denied he would send American boys to die in Asian jungles. In the summer of 1965, as Johnson prepared to escalate, some had even told reporters that "they would not support him in a full-scale ground war with heavy casualties."[77]

In the wake of Ia Drang, the Republican leadership predictably began talking about the large losses, tying them to the upcoming 1966 midterm campaign. "The war will have its impact," pronounced Gerald Ford (R-MI), the House leader who succeeded Halleck. "By election time, there will be three times the present number of casualties among American troops." Ford's House colleagues agreed. In September they even released a white paper accusing Johnson of covering up the truth about the scale of the war, including the extent of American losses.[78]

Ultimately, however, many key Republican leaders, in stark contrast to their more combative predecessors, were surprisingly restrained on the casualty issue. "We don't have to talk about it," insisted Ford. "It isn't good politics or good national policy to try to exploit the situation for political gains." "A political party doesn't make war an issue," agreed Dirksen. "People make it an issue because their youngsters are out there."[79] Of course, such statements might well have been nothing more than a common political trick to emphasize the very issue they were professing to dismiss. But Dirksen, in particular, truly wanted to take Vietnam out of the partisan debate. He got along well with Johnson, saw his duty as putting country before party, and thought Vietnam was a necessary war to check the spread of communism.[80]

Even in the wake of Ia Drang, then, Johnson faced surprisingly little danger from the places that had caused his predecessors such grief. Public support, while fragile, had been solidified by the bombing pause. Republican opposition, though occasionally bubbling to the surface, was more subterranean than in earlier wars—and definitely nowhere near as visible and as vehement as that faced by Truman in Korea. Increasingly, however, these familiar markers were no longer the most noticeable aspect of the home-front picture. In the foreground, and much more conspicuous, was dissent from a mass movement of antiwar protesters who were determined to oppose the Vietnam War outside the normal political channels—and who often placed American casualties at the heart of their unorthodox campaign.

Vietnam was not the first American war to generate domestic dissent. But the antiwar movement that exploded after 1965 was quite different from anything that had come before. This was partly a matter of timing. During the two world wars, opposition to American involvement had been most vocal and visible during the long periods of U.S. neutrality. As soon as Wilson and Roosevelt had asked Congress for a formal declaration of war, the high-profile isolationist movements had either collapsed or dissipated, as most Americans rallied behind their president—solidly after December 1941, more fractiously after April 1917. In Vietnam, by contrast, Johnson faced a mushrooming protest movement after U.S. forces had been sent into action.

Nor, more importantly, was the Vietnam era home front anything like Truman's audience during the Korean War. As the stereotype would have it, there was a vast difference between the consensual, convention-bound 1950s and the turbulent, rule-challenging 1960s. The Red scare, which had both fueled partisanship in Washington and discouraged dissent in the rest of the nation, was a thing of the past. In the Oval Office Democratic presidents might continue to fret about awakening the "great right-wing beast" if they lost a country to communism.[81] In the rest of the country most ordinary citizens were no longer so fearful of the stigma of disloyalty if they challenged basic Cold War orthodoxies. In fact many of the new "baby boom" generation—born in the immediate aftermath of World War II and raised in the affluence of the 1950s— felt they had little to fear from rebellion. They were inspired, instead, by the massive nonviolent civil rights campaign that began in the late 1950s. They were increasingly attracted, too, to the countercultural movement—a heterogeneous and inchoate impulse, comprising students, artists, radical intellectuals, and icons of popular culture. Some who fell within this orbit experimented with drugs and free love. Others embraced causes like women's rights and the environment. All were imbued with a sense of generational conflict built on impatience with the ideas of their elders.[82]

For those inclined to countercultural rebellion, opposing Vietnam held obvious attractions. The war's architects were the older generation at the top of the Johnson administration who had rarely leveled with the public when escalating the American commitment. The war's morality appeared questionable, especially as a combination of massive American air strikes and Westmoreland's search-and-destroy sweeps resulted in mounting civilian losses. The war's causes seemed debatable, particularly as South Vietnam's internal stability, democratic credentials, and willingness to fight scarcely bore scrutiny. To be sure, the anti-war movement that embraced such critiques was far from united or predictable. In scale, intensity, and sheer radicalism it constantly waxed and waned, rather than rising to a concerted crescendo. Yet, despite this volatility, the Americans who took to the streets, or who devised catchy chants and tunes, or who engaged in illegal acts like burning draft cards, all tended to place the casualty issue at the heart of their case against Vietnam.

The nature of war news was one reason for their casualty focus. During 1966 Vietnam quickly bogged down into a messy, complex, and unconventional fight. Although Westmoreland had sufficient troops to take the offensive by the fall, it was still a curiously shapeless war—a war neither with fronts nor an obvious march toward victory. As even Pentagon propagandists conceded, it was difficult for many faraway Americans

> to fit daily information into a clear picture of the progress of things. There are few battle lines, and much of the action occurs at villages whose place names are not on any map. These scattered and seemingly unrelated news reports, no matter how systematically assimilated, usually give only a superficial indication of what is happening.[83]

With few geographical signposts directing the way to ultimate success, the media followed a grim path paved with growing casualty statistics, its attention caught by a variety of ugly milestones during the course of 1966. As early as March, senior Saigon correspondents reported that U.S. losses for the first two months of the year were already more than half the entire casualty total for 1965. By June the U.S. KIA figure was regularly above a hundred a week, with overall casualties topping five hundred (it would start to exceed a thousand a week by January 1967). In September, moreover, U.S. losses were higher than South Vietnamese; a month later they would climb to more than double the amount of the ally that GIs were purportedly fighting to protect.[84]

Against this bloody backdrop, the antiwar movement started to proliferate. As protestors took to the streets with placards or chanted songs at sit-ins, they often simply amplified what mainstream voices were already saying about American losses. In February 1966, for instance, one leading peace demonstrator found a *New York Times* story predicting four to five hundred monthly American dead so "appalling" that he repeated it endlessly.[85] In June a major peace committee likewise latched on to a CBS broadcast by Eric Sevareid that had reached a shocking conclusion. "Every solider fighting in an active combat zone in Vietnam," Sevareid had declared, "has only a fifty-fifty chance of avoiding death or wounds

Figure 5.1 As the American troop presence in Vietnam grew, so inevitably did U.S. casualties. Here a medic comforts a wounded soldier in Operation Cedar Falls, January 1967. National Archives 111-CV-555.

during his twelve-month tour of duty"—a grim, if highly questionable, fact that the committee repeated in a range of fact sheets and flyers.[86]

As the peace campaigners obviously recognized, such news stories were an ideal antiwar recruitment tool, for they stoked youthful fears of dying in a far-away war. But the antiwar movement quickly proved to be more than a mere amplifier of traditional forms of media. It was also a modifier of this message, sometimes even a transformer, providing fresh perspectives and radical insights on recent news events. Ia Drang was a case in point. While mainstream news organizations generally took extreme care to balance their reports of large losses against the military's claim of a major victory, students marching on the East Coast adopted a very different refrain. "Your Daddy Died in the Ia Drang Valley," they chanted. "Where? Ia Drang Valley. Where? Ia Drang Valley. *Why?*"[87]

The accentuated "why" was crucial to antiwar protesters, even though their answer was eminently predictable: Vietnam had no purpose. It was simply, as one poster put it, a "senseless slaughter." The war, agreed a group of old soldiers who opposed it from the outset, was "not a worthy cause. . . . It is not worth a single life, American or Vietnamese. We need no more military graveyards. No more wounded. No more veterans." "Our leaders," added a group of Berkeley students,

> have blundered their way into this war. They have lied to us about their reasons for fighting it. And now they plan to put our lives on the line, while they sit back and continue the blundering and the lies. They want us to go to Vietnam to kill soldiers and civilians who are fighting for their national rights, or to be killed by them. To our leaders, we are plainly nothing but a natural resource—cannon fodder. They make the mistakes; we pay for them.[88]

Refusing to be cannon fodder in a senseless war was clearly a major motive for antiwar protesters. But many were driven by more than pure self-interest. Indeed, radical protesters, convinced that Vietnam was an immoral war, were not content to dodge or evade the draft and they began to resist it altogether. During 1966 and 1967 a diffuse movement of these draft resisters spread from Boston to Berkeley. Openly burning their draft cards and physically attacking draft board offices, they aimed to wreak so much havoc that the system would become unworkable. Some agitators even opposed student deferments. "To cooperate with conscription is to perpetuate its existence," declared one antidraft manifesto. "We will renounce all deferments."[89]

The extent and intensity of this draft opposition clearly took Johnson by surprise. Originally he had viewed the draft as the fairest and least contentious method of supplementing the professional army in Vietnam. In previous wars, after all, the draft had generated scarcely any complaints, even though the numbers affected had been much larger. During World War II almost the entire eligible population had entered military service; in the Korean War era this same figure was about 70 percent. Now, however, the situation had changed. The baby boomers were not only more radically inclined; they were also the largest youth generation in American history. The chance of being drafted was thus a lot slimmer than in the past. Of the 27 million who came of draft age between 1964 and 1973, just 2.5 million men went to Vietnam, a little under 10 percent.[90]

Ironically, though, the dwindling likelihood of getting drafted soon became a major bone of contention. The reason was simple: fairness. By the 1960s local draft boards had lost their reputation as impartial assemblages of the great and good; in cases where they had discretion, they were increasingly accused of making inconsistent, even arbitrary, decisions. For their part, middle-class Americans often had a good idea of how to play the system—how to get a student or a medical deferment, or even a place in a national guard unit that would not get sent to Vietnam.[91]

As a result, the draft was increasingly accused of bias along class or educational lines. Perhaps the biggest controversy, though, centered on its treatment of race. It was one area where Johnson thought his major domestic legislative achievements had given him a degree of protection from dissent. Once again, however, Johnson discovered that the rules of the game had suddenly changed.

Race, War, and Casualties

In 1917, 1941, and 1950 the United States had gone to war with a segregated army, and this had been the single most important factor shaping African American leaders' public posture. In all three cases most black spokesmen had supported the president's decision to intervene.[92] They had nevertheless complained loudly that too many black servicemen were being shunted off into service and support units, the victim of white racist attitudes that questioned their value as combat troops.

Here, in fact, was the crux. Determined to push for the "right to fight," these earlier African American spokesmen had had a strong incentive to play up the role of black troops whenever they did take part in bloody battles. In 1918, indeed, black newspapers had eagerly announced that black troops had proven "their value as fighters" when beating back "the Hun" in an area near Verdun. In 1944 they had boasted that "Negro marines are in the thick of America's bloodiest Pacific campaign, covering themselves with glory in the United States' battle for hard-won positions at Saipan."[93] In 1950, when the negative attitude of senior white officers toward the Twenty-fourth Infantry Regiment became notorious, the black American press had again extolled the "terrific" and "gallant" men who were in the vanguard of fighting the communist aggressor.[94]

Significantly these black voices not only lauded the combat role of black troops; they were even tempted to find an upside in black casualties. This was partly because, whatever the prejudices of white officers, the brutal reality of American losses was clearly exerting an integrating impact on the armed services. World War II began the trend. During the Battle of the Bulge, in particular, SHAEF was so short of replacements that Eisenhower agreed to accept volunteers from black service regiments who were then placed, forty at a time, into white companies of two hundred men.[95] The Korean War took this process a stage further. Although Truman had issued an executive order calling for integration of the military in 1948, not until the summer of 1951 did integration become reality. With casualties so high, and with large numbers of blacks volunteering or being drafted into military service, many white officers now conceded that the only way to meet the looming troop shortage was to mix up units.[96]

As well as these practical benefits, in earlier wars the African American media had tended to depict black casualties within a frame of heroic sacrifice. In this rendering, large losses, though a tragedy, gave lie to the racist canard that blacks were worthless fighters. More importantly they also provided an important and eloquent reason for ending discrimination inside the United States. A revealing moment came in the summer of 1944, when the *New York Herald Tribune* used the caption "No Color Line For Heroes" beneath a story detailing the bravery of two local soldiers. Black spokesmen seized on the tag with glee. "There is no color line for heroes," declared one, "there is no line a man may cross if he is big enough. And each member of a minority who lifts himself above the barrier, lowers that barrier for the worthwhile man that follows." Six years later, when the Twenty-fourth Infantry Regiment suffered badly during the bitter fighting in Korea, one headline put the same point much more pithily: CASUALTIES HIGH IN TWENTY-FOURTH REGIMENT, it boomed. BLOOD FOR DEMOCRACY.[97]

In previous wars, then, the black media's narrative on casualties had contained more than just shock, anguish, and grief. It had also included a strong sense that battlefield sacrifices were pushing the nation's fraught race relations in the right direction.

At the start of the Vietnam War some black leaders initially helped to create the impression that Johnson was still playing under these same rules. Vietnam, they insisted, was yet another equality-affirming crucible. In this war, argued Whitney Young in the *Baltimore Afro-American*, race "for all intents and purposes is an irrelevancy.... Colored soldiers fight and die courageously as representatives of all America."[98]

Eager to highlight the extent to which blacks had finally achieved the "right to fight," the Pentagon even reversed an old policy. The military had rarely broken down casualties by race or ethnicity in earlier wars. The basic military policy had been established in 1918, when the War Department had explained that "as well as the moral aspect of such distinctions, . . . a tremendous amount of clerical work would be entailed by the separation of the many names by racial or other group lines."[99] In 1966, however, the Pentagon for the first time published a list differentiated by race. Its goal was to demonstrate and celebrate the patriotism and bravery of black troops.[100]

During the Vietnam era, however, even such openness had a tendency to backfire. In the realm of race relations a large part of the problem stemmed, paradoxically, from the success of civil rights reforms. For one thing, with the military integrated and basic political rights granted, black leaders no longer had an incentive to extol black sacrifices on the battlefield. For another, the end of basic legal discrimination rapidly brought deeper forms of inequality into sharper focus: the lack of educational opportunities or living standards well below the

national average. As many black voices hastened to point out, America's fight in
Vietnam both reflected and compounded these basic inequalities.

The Pentagon's racially differentiated casualty lists starkly demonstrated that
blacks were fighting and dying in disproportionate numbers. In October 1966
the columnist Stewart Alsop provocatively publicized this fact. "Negroes," he
observed in an article for the *Post* magazine, "make up 11 percent of the population and 22 percent of the killed in action in ground combat in Vietnam." "There
is no question," he continued, "that the present system tends to push the poor
and the stupid up front, where they get shot at, and to keep the rich and the
bright back in the safe jobs." For black spokesmen, Alsop's implication that their
boys were "stupid" was highly offensive, but they still picked up on his central
point, giving it a highly significant twist. As the *Philadelphia Tribune* put it,
"What Mr. Alsop neglects to point out—whether intentionally or not—is the
rampant racism permeating all of [American] society which prevents large
numbers of Negroes from devising clever ways of being shot at."[101]

This indictment, so different from the public black position in earlier wars,
gathered pace during 1967. Some moderate organizations tried hard to swim
against the current. The NAACP leadership, for instance, decided to prioritize
domestic reform over taking a stance on Vietnam, but many of its members were
quick to protest. Typical was the cry of one local branch that the "high mortality
rate among our Negro fighting men" was ample evidence that white officers were
ordering black draftees to do the war's dirty and bloody work.[102]

By early 1967 Martin Luther King agreed. "We are willing to make the Negro a
100 percent citizen in warfare, but reduce him to a 50 percent citizen on American
soil," King declared publicly in February. "One-half of all Negroes live in sub-
standard housing and he has one-half the income of the whites. There are twice
as many Negroes in combat in Vietnam and twice as many died in action—as
whites in proportion to their numbers."[103]

As riots scarred many cities, King's indictment appeared too moderate to
many in a black movement that was becoming increasingly radicalized. Adam
Clayton Powell, the black congressman from Harlem, typified a more strident
opposition. The whole military system for sending boys to Vietnam, Powell
charged, was "reminiscent of Hitler. First we provide an inferior education to
black students," Powell claimed. "Next we give them a series of tests which
many will flunk because of inferior education. Then we pack these academic
failures off to Vietnam to be killed." As riots engulfed many ghettos, the Black
Panther leader Eldridge Cleaver used equally inflammatory language to com-
pare violence at home to violence abroad. "Those who turned the other cheek
in Watts," declared Cleaver, "got their heads blown off," just like the Vietnamese
who faced white-officered American troops. Both sets of corpses, he added,
"spoke eloquently of potential allies and alliances. A community of interest

began to emerge. . . . The blacks in Watts and all over America could now see the Viet Cong's point: both were on the receiving end of what the armed forces were dishing out."[104]

Casualties, the Credibility Gap, and Tet, 1967–68

For Johnson, the increasingly radical and rancorous nature of this antiwar challenge provided both a threat and an opportunity. The threat was obvious. As protests mounted, culminating in a massive October 1967 march on the Pentagon, they seemed to feed into a broader public frustration with the war. That same month Gallup recorded that 46 percent of Americans considered the war a mistake, up more than twenty points in the past two years. Worse, 57 percent now disapproved of Johnson's handling of Vietnam, compared to just 28 percent who approved.[105] "We've almost lost the war in the last two months in the court of public opinion," Johnson observed that grim October. "These demonstrators and others are trying to show that we need somebody else to take over this country."[106]

Yet these same demonstrators also provided Johnson with a major opening to regain the home-front initiative. He could certainly take heart from the numerous signs that radical antiwar agitators did not speak for most Americans. As one poll discovered, even among students the hawk-dove divide cleaved firmly toward the hawks, 49 to 35 percent, while only one-fifth of students polled had ever actually joined the protests. Across the country more generally, a surprisingly small minority told pollsters that they were personally affected by the war: just 5 percent, according to an October 1967 Gallup poll, which was way behind "the high cost of living, taxes" (60 percent) and even lagged behind "health problems" (8 percent).[107]

Implicit in such figures were two flickers of opportunity for the government. One was the shallowness of the public's frustration with the war. The other was the gulf between the public and the demonstrators, which only widened as rallies like the march on the Pentagon descended into violence. As Johnson realized, if he could equate such dissent with base treachery, he could in turn marginalize the protest movement—and he therefore pressed the CIA hard for evidence that the protesters were communist-funded.[108] At the same time, Johnson and his senior officials also hoped to place the blame firmly on the demonstrators for prolonging the war. As Westmoreland declared, "antiwar protests in the United States encourage a battered enemy to fight on despite 'staggering combat losses.'" Or, as the *Washington Post* paraphrased it, the government's message was "that antiwar protesters in this country are encouraging the enemy and costing American lives."[109]

Figure 5.2 American casualties were at the heart of the antiwar movement's opposition
to Vietnam. This slogan was daubed on the Pentagon wall during the mass protest there
in October 1967. National Archives 111-CCS-1196.

These speeches were part of a broader government public relations campaign,
launched with one eye on reviving support for the war and the other on securing
Johnson's reelection in a year's time. The White House had already set up a Vietnam
Information Group to serve as a "quick reaction team" and "strike a positive note."
In the fall of 1967 Johnson now reached out to establishment figures, sanctioning
the creation of Committee for Peace with Freedom in Vietnam to coordinate
pro-war statements by luminaries like Truman, Eisenhower, and Acheson. He also
summoned Westmoreland back home to undertake an intensive bout of public
speeches and media interviews.[110]

An integral part of all this PR activity was to counter a crucial dimension of
the casualty issue: the growing sense that American lives were being thrown
away in Vietnam for a worthless cause. Antiwar protesters clearly thought the
war was immoral and unnecessary, but even many GIs seemed to question the
cause, as their language about death implied. While counting down the days to
the end of their year-long tours, soldiers used numerous slang words to obscure
the awful reality that might prevent them ever returning home. In this vernac-
ular, their buddies were never killed; they were aced or greased, waxed or zapped.

By far the most common word, though, was "wasted"—a not-too-subtle reference to what many deemed the squandering of life in Vietnam's jungles.[111]

Worryingly for the administration, by late 1967 this same sense of wastefulness seemed to be seeping into the mainstream popular discourse. It was pumped in by the growing doubt that this was not a fight the United States could ever win. As Johnson admitted in November:

> [O]ur people are terrifically distressed and disturbed about Vietnam. They are disturbed for several reasons. It's costing us a lot of lives. The casualties are mounting. The coffins are coming home. They're seeing that flag too often in the family cemetery. And they just think that as intelligent as we are, if we can go to the moon, we ought to be able to find some way to get out of this mess.[112]

For Johnson, a crucial task was to convince the public that he was smart enough to end this "mess" soon. There was no stalemate in Vietnam, he insisted in a November press conference. "We are making progress. We are pleased with the results that we are getting. We are inflicting greater losses than we are taking." "The consensus," agreed Westmoreland in an interview with Steve Rowan on CBS, "is that the enemy is being weakened and our side is growing stronger."[113]

These claims, although vital to demonstrate progress, were not problem free.[114] In earlier wars the public had not been too squeamish about the destructiveness wrought by massive American firepower. Once again, though, Vietnam proved different. The nature of the war was one reason. In firefights with elusive guerrillas, American troops could not always be certain if their victims were VC regulars, irregulars, fellow travelers, or innocent bystanders. The media periodically picked up on this blurring of lines between combatants and civilians. As early as August 1965, for instance, the CBS correspondent Morley Safer reported on a search-and-destroy mission around the village of Cam Ne. Against the distressing backdrop of U.S. marines clearing the area, including burning houses and ushering away small children, Safer provided a chilling account of the day's kill ratio: the wounding of three women, the death of one baby, the wounding of one marine, and the capture of three prisoners.[115]

For those who questioned the righteousness of the American cause, such civilian deaths were a particular outrage, and the antiwar movement therefore placed them at the heart of its indictment against the war. But Americans on the ground were not the only ones killing Vietnamese civilians. As the U.S. air campaign gathered pace, seeking both to knock out North Vietnamese industry and to interdict communist supply lines, so protestors also focused on the collateral civilian damage.

Not that U.S. leaders admitted to such deaths. As in earlier wars, the air force was eager to insist that its bombers only attacked "strictly military" targets, with the goal to knock out enemy industry but not kill civilians.[116] This time, though, such claims did not go unchallenged. Antiwar protestors were always distrustful of official statements, and on this issue their innate skepticism was sharpened by the war's obvious asymmetry. North Vietnam, after all, was "a relatively small peasant nation that was not bombing the United States or even the South." At the same time protestors were also repelled by "technowar," with its brutal B-52s, whose bomb-load looked too large to discriminate between military and non-military targets, and its nasty napalm, which, as radical magazines and mainstream TV channels graphically showed, left a horrible effect on civilians.[117] Then came a pivotal moment: on Christmas Day, 1966, Harrison Salisbury, a senior foreign correspondent for the New York Times, published a dispatch from Hanoi that belied official claims that American bombers only targeted sites of military value. "Contrary to the impression given by United States communiqués," Salisbury wrote, "on-the-spot inspection indicates that American bombing has been inflicting considerable civilian casualties in Hanoi and its environs for some time past."[118]

The air force worked hard to retaliate, insisting that American pilots had only "accidentally struck civilian areas in North Vietnam while attempting to bomb military targets." Johnson tried to drive home the message, insisting publicly that this was "the most careful, self-limited air war in history."[119] But the domestic damage had been done. As cries of "civilian, civilian, napalm victims" became ever louder at antiwar rallies, senior officials started to question the wisdom of the air campaign. In the spring of 1967 McNamara even advised Johnson that the bombing campaign had created "a backfire of revulsion and opposition by killing civilians."[120]

By this stage, though, Johnson was increasingly preoccupied by a different fear. He was more concerned that the U.S. military was inadvertently exaggerating the number of American casualties, with announcements that were both too vague and too candid.

The vagueness stemmed from the MACV's desire to deny valuable information to the enemy. For this reason its daily briefings still used the terms "light," "moderate," and "heavy" to describe losses in a particular battle, but the result was increasingly troubling. Inevitably some media voices charged that the military was hiding casualty information—that it was claiming "light" casualties in fights that had been a bloodbath. Compounding the problem was the MACV's unwillingness to divulge how many men had been in action. Military spokesmen used the term "heavy" to denote losses of more than 15 percent of any unit, but this was meaningless without the knowledge of whether ten, one hundred, or one thousand men had been in battle. As a senior Pentagon official conceded in the spring of 1967, this procedure "resulted in news stories that our troops had suffered 'heavy' losses in actions where the actual losses had been only a few wounded and perhaps one or two dead. One page-one story in a major newspaper reported 'heavy' United States casualties in an action in which there was but one fatality."

The military found it relatively easy to rectify this media temptation to overstate the war's bloodiness. Brushing aside the complaints of intelligence officers, the Pentagon and MACV pledged to give out precise figures for each battle. Their reasoning was significant: the public need was paramount. "No subject is more important to us," the Pentagon explained. "The American people must be informed of every death of every American serviceman in connection with the war. Not only must the casualty reporting be accurate, the people must know it is accurate."[121]

This defensiveness was illuminating. Since the summer of 1965 neither the Pentagon nor the MACV had tried to conceal casualties. On the contrary, although their descriptions of battles had lacked precise figures, each week they had revealed statistics of extraordinary fullness and detail. Their motive had been partly to avoid the fractious Korean War debates about what precisely should be included in the casualty lists. By breaking down public releases so that they differentiated between enemy and friendly casualties or about the severity of a wound, the military hoped to head off partisan-inspired allegations that it was engaged in a cover-up.

Had this tactic been accompanied by another Korean-era innovation it might have worked. At the end of the Korean War the Truman administration, frustrated by the media's tendency to conflate the term "casualty" with "fatality," had tried to encourage a greater sense of media responsibility. It was vital, Truman's Pentagon had warned, for reporters to tell the public that only a small percentage of those on the casualty tolls would never return home. In 1967, with the MACV and Pentagon including even minor wounds in their press releases, it was even more vital for the media to operate with restraint. Otherwise the government's more liberal definition of casualties would greatly increase the total.[122]

The media was in no mood for restraint, however. Often editors and headline writers were too easily tempted to cite only the overall casualty figure, rather than breaking it down by dead, wounded, and missing. The most telling moment came in early October. With support for the war already starting to dip, the media was presented with a particularly eye-catching fact. As the *Los Angeles Times* blared in a typical front-page feature, CASUALTIES PASS 100,000.[123]

Johnson was troubled. The administration, he complained privately, had "killed" itself with "that announcement that we had one hundred thousand casualties." Why did officials not say that tens of thousands had been returned to duty? Westmoreland was equally concerned. The new accounting method, he realized, gave a WIA total of more than 106,000 between 1961 and 1967. Had his command used the Korean War definition, the same total would have only been 56,000.

Ten days later, still visibly upset by this stunning own goal, Johnson revisited the issue. He particularly wanted to ask his senior advisers why "we continue to release these statistics, especially since they make it appear that U.S. troops are suffering more casualties than South Vietnamese troops." The answer was revealing. The system had already been established, replied Westmoreland, who fully shared Johnson's concern. "We would catch hell from the press," he added plaintively, "if we were to change the system." McNamara agreed. "He dared not stop reporting these casualties," McNamara told his angry president, "because of the fear of a tremendous press attack."[124]

In the forefront of Westmoreland and McNamara's minds was the buzz phrase of 1967: the "credibility gap." The media, by this stage of the war, no longer trusted the Johnson administration to disseminate truthful information, and it would clearly explode if it thought officials were trying to cover up casualties. This endemic suspicion had a long genesis. It dated back to the early period of the war when the Kennedy and Johnson administrations had indeed tried to

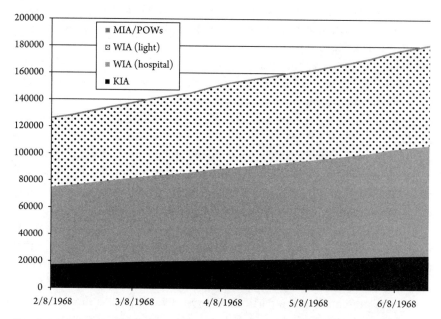

Graph 5.1 Breakdown of U.S. Casualties in Vietnam, February–June 1968.
Source: MACV, "Weekly Summaries," 1965–71, Entry 305, box 1, RG 472, National Archives.
As Johnson complained in October 1967, those with light wounds—who were included in the published figures for the first time—almost doubled the cumulative casualty total.

conceal the extent of American involvement in Vietnam. More recently it had been fueled by a sense that the war was bogged down in stalemate, which jarred with constant official claims of massive enemy "body counts." It had also been given further sustenance by the constant official predictions that the United States would soon win the war.[125]

In private, embattled officials were struck by the unfairness of it all. "Most of these charges are vague and unsubstantiated," one White House aide complained to Johnson. Moreover, he added, "no story in our lifetime has been covered more intensively—and more extensively—than Vietnam."[126] Casualties were a prime example. The Johnson administration had released more detailed information than any previous wartime government, but given the pervasive media skepticism it had received no credit. Worse, the government was now trapped into continuing to provide inflated figures. As even Johnson ruefully conceded, if officials suddenly tried to revert to the classification system used during the Korean War, they would doubtless be accused of yet another grand cover-up.

During the winter of 1967/68 the only saving grace was that, despite the intense media discussion about the credibility gap, Johnson still had sufficient standing to prompt a turnaround in the public's attitude toward the war. By January, in the wake of the government's concerted PR drive, Johnson's approval ratings had edged slowly upward, from a low of 38 percent in October to a respectable 48 percent—which placed him ahead of all the Republican candidates for the presidency. "People like his 'take-charge' approach," concluded Gallup on January 28. They were also more optimistic about the war, with 50 percent saying at the start of 1968 that the country was making progress, compared to just over one-third a few months before.[127] Then two days later came the great communist Tet offensive, which made these official claims of progress seem like a cruel government joke.

The communist effort to spark a general uprising in South Vietnam was impressive in scope. A series of assaults the length of South Vietnam, it included attacks on thirty-six of forty-four provincial capitals, five of the six main cities, and above all Saigon, where even the American Embassy was breached. As a military enterprise, however, Tet was a failure for the communists. South Vietnam survived, while the PAVN and VC troops, having exposed themselves to America's frightening firepower, suffered an estimated forty thousand casualties.[128]

For American troops Tet was a bloody affair—bloodier even than some previous conflicts. As the historian Ronald Spector observes, "during the first half of 1968 the *overall* Vietnam casualty rate exceeded the overall rate for all theaters during World War II, while the casualty rates for army and marine maneuver battalions was more than four times as high." For the American media, meanwhile, Tet was a gift. In Saigon even the most deskbound members of the press corps could scarcely avoid the fight to recapture the American Embassy, which unfolded just blocks away. Outside the capital, veteran frontline correspondents hastened to cover the long, hard fights at Khe Sanh and Hué in great detail.[129]

As well as witnessing some of this grim reality in televised Technicolor, the public's response was conditioned by a series of political prompts. The most important were Johnson's earlier claims of progress. Even before Tet, polls found that more than two-thirds of Americans thought Johnson was not telling the whole truth about Vietnam. Now Tet transformed this credibility gap into a yawning chasm. The massive communist effort, after all, seemed incontrovertible proof that the enemy was nowhere near collapse, despite more than two years of massive American pressure. As Cronkite famously declared on CBS, it "now seems more certain than ever that the bloody experience of Vietnam is to end in a stalemate."[130]

In March the start of the presidential primary season further magnified the impact of such doubts. In New Hampshire Johnson faced an antiwar rival, Eugene McCarthy, who few considered to be a real presidential contender. Johnson was therefore shocked when McCarthy polled surprisingly well, garnering 42.2 percent of the Democratic vote. His shock then verged on trauma when, four days later, Robert Kennedy announced his candidacy. Despite earlier involvement in his brother's Vietnam policy, Kennedy was yet another antiwar candidate anxious to tap into the deep sense of unease and frustration with the war. His basic position was that the war could not be won. Escalation, he insisted, would mean more death and destruction, but it would not break Hanoi's resolve to fight on. Negotiation, Kennedy declared, was the only way forward.[131]

In the complex post-Tet mood, this was not yet the majority position. At first, in fact, the hawk-dove split actually increased from 52 to 35 percent in December to 61 to 23 percent in February. Still, this rising support for escalation did not translate into personal support for Johnson, whose Vietnam job rating slipped to a paltry 26 percent. As frustration with Johnson's policy increased, even many hawks seemed prepared to consider de-escalatory alternatives. On March 12, as the votes were counted in New Hampshire's primary, Gallup found that 69 percent of Americans supported a "phase out" plan, in which the United States would slowly withdraw, handing over the fighting to the South Vietnamese as they left.[132]

Johnson's first response to this shifting mood was to hang tough. In the middle of February he conjured up the ghost of Abraham Lincoln, pointing out that his illustrious predecessor had seen 600,000 Americans die, "but steady—always convinced of his cause—Lincoln stuck it out." A month later he remained determined to do whatever necessary to secure victory. "The communists have made it clear that up to now," he declared, "they are unwilling to negotiate or to work out a settlement except on the battlefield. If that is what they choose, then we shall win a settlement on the battlefield."[133]

Yet Johnson's own advisers were increasingly skeptical about this message. Such statements "will cost the president the election," concluded one. They "had caused concern among thoughtful people," agreed another, "because the president seemed to be saying that he was going to win the war no matter what the cost in American lives."[134]

If ultimate battlefield victory was no longer tenable, an alternative had to be found. Westmoreland could not simply ask for more troops—certainly not the 206,000 additional men he requested in mid-March. As Clark Clifford, the new defense secretary, immediately pointed out, this new Westmoreland call was bound to lead to "significantly higher" casualties. It would also entail mobilizing the reserves, which many middle-class Americans viewed as a haven from the draft and service in Vietnam. If, as seemed likely, these moves stirred up massive new protests, Johnson would need to retain sufficient troops in the United States to maintain domestic order.[135]

Backed into a corner, Johnson adopted the only public position that was likely to jolt the public out of its skepticism, frustration, and creeping defeatism. On March 31, in a televised speech to the nation, Johnson offered Hanoi the chance to end the bloody stalemate. The United States, he began, was prepared to begin negotiations to end the war. In order to devote himself fully to this new enterprise, Johnson concluded, he would not seek reelection in November. The race for the White House was suddenly wide open.[136]

Johnson's offer to negotiate did not mean an immediate end to the fighting. On the contrary, he wanted to intensify the war in order to give his negotiators maximum bargaining strength with the communists. Nor were the other players in the unfolding drama of the 1968 presidential campaign calling for peace at any price. After Kennedy was assassinated in June, McCarthy lost the Democratic nomination to Vice President Hubert Humphrey in a chaotic Chicago convention. Humphrey, although deeply skeptical about the war, felt obliged to stay close to Johnson until very late in the campaign. This left the antiwar vote with little obvious option, for the Republicans picked Richard M. Nixon, long a Cold War hawk and a complete anathema to the Left.

Nixon's nomination meant that Johnson's Vietnam War would end as it began: with unsettling memories of the Korean War era. In 1952 Nixon had been the vice presidential candidate on Eisenhower's successful ticket. He therefore knew all about exploiting protracted and bloody limited wars for partisan gain. In Vietnam, to be sure, the fighting was at a more sensitive and unpredictable stage than it had been in Korea during the 1952 campaign. In public, Nixon therefore moved with extreme caution—certainly much more caution than he and

Eisenhower had employed sixteen years before.[137] Still, Nixon was not shy about using the Korean analogy to his advantage. As he told a delegate of southern Republicans at the party convention in August:

> I'll tell you how Korea was ended. We got in there and had this messy war on our hands. Eisenhower . . . let the word go out diplomatically to the Chinese and the North [Koreans] that we would not tolerate this continual ground war of attrition. And within a matter of months, they negotiated. Well, as far as negotiation [in Vietnam] is concerned that should be our position. We'll be militarily strong and diplomatically strong.[138]

What this meant in practice remained unclear, but one thing was certain: Nixon's slender election victory in November did not translate into a mandate to end the war immediately. Nixon was eager for the United States to extricate itself from Vietnam with its "credibility" intact. Like Johnson, he was determined not to lose. As long as the communists were prepared to fight, so was Nixon. Only he would try to fight in a way that reduced U.S. casualties and thereby defused the war as a political issue on the American home front.

6

Vietnam

De-escalation and Defeat, 1969–1989

In the months after Tet, while American politicians debated how best to withdraw gracefully from Vietnam, the fighting became increasingly bloody. In May and August North Vietnamese troops launched two new offensives to drive home what they thought was their battlefield advantage. The Americans fought back with a vengeance. Equally convinced that North Vietnam was "hurting," the U.S. military devised new tactics aimed at opening as much of the countryside as possible to South Vietnamese rule.

These new tactics were the work of Gen. Creighton Abrams, who replaced Westmoreland in June 1968. Although still under firm instructions to place maximum pressure on the enemy, Abrams adopted a very different approach to his much-maligned predecessor. One of his first decisions was particularly controversial. Sanctioning the withdrawal from static positions like Khe Sanh, which had been defended with so much bloodshed at the beginning of the year, Abrams wanted to free up troops "to attack, intercept, or take whatever action is most appropriate to meet the enemy threat." In practice this meant trying to protect populated areas from communist attacks. It also entailed placing less emphasis on big-unit sweeps, whose purpose had been to find the enemy units and force them into battle. Instead, Abrams preferred to deploy smaller patrols to disrupt and destroy the supply dumps that were so vital to continued communist operations. He was not totally averse to large operations, however. In early 1969, for instance, Abrams launched Operation Dewey Canyon, an eight-week sustained offensive to cut off the massive logistical buildup that American intelligence had detected in the northwestern regions of South Vietnam.[1]

As this new series of battles flared, the casualty toll inevitably mounted. American losses during Tet had been bad enough: more than 500 killed each week between February 17 and March 9, 1968. In May the fighting was even worse, with 616 combat deaths in the second week alone. And still the blood flowed. By the end of 1968 the Pentagon admitted that the year's American dead "almost equaled the figure for the first seven years of the Vietnam War and brought total combat deaths in Vietnam to about 30,543."[2] The new year, with another communist Tet Offensive in full swing, promised no respite. March 1969 was particularly grim, as successive weekly death tolls amounted to 453, 336, 351, and 226. "In a few weeks," reported James Reston in the *New York Times* that month, "more Americans will have been killed in Vietnam than in any other conflict in U.S. history except the Civil War and the two world wars."[3]

As it happened, this casualty landmark was totally eclipsed by another event: the battle to capture Dong Ap Bia, a stand-alone mountain 970 meters (more than a half-mile) above sea level in the A Shau Valley. To the American military this mountain went by the equally obscure name, Hill 937. In the United States it soon became notorious as "Hamburger Hill"—a term coined by weary troops who had witnessed their comrades ground up in a succession of bloody battles. Back home the moniker quickly caught on because, to the war's critics, it symbolized the futility of the whole Vietnam enterprise. Even to many hawks Hamburger Hill, and especially the domestic reaction to American losses on its slopes, confirmed that the time had come to change the way of waging war in Vietnam.

"I See Death Coming Up the Hill": Hamburger Hill, 1969

Despite the later public furor, American commanders had a clear rationale for seizing Hamburger Hill. The A Shau Valley was of key strategic importance. In enemy hands it had become "a natural conduit" for moving men and supplies in preparation for attacks on Hué and its surrounding areas—and as such it was a natural objective for Abrams's efforts to disrupt enemy logistics. "General Abrams emphasized," recorded one of his lunch guests in April 1969, "that it was essential to get out into the difficult western part of Vietnam in order to meet the enemy even as he begins his trek from sanctuaries in Cambodia and Laos."

Nowhere proved more difficult to get to than Dong Ap Bia's summit. As well as the mountain's height, the weather was poor. Tropical storms made it tough not only for the troops traversing the slopes but also for the crews in helicopter gunships who mistakenly fired on friendly forces. The enemy, having had years to develop elaborate defenses, was in a tenacious mood. The result was a series of grueling battles. Between May 11 and 20 four battalions of the 101st Airborne Division made no less than eleven attempts to evict the communist troops from this position, sustaining forty-seven dead and 308 wounded before finally succeeding.[4]

At first these assaults had little impact back home. With the Nixon administration still finding its feet, most commentators, analysts, and even protesters were prepared to give it time and space to search for a way out of the war. With media interest focused on the Paris peace negotiations, war correspondents found it difficult to get their editors interested in the fighting fronts. As Ward Just observed in the *Washington Post*, "The weekly casualty reports are buried in the paper, and the war stories are written from the afternoon briefing in Saigon. The war has lost its immediacy, which is to say it has lost its sense of intimate violent death."[5]

Then on May 19 Jay Sharbutt of the AP suddenly jolted the home front's attention back to the battlefield. Instead of relying on the terse and vague language of official briefings, Sharbutt used interviews with soldiers who had returned from one of a series of abortive assaults. These troops, he wrote, "came down from the mountain, their green shirts darkened with sweat, their weapons gone, their bandages stained brown and red—with mud and blood. . . . They failed and they suffered. 'That damn Blackjack,'" one of them complained of their commanding officer, "'won't stop until he kills every one of us.'"[6]

In Washington leading Democrats glimpsed a chance to turn the tables. Until now every twentieth-century war had seen Republicans hammering away at Democrats for wasting American lives in distant battles. The day after Sharbutt's article appeared Sen. Edward Kennedy (D-MA), the Democratic Party whip, demonstrated that exploiting casualties was a natural partisan reflex, rather than a GOP preserve. "I feel it is senseless and irresponsible to continue to send our young men to their deaths," Kennedy declared on the Senate floor, "to capture hills and positions that have no relation to ending this conflict." Hamburger Hill, he continued, "is only symptomatic of a mentality and a policy that requires immediate attention. American boys are too valuable to be sacrificed for a false sense of military pride."[7]

On May 28 the sense of the battle's futility was heightened when the MACV announced that Hamburger Hill had been abandoned to the enemy. "We feel we've gotten everything out of the mountain that we are going to get" was how one officer justified the withdrawal to the press. But Democrats were not satisfied. At a $100-a-plate party fund-raiser Kennedy again lambasted the battle's "cruelty and savagery," while Sen. George McGovern (D-SD) added his voice "against a truly senseless slaughter." On Memorial Day both Walter F. Mondale (D-MN) and Mike Mansfield (D-MT) joined the chorus of criticism. "Areas are won and lost many times on a temporary basis," observed Mansfield. "Lives are lost once and on a permanent basis."[8]

In the next few weeks this political uproar surrounding Hamburger Hill encouraged the media to frame the Vietnam debate around casualties. On television, ABC aired a report from Beallsville, Ohio, whose 441 residents were "hurt" by the "deaths of six of their town's sons in Vietnam—ninety times the U.S. average."[9] On the newsstands, *Life* was even more emotive. Losing money because television offered advertisers cheaper costs and bigger markets, *Life* had already exploited the casualty issue as part of its circulation-driven stance on the war.[10] But its post–Hamburger Hill coverage clearly broke new ground. While its earlier stories had aped TV's depictions of heartbreaking homecomings, now *Life* published an unprecedented twelve-page feature titled "Vietnam: One Week's Dead." Alongside the photographs of the 242 KIA the Pentagon had released in the week after the battle, *Life* ran some of their poignant last letters. "You may not be able to read this," one man had scrawled. "I am writing in a hurry. I see death coming up the hill."[11]

To the intensely political Nixon, this partisan point scoring and negative media reporting was deeply alarming. Although he had been elected on a pledge to secure "peace with honor," Nixon, like Johnson, was determined not to become "the first American president to lose a war." The scale of the sacrifice was just too large. "We simply cannot tell the mothers of our casualties," he remarked privately in 1969, "that it was all to no purpose."[12]

At first Nixon's strategy, which derived from the widely held myth of how Eisenhower had ended the Korean War, inclined toward applying different forms of pressure to force the communists to come to terms. His starting point was to pose as a "madman." Through hints, gestures, and actions Nixon played up his image as a Cold Warrior in an effort to convince Hanoi that he "might do *anything* to stop the war." Thus he leaked suggestions that the bombing of North Vietnam would be revived. In March he gave the go ahead to Operation Menu: the secret bombing of North Vietnam's sanctuaries in neutral Cambodia that resulted in 3,630 B-52 raids in the ensuing fourteen months. As one official explained, Menu was designed to "demonstrate to Hanoi that the Nixon administration is different and 'tougher' than the previous administration."[13]

At first glance Abrams's A Shau campaign fit snugly with these other elements of Nixon's strategy. Like Menu, it promised both to cut off PAVN infiltration into South Vietnam and to keep up the pressure on North Vietnam to negotiate. But there was one glaring difference: Menu was conducted in secret. As Nixon explained in his memoirs, "my administration was only two months old, and I wanted to provoke as little public outcry as possible at the outset."[14] When it came to Hamburger Hill, though, Nixon did not enjoy the same luxury. Instead this battle was waged under the full glare of public scrutiny even after the fighting had stopped.

Nixon was deeply troubled. Poring obsessively over media reports, he concluded that Hamburger Hill had lost him "time and tolerance with the American people."[15] He was particularly disturbed by a CBS interview with a wounded survivor who described the "battle as a turkey shoot . . . and we were the turkeys."[16] But the brunt of Nixon's legendary ire was reserved for Ted Kennedy. In Nixon's suspicious mind, Kennedy's exploitation of the casualty issue had only one purpose: it was his opening shot for the presidency in 1972.[17]

Nixon decided to act. At a press conference on June 19 he insisted that American commanders in Vietnam had very clear and simple instructions: "to conduct this war with a minimum of American casualties." Like many of Nixon's artfully constructed statements, what he said was strictly true. But in typically Nixonesque fashion what he failed to mention, or glossed over, was actually much more important. He was deliberately silent on the key matter of *how* his commanders were attempting to minimize American losses.[18]

This was an important omission because these commanders actually saw battles like Hamburger Hill as the most effective way of reducing casualties. In Saigon, Abrams and his team were heirs to a military tradition that viewed relentless campaigns as the best way of keeping down the final American death toll. It was a tradition with a long and illustrious heritage. In 1864, 1918, and 1944 Ulysses Grant, John Pershing, and Dwight Eisenhower had all sought to give their respective foes no respite. They feared that if they broke contact, the enemy would have time to recover, come back stronger, and inflict higher losses. But if they pressed on with a series of sustained and fierce battles, then the short-term casualties suffered in each specific engagement would be compensated by a speedier conclusion to the war as a whole.

Abrams was particularly comfortable with this inheritance. In early 1969 he even initiated a series of statistical studies that sustained the notion that it was less costly to attack than to defend in the particular conditions found in Vietnam. "Friendly forces suffer fewer casualties when they initiate actions than when the enemy initiates the action," Abrams reported to the Joint Chiefs in March. Moreover, because most American losses came from PAVN troops who enjoyed the "unimpeded use" of sanctuaries in Laos and Cambodia, Abrams was convinced that his air and ground campaigns in Cambodia and the A Shau Valley had protected American lives. In one private briefing session he even claimed that the five hundred tons of communist supplies captured in the valley had saved his command "five [or] six thousand in casualties."[19]

In the wake of Hamburger Hill, this old military tradition seemed dangerously out of step with the new political mood. Nixon certainly thought so. With both politicians and the press focusing on the hundreds of casualties actually sustained, rather than the thousands of lives that had perhaps been saved, Nixon turned to Henry Kissinger, his top national security official, for advice. In a memorandum revealingly titled "Impact of American Casualties on your Vietnam Policy," Kissinger was reassuring. The Pentagon, he reported, had now pledged to avoid the terms "sweep operations" and "body counts" in its press releases. More importantly the MACV planned to take technowar seriously in future. If any more enemy bases were found in the A Shau Valley, Kissinger wrote, the MACV would not send large numbers of ground troops to capture them. Instead, "artillery and air will play the dominant role in these operations."[20]

At the start of July, in a "big meeting" on the presidential yacht, Nixon then went a step farther and sanctioned a basic change in the MACV's mission statement. Rather than placing "maximum pressure" on the enemy, Abrams was instructed to focus on "protective reaction."[21] Although the Pentagon released no specific public statement about this change in emphasis, officials did brief the media. The new guidelines, it was widely reported, were "designed to cut down on the big search and destroy operations and to reduce American casualties."[22] Even the most traditional-minded commanders got the message. Melvin Zais, who had conducted the Hamburger Hill operation, now cautioned his subordinates to "recognize the atmosphere in our own country, recognize the political climate, recognize the difficulties under which the administration is operating insofar as public support is concerned, and recognize the impact of heavy casualties."[23]

The Politics of Withdrawal, 1969–70

In the summer of 1969 Hamburger Hill's impact extended beyond tactics and even the MACV's mission statement. It also influenced the timing and presentation of Nixon's whole strategy, which veered increasingly toward "Vietnamizating" the war.

In military terms, Vietnamization contained clear dangers. Four years earlier Johnson had Americanized the war because the Saigon government had been unable to confront the communists on its own. Since then, although the fighting had bogged down into a stalemate, some optimists believed that South Vietnam was becoming stronger. Its president, Nguyen Van Thieu, had been in charge for a couple of years. Its army had survived the major challenge of Tet. With Abrams and his team providing the spur, its regime was now enjoying some success with an accelerated pacification program aimed at securing more of the countryside. Yet South Vietnam's underlying fragility persisted. Corruption was rife, its army was plagued by demoralization and desertion, and Thieu's regime lacked legitimacy. As one journalist correctly observed, "after all these years of war, the Saigon government remains a network of cliques, held together by American subsidies, a group of people without a coherent political orientation, bent on their own survival."[24]

Any American withdrawal therefore raised an obvious question: was South Vietnam strong enough to stand alone? If not, North Vietnam simply had to wait for the Americans to leave before finishing off the Saigon government. This was Kissinger's bleak view. Kissinger worried that an American withdrawal, especially if it took place without any reciprocal concessions from the communists, would fatally weaken his hand at the negotiating table. He also believed that as soon as a withdrawal program began it would become "like salted peanuts to the American public: The more U.S. troops come home, the more will be demanded."[25]

Although Kissinger would become Nixon's dominant foreign policy adviser, on Vietnam he did not have things all his own way. Melvin Laird, the new defense secretary, was his biggest challenger. A pugnacious schemer, dubbed the "Midwest Machiavelli" by reporters, Laird was well matched to battling the equally conspiratorial Kissinger. A former nine-term Republican congressman from Wisconsin, he was savvy in the ways of Washington.[26] Acutely sensitive to the popular mood, he approached Vietnam with one clear goal. Americans, Laird was convinced, needed tangible proof that their boys would be coming home soon. In March, after a fact-finding trip to Vietnam, he returned confident that the United States could gradually hand the war over to the Saigon government without precipitating its collapse. He also insisted that a gradual American withdrawal was "an indispensable precondition . . . to the healthy growth of indigenous political institutions." In April Laird therefore pressed Nixon to accept a new directive that changed the U.S. objective to "the progressive transfer . . . of the fighting effort" from American to South Vietnamese forces.[27]

For most of May the details remained sketchy. Kissinger was still vehemently opposed to speedy withdrawals, which to his mind would result in "a cop out" or "a disguised American surrender." Nixon, for his part, was neither committed to a clear timetable nor willing to contemplate an end date for the last troops to leave.[28] But toward the end of the month, as the Hamburger Hill controversy gathered steam, he became convinced that he had to move publicly on Vietnamization. On June 8, after meeting Thieu at Midway, he therefore announced that he was bringing home twenty-five thousand U.S. troops. But he added a clear caveat. Additional troop withdrawals would be made on the basis of the training of South Vietnamese forces, progress in the peace talks, and the level of enemy activity.[29]

Nixon was buoyed by the announcement. He considered it "a political triumph," Kissinger recorded. "He thought it would buy him time"—perhaps even some of the time recently lost by the political eruption over Hamburger Hill. For Nixon, the policy's appeal stemmed from a simple insight. Americans, he believed, were not opposed to the Vietnam War as such; they were simply opposed to their boys dying in Vietnam. Nixon therefore reached the obvious conclusion. If he could place more American boys out of harm's way, he could in turn eradicate most of the antiwar protest.[30]

* * *

That Nixon wanted to end the divisions that had destroyed Johnson was only natural. As well as avoiding his predecessor's fate, Nixon recognized that a more united America could provide Kissinger with some compensatory strength at the bargaining table. While withdrawing troops weakened Kissinger's hand, widespread domestic support for a lower intensity war might make Hanoi question whether it could outlast the United States in a protracted war. As Nixon put it in one of his pithy yellow-pad jottings, he could gain leverage over Hanoi in two ways: "Give them a jolt & they'll talk" or "Stop U.S. dissent & they'll talk."[31]

But how to stop dissent? Together with the troop withdrawals, one possibility was to defuse and depoliticize the political discourse on the war. At the start of his presidency Nixon seemed primed to adopt such an approach. In 1968 he had campaigned as a "new" Nixon, so different from the Cold War ideologue and partisan bruiser of the 1950s. In his inaugural address he then adopted the mantle of "peacemaker," both foreign and domestic, who would heal the wounds of the Johnson era. "We are caught in war, wanting peace," Nixon declared. "We are torn by division, wanting unity." In recent years, he continued,

> America has suffered from a fever of words; from inflated rhetoric that promises more than it can deliver; from angry rhetoric that fans discontents into hatreds; from bombastic rhetoric that postures instead of persuading. We cannot learn from one another until we stop shouting at one another—until we speak quietly enough so that our words can be heard as well as our voices.[32]

On casualties, this logic pointed in one direction: starting afresh and ignoring the high death toll of the Johnson years. This, at least, was Laird's view. "The decisions which committed more than half-a-million troops, nearly $100 billion of resources, and more than thirty-three thousand American lives are behind us," Laird told Nixon in March. "They represent 'sunk' costs." An administration committed to forging a new sense of unity had nothing to gain by constantly alluding to them.[33] On occasion Nixon seemed to agree. In one unscripted speech to Congress he even declared that "when the security of America is involved, when the lives of our young men are involved, we are not Democrats, we are not Republicans, we are Americans."[34]

Yet this "new Nixon" persona was only ever a mask. And the mask was apt to slip at any moment, especially since Nixon had a series of political incentives to shout rather than whisper, to divide rather than heal.

One incentive was obvious. With the first American troops heading home, and with those still in Vietnam operating under new guidelines, weekly American losses started to decline in the second half of 1969—down to 190 on August 23, 137 on September 6, ninety-five on September 27, and sixty-four on October 4.[35]

Despite Laird's advice about "sunk" costs, Nixon could not resist the temptation to contrast these heartening figures with the bloodiness of Johnson's war. Before major speeches, Nixon asked advisers for specific monthly numbers so he could make a "pointed reference" to how much lower casualties were compared to Johnson's last year in office.[36] The speeches themselves then included skillfully worded, but barbed, passages that underlined how much had changed since he had taken over. "This week," Nixon told a national audience in November, "I will have to sign eighty-three letters to mothers, fathers, wives, and loved ones of men who have given their lives for America in Vietnam. It is very little satisfaction to me that this is only one-third as many letters as I signed the first week in office."[37]

As well as such implicit attacks on Johnson's war, Nixon saw the declining death toll as a way of defusing the sudden revival of the antiwar movement. Despite the first troop withdrawals in the summer, peace protesters prepared for action in the fall. Always suspicious of Nixon, they were frustrated by the slow pace of his disengagement from the war and responded with a burst of new activity. The Moratorium came first: a daylong effort in mid-October 1969 to draw attention to the war by staying away from work or school. This was the moderate face of the movement, attracting the support of "at least two million people in more than two hundred cities. It was successful," writes one historian, "because it was unique, peaceful, and highly telegenic—images in the media were generally positive."[38]

Then during November and December the New Mobilization Committee to End the War in Vietnam sought to maintain the momentum. Known as "the Mobe," it was more radical. Although adopting the familiar tactic of protesting on Washington's streets, it employed an eye-catching twist. In freezing rain, thousands of demonstrators began a "March Against Death." While drummers hammered out a solemn beat, protesters carried placards with the names of Americans killed in Vietnam. Edging past the White House, candles in hand, they also shouted the names of the fallen over the fence, in an emotional scene that had echoes of *Life's* July casualty coverage.[39]

Nixon's response was complex. On the surface he was disdainful of the Mobe marchers and pointedly retreated to the White House bowling alley rather than hear them shout out the names of dead GIs. But the edgy and brooding Nixon was temperamentally unable ignore the campaigners for long. Soon he was discussing all sorts of ideas to hit back, from using helicopters to blow out the protestors' candles to pressuring the media to scale back its coverage of the event.[40]

While such tricks, dirty or otherwise, were a Nixon hallmark, his ultimate response to the antiwar movement was much more straightforward. Like Johnson, Nixon viewed the protests as an opportunity as well as danger. He

hoped, in particular, to blame the demonstrators for prolonging the war and in-creasing the casualty lists. Unlike Johnson, Nixon also had an additional partisan motive: to equate liberal Democrats with radical hippies whose countercultural lifestyle was anathema to "middle America." If successful, he might even be able to use the war, and the protest against it, to create a new Republican majority.[41]

All these calculations combined on November 3, when Nixon delivered a major national speech on Vietnam. The protesters, he told a massive television audience, were a minority who sought to impose their antiwar stance on the rest of the "nation by mounting demonstrations in the street." The "great silent ma-jority," by contrast, wanted an honorable end to the war. This end would come only if the whole nation rallied behind their president. "The more support I can have from the American people," Nixon insisted, "the sooner that [the] pledge [to achieve 'peace with honor'] can be redeemed; for the more divided we are at home, the less likely the enemy is to negotiate at Paris."[42]

The speech was a public-relations triumph. Initial polls suggested that more than three-quarters of Americans approved. With the White House developing a game plan to attack the protesters and foster pro-war demonstrations, Nixon also took some comfort from additional surveys that found that 72 percent believed "moratoriums and public demonstrations" were "harmful to the attainment of peace."[43] Ever restless, he was eager to exploit his advantage.

Nixon began with the military draft. Convinced that a system based on ran-domness rather than universality would defuse student protest, on December 1 he hurriedly introduced a new lottery system. From this point on an entire generation was no longer vulnerable to being sent to Vietnam. Now it would be only those nineteen-year-olds whose birthdays were picked out of the bowl.[44]

Even many of these nineteen-year-olds would never see action. As this was Vietnamization's crucial corollary, Nixon desperately wanted to drive the point home. On top of the twenty-five thousand withdrawals announced in June, Nixon unveiled a total of eighty-five thousand more in September and December. Then on April 20, 1970, he made another major speech. This time he revealed "the withdrawal of an additional 150,000 American troops to be completed during the spring of next year." Put another way his government planned to reduce the American military presence in Vietnam by more than a quarter of a million men in just over two years.[45]

With casualty figures continuing their steady decline, Nixon's April 20 speech had a major impact on the home-front mood. The TV networks were generally positive. CBS, for instance, expressed "surprise" at the size of the announcement, before concluding that Nixon had overridden the military, which wanted to retain more men in Vietnam. On Capitol Hill, although prominent doves stressed that Americans would continue to die in a worthless war, Republicans rallied strongly behind their president. Even many moderate Democrats, including

Mansfield, expressed their "pleasure" at the high number of men that would soon be coming home.[46]

Nixon's surprise announcement seemed to sap the strength of the antiwar movement too. As the *New York Times* concluded, "the galvanizing appeal once provided by the Vietnam War appears to have been blunted by President Nixon's pullout of troops, the advent of the draft lottery, the general psychic release provided by last fall's Moratorium, and a general feeling that antiwar protest has become futile." As Nixon unveiled his plan to withdraw 150,000 troops, he certainly appeared to have outmaneuvered at least one key antiwar organization: on April 20 the press reported that the Vietnam Moratorium Committee was closing its Washington office due to lack of funds and support.[47]

The Politics of Escalation, 1970–71

Ten days later Nixon suddenly appeared on the nation's television screens again, this time to announce a ground incursion into Cambodia.

Nixon's motives were mixed. He had always been tempted toward escalatory measures, which he thought were essential to pressure Hanoi to come to terms at the negotiating table. He had long been lured by operations that promised to eradicate communist sanctuaries in neutral Cambodia and Laos. A year earlier, Nixon had begun bombing Cambodia for these very reasons, but this air campaign had triggered "profound military, social, and political perturbations in eastern Cambodia." In particular, as North Vietnamese troops pushed west to avoid American bombs, the Cambodian elite had divided on how best to respond. The culmination came in mid-March when Lon Nol, the pro-American prime minister, ousted the Cambodian king and appealed to Washington for help. Faced with this sudden opportunity, Nixon believed that a bold move into Cambodia promised numerous payoffs. It would send a powerful signal to Hanoi and destroy important North Vietnamese sanctuaries; it would safeguard South Vietnam in the midst of continued American withdrawals and help shore up the fragile new Lon Nol regime. Determined to "go for broke, for the big play," Nixon decided to use both American and South Vietnamese troops. While Saigon's forces attacked the much larger region known as Parrot's Beak, a joint U.S.-South Vietnamese operation would target a second area dubbed Fishhook.[48]

This use of U.S. soldiers was bound to be deeply controversial. Whereas Nixon's gradual troop withdrawal had sapped the strength of the antiwar movement, his sudden escalation was likely to reenergize the protesters. At a deeper level, moreover, the Cambodia operation harked back to the way of war that had been discredited a year earlier. Laird certainly thought so and grimly estimated five hundred KIA a week.[49] Ominously, so did leading Democrats, who were primed to reprise their earlier opposition. As one charged in the initial outpouring of angry protest, the Cambodian operation was "Hamburger Hill all over again."[50]

Unlike the spring of 1969, this time Nixon was determined to confront this public opinion danger head on. Indeed the main purpose of his April 30 speech was to frame the domestic debate around the large number of lives likely to be saved, rather than the relatively few that would actually be lost. Thus on nine separate occasions Nixon stressed that the operation was designed to save American lives. "A majority of the American people want to keep the casualties of our brave men in Vietnam at an absolute minimum," he declared in a typical comment. "The action I take tonight is essential if we are to accomplish that goal. . . . We will not allow American men by the thousands to be killed by an enemy from privileged sanctuaries."[51]

In the next few days Nixon's subordinates and allies amplified this message. In Saigon, Abrams instructed MACV spokesmen to emphasize "the threat to American lives posed by the sanctuary strongholds and the fact that the objective of the operation is to save American lives."[52] In Washington Republican Party literature likewise trumpeted what it dubbed a "Courageous Move to Save American Lives."[53]

Then Nixon's public leadership suddenly faltered. At a Pentagon briefing the day after his speech he was edgy and nervous. Applauded by a secretary whose husband was in Vietnam, Nixon proffered a provocative off-the-cuff observation. Those young Americans who were fighting overseas, he declared, were "the greatest," while those who were demonstrating at home were "bums."[54]

The negative response was instantaneous. Thousands of students, already incensed by the incursion, rose up in protest. "We're coming angrily, urgently, and non-violently," declared the Mobe leaders. Passions were running too high, however, to be channeled entirely peacefully. In Madison, Wisconsin, national guard units fixed bayonets and dispersed crowds with tear gas. At Kent State University in Ohio, another national guard unit was less restrained: it opened fire on student protestors. When the clamor finally subsided, four students were left dead and another eleven wounded.[55]

This sudden connection between the killing in Cambodia and the deaths at Kent State would long linger in the American memory. Within weeks Crosby, Stills, Nash, and Young would record "Ohio," a eulogy to "the Kent State victims as the casualties of the president's domestic war."[56] Within months the filmmaker Paul Ronder would make a TV documentary titled *Part of the Family*, which told the tragic story of three Americans killed at the same time—one GI in Vietnam and two students in the United States—to create "a relationship based on death."[57] But it was Kent State's short-term impact that was most searing. On television CBS and NBC both broadcast an emotional interview with the father of Allison Krause, one of the four Kent State victims. "Is this a crime for which

Figure 6.1 Nixon placed the number of American lives that were likely to be saved at the heart of his efforts to sell the Cambodian incursion. The Republican National Committee extensively used this photograph and caption. Nixon Library.

my daughter should be shot," he asked despairingly, "that she opposed the killing of Americans in Cambodia?"[58] ABC, meanwhile, carried a speech by Lawrence P. O'Brien, chairman of the DNC and a long-time Nixon bête noire. Abandoning even the veneer of partisan etiquette, O'Brien charged that the Cambodian incursion would result in higher combat casualties. He also claimed that Nixon's "sidewalk language" was responsible for the Kent State deaths. "I can only won-der," he declared, "whether those triggers would have been pulled if the elected leaders in this country had acted differently."[59]

In some major media organizations senior figures worried that passions were finally careening totally out of control. At the AP, Wes Gallagher, the general manager, therefore decided to spike at least one "inflammatory" story from Cambodia. At the *Washington Post*, publisher Katharine Graham similarly asked her reporters to "cool down" their Kent State reporting.[60] But such strictures did little to alter the temperature on the nation's campuses, where the fighting in Cambodia and the shootings in Ohio forged a temporary alliance of radicals, liberals, and formerly apolitical students. Within days almost five hundred col-leges had closed, more than a thousand demonstrations had taken place, and "two million students were on strike." At Berkeley alone, twelve thousand marched, some with a huge banner that read simply "Nixon's Slaughter."[61]

As the protests multiplied and intensified, Nixon adopted a two-prong response. Behind closed doors he was typically combative, pressing his advisers to find any link between Hanoi and the demonstrators that could be used to smear them.[62] In public he tried to revive his emollient persona. In a rare meeting of minds with the *Washington Post*, the White House press office advised reporters that it too would "cool down" its rhetoric. "Those who protest want peace," Nixon told the nation in a televised press conference on May 8. "They want to reduce American casualties and they want our boys brought home. . . . I agree with everything that they are trying to accomplish."[63]

To drive home the fact that the operation was saving American lives, Nixon also reverted to an old Johnson-era device: number crunching. He wanted official spokespersons at all levels to specify precisely how much enemy materiel the operation had captured. The implication, he believed, would be clear: the thousands of weapons taken out of communist hands would no longer be threatening GI lives.

At first, however, the media predictably focused on a very different set of figures. With Nixon framing the incursion in terms of American lives saved, reporters were anxious to emphasize the actual new casualty totals. As early as May 7, ABC's evening news show announced that twenty-nine Americans had been killed and another sixty-four wounded, adding controversially that ten of these GIs had been killed by friendly fire. The next night all three networks ran with the story that casualties were suddenly up, with 123 KIA in the first week of the campaign.[64]

For Nixon, the one saving grace was that, ultimately, American casualties were relatively low, and certainly nowhere near the five-hundred-a-week pre-diction that Laird had made in April. In Saigon the MACV press office was particularly anxious to get this point across. Although still releasing its usual weekly casualty figures for the whole theater (which during May showed KIA totals of 123, 168, 217, and 142), the MACV also handed out a specific break-down for those sustained specifically in the Cambodian operation, which were substantially lower.[65]

By the end of June, as the operation came to an end, Nixon was ready to declare success. In a detailed report to the nation he stressed that American troops were leaving Cambodia, that the communist sanctuaries had been destroyed, and that this operation "will save American and allied lives in the future."[66] But the political cost had been high, and not just on the nation's campuses. In the Democratic-controlled Senate, doves pushed for the Cooper-Church amendment, which would have cut off funding for the Cambodian operation had Nixon not withdrawn American troops. They also began a drive to terminate *all* funding for the war if it lasted beyond June 30, 1971. McGovern, a main sponsor of this second initiative, even mortgaged his house to fund an NBC antiwar show. In Congress he took the whole casualty issue to a new level, abandoning both the senatorial norm of politeness and the partisan incentive to blame the president. Indeed, McGovern tore into his colleagues: "Every senator in this chamber," he declared, "is partly responsible for sending fifty thousand young Americans to an early grave. This chamber," he charged, "reeks of blood. Every senator here is partly responsible for the human wreckage at Walter Reed and Bethesda Naval and all across our land—young boys without legs, or arms, or genitals, or faces, or hope."[67]

While dovish Democrats grabbed attention with impassioned appeals, a mistrustful media started to wonder whether Nixon was falling into the same PR trap that had plagued his predecessor: at best skirting the truth; at worst actually lying. Since assuming office Nixon had not been deaf to this danger. He knew full well that he was president partly because the so-called credibility gap had destroyed Johnson, and for this reason he had initially struck a

Table 6.1 **U.S. Casualties in Cambodia, May 1970**

					Cumulative
	Apr 29–May 9	May 10–16	May 12–23	May 24–30	Apr 29–May 30
KIA	34	77	61	55	227
Total WIA	64	199	249	236	748
(Hospitalized)	(38)	(74)	(124)	(128)	(364)
(Non-hosp.)	(26)	(125)	(125)	(108)	(384)

Source: MACV, "Weekly Summaries," 1965–71, Entry 305, box 3, RG 472, National Archives.

refreshing new pose. His frequent speechmaking on Vietnam was the core of this effort. In stark contrast to Johnson, who had been reluctant to dramatize the war by televised Oval Office addresses, Nixon was determined to portray himself as a candid presidential educator. In no less than seven televised appearances between 1969 and 1971 he sought to explain why the United States was at war, why it could not afford to lose, and what actions were being taken to ensure peace with honor.

At first, it seemed to work. After one hundred days in office, the media gave Nixon high marks for his "measured and deliberate manner." He had projected "an image of thought instead of motion," Dan Rather declared on CBS; "candor and direction instead of wordiness and evasion."[68]

All too predictably, however, an increasingly inquisitorial media started to discover that Nixon's private actions often belied his public pose. Although the secret bombing of Cambodia remained largely under wraps, in February 1970 Nixon's policy in Laos, another neutral state, came under withering media scrutiny. When the *New York Times* revealed that Nixon had ordered bombing raids over Laos, Nixon's private response was typical. "No one cares about B-52 strikes in Laos," he insisted. "But people worry about our boys there." Nixon therefore tried to reassure the public by claiming that "no American stationed in Laos has ever been killed in ground operations." Unfortunately, however, the press soon unearthed numerous American deaths in Laos—seven since the start of 1969 and about four a year between 1965 and 1968. Although the White House immediately issued a sheepish correction, this did little to assuage mounting media misgivings that Nixon was falling into the same bad habits as Johnson. The *Philadelphia Tribune's* conclusion was typical. "To say that a credibility gap is developing with regard to administration statements on U.S. involvement in Laos," it editorialized, "is to understate the case."[69]

By the time of the Cambodian incursion, then, an intensely suspicious media was already eager to expose falsehoods. As Laird cautioned, this made Nixon's attempt to use figures to demonstrate success highly risky, for prying and doubting reporters were bound to spend much of their time searching for errors and distortions. It was a prescient warning. Within days, the *Washington Post* was comparing the administration's new focus on numbers to the ill-fated statistical barrage of the Westmoreland era. Within weeks, *Time* was charging that some of Nixon's figures of captured material were "downright misleading."[70]

In this corrosive atmosphere, the Pentagon's official casualty figures soon came under renewed inspection. On the surface these numbers continued to show big improvements, especially once the Cambodian incursion was over. As the MACV emphasized in September 1970, the weekly death toll was now half of what it had been a year earlier, and for the past three months it had been consistently below a hundred.[71] On November 2, in an unexpected announcement, the Pentagon then gleefully observed that another landmark had been passed: American losses had hit a five-year low.

Rather than rejoice, though, reporters responded with a barrage of barbed questions. On November 2 they accepted that the headline figure was probably accurate, but they were still quick to question the manner and timing of the announcement. After all, casualties were normally released in Saigon on a Thursday. Why was the Pentagon getting into the act on a Monday? Could this early disclosure possibly have anything to do with "with tomorrow's [mid-term] election?" asked one journalist, knowing full well that Nixon was desperate to shake the Democrats' hold over Congress.[72]

As this question suggested, the Pentagon's release of good casualty news on election eve was such a transparent ploy that it merely ratcheted up the level of media cynicism another notch. It was scarcely surprising, therefore, that within two weeks suspicious reporters were questioning more than the timing of releases. They were also challenging the veracity of the actual figures.

Initially this challenge stemmed from the fact that the military routinely issued three different types of press release. While the MACV dispensed daily reports that reported the level of intensity of major fights, the Pentagon handed out daily releases, which contained the names of casualties whose next of kin had been notified. In both Saigon and Washington, moreover, press officers also provided the media with weekly casualty totals, normally on a Thursday "to reflect casualty statistics reported during the week ending the previous Saturday." Because of their different purposes, the three official releases rarely tallied. This had long been the case, but by the middle of November 1970 media mistrust had reached such a pitch that the military was forced to offer a defensive explanation. There was nothing sinister behind the disparity, it insisted. "Each of the three reports has been developed to satisfy military, public, or news media requirements." "Every effort," it concluded, "is being made to report all casualties as rapidly, accurately, and meaningfully as possible."[73]

Some war correspondents remained skeptical, however, especially when they witnessed bloody events that did not appear in MACV communiqués. In February 1971, for instance, an enemy rocket hit a bunker killing three Americans. When reporters pointed out that the military had failed to include this incident in their daily release, an MACV spokesman insisted that the omission was "inadvertent." Reporters were unconvinced. Some began compiling lists of known enemy attacks or unofficial field accounts of helicopter losses, which had not appeared in MACV handouts. In the *New York Times* Ralph Blumenthal even went as far as to claim that the disjunction between military statements and media observations called "into question again the accuracy of American casualty reports."[74]

With such suspicions intermittently hitting the headlines, some Democrats in Congress were emboldened to challenge Nixon's emphasis on declining casualties. In April 1971 Representative William D. Ford (D-MI) charged that the official totals for the Nixon years were false. His reasoning was simple. In an unconscious echo of the arguments Republicans had leveled against Truman in the latter stages of the Korean War, Ford focused on non-battle casualties. In his controversial claim (which the Pentagon vigorously denied), while combat casualties had declined 70 percent between 1968 and 1970, non-combat deaths had risen dramatically: from 1.95 per thousand under Johnson in 1965 to 5.5 under Nixon in 1970. Ford's conclusion was blunt. Nixon's Pentagon, he charged, was "playing a numbers game on casualty figures 'for [a] political purpose.'"[75]

Ford's attack was a foretaste of what was in store in the upcoming presidential campaign, when the Democrats would hammer away at the casualty issue. Nixon, though, would weather this particular assault, winning reelection in a landslide. He would then finally extricate the United States from Vietnam, claiming that he had achieved "peace with honor." Almost immediately, however, both these victories would prove hollow, setting the stage for the final tumultuous episodes of this period: the Watergate scandal, Nixon's resignation in disgrace, and South Vietnam's collapse.

A Pyrrhic Victory, 1972–75

In 1972, with the Vietnam War still raging, Democrats certainly hoped to make the large loss of American life a pivotal issue in their effort to oust Nixon. *Washington Post* cartoonist Herblock led the way. A long-term Nixon-hater, he graphically emphasized that Nixon's war had cost twenty thousand lives. George McGovern, the Democratic nominee, ardently sought to exploit this large death toll. The only out-and-out antiwar presidential candidate of the entire Vietnam era, McGovern implored the electorate to "choose life, not death" when they voted in November. "Someone," he insisted, "must answer for [the] 20,000 more dead, for 110,000 more wounded, for 550 captured or missing, for $60 billion more wasted in the last four years."[76]

Ultimately the most striking characteristic of McGovern's candidacy was its spectacular lack of success. In 1972 the Vietnam War—and the high death toll of the Nixon years—simply failed to resonate with the electorate. Part of the reason was unconnected to casualties. The two main candidates simply ran very different campaigns. McGovern's was a liberal insurgency that initially benefitted from the opening up of the nominating process to state primaries in which activists made a decisive difference. McGovern had trouble, however, transforming his primary momentum into the fall. At the Democratic Convention, in particular, he was slack and disorganized. His acceptance speech was made to a tiny audience in the

"Now, As I Was Saying Four Years Ago — "

Figure 6.2 In the 1972 campaign, Nixon's critics pointed to the high number of casualties sustained since the start of his presidency. A 1972 Herblock Cartoon, © The Herb Block Foundation.

early hours of the morning. He also picked a vice-presidential running mate who soon had to withdraw after he admitted undergoing electroshock therapy.[77]

Nixon, meanwhile, sought to soar above the fray. He had already established his credentials as a successful international statesman, visiting both China and Moscow within the space of four months in the first half of the year. In the summer and fall he then implemented a detached Oval Office–centered campaign, while his aides played dirty. On presidential orders Nixon's underlings worked hard to tarnish McGovern as a radical in cahoots with the most extreme antiwar protestors—those long-haired, and sometimes violent, demonstrators who "the great silent majority" had so little time for.[78]

While this unseemly Watergate-tarnished campaign grabbed the nation's attention, the actual fighting in Vietnam slipped into the background. This was surprising, for throughout 1971 the war had remained a major topic. In February and March, Nixon had seemed particularly vulnerable after media reports depicted South Vietnam's incursion into Laos as a spectacular fiasco. Correspondents had been particularly eager to criticize the government's clumsy efforts to minimize helicopter losses and use "misleading evidence" to claim the South Vietnamese had performed well. Then in the spring, with opinion polls revealing that 61 percent considered the war a mistake, the antiwar movement launched another bout of mass protests.[79] The actions of veterans who opposed the fighting were particularly striking, as they discarded their medals and appeared on the media and before Congress. When John Kerry, the future senator, presidential candidate, and secretary of state under Obama, was called before the Senate Foreign Relations Committee, he dubbed the war "the biggest nothing in history," adding, in a subtle rephrasing of the Korean War sound bite, "How do you ask a man to be the last man to die for a mistake?"[80]

A year later, Nixon was able to prevent Vietnam from igniting as a major campaign issue. He began his reelection campaign by readopting the mantle of peacemaker. On January 25, just weeks before making the historic trip to China, he went on television to reveal that Kissinger had met a North Vietnamese negotiator on twelve occasions. In these secret sessions, Nixon explained, Kissinger had unveiled numerous initiatives to break the deadlock, but each one had been rebuffed by North Vietnam.[81]

If this speech helped to defuse the charge that Nixon had made no moves to end the war, then his next televised address, on April 26, emphasized the success of Vietnamization. On the day he had assumed office, Nixon reminded his national audience that

> the American troop ceiling in Vietnam was 549,000. Our casualties were running as high as three hundred a week. Thirty thousand young Americans were being drafted every month. Today, thirty-nine months later, through our program of Vietnamization—helping the South Vietnamese develop the capability of defending themselves—the number of Americans in Vietnam by Monday, May 1, will have been reduced to sixty-nine thousand. Our casualties—even during the present, all-out enemy offensive—have been reduced by 95 percent. And draft calls

now average fewer than five thousand men a month, and we expect to bring them to zero next year.[82]

As Nixon pointed out, even a major new North Vietnamese offensive failed to halt the inexorable decline in American losses. Vietnamization was one obvious reason. The other was that Nixon unleashed a true technowar campaign, especially in the air, to bolster South Vietnam and counter the communists.

Hanoi had launched its Easter Offensive on March 30. It was a sustained three-pronged attack that placed intense pressure on South Vietnam during the spring and into the summer, but Nixon hit back hard. As he told his advisers, he was determined to "bomb those bastards like they've never been bombed before"— and he certainly had sufficient power at his disposal. Alongside the massive B-52s, which each had a payload of about twenty-two tons, the U.S. Air Force was now equipped with high-precision weapons that had been waiting for action since the 1968 bombing pause. As the historian Stephen P. Randolph points out, American aircraft could now "strike accurately from a higher altitude, avoiding the antiaircraft fire that had always been the greatest threat to strike aircraft. More significantly, perhaps, a single aircraft could attack with greater assurance of destroying a target than had been possible" during the 1960s. Nor was this all. On May 8 Nixon announced the mining of Haiphong Harbor. Within the space of just two minutes U.S. planes laid thirty-six mines. Without suffering any losses, they closed the major port through which North Vietnam brought in crucial supplies.[83]

From Nixon's perspective, this technowar response was a clear success. By June it had helped halt the Easter Offensive, at a cost to Hanoi of about half the 200,000 troops it had thrown into battle. By October it had even contributed to a breakthrough in the negotiations. For the first time Hanoi agreed to a settlement that would leave Thieu in place. During November and December Thieu himself was the main obstacle to a deal: he balked, in particular, at an agreement that would permit communist troops to remain in the South. But after Nixon launched the massive Christmas bombing raids in December, Thieu was somewhat reassured both by minor additional North Vietnamese concessions and by the prospect that the United States would again bomb if North Vietnam violated the deal. On January 23 the Paris Peace Accords were finally signed. Four days later a ceasefire went into effect, bringing an end to the United States' protracted involvement in the Vietnam War.[84]

At home, meanwhile, Nixon's way of war was, if not popular, then at least sufficiently blood-free to head off the type of domestic eruption that had brought down Johnson four years before. Indeed, although a series of big battles unfolded throughout Vietnam, it was the South Vietnamese army that was doing the fighting and dying on the ground. American casualties, by contrast, dwindled to a point where on September 21 the MACV could happily announce that the past week had seen no combat deaths—the first time this had happened in seven years.[85]

Nixon had long ago calculated that most Americans were prepared to endure such a war. He now appeared vindicated by opinion polls, which showed support for his Vietnam policy veering sharply upwards, from a low of around 45 percent just before the Easter Offensive, into the 50, 60, and even 70 percent range as a peace deal loomed. Then in November, in the only poll that really mattered, Nixon won reelection with a massive landslide victory. As a rueful McGovern conceded, Vietnam simply did not work for him as an issue. Why, he was asked? "When the corpses changed color," McGovern acidly responded, "American interest diminished."[86]

For once Nixon wholeheartedly agreed with his political rival, but he had not been prepared to let this interest diminish of its own accord. When it came to discussing U.S. casualties in public, Nixon's team was acutely aware of what to avoid, down to the smallest details. White House advisers, for instance, shied away from using casualty charts when briefing the press, fearing they would be too impersonal and set "the wrong tone."[87]

The Pentagon, meanwhile, was much more media savvy than at the outset of the war. Back in 1965 it had unwittingly helped to dramatize the bloody start of the fighting by helping ABC and CBS produce special TV broadcasts that vividly showed returning coffins and military funerals after the Ia Drang battle. By the 1970s it was much warier. When one network asked for official help to produce a ninety-minute color documentary that explored the reactions of families to the death of their next of kin in Vietnam, the Pentagon's response was curt. It considered "such coverage in extremely poor taste," explained the army's PI chief, who added that no one in the military should give "any encouragement to such a morbid project."[88]

As well as realizing what to avoid, Nixon also knew what to stress. By 1972 his central calculation was that the public cared only about current losses. This might seem patently obvious, but other key players often reached a very different conclusion. The military, for one, tended to think about the future. In devising military campaigns, commanders kept one eye on ultimate cost of the war. In their firm view the overall death toll would be much lower if they maintained relentless pressure on the enemy. Nixon increasingly dissented, however. He recognized that Hamburger Hill had starkly exposed the domestic danger of this logic. Although he subsequently sold the Cambodian incursion as a way of saving future lives, he had long since instructed his commanders to fight the war with one eye firmly fixed on each week's casualty total.

The Democrats, meanwhile, increasingly focused on past losses. Throughout 1972, in particular, they talked constantly about all the casualties suffered since

Nixon had taken office, in an effort to emphasize his broken pledge to end the fighting. Nixon, of course, was not averse to delving back in time, but his reference point was quite different. He emphasized the bloodiness of Johnson's war as a way of drawing attention to the happier state of current affairs. As one of his 1972 campaign posters starkly declared, under Nixon American casualties had declined 95 percent.[89]

When the peace accords were signed in January, Nixon could also boast another casualty success: the return of the American prisoners of war from communist captivity.

From the start of his presidency Nixon had recognized the power of this issue. In May 1969, abandoning Johnson's "quiet" diplomacy, Laird had launched a "go public" campaign. Ostensibly its aim was to "influence world opinion to the point that Hanoi will feel compelled to afford proper treatment to U.S. POWs." But Laird also had one eye fixed firmly on the home front. He hoped to "marshal public opinion," according to one account. So did Nixon. By the end of 1969 the two men were no longer content to rely just on Vietnamization to defuse the antiwar movement. They also wanted a positive rallying cry to energize their base. The American POWs seemed ideal. By emphasizing that the United States would fight until every prisoner was returned, Nixon hoped to remobilize the home front—or at least his "great silent majority." With public support solidified, he believed that Hanoi would come to terms at the peace table. Because these terms would include the prisoners' return, he could then show Americans a clear success.[90]

Although Nixon's publicity campaign was intensive, he never completely controlled the debate. North Vietnam itself tried to manipulate POWs. Long before Nixon's election Hanoi had threatened to try downed airmen for war crimes—a clear way of pressuring the United States to halt its bombing campaign. It then continued intermittently to release small groups of prisoners into the hands of prominent American antiwar activists—with the obvious intent of trying to compound the war's divisiveness inside the United States. Increasingly, moreover, Nixon also found that the POW issue was a double-edged weapon at home. Although the League of Families—the most powerful of the prisoner groups—was behind him for much of the time, other relatives argued that the prisoners would return home quicker if he simply ended the war. Increasingly, even the league itself was impatient, and in 1971 it began pressing him for a firm date for an American withdrawal.[91]

Whatever the daily frustrations, Nixon's "go public" campaign clearly helped to make the POWs a dominant issue in American politics. By the early 1970s tens of thousands of bumper stickers appeared on cars. Hundreds of supportive resolutions were introduced in Congress. And no presidential speech on Vietnam was complete without a pledge not to "abandon our POWs and our MIAs, wherever they are."[92] In 1973, when the peace accords finally brought these prisoners home, Nixon was naturally quick to declare victory. But he also claimed much more: vindication. In May, after hosting a special White House dinner for the returned POWs, he recorded feeling a sense of "joy and satisfaction . . . that they, who were so completely courageous and admirable, seemed to consider the decisions I had made about the war to have been courageous and admirable ones."[93]

Nixon's achievements—if not his sense of vindication—were to prove extremely fleeting. Within months, in fact, they would turn out to be pyrrhic victories, which not only constrained American power and credibility but also helped to destroy his presidency.

Vietnamization was a case in point. Inside the United States the slow withdrawal might have numbed the political debate. But for many of those Americans who still had to fight Nixon's war the pointlessness of the exercise engendered a profound sense of disillusionment. This was an "army in anguish," according to a series of *Washington Post* special reports published in the fall of 1971. No one wanted to be the last American killed, the *Post* revealed, a conviction so strong that some troops now reported "false positions to avoid combat." In one widely reported incident, fifty-three men even refused to launch a dangerous nighttime mission—a refusal that became a cause célèbre when the general in charge refused to discipline them. Even such insubordination paled next to stories of "fragging." It was a term the military hated and tried to dissuade reporters from using, on the grounds that it "trivialized a serious offence." By 1971, however, officials had to concede that the intentional targeting of friendly soldiers had occurred, although they challenged the claim that it had "become fairly commonplace."[94]

Drug abuse presented a similar problem. During 1970 and 1971 media reports of a drug epidemic were rife, as soldiers apparently turned to narcotics to blot out the whole Vietnam experience. The Pentagon was quick to demolish the more exaggerated of these reports—such as stories of stoned soldiers shooting down an American helicopter gunship. But faced with TV reports showing GIs at a "pot party," military spokesmen were again forced to admit there was a problem, this time with the qualification that the rest of American society faced a similar problem.[95]

In June 1973 the Pentagon's final accounting provided statistical evidence to demonstrate the extent of the army's anguish. As well as the overall figure of 45,958 Americans KIA during the war, officials announced that a further 10,303 U.S. servicemen had died of non-combat causes. Although almost half of these were from aircraft or motor vehicle crashes, a significant proportion stemmed from the specific problems of the Nixon years. Thus there had been 1,172 suicides, 1,163 homicides, and 102 deaths from drug abuse. Fragging fatalities had actually declined toward the end, from a high of thirty-seven in 1969 to twelve in 1971 and three in 1972. But the overall trajectory of fragging incidents was still worrying, leaping from 126 to 333 between 1969 and 1971.[96]

While this sense of decay ate away at the military in Vietnam, Nixon's technowar escalation increasingly riled political elites at home. Determined to prop up South Vietnam in an election year, Nixon's casualty sensitivity had not extended beyond American lives to enemy noncombatants. "Now, we won't deliberately aim for civilians," he told his senior advisers at one point in 1972, "but if a few bombs slop over, that's just too bad." In Nixon cold calculation the American electorate was principally concerned with U.S. losses; it cared far less about what happened to civilians.[97]

In a narrow sense Nixon was correct, for he won reelection by a landslide in November. But the consequences of his deeply cynical war-making strategy were profound, especially for the more than 1,500 civilians who died in the Christmas bombing raids.[98] Nor in the Vietnam era was the domestic mood entirely inured to such deaths. While protestors had long placed the impact of bombing at the heart of their indictment against the war, the death of 109 civilians in the village of My Lai had been a black stain for most of Nixon's presidency, with the antiwar movement predictably seizing on it to claim that the United States was no worse than its reviled enemies of the past.[99]

Nixon's Christmas bombing naturally rallied these protestors in another bout of rage against the war, where they were joined by a growing number of mainstream voices who dubbed these raids a "shameful" and "monstrous deed." "The rain of death continues," declared the *Boston Globe* in a typical comment. "Are we now the enemy—the new barbarians?" asked the *New York Times*. On Capitol Hill the mood was particularly heated. Even Hugh D. Scott (R-PA) the Senate Republican minority leader, stated publicly that he was "heartsick and dispirited." On the other side of the aisle Mike Mansfield, the Democratic majority leader, said that patience had finally collapsed. As soon as the new Congress convened in January he pledged to press for legislation to end the war immediately.[100] Nixon was often dismissive of opposition from these quarters. The media and Congress, in his eyes, were liberal bastions to be outwitted, smeared, and beaten. But with an increasingly assertive Democratic Party in charge on Capitol Hill, Nixon recognized that he had to conclude a peace deal before the end of January. He also knew that Congress was unlikely to support future efforts to bolster South Vietnam with American force. The poison his Christmas bombing had injected into the congressional debate had seen to that.

Soon after, Nixon's authority over Congress collapsed entirely, as Watergate shifted from a minor campaign issue to a major political scandal. In Nixon's jaundiced view, Watergate was the central reason why Vietnam was finally lost in April 1975. The Democrats in Congress, he charged, were so emboldened by the scandal that they denied both him and his successor "the means to enforce the Paris agreement at a time when the North Vietnamese were openly violating it."[101]

Yet Nixon's postwar scapegoating ignored two crucial facts. One was that his own bombing, especially during December 1972, had already destroyed congressional support for bolstering South Vietnam. Even without Watergate Nixon would have found it difficult to revive his technowar campaign in response to a new North Vietnamese attack.[102] The other was that the relationship between Vietnam and Watergate was one of cause as well as consequence. While the specific break-in stemmed from the Nixon White House's desire for dirt on the Democrats, the overall scandal was inextricably entwined with his way of waging war in Vietnam. Indeed, the administration's first steps along the path of illegality had come in the spring of 1969, when it used wiretaps to trace who had leaked the story of the secret Cambodian bombing. Later the president's men had lengthened their stride with efforts to smear antiwar radicals, including burgling the office of a leading antiwar figure's psychiatrist in an unsuccessful effort to get damaging material to use against him.[103]

These were just two of the "White House horrors" that Nixon was desperate to cover up after June 1972, when the Watergate burglars were caught. When this effort crumbled, Nixon left behind a debilitated presidency. In 1973 alone, Congress cut off funding for the continued bombing of Cambodia and passed the War Powers Act that limited the president's power to deploy troops overseas. Then in 1975, with a new North Vietnamese offensive poised to overrun South Vietnam, legislators refused to vote for aid, let alone any new use of air power. Amid political recriminations in Washington and television images of a chaotic evacuation in Saigon, the United States finally lost its war in Vietnam.

The Vietnam Syndrome

This dismal end was an important contrast to earlier wars. Casualty debates had often spilled over into the postwar era, most notably after 1918 when many Americans had recoiled from the prospect of ever sending their boys off to another European slaughter. Yet at least World War I had had the saving grace of ending in victory. Vietnam had no such upside. After 1975 one of the few things ex-doves and ex-hawks could agree on was that the lives lost in Vietnam were "utterly wasted"—doves because they still thought the war immoral and unnecessary, hawks because they believed that battlefield deaths ought to have been sustained in a winning cause.[104]

In the years after Vietnam this sense of utter waste permeated the political debate. As well as the war's miserable outcome, memories lingered of bloody battles waged for no purpose, with Hamburger Hill as the prize exhibit. In this sense the 1970s were an eerie reprise of the 1920s. Although few embraced the term "isolationist," many did agree that American boys should "never again" be sent into a similar war. It was a belief that, as in the 1920s, was reinforced by an influential strand of popular culture, as veterans, novelists, and filmmakers all emphasized the wounds the war had created and then left to fester. But this time the "never again" mentality was also stiffened by statistically based academic research.

In 1972, while the war still raged, the political scientist John Mueller published a book that contained a simple and powerful idea. Popular support for the Korean and Vietnam wars, Mueller argued, had declined as casualty figures mounted. Chiming neatly with the prevailing mood, Mueller's thesis quickly became accepted conventional wisdom. Thereafter many prominent voices not only believed that "support for Vietnam [had] buckled as the body-bag toll mounted," but also projected this idea forward into future wars, claiming that the casualty-sensitive public would no longer accept conflicts with a large number of American losses.[105]

Cold War hawks were horrified. Convinced that the United States still had to wield every weapon in its arsenal to contain—and even rollback—communism, these hawks tried to confront this new mood head on. Ronald Reagan was their cheerleader. "For too long," Reagan declared during his successful presidential campaign in 1980,

> we have lived with the "Vietnam syndrome". . . . We dishonor the memory of fifty thousand young Americans who died in that cause when we give way to feelings of guilt as if we were doing something shameful, and we have been shabby in our treatment of those who returned. They fought as well and as bravely as any Americans have ever fought in any war. They deserve our gratitude, our respect, and our continuing concern.[106]

As this speech suggested, a key component of Reagan's agenda for ending the Vietnam syndrome was to honor the war's casualties, both living and dead. The former were a particularly big group, largely because better medical facilities insured that the wounded-to-killed ratio had been massively improved. After the war, however, this tremendous achievement meant that a higher proportion of veterans still carried some form of physical disability. They were not the only lingering sufferers. Some veterans also came down with serious illnesses, including cancer, which they traced to their exposure to chemicals used against the enemy, especially Agent Orange.[107] Many more were physically fine but mentally scarred. Unlike in World War II, where most psychiatric cases had occurred under extreme battlefield conditions, in Vietnam the problem was the exact opposite: relatively few instances in the fighting theater, but a delayed reaction when veterans returned home.[108]

During the 1980s the United States tried to come to terms with these casualties. While Reagan publicly challenged the "unjust stereotype" of the traumatized outsider, veterans groups were now better organized and Congress more open to meeting their demands than after previous wars. The result was a series of practical gains. Agent Orange victims received compensation in a court settlement, health care providers recognized post-traumatic stress disorder, and the government made some effort to improve veterans' facilities. In 1982 the Vietnam dead even received their own national monument. Conceived in controversy, the memorial's moving simplicity soon proved a hit with families, veterans, and tourists alike—so much so that it rapidly became Washington's most visited monument.[109]

Yet talking about or memorializing Vietnam was one thing. Overcoming the nation's acute sensitivity to fresh combat casualties was quite another. Even Reagan, for all his much-vaunted gifts as the "great communicator," was unable to shift the debate away from the likely human cost of Cold War interventionism.

Reagan, in fact, could not even drum up domestic support for the use of force in Central America. This was significant. El Salvador or Nicaragua were not distant flashpoints like Korea or Vietnam. They were in America's "own backyard." Even in the casualty-shy 1920s, when memories of World War I had hung heavily over U.S. foreign policy, the United States had sent marines to Nicaragua.[110] In the early 1980s, though, when Reagan wanted to roll back communism in the region, public opinion remained a major obstacle. In March 1981 one poll found that only 2 percent favored sending U.S. troops to El Salvador. A year later a string of other polls reported that between 60 and 74 percent thought that El Salvador was likely to become another Vietnam. As Reagan later conceded, "after Vietnam, I knew that Americans would be just as reluctant to send their sons to fight in Central America, and I had no intention of asking them to do that."[111]

Although the military largely agreed, during the 1980s it had to work on the assumption that at some future point a president would again place America's boys in harm's way. Given the public's casualty shyness, Pentagon planners searched for ways to make such a war domestically palatable. They began by revamping media relations. In Vietnam the lack of censorship had enabled reporters like Neil Sheehan and Jay Sharbutt to emphasize the bloodiness of battles like Ia Drang and Hamburger Hill. The military was desperate to avoid a repeat, so desperate, in fact, that when Reagan invaded Grenada in 1983 the Pentagon implemented a complete news blackout. There was no press pool, no accreditation, and not a single reporter with American forces during the operation.[112]

The media immediately remonstrated. With powerful owners, editors, and reporters all emphasizing the public's right to know, the military was forced to rethink. Within weeks the Pentagon's press office pledged to allow the media "complete access" to future operations "so long as it [did] not violate the security of our operation or endanger the lives of our forces." To work out the details the Pentagon created a panel of fourteen PI officers, former journalists, and academics. Headed by a former MACV PI chief, it soon unveiled a range of improvements, including granting correspondents access to the war zone in press pools and a voluntary set of guidelines that all news organization ought to subscribe to.[113]

This attempt to forge a new military-media relationship was by no means successful. By the 1980s there were simply too many lingering resentments on both sides of the divide, which were apt to erupt in controversy even without a major war. The military complained first. In the spring of 1985, when the Pentagon trialed its new censorship system, flying ten reporters to Honduras to watch a secret training exercise, officials were appalled when one section of the media produced unauthorized and "speculative stories."[114] But the media soon hit back. A year later, when Reagan launched a strike against Libya, correspondents on board one carrier were in uproar when the navy first kept them in the dark about the missile launches and then outright lied to them.[115]

Faced with these failures, the military could at least take some comfort from internal studies suggesting that media reporting was *not* the main danger to future operations. Casualty totals still held this dubious distinction. "What alienated the American public in both the Korean and Vietnam Wars," an army study concluded in 1989, "was not news coverage but casualties. Public support for each war dropped inexorably by 15 percentage points whenever total U.S. casualties increased by a factor of ten."[116] If this were true, tinkering with media relations would not fix the problem. What was needed was a whole new approach to modern warfare. Under Nixon, the military's mission statement in Vietnam had included a clear injunction to keep losses to a minimum. Under Caspar Weinberger, Reagan's defense secretary, an even deeper change was introduced. In a major speech in November 1984 Weinberger revealed six "tests" to be applied when "weighing the use of U.S. combat forces abroad." The so-called Weinberger doctrine included using force only as a last resort, devising objectives that were clear and attainable, ensuring that troops had sufficient resources to win, and obtaining the full support of Congress and the public.[117]

As the Cold War came to an end, then, the searing Vietnam experience continued to linger. For Johnson and Nixon, it was a war that had thrown up different problems, and not just because Johnson had steadily expanded the

U.S. commitment while Nixon had sought to gradually withdraw. Johnson's war had also been plagued by paradoxes—the playing down of American involvement while drawing attention to the tragedy of mounting casualties; the presiding over a military that provided unprecedented amounts of casualty information but was still dogged by major questions about its credibility. Nixon, too, had faced his own paradoxes, not least in escalating a conflict at the same time he was seeking to disengage. But the central theme of Nixon's war was the pyrrhic nature of his victories. From Nixon's narrow perspective, his strategy worked perfectly in 1972. His attempt to reduce American casualties without precipitating South Vietnam's collapse helped him achieve the central goal of his first term: reelection. Within months of his resounding landslide, though, Nixon's presidency—and its legacy—was in ruins. The complicated consequences of trying to bomb in secret were part of the cause, but so were other strands of his strategy. Nixon's Christmas bombings might have helped force a deal, but they further eroded congressional support not just for Vietnam but for all forms of presidential war-making. His Vietnamization strategy might have muted the public's opposition to the war, but it generated major problems for the U.S. military and, above all, proved ineffective against the renewed communist onslaught in 1975.

In the wake of defeat, the U.S. government tried to learn the appropriate lessons. As well as reconsidering military-media relations, officials thought long and hard about the conditions under which the public would support the use of force—and the prospect of casualties—in the future. Sometimes, they looked back beyond Vietnam to an earlier era when the media had appeared more manageable and the public less skeptical. Of course, even during the two world wars and Korea, the government had always faced searching questions about the veracity of its casualty information. But Vietnam had clearly changed the rules of the game. Trust in government was much lower. The media was even keener to probe for the story behind the official narrative. And the whole debate was now even more sensitive to the human cost of war. These were all legacies that the two Bushes would have to grapple with in the post–Cold War era, as they took the United States into war against a new set of enemies.

‖ 7 ‖

Gulf Wars

Iraq and Afghanistan, 1990–2011

Behind the nameless casualty numbers that so often dominate American wartime debates lay tragic stories. The main reason why the Vietnam Memorial has been such a success is that it not only gives a sense of the size of the human tragedy but also rescues the individual victims from anonymity.

New technologies can perform a similar function. Television has always been eager to focus on war's human angle. Now, in the Internet age, almost anyone can tell her own story, as the founders of the Iraq Veterans Memorial recognized. Constructing their own commemoration four years into the Iraq conflict, they were consciously "inspired by the Vietnam Memorial," which, they explained, brought the "tremendous loss of life to a human scale." But they also wanted to exploit the possibilities presented by the Internet. Thus their website featured videos that provided "a human face, not just of those who have been killed, but of the people they left behind—brothers and sisters, parents, children, friends, lovers, cousins, comrades."

The result was a particularly moving set of tributes. One was for Lt. Seth J. Dvorin, twenty-four, who was married and wanted children; another for Pvt. Steven F. Sirko who was only twenty and had "eyes that laugh." Lt. Kenneth Michael Ballard was just twenty-six when he was killed. An only child, his mother described him as "the brightest star in my darkest night." The sister of S. Sgt. Paul M. Neff II remembered him as "more than just a name etched in cold stone. And he wasn't just my brother. He was our father's best friend. He was our mother's baby boy."[1]

This way of commemorating the fallen is not just a crucial reminder of war's heartrending consequences; it also demonstrates an important shift in American casualty debates. In the twentieth century, when U.S. losses were counted in the tens of thousands, the individual human tragedy was often obscured behind the sheer scale of the figures. In America's recent wars, when the death toll has been

much lower, these personal narratives have tended to receive far greater prominence. They have also become entwined with a variety of other post-Vietnam
developments: the growing focus that political scientists, pollsters, and the press
have given to measuring and monitoring the public's casualty tolerance; the new
media's obsession with celebrity and its associated propensity to identify warrior
celebrities; and the recognition by officials and officers that they not only have to
take the public's casualty sensitivity into consideration before unleashing American military power but also face pressure to mourn with the families of those
who never return.

From Iraq I to Iraq II

During Persian Gulf War, George H. W. Bush was the first president to grapple
with this newly emerging environment. His problems began in August 1990,
when Saddam Hussein invaded Kuwait—an action he was not prepared to
countenance. Bush therefore spent the next five months forging an international
coalition and getting U.S. forces into position. All the while the American debate
was fixated on prospective casualties.

The Mueller thesis loomed large. "Our reaction to wars is surprisingly consistent," insisted Richard Morin in the *Washington Post* in September 1990. "Of all
the complex variables governing public opinion, the single overwhelming fact is
the casualty total."[2] As war became more likely, pollsters even constructed surveys around this insight. In early January one survey found that while 63 percent
supported the need to fight, this figure dropped to 44 percent on the assumption
that one thousand American troops were killed and went down to 35 percent if
ten thousand were killed.[3]

Other types of statistics fueled this casualty obsession. In the computer age a
range of organizations and individuals devised programs to generate casualty
projections. According to news reports, one Pentagon computer simulation
claimed that as many as thirty thousand Americans would be killed in less than
a month. At the other end of the spectrum, the Brookings Institution's deceptively precise figures were less alarmist, predicting "between 1,049 and 4,136
U.S. fatalities after fifteen to twenty-one days of intense combat."[4] Even this
smaller figure spooked many influential voices, especially on Capitol Hill. Here
a number of leading Democrats, stressing that the public was "very, very strongly"
opposed to casualties, increasingly pushed for a Nixon-style technowar air campaign that would keep friendly fatalities low.[5]

With diplomacy failing and war impending, Bush was troubled. In November
1990 he tried to reassure Americans that "this will not be another Vietnam. This
will not be a protracted, drawn-out war." "I will do my level-best," he promised,

"to bring those kids home without one single shot fired in anger. And if a shot is fired in anger, I want to guarantee each person that their kid, whose life is in harm's way, will have the maximum support, will have the best chance to come home alive."[6]

In planning for battle, meanwhile, Bush's generals relied on America's immense technological superiority to keep casualties low. Colin Powell, the chairman of the JCS, rejected the idea of an air-only campaign. But Powell, who had played a key role in the development of the Weinberger doctrine, also shied away from a potentially costly frontal attack on Iraq's defenses. Instead, he was convinced that long air campaign should first prepare the battlefield. Following that, a combination of air support and ground mobility would be deployed to overwhelm Saddam's forces.

In short, then, the war that Bush and Powell unleashed in January 1991 was not designed to be a series of grinding battles aimed at placing unremitting pressure on the enemy. It would be more akin to a rapid blitzkrieg campaign, with every effort made to minimize the death toll. Lower down the chain of command, officers took note of the prevailing mood. Rather than relentlessly pursuing the enemy, at least one ordered a halt when it got dark, fearing that battlefield debris and the prospect of friendly fire might result in unnecessary casualties.[7]

While combat commanders kept one eye on losses, the Pentagon fixed its gaze on the media's coverage of the fighting. Based on the post-Grenada planning, the new media system was actually something of a throwback to World War I. As in World War I, the media was grouped into pools. To join, reporters had to pass a "security review." They also had to subscribe to a set of guidelines that proscribed, among other things, the filming of soldiers in "agony or severe shock" and the writing of stories that "could be used against U.S. forces, such as details of major battle damage or major personnel losses." Only then were they permitted access to the war zone. And even here they invariably encountered officers who were extremely careful about what they divulged. The "game" of counting bodies was definitely off limits. "I'm anti-body count," Norman Schwarzkopf, the senior U.S. commander, told reporters at one point. "Body counts mean nothing, absolutely nothing." The filming of coffins was also blocked. With vivid memories of those Vietnam television stories detailing family heartbreak at military funerals, the Bush White House was quick to place a complete media ban on the return of all dead soldiers to American soil.[8]

Ultimately these measures were not necessary, for the actual fighting could not have been more different from Vietnam. Rather than a protracted and bloody fight, victory was swift. Although the United States deployed more than half a million troops, only 148 were killed in action and a further 458 wounded. Bush was ecstatic. "By, God," he declared in March after Iraq's resistance rapidly crumbled, "we've kicked the Vietnam syndrome once and for all." "The specter of Vietnam," he added, "has been buried forever in the desert sands of the Arabian Peninsula."[9]

This was overly optimistic. For one thing, while the fighting rapidly ended, victory proved elusive. Most obviously Saddam remained in power, much to the chagrin of many Bush advisers who viewed him as a major threat to peace and stability. For another, Americans had not suddenly forgotten the Vietnam trauma: according to one poll, even in March 1991 more than half still felt that success against Iraq had failed to wipe out the memory of this earlier defeat.[10]

Bush's successor certainly did not think the nation had kicked its Vietnam-inspired casualty obsession. Bill Clinton had come of age during the Vietnam era. He had been one of those many Americans whose educational attainments had gained a draft deferment. Deeply reluctant to fight in the 1960s, Clinton was equally loath to commit American boys to battle during the 1990s. Instead he became an enthusiastic advocate of technowar. As a series of conflicts erupted in the post–Cold War world, he used cruise missiles or air strikes on numerous occasions, from Iraq to Afghanistan, but he was deeply reluctant to send in ground troops. Perhaps the telling moment came in March 1999, when he decided to intervene in Kosovo. As well as insisting that American interests justified the "dangers to our armed forces," Clinton explicitly ruled out sending ground troops. His reason was simple: more than twenty-five years after the end of the U.S. involvement in Vietnam, Clinton believed that there was still a strong public consensus against shedding American blood in distant wars.[11]

One group of thinkers, policymakers, and politicians vehemently dissented from the consensus of the Clinton years. These were the neocons, and they viewed the 1990s as "a squandered decade." By allowing "dangerous dictators" in Iraq, Serbia, and North Korea to survive, they argued, both Bush and Clinton had established a "disturbing principle": that such regimes "can challenge the peace, slaughter innocents, threaten their neighbors with missile attacks—and still hang on to power. This constitutes a great failure in American foreign policy," William Kristol and Robert Kagan declared in 2000, "one that will surely come back to haunt us."

On the cusp of a new millennium the neocons pressed for a more assertive foreign policy. As the sole superpower in a unipolar world, they called for the United States to act without the restraints imposed by awkward allies or inconvenient institutions. Convinced of America's exceptional virtue and unparalleled strength, they wanted it to create a stable international order in its own image. "Dangerous dictators" were their first target. In the neocons' uncomplicated view, it was crucial to overthrow such regimes and replace them with a string of peace-loving democracies.

As the neocons realized, regime change would not be cost-free. It could only be achieved by the effective deployment of military power—not just by lobbing a few missiles or half-heartedly imposing economic sanctions. The neocons were particularly disdainful of Clinton's decision to adopt these lesser means against Iraq. He had failed to unseat Saddam, they complained, making the United States appear weak in the process. Instead of such ineffective technowar, they argued, American leaders had to be prepared to put soldiers in harm's way. Only then would the United States demonstrate that it had the resolve to defend its interests. Only then could it preserve what the neocons dubbed "America's benevolent global hegemony."[12]

In crucial respects these riffs, although purporting to be modern, came from a disconcertingly familiar sixties' tune. In their own minds the neocons were consciously trying to banish the enervating memory of the Vietnam era. In reality, however, key elements of their agenda were ominously similar to ideas that had mired the United States in Vietnam in the first place. The notion that credibility had to be reinforced by a willingness to accept casualties was the most obvious throwback. In 1965 McNamara's minions had talked specifically about communicating American resolve by "bloodying" U.S. troops.[13] While few neocons had actually fought in the resulting Vietnam battles, thirty-five years later most had a fascination with war. They were convinced that the United States had "to risk the lives of its sons and daughters . . . to preserve the global stability on which peace and prosperity rest."[14]

The neocons' opportunity to pursue their agenda came in 2001. With George W. Bush's narrow election they acquired a key ally in the White House. As well as agreeing that the Clinton years had been a disaster, Bush shared the neocon commitment to rebuilding U.S. military power while listening less to allies. So did the heavy-hitters Bush recruited to top positions. To be sure, old Washington hands like Dick Cheney, the influential vice president, and Donald Rumsfeld, the driving defense secretary, were not neocons in the strictest sense. But they were robust nationalists who hankered for the old days of vigorous presidential leadership, and they were happy to recruit leading neocons who shared important parts of this vision, men like Paul D. Wolfowitz, who became Rumsfeld's deputy.[15]

It took the events of September 11, 2001, before the neocons were really in a position to implement their agenda. On that day Osama bin Laden's Al Qaeda launched terrorist attacks on the World Trade Center and Pentagon, which immediately transformed the public's attitude toward war. With thousands killed, Americans demanded action. According to one poll, a massive 92 percent believed the United States had to respond militarily to the 9/11 attacks—a figure that only dipped to 72 percent if military action resulted in thousands of U.S. battlefield casualties. At long last the Vietnam syndrome seemed dead. Or, as one official emphatically put it, "History starts today."[16]

Bush fully agreed. Just before he went to bed on September 11 he jotted some thoughts in his diary. "The Pearl Harbor of the twenty-first century took place today," he began, and as with the aftermath of Pearl Harbor, the United States was now at war—"a war in which people were going to have to die."[17]

As Bush recognized, the parallels were by no means exact. For a start, the events of 9/11 were more unexpected, more shocking, and more filmed even than the Japanese attack of 1941. They also resulted in an unprecedented number of American civilian casualties: men and women who had simply gone to work in the heart of the financial and government districts, or who had boarded planes. "Now come the names, the list of casualties we are only beginning to read," Bush told his compatriots three days later, when leading them in a day of prayer and remembrance:

> They are the names of men and women who began their day at a desk or in an airport, busy with life. They are the names of people who faced death and in their last moments called home to say, "Be brave," and, "I love you." They are the names of passengers who defied their murderers and prevented the murder of others on the ground. They are the names of men and women who wore the uniform of the United States and died at their posts. They are the names of rescuers, the ones whom death found running up the stairs and into the fires to help others. We will read all these names. We will linger over them and learn their stories, and many Americans will weep.[18]

Bush believed that these deaths had to be avenged, but he also thought he faced a trickier situation than at the start of any previous war. Unlike the Axis powers, or even the Viet Cong, Al Qaeda was an elusive enemy. It was sheltered by the Taliban regime in Afghanistan, but not tied to any state. It was geographically diffuse and difficult to locate. Above all it posed a far more direct danger to the American homeland, especially if the next terrorist attack was with biological weapons or a dirty nuclear bomb. "We're in for a difficult struggle," Bush admitted soon after, "it is a new kind of war; we're facing an enemy we never faced before; it is a two-front war initially—Afghanistan and at home."[19]

These themes would be ever-present in the months ahead, as Bush and his team struggled to develop a response to the 9/11 attacks. The Taliban regime in Afghanistan immediately became the target. By eradicating this save haven, Bush hoped to expose Osama bin Laden and his Al Qaeda supporters to withering American firepower; he also wanted to send a message to the world that the United States had the wherewithal and will to "end" any state that supported terrorism.

If crushing the Taliban and Al Qaeda was the objective, military power—including U.S. troops on the ground—were the preferred means. On September

14 Bush signed an order that made reservists available for up to two years of active duty. The next day he sent a public message to "everybody who wears the uniform: Get ready. The United States will do what it takes to win this war." Bush's message was designed to tell the world that he was prepared to deploy "boots on the ground," rather than rely merely on surgical air strikes. He considered this a crucial point. In a series of meetings over the next few weeks, he reacted with "palpable disgust" when anyone suggested responding only with technowar gestures. As Bush explained to one reporter, "The antiseptic notion of launching a cruise missile into some guy's, you know tent, really is a joke. I mean, people viewed that as impotent America . . . that when struck, we wouldn't fight back. It was clear that bin Laden felt emboldened and didn't feel threatened by the United States."[20]

To disabuse terrorists of the dangerous notion that the United States lacked the will to fight, Bush and his national security team were ready to place ten thousand to twelve thousand soldiers and marines in Afghanistan. To calm a home front clamoring for immediate and decisive action, the Pentagon was more than a little eager to emphasize that American soldiers were "ready to spill their own blood." Rumsfeld, fast becoming the media face of America's new wars, was characteristically blunt. Air power had only limited value, he told reporters in mid-October. War planes, in particular, "can't crawl around on the ground and find people." Only troops could do that.[21]

Still, the problems of placing troops in Afghanistan were daunting. Everyone knew the sobering recent past: that the Soviet Union had suffered its own Vietnam in Afghanistan's mountain fastness, its troops treated as infidel invaders in a long and bloody war of attrition. The Soviets had at least enjoyed the advantage of bordering on Afghanistan. To the Americans, it was a landlocked country. The Bush administration therefore undertook an intensive round of diplomatic bargaining to acquire the fragile support of Pakistan, as well as base rights in Uzbekistan, Tajikistan, and Kyrgyzstan. But this diplomacy took time. By October 8 Bush and his team were only in a position to launch an air campaign. On the ground the most they could deploy was three hundred members of the special forces, together with 110 CIA officers, whose job was to work with indigenous anti-Taliban fighters, labeled the Northern Alliance.[22]

In the hawkish post-9/11 mood some media voices were distinctly unimpressed. On the *Jim Lehrer NewsHour* one analyst even dredged up the dreaded 1990s analogy, charging Bush with practicing "the Bill Clinton approach to warfare . . . thinking small." In mid-December this seemed a valid criticism when American forces failed to capture or kill bin Laden, who had been located in a cave complex in the forbidding Tora Bora region. The Afghan forces surrounding him were too ridden with factions, their leaders too willing to sanction a brief ceasefire. Without an adequate number of U.S. troops to finish the job, the Al Qaeda leader slipped into Pakistan, casting a pall over the entire campaign.[23]

At the time, the media inquest into bin Laden's escape was muted. Some press reports did pin the blame on "dubious military tactics" or quoted unnamed officials complaining that "despite all the brave talk" the administration had not been prepared to put troops on the ground to bag its target. But the precise details were still too murky for such stories to spark a major controversy.[24]

Meanwhile, Bush could point to some impressive victories. Air power had certainly taken a big toll on the Taliban. American special forces had also successfully worked with the indigenous Northern Alliance, who seized Afghanistan's main cities as Taliban resistance crumbled. With a stunning and surprisingly rapid victory in the offing, the death toll was small: just seven Americans killed between October and December, by which time Kabul had been liberated. Although American fatalities then increased to twenty-four during the first three months of 2002, as U.S. forces engaged in a fierce battle with the remnants of the fighters that had escaped from Tora Bora, popular support remained robust. A month into the conflict 90 percent endorsed military action in Afghanistan. According to another poll, 81 percent thought the military was "doing all it reasonably can to avoid U.S military casualties."[25]

Even to some of those relatives who suffered the modern agony of casualty notification, the sacrifice seemed to be for a worthwhile cause. At the start of this war the Pentagon's process for informing next of kin was generally smoother and more compassionate than in the past. Gone were the days when the military had received a bad press for entrusting this sensitive task to yellow taxis delivering Western Union telegrams. Now it sent out trained officers in martial dress greens who arrived in black SUVs. For the newly informed relatives, the agony was just as intense. It was "the nightmare that all military wives have had," said one after being given the dreaded news, but in the wake of 9/11 those whom the media interviewed tended to think the Afghan fight was necessary and just. My husband was "a hero," the widow of one special forces officer told reporters in a front-porch interview, "and he wouldn't have wanted it any other way."[26]

While the relatives of the first battles grieved, the Bush administration planned the next phase of the fight. Rumsfeld was often in the vanguard. Dynamic and domineering, he was so pleased with the manner of the Afghan success that he intended to use it as a template for the future.

Rumsfeld's delight was hardly a surprise. At the onset of the Bush presidency he had arrived at the Pentagon determined to remake the military so that it was relevant to the post–Cold War world. Its hallmarks would be speed and agility. "For Rumsfeld," as one analyst explained, "the future belonged not to the GI slogging it out in a foxhole, but weapons from space and more use of air power." While such ideas seemed to place him firmly in the technowar camp, there were important qualifications. Like the neocons, Rumsfeld detested what he considered the impotent futility of Clinton's overreliance on missiles. Like the neocons, too, he thought that America's big lumbering military establishment had essentially become an excuse for inaction. He wanted to make it leaner so that it could be deployed.

To Rumsfeld and Wolfowitz, his deputy, the Weinberger-Powell doctrine was particularly pernicious. Both men thought that the notion that the United States had to use "overwhelming force" in any military engagement was overly cautious. It also tended to unnerve already-anxious presidents who balked at the expense of sending hundreds of thousands of men to deal with distant threats like Saddam in Iraq. By scaling down the size of divisions, emphasizing the speed of deployment to and on the battlefield, and upgrading to a new generation of weapons, Rumsfeld hoped to make the military more usable again. But, he hastened to add, it would usable in a decisive way. There would be no going back to the other extreme and uselessly lobbing a few missiles at tents in the desert.

By the end of 2001, with the Afghan fighting coming to a swift end, Rumsfeld claimed his new style of war had been vindicated. Ignoring the Taliban's weakness, the role played by the Northern Alliance, and the failure to capture bin Laden, Rumsfeld insisted that the combination of hi-tech weaponry in the skies and special forces on the ground had won the day. And so did Bush. In a speech at the Citadel, in Charleston, South Carolina, on December 11, Bush declared that the United States was "finding new tactics and new weapons to attack and defeat" the terrorists, in a "revolution in our military" that "promises to change the face of battle. Afghanistan," Bush added, "has been a proving ground for this new approach." The combination of "real-time intelligence, local allied forces, special forces, and precision air power . . . has really never been used before." The Afghan conflict, he therefore concluded, was a vital testing ground as well as an important first victory, having "taught us more about the future of our military than a decade of blue ribbon panels and think-tank symposiums."[27]

As well as a sense of vindication, Rumsfeld and Bush had obvious bureaucratic and policy motives for equating the apparent triumph in Afghanistan with their new vision. Before 9/11 the defense secretary had effectively been at war with his own defense department. On the day before the terrorist attacks Rumsfeld had even declared publicly that the Pentagon bureaucracy was "an adversary that poses a threat, a serious threat, to the security of the United States." The reason for this extraordinary judgment was the bureaucratic hostility to his plans for remaking the military. Inside the Pentagon many officers resented Rumsfeld's bruising, hectoring style, especially when it targeted their budgets or pet projects. Before 9/11 some had fought back with leaks, others with open dissent. Now Rumsfeld hoped to use the Afghan success to place these critics on the defensive.[28]

The combative Rumsfeld also considered Colin Powell, the secretary of state, an adversary, especially since Powell had coauthored the doctrine on overwhelming force that he thought too "soft-line." In reality Powell was no dove, but he clearly had qualms about some of the neocons' more grandiose ideas. Rumsfeld therefore recognized that Powell would have to be outmaneuvered if the United States was to eradicate the threat that he thought was the most menacing: Iraq.[29]

Saddam had always been in the Bush administration's sights. He posed a major threat, senior officials believed, because he possessed weapons of mass destruction (WMD). Containment and inspection had not deprived him of these weapons, they believed, and so to keep them away from terrorists who might be prepared to detonate a dirty bomb inside the United States, the only option was forcible regime change. As Bush increasingly argued, using words straight from the neocon lexicon, removing Saddam would remove a major threat to the American homeland. It would also send a powerful positive message to the rest of the Middle East. "A liberated Iraq," Bush declared in February 2003, "can show the power of freedom to transform that vital region, by bringing hope and progress into the lives of millions. America's interests in security and America's belief in liberty both lead in the same direction, to a free and peaceful Iraq."[30]

Rumsfeld fully agreed with this reasoning, but he added a further twist. In his view the liberation of Iraq was not only essential and desirable; it would also be easy—"a cakewalk"—given the ongoing transformation of the American military.

When Rumsfeld first looked at the Pentagon's existing Iraq war plan, he was aghast. It called for half a million troops, he complained, and was "cumbersome." The general charged with finding an alternative agreed. The plan, observed Tommy Franks, was "the classic kind of plodding, tank-heavy, big-bomb massing of military might from another era. Just the thing that drove Rumsfeld nuts." During 2002 and early 2003 Rumsfeld pushed for a much slimmer operation: only 145,000 troops. Speed and agility would take the place of overwhelming force. Modern technology would compensate for fewer men on the ground, especially "information superiority" to outfox the enemy and "shock and awe" to demoralize its leaders and elite units. In planning and execution, then, Iraq would be Rumsfeld's war with a vengeance: a new type of campaign that would both sustain and showcase his drive to remake the American way of war.[31]

Iraq, 2003—New War, New Problems

Not everything about the Iraq War would be new, however. The Pentagon's public relations policy, in particular, would lean heavily on past precedent. Eager to avoid the problems of the Vietnam era, the military planned to exert tight control over the media. War correspondents would be prevented from traveling on their own. They would also be prohibited from divulging certain types of sensitive information, including troop numbers and operational plans. And they would be reminded of "the sensitivity of using names of individual casualties or photographs" until the next of kin were notified.

Harking back to the older lessons learned during the two world wars, however, the military decided that restriction would not be the only method of control. Public information officers would also seek to co-opt the seven hundred or so accredited journalists, turning them into a "band of brothers with our troops." With a clear nod to the first system Palmer had devised in 1917–18, these "embedded correspondents" would live and travel with the troops. They would be provided with "training, transportation, food, shelter, and of course protection." In return, the military hoped that they would so identify with their new military comrades that they would "dominate the information market" with friendly war stories, loudly extolling the virtues of American warriors, sensitively explaining problems from their perspective, and quietly downplaying the more gruesome aspects of the battlefield.[32]

From the administration's perspective this system initially worked quite well. According to one study, most stories in the first weeks of the war "avoided graphic material" and none "showed pictures of people being hit by weapons fire."[33] Yet even for an administration so keen to dominate the public's consumption of war news, Iraq soon proved a tough sell. Part of the reason was its novelty. At first, Iraq was new not only in the way Bush and Rumsfeld sought to fight it; it was also new in how it was experienced by Americans on the home front.

The nature of the media was perhaps the biggest change. Although Vietnam had been the first televised war, during the 1960s and 1970s television coverage had been confined to three networks, which invariably carried just thirty-minute nightly news shows and the odd hour-long special. In 1990–91 the Persian Gulf War had given a major boost to CNN, the pioneer of rolling twenty-four hour cable news channels. A decade later the landscape of cable narrowcasting had altered dramatically. CNN looked somewhat dated and tired next to its overtly partisan rivals: Fox on the right and MSNBC on the left, both of whom replaced many tenets of objective journalism with open editorializing.

All these television networks were also up against the speed, the unpredictability, and the sheer size of information emanating from the Internet. As well as the efforts by television and newspapers to develop their Web presence, a vast number of bloggers were in a position to push their own agendas. In the first weeks of the Iraq War traffic to news websites jumped by 6 percent, with major news organizations reporting anywhere from 30 to 100 percent more visits. Chat rooms and discussion forums also flourished, while bloggers hastened to offer their own, unmediated take on the war. In this new blogosphere, partisan mudslinging was rife, but so was speculation and fiction. Some bloggers were prepared to pedal unfounded rumors, others circulated stories that traditional media outlets were loath to touch, and still others sometimes scooped everyone with their ability to instantaneously publish news.[34]

Equally controversial was the challenge posed by overseas cable networks, especially Al Jazeera, which adopted a very different frame to U.S. news organizations. In important respects Al Jazeera was doing nothing new. In earlier wars each national media had developed its own narrative, and on a number of occasions these narratives had spilled over into the American discourse. In World War I, for instance, the U.S. media had often been influenced by the British and French military, largely because their censors had first controlled what could be written and had later provided U.S. censors with vital tips on what divulge. In World War II, moreover, Axis-originated stories had intermittently appeared in the American press, particularly when the army and navy had failed to provide timely casualty information.

Yet Al Jazeera was different for two reasons. Its filmed footage was far more vivid, and it could be accessed with much greater ease. Already in Afghanistan, Al Jazeera had focused its war coverage on death and destruction. Whereas the majority of U.S. cable news stories had relied on "clean language" that removed "the idea that lives were being lost in the battles," Al Jazeera's reporting provided a contrasting perspective. According to one content analysis, it concentrated on "the damage caused by the bombing of schools, homes, mosques, as well as the . . . loss of innocent Afghani life 'that had nothing to with bin Laden or the Taliban.'" Crucially, moreover, Americans no longer depended on their own media to discover what a foreign organization was saying. Now anyone with Internet access could see an Al Jazeera report for themselves.[35]

While foreign news networks showed graphic images, the American media was united by more than just a desire to sanitize the war. It was also obsessed with personality. Again, this was not entirely new. Newspapers had long sought wartime human-interest stories; invariably they had also reserved a prominent spot for American heroes who had died in battle. Television, too, had always been a medium that prioritized the dramatic over the analytic. As early as the Korean War, CBS had been roundly criticized for a stunt in which a shocked mother was unexpectedly confronted with her wounded son. But it was during the Vietnam era that television had really pioneered its emphasis on individuals. Indeed, during the 1960s, network coverage often revolved around hero narratives: short vignettes about brave leaders of brave men, willing to sacrifice all for a noble cause.[36]

Since Vietnam, though, the media had become even more fixated on personality. The 1970s saw a growth in celebrity magazines. Then the advent of cable TV produced numerous channels devoted specifically to entertainment news and celebrity biographies. In an ever more crowded market, media bosses concluded that celebrity sells. By the start of the twenty-first century, as serious reporters complained openly about the blurring of "lines between news and entertainment," the AP expanded its entertainment coverage to cater to a growing demand for more celebrity-based stories. Even 9/11 failed to halt the trend. According to one survey, by the spring of 2002 the volume of "hard" news on network television had dwindled from 80 to 52 percent in the past six months, while "lifestyle stories made up almost 20 percent of all output."[37]

With the outbreak of the Iraq War, editors were clearly primed to cover the fighting in a similar way. Their calculation was simple: If personalities increased circulation or viewing figures during times of peace, then it was only natural to focus on the new warrior celebrities who were bound to emerge during the course of the fighting.

At the start of the Iraq War all these developments came together to shape the way the media covered the human cost. In the first weeks, the war appeared to be a stunning success. Unlike the five-week-long air campaign in 1991, this time there was only a short nine-hour "shock and awe" bombardment. Although the Iraqi fedayeen militias initially fought well, especially when poor weather whipped up suffocating sandstorms, U.S. forces were soon making a series of rapid thrusts into Baghdad, effectively utilizing the vast gap between the quality of their own equipment and training, and that of the enemy. Caught by surprise at the speed of the advance, Saddam was unable to turn the city into a fortress that would bleed U.S. forces and undermine the American public's will to fight. Within weeks his regime was on the verge of destruction, at a cost to the United States of just 131 battlefield deaths.[38]

This toll was nothing like the hundreds the Pentagon had announced week and after week during the Korean and Vietnam wars. It even paled next to the 148 killed during the Persian Gulf War in 1991. Yet this relatively small number still resonated loudly on the home front.

Rumsfeld's way of war was one reason. Although the remarkable swiftness of the American advance left the enemy flat-footed and bewildered, it also placed a number of American support troops in vulnerable positions, as they struggled to keep pace with the frontline units in areas that were not yet fully secured. On March 23 the 507th Maintenance Company paid the price. Consisting mainly of mechanics charged with repairing transport vehicles, the 507th was unprepared for battle. Disorientated and lost after rushing to catch antimissile units dashing into the heart of Iraq, it soon fragmented into several groups, came under enemy fire, and sustained high casualties. In an ambush at An Nasiriyah one column containing thirty-three soldiers suffered eleven killed and seven captured, while several of those who escaped were wounded.[39]

As in earlier wars, the Pentagon was reluctant to promptly divulge details about such casualties. It preferred to wait until it was clear exactly how many of the missing had been killed or taken prisoner. Once again, however, the media balked at this delay. Journalists, driven by ever more intense deadlines, were desperate for information, and this time they did not have to wait for their own government to divulge details. In the age of the Internet and twenty-four-hour cable news, first Al Jazeera and then a range of American outlets immediately picked up an Iraqi news broadcast that showed "gruesome images of bodies and interviews with stunned and anxious soldiers who said they were in the 507th Maintenance Company."[40]

Jessica Lynch was by far the most newsworthy of those captured. A nineteen-year-old who had not even seen her state capital of Charleston, West Virginia, before graduating from high school, the media viewed Lynch as an unusual warrior, at least compared to earlier wars. For one thing, as a young woman, she represented a significant component of the all-volunteer force that had emerged after Vietnam. Women now comprised about 10 percent of the forces sent to Iraq and Afghanistan. On paper they still faced gender restrictions that were meant to keep them away from the front line. But in the midst of the rapid advance toward Baghdad, such limitations had little practical effect.[41] In fact, Rumsfeld's way of war had exposed to capture soldiers who had never dreamed they were joining the army to place themselves in dire danger. Lynch was one. As her parents told reporters, she had only signed up to see a bit of the world, acquire a college education, and then become a kindergarten teacher.[42]

On April 1 Lynch's fame grew rapidly when the AP announced that she had been rescued from Iraqi captivity in a daring night raid. The next day an army spokesman announced that she would be flown to a hospital in Germany to be treated for wounds sustained during the initial An Nasiriyah ambush. The media's response was frenzied. Soon mainstream newspapers reported that Lynch had received "multiple gunshot wounds" in a vicious firefight. "She was fighting to the death," one official explained. "She did not want to be taken alive." Avidly latching on to this lead, some newspapers portrayed her as a "female Rambo," while others suggested that her exploits were proof that women could excel in combat. Looking for an even more eye-catching angle, at least one tabloid speculated that the Iraqis must have tortured her. Back in West Virginia, though, her father was more down to earth. "The little brat's caused a big stir in this country," he told a media scrum outside his house. "As soon as she's capable, we're planning a big shindig."[43]

The media's handling of the Jessica Lynch story was just the most extreme example of its growing personalization of casualty stories. In the first weeks of the Iraq War the numbers of dead, wounded, and missing were not high. But this fact itself encouraged many news organizations to give greater attention to the backstory of each individual victim. The main TV networks led the way. At the start of most days, ABC's *Good Morning America* listed the names of the confirmed dead; later, NBC's *Nightly News* focused "its casualty coverage on in-depth reports about individuals and their families." On April 4 CBS's *Early Show* ended with "a four-minute display of the names, ages, and photographs of all the casualties in order of their deaths."[44]

These galleries were apt to showcase another new development: the wide age-range of casualties. The forces that fought in Iraq and Afghanistan were not drawn from draftees, as they had been in earlier wars. The reason was simple. During Vietnam the draft had become so controversial that Nixon had killed it, and none of his successors wanted a resurrection. Instead the army that now went to war was increasingly composed of reservists. Since these reservists came from a relatively small pool, they were forced to make repeated tours of duty.

The result was twofold. Critics of the war soon started complaining of a "backdoor draft," especially when the army began handing out "stop-loss" orders to troops in units bound for Iraq or Afghanistan.[45] Furthermore, because many reservists were older than the men who had been formally drafted in earlier wars, those that became casualties were more likely leave behind spouses and children— a fact that the media frequently latched on to. In July, for instance, *Time* published a five-page special on the life and death of an army sergeant in his fifties who had been killed trucking supplies along the dangerous road between Kuwait and Baghdad; it began with the moving story of how he had tried to stay close to his wife while in the warzone.[46] Across the country, meanwhile, smaller newspapers focused on the tragic losses in their communities, often with accompanying photographs and moving captions that highlighted the void left behind. Particularly poignant was the poster-size image of a wife and three young children holding a banner reading "Happy Birthday Major Dad." It was a present they had planned to send him before they got news of his death.[47]

This was not the only way the print media now reported casualties. Struggling to come to terms with the Internet challenge, major newspapers also used their web pages to publish the latest casualty stories in various eye-catching ways. On the West Coast, for instance, the *Los Angeles Times* compiled portraits of every Californian killed in Iraq. On the other side of the country the *New York Times* used graphs and maps to break the numbers down by service, race, and home state. Both the *Times* and the *Washington Post* also had links to pictures of the dead, next to which they placed moving tributes detailing their careers, "from training to their deaths to the final journey home."[48]

Nothing on this scale had occurred before. Back in 1969 *Life* had published pictures and profiles of one week's KIA after Hamburger Hill, but this story had been highly unusual and deeply controversial. Now it was not only the norm but also helped to fix the domestic debate even more firmly onto the subject of casualties.

Since Vietnam all media organizations had imbibed the conventional wisdom about the public's apparent averseness to casualties. Leading political scientists, they knew, taught that the public was casualty-intolerant; that popular support would inevitably ebb when the country lost a particular number of troops. Whatever the accuracy of this thesis—and a number of political scientists were in the process of offering refinements or serious challenges—its eye-catching simplicity made it a staple of the media discourse. Whenever troops were committed to war and the first casualties were sustained, many editors turned to John Mueller and his followers for comment. They also published polls that sought to establish if casualties were influencing domestic levels of support for the fight. And they sent reporters on to the streets to monitor the public's sensitivity to losses in the current fight. What did the average voter think about the present casualty totals? What if casualties rose precipitously? What level did they think was acceptable?

At first, the Bush administration found the results reassuring. Before the invasion, opinion polls found that a majority of Americans thought that removing Saddam from power was "worth the potential loss of American life." In early April, when the death toll was eighty-eight, a voter-in-the-street interview found the dominant mood even more robust. "Casualties had not eroded . . . support for the war," the interviewer recorded, and most people "could accept two, three, or even ten times as many deaths in the coming weeks, as long as success was in sight." These last six words were a potentially significant caveat, but they were by no means the only warning sign. The new type of media coverage also appeared to be exerting an impact. "Many people," the interviewer added, "said the limited number of casualties, as recorded by the twenty-four-hour news coverage, has made each life lost seem more poignant." It remained to be seen how the public would react to such poignancy, especially if success in Iraq no longer appeared imminent.[49]

Iraq, 2003–4: New War, Familiar Problems

On May 1 this did not seem a problem. That day, in a speech aboard the USS *Abraham Lincoln*, Bush declared that the Iraq mission had been accomplished. After praising the skill and devotion of America's soldiers, as well as mourning those who would never return, Bush went on to emphasize the advantages of his new type of warfare. In the world war era, he observed, the United States had relied on massive military power "to end a regime by breaking a nation." Now, he declared, "with new tactics and precision weapons, we can achieve military objectives without directing violence against civilians. No device of man can remove the tragedy from war; yet it is a great advance when the guilty have far more to fear from war than the innocent."[50]

Unfortunately for Bush, even as he spoke, his way of war was unraveling fast. In April the lightning advance might have ended Saddam's regime, apparently at little cost, but by May it had also created numerous unforeseen problems. One was the survival of units loyal to Saddam. In their dash for Baghdad, American forces had bypassed many fedayeen militias, in the belief that they would "die on the vine" when Saddam was overthrown. In actuality, the fedayeen ultimately survived to fight another day. Worse, these Iraqi militias were now primed to fight an unconventional insurgency of the type that U.S. forces were ill prepared to counter. They could also rely on outside support, partly because Rumsfeld's army on the ground was much smaller than the 380,000 that some military planners had estimated would be required to both police Iraq and seal its borders.

Nor had Bush anticipated the internal problems that soon erupted inside Iraq. Before the invasion Bush and his team had scarcely considered postwar planning, blithely convinced that Iraqis would greet U.S. forces as "liberators" before creating a stable democracy that would become a key American ally. The reality was quite different. Saddam's sudden ouster initially resulted in wave of massive looting. When the Americans then abruptly removed all former Baathist Party members from positions of authority, many ministries, hospitals, and schools stopped functioning. In a country divided between Sunnis, Shiites, and Kurds, membership in Saddam's party had provided not just work but also one of Iraq's "few unifying national institutions." As a vacuum developed at the center, Iraq threatened to divide into ungovernable—even warring—factions.

For American troops on the ground it was a bewildering time. Trained for combat, they suddenly faced a disconcerting array of requests from Iraqi civilians about water supplies, garbage collection, and freedom of movement. Given orders to oust Saddam, secure Iraq's oil fields, and locate the WMD, they had no instructions for dealing with the endemic looting. Then they started to come under attack from insurgents. Throughout the summer, as temperatures soared well above 100ºF, violence flared across Iraq. Instead of a quick return home, the 130,000 soldiers and marines faced a new war, albeit one that varied from region to region. In the north the 101st Airborne under Gen. David Petraeus emphasized nation building as well as insurgency fighting. In the region west of Baghdad, by contrast, a savage war was underway, while Baghdad itself became the scene of a growing number of terrorist bombings. Nevertheless, wherever they were based, all American troops faced roughly the same outlook: a growing chance of becoming a sudden casualty in a new and unpredictable conflict.[51]

The Bush administration struggled to find a coherent response to these unexpected developments. When reporters first asked Rumsfeld about the looting, he was breezily dismissive. "Stuff happens!" he replied, adding "it's untidy, and freedom's untidy, and free people are free to make mistakes and commit crimes and do bad things," but "they're also free to live their lives and do wonderful things." What was certainly *not* happening, Rumsfeld insisted throughout the early summer, was a full-blown insurgency. In mid-June he blamed the violence on "pockets of dead-enders" left over from the invasion. His commanders, meanwhile, insisted that a deployment of four thousand U.S. soldiers in central Iraq "would curb the threat," adding that the violence was not a sign that they now faced organized nationwide resistance.[52]

But the violence continued to escalate. In June U.S. forces initiated roughly half of the thirty-five daily incidents. On a single day in August, by contrast, insurgents were responsible for upwards of 80 percent of incidents. As a result American losses rose dramatically, hitting thirty-three in October and rising to sixty-eight in November. On November 3 alone, seventeen Americans were killed, sixteen of them in a Chinook helicopter shot down by insurgents. The next day, even relatively staid newspapers like *USA Today* ran with alarming banner headlines, pronouncing: VIOLENCE IN IRAQ REACHES NEW LEVEL.[53]

Just like Johnson thirty-eight years earlier, Bush was at his Texas ranch as this major spate of new casualties was announced. Whereas Johnson had spoken publicly about the pain he felt at every new death, Bush was deeply reluctant to embrace, or even talk about, the casualty issue. Determined not to engage in public displays of grief, he initially rejected any suggestion that he appear at funerals or memorial services. He even waited two days before making a statement on the Chinook loss.[54]

To the twenty-four-hour cable news channels that lived off breaking news, this time lag seemed an eternity. Even to more traditionally minded journalists, Bush's reluctance to connect himself openly with a tragic event marked a clear break from the past. For at least a generation the sitting president had acted as mourner in chief. In 1965 Johnson had led the way, telling the public of his pain at the Ia Drang losses. Nixon had then spoken frequently about recent losses, albeit tinged with a partisan desire to attack the Democrats and justify his own policies. Then after the Vietnam War the president's public grieving role had become fully established. As reporters now hastened to remind Bush:

> President Jimmy Carter attended ceremonies for troops killed in Pakistan, Egypt and the failed hostage rescue mission in Iran. President Ronald Reagan participated in many memorable ceremonies, including a service at Camp Lejeune in 1983 for 241 Marines killed in Beirut. Among several events at military bases, he went to Andrews in 1985 to pin Purple Hearts to the caskets of marines killed in San Salvador, and, at Mayport Naval Station in Florida in 1987, he eulogized those killed aboard the USS *Stark* in the Persian Gulf.

In the next decade Clinton had taken public mourning to a new level. Always adept at publicly empathizing with victims, Clinton had attended a number of military funerals, including a service for seventeen soldiers killed by Al Qaeda on the USS *Cole*.[55]

Bush, however, was determined to be different. With the exception of Reagan, he found these past precedents unappealing. Clinton was always a particular Bush bête noire; and, as one of his aides revealed, Bush had long been offended by what he saw as Clinton's "exploitation of private grief for political gain." Johnson's example was even more troubling. Bush's aides were acutely aware of the obvious parallel of two Texan presidents presiding over bloody insurgency wars. Behind closed doors Bush also craved detailed information on losses in a way that rekindled ominous memories of Johnson's obsession with body counts. Ever eager to avoid a PR disaster, Bush advisers were highly sensitive about what they told the media. "Not once in this building have we ever discussed the number," the chairman of the Joint Chiefs maintained on one occasion, under intense questioning from a skeptical reporter. Bush, agreed another official, had never "become hostage to daily body counts."[56]

As reporters continued to probe Bush about this tendency to shy away from casualties, they received various responses. The president simply lacked the time to attend all the military funerals, declared one White House official. He was also wanted to let grieving families "have their privacy," insisted another. Nor, averred a third, did he think it fair to single out specific deaths. As Bush's communications director explained, "He never wants to elevate or diminish one sacrifice made over another."[57]

To the skeptics, however, Bush's motives were much more brazenly political. A presidential election was just a year away. The media was already focusing intensively on casualties in the unexpected guerilla war, and pollsters were increasingly making the disturbing connection between mounting losses and Bush's approval ratings. As early as July 2003 opinion polls started to record that a majority of Americans thought the level of casualties was "unacceptable"—a figure that rose at precisely the same time that Bush's personal approval ratings began to dip alarmingly.

Against this domestic backdrop, Bush had an obvious incentive not to dramatize the growing death toll. Faced with domestic criticism over his tardy response to the Chinook downing, he did fly to Fort Carson, Colorado, at the end of November where four of sixteen dead soldiers had been based. In a tearful two-hour meeting with relatives, he offered condolences and comfort. But this visit proved an exception rather than the rule. For the most part Bush focused on doing nothing to dramatize the casualty issue. Most controversially he continued to uphold the ban, introduced by his father in the Persian Gulf War, on media coverage of the return of flag-draped coffins. "There will be no arrival ceremonies for, or media coverage of deceased military personnel returning to or departing from Ramstein [Germany] airbase or Dover [DE] base, to include interim stops," the Bush administration insisted.[58]

If the past was any guide, Bush's effort to defuse the casualty issue was unlikely to succeed. In earlier wars similar PR strategies had simply created an information vacuum, which was filled by partisan politicians and speculating reporters. This time, as well as adding uncontrolled bloggers to the equation, these competing voices in the polity had clear reasons to develop their own casualty narrative.

Their most powerful motive was a growing skepticism about the Bush administration's entire case for war. Before the invasion, the unifying threat in Bush's propaganda had been that Saddam's WMD posed a clear and present danger to the United States. "It was the one justification for war on which everyone could agree," according to the historian Susan Brewer. It was also the justification that did most to rally overwhelming popular support for the war. Unfortunately for Bush, it proved glaringly erroneous. Although the administration sent teams of WMD hunters into Iraq, weapons were never found. Saddam had sustained the illusion of still having stockpiles partly because he thought this would instill fear in his enemies in the region and partly because believed he believed the Americans would never invade. By January 2004 David Kay, the head of the WMD-hunting operation, publicly admitted failure. "We were almost all wrong," he conceded to the Senate Armed Services Committee.[59]

This stunning admission had a clear, if complex, impact on the casualty debate. At the beginning of the war, some relatives of the fallen had told reporters that the discovery of chemical and biological weapons would help them make sense of their loss. If they were not found, warned Jeremy Rosner, a Democratic pollster, Bush was in for a hard time. "The American tolerance for casualties," Rosner told the New York Times in April, "is going to change a whole lot depending on whether you find a weapon of mass destruction."[60]

A year later this appeared, at first glance, to be a prescient prediction. As casualty totals increased, while the WMD proved nonexistent, the public mood appeared to be shifting. Only a third of Americans, for instance, thought that the level of casualties was acceptable. Although Saddam's capture at the end of 2003 fulfilled one war aim, the number thinking Iraq was a mistake continued to rise, as did the percentage who no longer thought the war worth fighting.[61] And yet, domestic support did not collapse entirely. Most notably the public's tolerance for casualties remained fairly robust. According to a specific series of polls undertaken on the subject, the number stating they would *not* tolerate more than a thousand casualties only jumped from 24 to 32 percent during the period when the administration admitted there were no WMDs. During the winter of 2003/4, moreover, overall support for the war continued to hover just above the significant 50 percent threshold.[62]

The failure to find WMD, though not directly undermining popular support for the war, did exert a clear influence over the elite discourse. In particular it provided the war's critics with an obvious new rallying cry. Back in 1952 opponents of Korea had decried Truman's "die for a tie" stalemate war. Now this slogan was revamped into the catchy "die for a lie" sound bite, and reiterated by politicians, protesters, and bloggers. Perhaps its most telling use came on the anniversary of the Tonkin Gulf incident, which Johnson had used as legal cover to escalate the Vietnam War. Forty years later antiwar protesters gathered next to the USS *Admiral Turner Joy*, one of the ships that had been involved in the incident and was now docked permanently at Bremerton, Washington. On their placards was the barbed question: "How do you ask a soldier to be the last to die for a lie?"[63]

During the Vietnam War, of course, the murky nature of the Tonkin incident had generated suspicions of a "credibility gap" between Johnson's public statements and the reality on the ground. In the wake of the failure to locate WMD, Bush faced a similar problem. Like Johnson, moreover, he then widened the credibility gap by making constant claims about progress in Iraq, which jarred with repeated media stories of violent incidents and mounting casualties. Some experts were quick to note the similarity. As early as November 2003, for example, Ernest May, the influential Harvard historian, declared ominously that "the gap between official assessments of the situation and reports from the ground is 'eerily reminiscent' of the Vietnam era."[64]

Just like in the 1960s, these "credibility gap" claims threatened to have a deeply corrosive impact on presidential leadership. Ever since Bush's ill-fated decision to declare victory on May 1, the media had been gifted the opening to frame every casualty story around the same refrain: How many Americans had died "since the president declared major operations were over?" Such an opening hardly inspired confidence in Bush's leadership, especially when the media reported in late October 2003 that the "postwar GI death toll" now exceeded the wartime total. As skepticism grew, the media predictably began to shine its investigative spotlight on a whole range of government pronouncements.[65]

It soon emerged, for instance, that Jessica Lynch had not been captured during a last-ditch Rambo-style shoot-out, as official spokesmen suggested and the media avidly reported. The reality was much more prosaic. According to the *Washington Post*, which had run one of the most influential early stories, "Lynch tried to fire her weapon, but it jammed. . . . She did not kill any Iraqis. She was neither shot nor stabbed." In the aftermath of this effective retraction, other media organizations began to ask, as Jim Lehrer did on his *NewsHour*, "whether the American media too willingly accepted the story of the rescue of Jessica Lynch as presented by the Pentagon."[66]

This was not the last time that media mistrust would interact with a celebrity casualty story. A year later, when the football star Pat Tillman was killed in Afghanistan, the Pentagon initially tried to conceal that he had been a victim of friendly fire. It was a cover-up that failed disastrously, magnifying distrust in official statements and leading ultimately to a House of Representatives investigation into why the Defense Department had sought to mislead the public about both Tillman and Lynch.[67]

Prompted by both incidents, a number of families came forward "to recount similar experiences in which the Pentagon provided misleading information about a battlefield casualty."[68] As the inquest dragged on, some media voices charged that the Tillman case had disturbing echoes in how Johnson and Nixon, "drunk with power," had repeatedly lied to the American people. Others concentrated on the Lynch episode, arguing that it raised equally profound questions about the modern personality-obsessed media culture that the Pentagon had manipulated so easily. In this view, rather than being a real hero distinguished by achievement, Lynch was the archetypal celebrity-hero created by an unholy military-media alliance. "Jessica Lynch is but a puppet," opined Mark Morford, a columnist and culture critic for the *San Francisco Chronicle*, "a toy, a convenient TV-ready canvass [sic] onto which we can project our impotent myths of patriotism and war, spit forth by the BushCo military machine to ease America's pain, to assuage the increasingly nagging fear that we have committed this horrible thing, this irreversible atrocity."[69]

While Morford's trenchant scorn for the official line had little resonance outside liberal circles, the growing mood of distrust that it fed into did present Democrats with an obvious opportunity. At the very least those who had always opposed the invasion felt vindicated. Ted Kennedy, who had caused Nixon so much anxiety over the Hamburger Hill casualties in 1969, was now a similar thorn in Bush's side. In October 2002 Kennedy had voted against the congressional resolution for war on the grounds that Bush had neither made a "convincing case that we face such an imminent threat" nor had "laid out the cost in blood and treasure for this operation." Now he branded the Iraq War "an unnecessary war, based on unreliable and inaccurate intelligence," which "has brought new dangers, imposed new costs, and taken more and more American lives each week."[70]

As casualties mounted over the winter of 2003/4, those Democrats racing for their party's presidential nomination intensified this partisan assault. Some targeted Bush's reluctance to act as mourner in chief, depicting him as "isolated from the real pain of war." Others invoked casualties to highlight what they dubbed the war's mismanagement. In an op-ed piece in the *Boston Globe*, Wesley Clark began with the tragic story of Sgt. Ernest Bucklew—one of the sixteen killed in the downed Chinook, who had been heading home to attend his mother's funeral—to call for a new plan to end the Iraq War.[71]

In the spring, as the situation in Iraq continued to worsen, this line of attack seemed likely to gain more traction. April was a particularly bloody month. Whereas U.S. forces had normally faced about two hundred incidents a week, this figure jumped to 370 one week, followed by 600 the next. The city of Fallujah became the central flashpoint. More aggressive patrolling by the marine corps, which had just taken over responsibility for the city, resulted in a series of intense firefights, but the most explosive episode came when four American contractors were ambushed by insurgents. Dragged from their cars, they were beaten and dismembered, before their blackened corpses were left hanging from a bridge. As Peter Jennings began on that evening's ABC news, "[T]he cameras were there for the gruesome aftermath." The pictures they recorded, he added, were "pretty repugnant, but they are the reality of war."[72]

On many occasions such contractors' deaths remained effectively hidden from public view. As private employees, they certainly did not appear in official casualty statistics. This time, however, the public was appalled. According to one survey, the footage of their corpses was so gruesomely eye-catching that more than 80 percent had "seen or heard something about the attacks." Democrats now glimpsed an opportunity. While leading congressional critics branded Iraq "George Bush's Vietnam," John Kerry, the Democrats' presumed presidential nominee, declared that Bush's handling of Iraq was both "inept" and a "mess."[73]

Yet the Fallujah incident would soon reveal, in microcosm, all the problems Kerry would face trying to turn this new spate of Iraq violence into a winning electoral message. Part of the problem stemmed from the reckless and objectionable comments of some of his liberal allies. Soon after the networks had aired gruesome footage of the dead contractors, the *Daily Kos*, a progressive political blog, published a comment by Markos Moulitsas, its founder. "I feel nothing over the death of merceneries [*sic*]," Moulitsas provocatively wrote. "They aren't in Iraq because of orders, or because they are there trying to help the people make Iraq a better place. They are there to wage war for profit. Screw them." Kerry was immediately forced on the defensive. In the next few days, instead of sharpening his political attack on the war, he was forced to disavow these comments as "unacceptable" before removing a link to them from his campaign website.[74]

In the late summer Kerry was again was thrown off balance, this time by some of his former Vietnam military comrades. These men, angered by Kerry's role in the Vietnam antiwar movement during the early 1970s, produced contentious TV ads and a video "documentary" that questioned both Kerry's patriotism and the incident that won him a third Purple Heart.[75]

Kerry struggled to find an effective retort. By mid-September even Democratic consultants admitted that he "had been too slow to respond to Republican attacks on his military record." To make matters worse, when Kerry tried to shift the focus back to Iraq, he was easily caricatured as lacking consistency.[76] Why, Republicans asked, had he voted against the first Iraq War in 1991 but for the second one in 2003? Was his current criticism of Bush's handling of the conflict just another example of his muddle-headed opportunism? If Kerry had been president, Cheney declared, Saddam would not only still be in power, he would still be in control of Kuwait. Was this the man to be president at such a dangerous moment?[77]

Although Kerry tried to hit back hard, his campaign statements often lacked focus and fire. The first presidential debate was particularly telling. Held just after the American death toll had passed the landmark one-thousand threshold, it should have presented Kerry with a prime opportunity, especially when Lehrer, the impartial moderator, asked both candidates whether the war had been worth such a cost. But Kerry muffed his lines. While Bush spoke movingly of meeting with widows who understood the need to remove Saddam, Kerry said somewhat cryptically that Lehrer's question was a timely reminder that Americans should never confuse war "with the warriors." He then went on to speak stolidly of his plan to end the fighting by holding a summit meeting and bringing in the UN.[78]

For Democrats it was all very frustrating. The public clearly distrusted Bush on Iraq. In mid-September about 80 percent said he was either "hiding something" or "mostly lying" about the war. A plurality also said that the fighting had "produced more casualties than originally expected." And still the death toll continued to rise. The fighting, which spread from Fallujah during the spring, remained intense in the city itself. Although the marines launched a major campaign, this merely resulted in a costly stalemate on the ground. In April alone, 126 Americans were KIA, making it the bloodiest month of the war.[79]

For Bush, however, the sheer size of this mess contained at least one advantage. As the security situation deteriorated, American correspondents found it almost impossible to cover the war. "It was journalism under siege," reported one correspondent, "with hotels being mortared and every trip out of them risky, made in armored SUVs and wearing body armor." As the country descended into chaos, ambushes and kidnappings became depressingly common, and many correspondents stopped making even these heavily chaperoned trips. "The whole world of foreign correspondence changed," observed the Washington Post's Baghdad bureau chief. "We started out like other reporters—go out, report, do a day trip, come back, write the story. By the end, I wasn't going anywhere much."[80]

With "cowed reporters" often failing to depict the ugly reality of events on the ground, Bush's constant claims of progress started to stick. Even at the beginning of the year popular support, though dipping, had remained relatively robust. It continued to edge downward during the spring, with the balance between those

Americans approving and disapproving hitting a low of 40:58 in May. But the decision to hand over power to an Iraqi government a month later halted the trend. In July this ratio then increased to 45:53, before nudging up to 47:50 just before the election. With the country about to vote, Bush also led Kerry on the question of who would best deal with an international crisis and who could best protect the homeland from another terrorist attack.[81]

As reporters went out into the American heartland to interview friends and relatives of the fallen, they discovered similar pattern. "I don't think I like what John Kerry has to say," said the best friend of a Nebraska corporal recently killed in Iraq. In fact, throughout this admittedly Republican-leaning Nebraska neighborhood, the journalist found that most people did not see the corporal's "death through the prism of politics." "I sense no bitterness or contrition whatsoever," observed another inhabitant of this small town. "I think the overall feeling is that we're grateful he died the way he did—serving his country."[82]

The Worsening War, 2004–6

Although Bush's reelection victory was narrow, he was determined to make his second term count. At the outset he even envisaged it becoming a decisive turning point in American history. Domestically, he believed, a new partisan realignment could be forged around the issue of privatizing social security. In the Middle East, the Iraq War would be just a starting point for a vigorous effort to spread freedom and democracy. As Bush declared in his inaugural address on January 20, 2005, "It is the policy of the United States to seek and support the growth of democratic movements and institutions in every nation and culture, with the ultimate goal of ending tyranny in our world."[83]

The situation in Iraq, however, quickly undermined such grandiose ambitions. Immediately after the election U.S. forces tried to take the battle to the insurgents. Launching a second campaign in Fallujah, their aim was clear: to defeat the enemy in this city so decisively that insurgents in other areas would think twice before taking on the Americans. In a narrow sense the battle was a success. Fallujah was retaken and more than one thousand insurgents were killed. But the U.S. casualty toll was high: 54 dead and 425 seriously wounded. And it soon became evident that the larger goal of deterring attacks across Iraq had failed.

The violence certainly continued unabated. By the winter of 2005/6 weekly attacks on U.S. troops were up to five hundred. Six months later they had increased still further, to eight hundred a week, and the worst was still to come. Sectarian killings became more and more commonplace, as divisions between Shiites and Sunnis sharpened. Al Qaeda, rather than being put on the defensive throughout the world, also had a foothold inside the country. All the while American troops were the target for ambushes, suicide bombers, and above all ever more sophisticated roadside bombs that inflicted 73 percent of the 767 casualties during 2007.[84]

Back home, Americans witnessed this war through a media whose coverage was neither graphic nor copious. If in 2004 the intensifying levels of violence had deterred correspondents from touring the country, by 2006 simple economics discouraged editors from sending them to Iraq in the first place. With a U.S. reporter in Iraq costing about $30,000 a month, most news organizations now operated "largely through inexpensive stringers." By September 2006 there were only 11 correspondents embedded with the military, down from more than 600 during the invasion and 114 a year before. At the same time the major networks were devoting 60 percent less time to Iraq than they had in 2003, although this could sometimes have a perverse effect. On one occasion, for instance, NBC had such a guilt spasm about its effective neglect of Iraq that Brian Williams, its news anchor, read on air a "'shame you' email complaint from the parents of two military sons anguished that his broadcast had so little news about the war."[85]

Figure 7.1 Although media coverage of the bloody fighting in Iraq declined after 2003, reporters were always eager to emphasize landmark U.S. casualty totals. By permission of Mike Luckovich and Creators Syndicate, Inc.

As the airing of this email suggested, the public still received a steady diet of disturbing casualty news. Although media coverage lacked graphic footage of the fighting, TV newsreaders still had plenty of landmark numbers to emphasize. Perhaps the most striking was the three-thousandth American death on the last day of 2006—the day after Saddam was hanged.[86] Nor was this the only way that casualties continued to play a prominent role in the nation's debate. Also vital was a casualty story closer to home. This was Cindy Sheehan's vigil outside Bush's ranch in 2005, an event that symbolized so much about modern casualty debates.

At one level Sheehan was simply an anguished mother who thought her twenty-four-year-old son had died in an "illegal and immoral" war. As such, she not only became a darling of the antiwar movement, but she also personified the public's growing anger at the loss of life in Iraq. At deeper level, though, Sheehan was much more than a grieving mom. She was also at the heart of a new type of political campaign, which integrated political consultants, PR teams, and social networking to develop a powerful antiwar message.

What really grabbed the nation's attention was the way that Sheehan tapped into two deeper trends that had characterized casualty debates since 2003. One was the growing sense that Bush, who often shied away from public meetings with relatives, was too remote from the consequences of his war. The aim of her vigil, Sheehan proclaimed, was to tell Bush "face to face how much this hurts"— how much "devastation" she had experienced since her son's death. The other was the personalization of contemporary casualty debates. Sheehan, on the left, was lionized by those who depicted her as a brave, impassioned, and principled protester. On the right she was castigated by those who claimed she wanted "the U.S. government to surrender to Muslim terrorists." But to all, Sheehan was undoubtedly a major media celebrity; her story often told more comprehensively than the actual fighting still ongoing in Iraq.[87]

Sheehan posed a problem for Bush. Although a Gallup poll found that her tactics had not increased public opposition for the war, most sympathized with her plight and thought that Bush ought to meet her. By the fall of 2005 a clear majority also considered the war was a mistake, while 53 percent favored a reduction of U.S. troop levels in Iraq.[88]

Bush had to respond. Like previous presidents faced with an increasingly unpopular war, he decided to hammer away at the progress being made in the struggle against an evil enemy. But Bush's 2005–6 publicity campaign was also subtly different from these earlier efforts, since it revealed just how deeply the political-science research on casualties and opinion had seeped into the mainstream public discourse. In mid-2005 Bush recruited Peter D. Feaver, an academic expert on public opinion during wartime, to his NSC staff. Challenging

Mueller's thesis, Feaver and two colleagues had published eye-catching research arguing that Americans were willing to tolerate a significant number of casualties if they were confident the government had a winning strategy.[89]

Against the grim backdrop of ebbing support for the Iraq War, this was just what Bush wanted to hear. In 2005 he began incorporating Feaver's ideas into keynote speeches. The United States was on course to win, Bush declared on numerous occasions. "I think they're on the last throes, if you will, of the insurgency," agreed Cheney on *Larry King Live* in May. Six months later, when the White House unveiled its "National Strategy for Victory in Iraq," Bush's accompanying speech confidently used the word "victory" no less than fifteen times.[90]

Still, even with a public opinion expert at his side, this was a tough sell. One obvious drawback was that such claims immediately rekindled uncomfortable memories of Johnson's attempts to demonstrate progress in Vietnam. Another was the clear clash between Bush's upbeat rhetoric and the continued chaos in Iraq—which again had an obvious echo in the Vietnam era. By 2006 even Feaver recognized the problem. According to one account, Feaver "cringed" when Bush declared during one press conference that "absolutely, we're winning"— explaining that this "wasn't the way it felt from where I sat at the time." Some Republicans agreed. As early as June 2005, for instance, Chuck Hagel (R-NE) publicly suggested that "the White House had departed from reality with its optimistic assessments of Iraq."[91]

On the other side of the aisle, meanwhile, Bush's critics were not content to depict him as too upbeat or excessively delusional. Given the credibility gap over WMD, they also labeled him a plain liar. As partisan debate became angrier, some Democrats even revived a charge similar to that used by nationalist Republicans during the Korean War. On December 7, 2005, seven Democratic lawmakers wrote a public letter to Bush, accusing him of deliberately underreporting American losses. The problem, they insisted, was the government's excessively narrow definition of a casualty. Official figures, they insisted, only included those wounded in combat and omitted those suffering from illness, especially "medical afflictions," caused by their time in Iraq. As a result, these Democrats declared, the Pentagon's official toll of 2,082 killed and 15,477 was "inaccurate by several multiples." "Based on the data that have been released by your administration," they continued,

> and the unofficial data that are coming out of the Pentagon, what we can be certain of is that at least tens of thousands of young men and women have been physically or psychologically damaged for life. To be exact, the figure ranges somewhere between 15,000 and 101,000 today. This is a staggering range of casualties by any standard, as these casualties will affect the lives of at least hundreds of thousands of family

members and others. We cannot emphasize enough how important it is that we understand the gravity of the situation that we are faced with.[92]

The Bush administration, which had always played political hardball, hit back. Although Bush and Rumsfeld were careful to avoid a public debate over misleading casualty totals, they continued to insist that progress was being made in Iraq. The problem, they now emphasized, was a biased media. Television and the press, Rumsfeld declared, were feeding the public a depressing diet of excessively downbeat news that ignored the big improvements.[93] It was a charge that infuriated liberal commentators. The "images of violence are real," responded Frank Rich, the *New York Times* columnist. "Americans are really dying at the fastest pace in at least a year, and Iraqis in the greatest numbers to date. To imply the carnage is magnified by the news media . . . is to belittle the gravity of the escalated bloodshed and to duck accountability for the mismanagement of the war."[94]

This was a mudslinging match Bush was unlikely to win, and not merely because the daily headlines belied his claims of imminent victory. He also faced a new set of practical problems that sharpened public suspicions about his overall candor. In this sense Bush was unfortunate. Since the Korean War the military had made great strides in tackling many of the practical difficulties surrounding casualty reporting, thereby reducing the gap between official totals and the battlefield reality. In the Internet age, however, as the government tried to keep pace with the growing demand for web-based news, it faced a new practical headache: how to coordinate casualty publication across multiple websites.

The Pentagon remained the fulcrum of the casualty-reporting system, and its website had a special page containing the most up-to-date casualty releases. But other related departments and agencies also published web-based casualty information, increasing the chance of a major discrepancy. In early 2007 numerous newspapers duly spotted such a difference. On January 5, an op-ed in the *Los Angeles Times* stated that 50,508 Americans had so far been wounded in Iraq and Afghanistan, basing this on a recent figure on the Veterans Affairs Department's website. Less than a week later, however, this same website suddenly dropped its wounded total to 21,649 without offering any explanation. When questioned, Veterans Affairs officials initially tried to dismiss the higher number as a mere clerical error. As suspicions grew, it became clear that the real reason was that the Defense and Veterans Affairs departments had used different definitions for wounded and that Veterans Affairs had lowered its total to conform to Pentagon practice.[95]

It was an explanation that scarcely satisfied the skeptics. At a time when the Pentagon's reputation for veracity was at a particular low, the antiwar blogosphere was soon awash with claims that the government was trying to massage the figures. Some continued to question why the more than seventy-three thousand veterans who had "sought treatment for mental problems like post-traumatic stress disorder" were nowhere to be found in either total. Others placed their own estimates beside official statistics, claiming that the real casualty total was more than triple the figure provided by the military.[96] Ted Rall, the political cartoonist, even depicted a soldier carrying a badly wounded comrade to a helicopter. Beneath, the caption read: "You don't count as war dead unless you die IN Iraq. If you die in Germany, or even on the plane leaving Baghdad, you're not counted." According to Rall, this particular accounting trick reduced the official KIA figure by more than seven thousand.[97]

Change, 2007–11

As America voted in the 2006 midterm elections, even the official casualty figures were bleak enough. In October, when the political campaign reached its climax, American troops suffered their third bloodiest month of the war—a grim statistic that clearly worried Republicans. "The really big issue here is Iraq," admitted one GOP consultant. "A large segment of the American people are frustrated by Iraq and impatient about it. That's definitely hurting Republicans politically. It's probably 80 percent of all our problems." Polls supported this conclusion. After the Democrats duly won control of Congress, one analysis found that "a state's casualty rate of five casualties per million residents cost the Republican candidate about five percentage points at the ballot box."[98]

To some extent, and somewhat paradoxically, this drubbing at the polls helped Bush during his last two years in office. The day after the election Rumsfeld finally resigned. Robert M. Gates, his successor, was a less polarizing figure who would work more comfortably with Democrats; he was also willing to sanction a strategy change. With Petraeus in command, in early 2007 the American military launched a "surge" in Iraq, sending thirty thousand additional troops and using them principally to protect Iraqi civilians from the insurgents.

In the first half of 2007 American troops went on the offensive. Rather than prioritizing their own security, they were encouraged to take risks. Instead of remaining in their well-protected Humvees, they were now, as one general explained, "literally putting boots on the ground." American troops were even sent into hitherto no-go Baghdad neighborhoods like Doura, despite the obvious danger. "Doura was a meatgrinder," complained one soldier, as was much of Iraq—a judgment confirmed by the stark numbers. With the surge gathering pace, U.S. forces were subject to 180 attacks a day, and casualty figures rose accordingly: 71 KIA in March, 96 in April, and 120 in May.[99]

It was all so different from Vietnam, despite the growing temptation of many critics to stress the parallels between the two "quagmire" wars. After all, in 1969

Nixon had responded to flagging domestic support by withdrawing troops and instructing those that remained to avoid excessive losses. After numerous permutations, Nixon's low-casualty obsession had morphed into Rumsfeld's attempt to focus on technology and speed, rather than mass armies. Now that Rumsfeld was gone, however, this particular way of war was being discarded. In late 2007 Bush was prepared to listen to generals who wanted more men in Iraq. Unlike Nixon, he was also ready to sanction a mission change that put these men in harm's way.

As the violence escalated and casualties grew, the domestic response was predictable. The media renewed its interest in the story. In and around Baghdad, war correspondents faced a situation that was as dangerous as ever. Although largely for this reason news organizations continued to rely heavily on Iraqi staffers, these locals were under clear instructions to focus on stories of interest to the American audience. They therefore reported on the day-to-day violence suffered by GIs and marines, rather than the problems faced by Iraqi civilians. And their stories duly found their way to American screens. Indeed, while the cable news networks spent almost a quarter of their time on the surge, reports of the fighting "averaged thirty minutes of coverage . . . on the three network evening newscasts" between January and September 2007.[100]

Back home, support for the war threatened to collapse entirely. In May 76 percent said the war was going badly, 61 percent thought the United States should never have gotten involved, and only 30 percent approved of the job Bush was doing. On Capitol Hill, high-profile Republicans started to voice their doubts. "The costs and risks of continuing down the current path," declared Sen. Richard Lugar (R-IN) in June, "outweigh the potential benefits that might be achieved of doing so." Even Sen. John McCain (R-AZ), perhaps the surge's highest profile congressional supporter, now talked of being "sick at heart by the terrible price we've paid for nearly four years of mismanaged war."[101]

For the Democrats this rapidly shifting situation provoked mixed feelings. While the war's growing unpopularity provided party presidential hopefuls with an excellent opportunity in the upcoming 2008 election, Democratic congressional leaders faced a quandary. Simply put, these leaders wanted to oppose, but not own, the war. They wanted the fighting to an end but were leery about being blamed for the war being lost.[102] On Capitol Hill the Democratic response was therefore rhetorical rather than substantive. Although party leaders pushed through a vote condemning the surge, they insured it was nonbinding. They also shied away from any action that could be construed as endangering the troops who were still fighting.

Campaign speeches by the junior senator from Illinois symbolized this dual nature of the Democrats' opposition. Barack Obama rose to national prominence partly because he had condemned the war from the outset. In 2007 he was eager to focus on the war's tragic cost. "Families have lost loved ones," he observed on MSNBC. "But the best thing that we can do for those families," he carefully added, "is to make sure that for those young men and women who are still there, we are coming up with the most effective strategy, compatible with our national security."[103]

As his campaign gathered momentum, Obama continued this twin track. He was *the* antiwar candidate, Obama stressed to the Democratic base throughout the primaries: the only one with a pure record of opposition to Bush's war of choice. But, Obama hastened to explain, he was not opposed to all war. In fact he was anxious to build a relationship with the armed forces, in order to resolve the ongoing conflict in Afghanistan. This was the forgotten war of the Bush years, the war of necessity, as Obama described it. Afghanistan and Pakistan, Obama stressed in a major campaign speech in March 2008, were where the 9/11 attacks had been planned, where extremism still posed "its greatest threat," and where "bin Laden and his lieutenants still hide."[104]

After winning the election, Obama was determined to reorient American policy toward Afghanistan. With Petraeus's surge stabilizing the situation in Iraq, Obama's first months in office were dominated by an internal strategy review on Afghanistan, which generated two conflicting—and familiar—positions. The more politically attuned officials, such as Vice President Joe Biden, thought the public would not accept the higher casualties that would inevitably accompany a new surge. Rather than employ large numbers of troops to protect the Afghan population from the Taliban, Biden wanted to deploy a limited number of special forces and counterterrorism teams to target Al Qaeda. Many senior military officers dissented; they pushed strongly for more boots on the ground. Although conceding that this might result in a short-term spike in casualties, they argued that trying to muddle through with insufficient numbers would ultimately prove costlier. "Failure to provide adequate resources," concluded the senior Afghan commander, " . . risks a longer conflict, greater casualties, higher overall costs, and ultimately, a critical loss of political support."[105]

While Obama instinctively inclined toward Biden, his own political antennae pushed him toward supporting the military, who were asking for forty thousand more troops. To an inexperienced commander in chief, the consequences of flatly turning down the military were certainly unappealing, but Obama did not cave in entirely.[106] Although he agreed to send thirty thousand fresh troops, he carefully circumscribed their mission. Instead of nation-building, they would simply seek "to disrupt, dismantle, and defeat Al Qaida in Afghanistan and Pakistan." They would do so within a limited time frame, handing over to indigenous Afghan forces by the summer of 2011.

In announcing this decision, Obama took the American people back to 9/11—to the terrorist attacks, the civilian casualties, and the sense of unity that had emerged all those years before. Bush had squandered this unity, Obama declared, on his unnecessary war in Iraq. Now it was vital for the nation to come together, in one final push in Afghanistan. In an effort to heal the fractures of Bush's wars, Obama also signaled that he shared the nation's pain at the losses of the past eight years. Of course, so had Bush—but his private mourning had been roundly criticized. Obama was determined to be different. When announcing his Afghan surge, Obama flaunted his own casualty actions. "As president," he pointed out,

> I have signed a letter of condolence to the family of each American who gives their life in these wars. I have read the letters from the parents and spouses of those who deployed. I've visited our courageous wounded warriors at Walter Reed. I've traveled to Dover to meet the flag-draped caskets of eighteen Americans returning home to their final resting place. I see firsthand the terrible wages of war. If I did not think that the security of the United States and the safety of the American people were at stake in Afghanistan, I would gladly order every single one of our troops home tomorrow.[107]

The resulting fight in Afghanistan was neither easy nor popular. American forces suffered 266 fatalities in 2010 and a further 440 in 2011. Support also dropped precipitously, down below the 40 percent range by the fall of 2010, from which it never recovered.[108] Still, by defining the Afghan mission narrowly, Obama was able to achieve a major success just before his self-imposed deadline.

In the spring of 2011, almost ten years after the terrorist attacks that started the war, Obama sent in a squad of navy SEALs to get bin Laden. With no American losses, the Al Qaeda leader was killed. On May 1 Obama addressed the nation. He again emphasized how painful all the casualties had been, but he stressed that at least the sacrifices in his own war had not been in vain. "On nights like this one," he intoned, "we can say to those families who have lost loved ones to Al Qaida's terror: Justice has been done."[109]

Conclusion

On September 11, 2011, Barack Obama and George W. Bush stood side by side as the nation remembered the terrorist attacks a decade earlier. While their physical proximity implied that wartime politics stopped at the water's edge, Bush's brief and somber comments suggested that American leaders had publicly confronted war's human cost in a similar manner across the centuries. Turning to the greatest of all American war leaders, Bush read out a letter Abraham Lincoln had written to a widow of five sons killed in the Civil War. "President Lincoln," Bush observed, "not only understood the heartbreak of his country, he also understood the cost of sacrifice and reached out to console those in sorrow."[1]

Although this was a deeply moving moment, on close inspection its political symbolism had a jarring quality. Politics, after all, rarely stops at the water's edge, and presidents have not always handled its human cost in the same way. In their time in the White House, Bush and Obama were prime examples of both traits. Not only did they clash over the necessity of the Iraq War, they also represented two very different models of how presidents deal publicly with casualties.

Mobilizers and Mourners

As president, Bush's instinct was to refer publicly to casualties when trying to mobilize the population. In this sense his harking back to Lincoln was ironic but apt. It was ironic because both Bush and Lincoln shied away from public displays of grief. When they reached out to those who suffered a loss, it was in private letters and meetings—at least until Bush read Lincoln's letter at the 9/11 memorial. It was apt because the central purpose of their public references about casualties was the same. Both sought to stress that the sacrifices would be worthwhile—that, as Lincoln famously put it in his Gettysburg Address, "these dead shall not have died in vain."[2] Indeed, along with Wilson, Roosevelt, and Truman, these presidential mobilizers insisted publicly that their wars fulfilled a deeper purpose: the safeguarding and spreading of liberty. But often their references to casualties had a more prosaic quality. On a variety of occasions they emphasized that losses in recent battles, however large, had brought the day of victory closer—that, as Roosevelt declared in the summer of 1944, they helped the United States "achieve the impossible."[3]

Obama did not ignore this mobilization model, but the balance of his public actions often tilted toward a newer concept: the president as "mourner in chief" as well as commander in chief. This model was not entirely new. Indeed, Lincoln's Gettysburg Address was delivered next to a military cemetery. Eighty years later Roosevelt, the next president to visit a war zone, also paid public tribute at the graves of GIs killed in the first North African battles. But these earlier events were exceptions. Not until the Vietnam era and its immediate aftermath did Johnson, Reagan, and Clinton try, to varying degrees, to feel, channel, and give expression to the nation's pain. In public they empathized with relatives' grief and attended military funerals. Obama followed suit. Indeed, when he was photographed saluting as flag-draped coffins returned home, he was merely playing out a presidential role that had developed in the past thirty-five years, albeit one that had atrophied during the Bush presidency.

The reasons for these two different models are not difficult to discern. All presidents who face long and costly wars need to sustain popular support. As a number of historians have observed, whenever domestic morale threatens to buckle under the weight of mounting casualties, governments have not stood

Figure C.1 Unlike Bush, Obama allowed the publication of photographs of returning coffins. In October 2009 he even publicly attended the return of eighteen men recently killed in Afghanistan. Official White House photograph.

idly by. Rather, they have tried to "remobilize" the home front, devising more eye-catching goals that turn the war into some sort of crusade for basic American values.[4] But this is not the only way mobilization has operated. As well as using new rhetorical strategies to numb the pain of large losses, presidential mobilizers have used casualties to insist that the war can and must be won. Even the "mourners" have seen this necessity. Lyndon Johnson, the first president to tell his compatriots just how heavily every loss of life weighed on his mind, also spoke constantly of how American casualties were allowing the United States to progress toward inevitable and vital victory in Vietnam.

More recently, however, as the American debate has become ever more fixated on whether the public will tolerate high casualties, presidents have often felt the need to go beyond such statements. In an age of 24/7 breaking news, the White House is asked, as a matter of course, to comment on the fresh losses in recent battles. The media, too, increasingly frames its casualty coverage around moving biographies of the fallen and searing interviews with their next of kin. In a culture ever more geared toward public displays of grief, presidents feel the pressure to take the lead. Hence the instinct to mobilize has been accompanied by a demand to mourn. And those who try to buck the trend pay a stiff price.

Bush certainly did. In his defense, he cited various practical reasons for not publicly seeking to console the families of the fallen. These relatives needed time and space to grieve without presidential interference, Bush insisted. In his memoirs he referred to numerous occasions when he met privately with widows of the dead or the wounded in hospitals. But, he added, to single out some in public would not be fair to those he had no opportunity to mention. Bush's critics, however, adopted a more jaundiced view of his actions. Some accused him of being isolated from the most painful aspect of war. Others alleged that he was deliberately downplaying the extent of U.S. casualties for brazenly political reasons.[5]

The Political and the Practical

This clash between Bush's reference to practical constraints and his critics' insistence on political motives is not a new phenomenon. It has been a recurring theme throughout America's wars.

The critics clearly have a point. All presidents act with one eye fixed firmly on the electoral calendar. In 2003 Bush's reluctance to meet with relatives or allow pictures of returning coffins suggested a clear desire to minimize the public's awareness of the war's cost in the run-up to a presidential election. Nor, if this were his aim, would Bush have been unusual. In 1972 the intensely political Nixon worked hard to ensure that actual U.S. casualties in Vietnam dropped to zero before election day. During the 1964 campaign Johnson repeatedly downplayed the level of American military activity in Vietnam and carefully shied away from any association with the dead and wounded. Before that, both Roosevelt and Truman were sensitive to casualty accounting during the closing stages of presidential campaigns. Indeed, while Roosevelt postponed a bookkeeping change that would have increased the casualty total by about twenty thousand until after the 1944 vote, Truman tried to get the military to differentiate between fatalities and casualties just weeks before the 1952 election.

In earlier wars, moreover, such political motivations were not confined to the politicians. Although generals have no elections to fight, they do have careers to protect and reputations to burnish, both of which can be damaged by bloody battles. As a result generals also have an incentive to mute the impact of high casualties. Perhaps this explains why, during World War I, Pershing's basic preference was to provide the public with as little casualty information as possible. It was certainly the reason for MacArthur's persistent efforts to spin the figures during World War II and Korea—as shown by his tendency to release losses on the same day as major victories or announce American casualties alongside a far bigger enemy toll.

Given the level of cynicism that has entered the political discourse since Vietnam and Watergate, few would be surprised by the notion that the government has, from time to time, intentionally minimized the number of American battlefield losses. But in fact this has not been its only motivation. Surprisingly, officials have sometimes had clear political incentives for doing the exact opposite: making the public fully aware of the bloodiness of war. The fall and winter of 1943 was one such occasion. With the Roosevelt administration fearful that the public was too complacent about the prospects for victory, many officials engaged in a concerted effort to publicize the reality of war. While the military allowed the press to publish pictures of dead American soldiers, James Byrnes briefed reporters about the prospect of hundreds of thousands of fresh casualties in the next few months.

Byrnes's press briefing was not just a perverse attempt to worry the public about upcoming losses. On closer inspection it also reveals another important point: casualty reporting has stemmed from error as well as design. Clearly Byrnes did not intend the press to report that half a million new casualties were in the offing. Nor did he anticipate the savage reaction from other government departments and the press that would greet his prediction. His press briefing was a mistake, pure and simple, and he immediately set about trying to limit the damage. But Byrnes was by no means unique. In October 1967, at a particular low point of the Vietnam War, Johnson was shocked to learn that the Pentagon had announced that casualties had now passed 100,000. As Johnson lectured his senior officials, this announcement was a major blunder because it misleadingly inflated the total by including thousands whose wounds were so light they had been able to return to duty.

To emphasize these episodes is not to claim that the government has been crassly incompetent rather than cynically political. It is, instead, to suggest that often the principal reason why the government's casualty reporting has not always been prompt or accurate is that the task is inherently complex—and mistakes are easily made.

Over time, to be sure, the government has instituted major improvements. After establishing an effective media system during World War I, the military retained its core elements during the wars of the 1940s and 1950s. It also embraced new technologies to speed up the whole process of gathering casualty information, using IBM tabulators in World War II, state-of-the-art electrical messaging in the Korea, and the Internet in Iraq. Above all, casualty reporting became more efficient for the simple reason that the military became more firmly ensconced in the American state. At the turn of the twentieth century the War and Navy departments were still run on a skeleton-staff basis. Fifty years later not only had they been unified in a single Defense Department; they were now so big they were spilling out of the massive Pentagon structure into other buildings in and around the capital.

Still, even with all of these steadily accruing advantages, the military has always found casualty reporting a tough job. To begin with, it has to ascertain precisely who has fallen. Under the enormous stress of battlefield conditions, it has sometimes lacked sufficient qualified personnel to undertake this grisly job. During the great Normandy campaign in 1944, for example, some units were involved in such fierce and sustained combat that they provided no casualty figures for about a month. When Patton then spearheaded the breakout that led to the liberation of Paris, his command, as one official investigation revealingly recorded, provided no "reliable daily casualty estimates" for two weeks, "for all priorities went to operations."[6] In the aftermath of a retreat or a defeat, moreover, the enemy controls the battlefield. American troops find it difficult to recover bodies. They also have to wait to see who will make it back to friendly lines and who has been taken prisoner. Such problems were particularly acute during the Korean War retreats of 1950–51, and they helped to account for the long delay in publishing accurate totals at these crucial periods of fierce fighting.

Once the totals have been computed, the military then has to decide who to include in each category. Should it announce only those killed in battle? What about those victims of accidents and other noncombat incidents? The wounded category is just as problematic. By only including flesh wounds, the military has long ignored psychological casualties—the estimated extra 25–30 percent during the Normandy campaign of 1944 or the large numbers of post-traumatic stress victims of the Vietnam and Iraq wars. Over time, though, its handling of minor and noncombat wounds has differed: during the world wars and Korea neither was included in all the totals. Then in 1965 the Pentagon adopted a new practice. As well as providing a separate list of battle and non-battle casualties, it also included all types of flesh wound, even those not serious enough for hospitalization—much to Johnson's chagrin in October 1967 when he discovered this was the reason why the Vietnam casualty total was so high.

Even after the military has decided precisely what to include in each category, it still has to package the information for public consumption, but without revealing vital intelligence. In 1918, following suggestions from the British and French Allies, the AEF staggered the publication of casualty lists so that the Germans could not connect individual totals with a particular operation. In 1965 the MACV adopted a slightly different system. Alongside staggered lists, it published daily reports on specific battles, but these only used the terms "light," "moderate," or "heavy" so that the communists could not piece together the precise toll of any single engagement.[7]

At the same time the military has not wanted to upset the next of kin. For this reason it has insisted on delaying the release of names until families have been informed. It has also repeatedly reminded the media of the "the sensitivity of using names of individual casualties or photographs" until the next of kin have been notified. Often too, it has used censorship or heavy persuasion to prevent the publication of graphic images that would cause anguish to relatives.

These practical constraints are crucial because they provide other voices in the polity with grounds to complain about, or even challenge, the official figures. For a start, the complex task of ascertaining who has fallen on the battlefield takes time. But the media is desperate for a story each day—or, at a time of 24/7 breaking news, after each ad break. If the government fails to provide timely information, news organizations have a tendency to look elsewhere. Most obviously during the Iraq War they could use Al Jazeera pictures of American dead, wounded, or captured. But this is not a new phenomenon. It even happened during the "good war," when the enemy was the hated Axis powers whose propaganda machinery spewed out misinformation on a regular basis. In the winter of 1941/42, when the Roosevelt administration failed to provide details of the Pearl Harbor casualties, many newspapers turned to Japanese propagandists. Three years later, when the Pentagon imposed a blackout on stories about the Battle of the Bulge, even many mainstream titles printed German figures of American losses. Needless to say, on both occasions the figures were much higher than the reality U.S. officials revealed later.

To make matters worse, however hard the government strives for accuracy, its casualty figures are likely to be soft at the edges. Critics therefore have various opportunities to allege that officials are deliberately misleading the nation. Not surprisingly, opposition politicians have often been in the vanguard. Korea and Iraq were prime examples: both were fought at a time of vicious partisan brawling, and in both wars prominent legislators accused the government of covering up the true human cost of the fighting. In 1951 Republicans constantly questioned why the Truman administration omitted non-battle casualties from its figures, claiming that by so doing it was consciously concealing about sixty thousand wounded fighting men from the total. Just over fifty years later the Democrats similarly asked why the Bush administration refused to include returning soldiers with psychological wounds, charging that as a result its casualty announcements did "not accurately reflect the true toll that this war has taken on the American people."[8]

While the intensity of partisan conflict has been a major reason for the level of skepticism directed at official casualty figures, it has not been the only cause. During the early stages of the Vietnam War, Johnson enjoyed surprisingly high levels of bipartisan support, but he still could not avoid growing claims that he was covering up the reality of war. This was partly because of the way he took the country to war. In earlier conflicts Wilson, Roosevelt, and Truman had committed the United States fully to the fight only after a clear-cut act of aggression: the German U-boat sinkings in 1917, the Japanese attack on Pearl Harbor in 1941, and the North Korean invasion of a U.S. ally in 1950. In 1965, however, the situation was different. Johnson used the congressional resolution passed after the earlier Tonkin Gulf incident to provide him with political cover, but apart from that he went to war quietly, without a major and direct provocation from North Vietnam. When the Tonkin Gulf incident then proved to be far murkier than the administration had claimed, question marks started to hover over the veracity of all official information, including casualty totals. It was a process that would be repeated in 2003, when Bush took the United States to war on the back of claims that Iraq possessed WMD. When these claims proved false, domestic support for the war did not suddenly collapse. But media critics and congressional Democrats did start to doubt any public information emanating from the White House and Pentagon, from the overall totals of KIA and WIA to details about what had happened to high-profile casualties.

Success and Failure

The result was a series of casualty debates, which were rarely based on accurate official information. On a number of occasions government figures were tardy, too low, or even too high. Often the media challenged these official totals; at certain moments it even published enemy claims about American casualties. Almost always the partisan opposition claimed that the government was responsible, if not for excessive losses, then for trying to conceal the bloody reality of its war.

When the government has got things wrong, the consequences have been particularly pronounced. Indeed, at tense moments, all this sound and fury surrounding casualties created powerful spasms of panic. During the Battle of the Bulge, for instance, speculation of a hundred thousand fresh casualties was accompanied by growing pressure to reformulate the unconditional surrender war aim. In the wake of exaggerated stories that China's intervention in the Korean War had resulted in a bloodbath, two-thirds of the public suddenly wanted to pull U.S. troops out of Korea as soon as possible.

In both cases, as the battlefield situation stabilized and the true scale of American losses was reported, so the sense of panic started to fade. But these brief spasms still had lingering effects. During the Korean War, Truman's own personal approval ratings never recovered from the low administered by China's intervention. The controversy over casualties also left a strong impression that Korea was a particularly costly war. In 1952 this impression helped to sweep in the Republican Party to victory. In the longer term, it insured that the Korean legacy lingered in the public mind.

Other wars had similar casualty-driven syndromes. After the guns fell silent in 1918 the prevailing popular mood was even more vehemently antiwar. With the sudden end of censorship, coupled with the government's continued announcements of fresh casualties, most Americans reached the straightforward conclusion that modern war was so bloody it ought to be avoided at all costs. Something similar happened fifty-five years later, when a fragile agreement ended the United States' searing involvement in the Vietnam War. For the next thirty years, the public was gripped by an equally intense impulse to avoid future military interventions.

In short, then, casualty debates have often mattered. They have influenced the public's support for war at key periods, shaped the dynamics of certain presidential election campaigns, and underpinned the country's longer-term attitude toward the use of force. But the government has not been entirely powerless. Under certain conditions, it has been able to mute the domestic impact of large losses and thereby maintain an impressive degree of domestic unity. What are these conditions?

Presidential mobilization is a key prerequisite. Those presidents who cogently demonstrate that the war is progressing well and that casualties are being sustained for a victorious cause tend to emerge politically unscathed. Roosevelt is the prime example. In 1944 his fourth-term bid coincided with one of the bloodiest phases of World War II, as the Allies invaded Normandy and U.S. forces pushed across the Pacific. Despite the lengthening casualty lists, Roosevelt could plausibly stress that these battles were having a decisive impact on the course of the war. It was all very different to the election campaigns in 1952 and 1968, when Roosevelt's Democratic successors were exposed to the charge that they were asking Americans to "die for a tie."[9]

So far, so familiar: the idea that success works is hardly novel. It is also similar to Feaver's argument that Americans will tolerate significant numbers of casualties if they are convinced that progress is being made—an argument that influenced Bush's rhetoric in 2005 and 2006.[10] But this is by no means the only crucial variable. Presidents, after all, rarely exert absolute authority over their entire administrations. Most obviously they tend to give the military the job of regulating the media's access to battlefield stories. The military in turn has adopted one of three basic approaches: control, co-option, or informal guidance.

On the surface, total control appears the most promising way of deadening the impact of battlefield death, but the reality has been quite different. When the military completely clamps down on information—as it did three of the twentieth century's biggest battles, the Ludendorff Offensive, the Battle of the Bulge, and China's intervention in the Korean War—the media tends to bristle at what the *New York Times* dubbed in 1918 "an arbitrary and stupid censorship."[11] Moreover, rather than remain mute, media organizations invariably turn to sources other than the government. After China entered the Korean War, for instance, many newspapers speculated or pedaled rumor. In the midst of the Battle of the Bulge some even published inflated enemy figures.

Nor, at the other end of the spectrum, have informal guidelines worked much better. The popular conventional wisdom surrounding media coverage of the Vietnam War contains many myths. It was not the case that television beamed hours of images of battlefield death into American living rooms: the equipment was too bulky and advertisers too nervous for that to happen on a regular basis. But, as had also happened during the first six months of the Korean War, the absence of censorship did allow many reporters to print stories of savage firefights, disillusioned GIs, and the "slaughterhouse" of war.[12] As such, total press freedom clearly magnified the domestic impact of American losses.

The only time the military has exerted effective control over war correspondents, and their casualty-related stories, has been when it has co-opted them. This was the goal in 1918, when Palmer set up the first military press camp with the aim of developing an understanding between journalists and soldiers. It was repeated in 1942, when the U.S. military relied heavily on its World War I system. It was then revived in a modern form in 2003, when the Pentagon embedded its accredited correspondents in particular units. On each occasion, because many reporters came to understand the problems and dangers GIs faced on the battlefield, they tended to be more cautious about what they wrote. In 1918 they were "enthusiastically" silent about the American units who suffered the heaviest casualties. Ninety years later only 21 percent of embedded TV reporters' stories focused on combat coverage, and not one showed an American casualty of war.[13]

For both the White House and the military, however, even demonstrating progress and embedding correspondents are not sufficient on their own. In fact, neither initiative is likely to work if officials acquire a reputation for spinning, manipulating, or even lying. This is the most obvious lesson of Vietnam and Iraq. On both occasions, the growing sense that Johnson and Bush had misled the country into war exerted a deeply corrosive effect over their governments' entire publicity efforts, including their reporting of casualty figures.

Instead of trying to spin, governments have been more effective when they have tried to depoliticize the whole casualty publicity process. In 1969 Melvin Laird was correct to advise Nixon that he ought to treat the casualties sustained during Johnson's war as a "sunk cost," which an administration committed to unity ought to avoid mentioning. It was a suggestion that the instinctively political Nixon completely ignored—ultimately to his own expense, because the increasing Democratic sniping at his Vietnam policy gradually reduced his room for maneuver. Other presidents have been shrewder. At key moments, Roosevelt, Truman, and Obama all worked with Republicans or nonpartisans in the Pentagon. In the heat of political battle, these commanders in chief did not always thank their advisors for standing above the fray, especially when in 1944 a Republican war secretary and in 1952 a nonpartisan defense secretary resisted White House pressure to tinker with the casualty accounting methods just weeks before an election. But herein lay their strength. As well as immunizing their political masters from partisan attack, they helped to protect the White House from misguided electoral maneuvers.

Some generals have performed an even more important function. During World War II Marshall's enormous influence on Capitol Hill provided Roosevelt with further political cover, but this was by no means his only asset. As well as organizing the American army, George C. Marshall was more than eager to inform his boss of the cost of war. "It must be remembered," Marshall once told an interviewer, that

> the military responsibility in operations is very, very large, and it has with it a terrible measure of casualties. I know I was always very careful to send Mr. Roosevelt every few days a statement of our casualties and it was done in a very effective way, graphically and . . . in colors, so it would be quite clear to him when he only had a moment or two to consider. I tried to keep before him all the time the casualty results because you get hardened to these things and you have to be very careful to keep them always in the forefront of your mind.[14]

This is indeed a crucial point to remember. It is not only top policy makers who are apt to become hardened to the human cost of war. Often, propagandists are preoccupied with how the numbers look to the public, news organizations are obsessed with getting the bottom-line figure for their next edition, and opposition politicians are intent on accusing the government of covering up the human cost. Still, casualties are not just numbers or images to be manipulated at will. Each one is a tragedy—a life curtailed, a family left grieving, a community made emptier. As Marshall understood, this is the most important wartime lesson of all, and it needs to be at the forefront of leaders' minds whenever they commit the nation to battle.

ABBREVIATIONS

In notes, *NYT* for *New York Times*; *LATimes* for *Los Angeles Times*; *WP* for *Washington Post*; *WSJ* for *Wall Street Journal*

AEF	American Expeditionary Force
AP	Associated Press
ASF	Army Service Forces
BPR	Bureau of Public Relations
CPI	Committee on Public Information
JCS	Joint Chiefs of Staff
KIA	Killed in Action
MACV	Military Advisory Command Vietnam
MBS	Mutual Broadcasting System
MHI	Military History Institute
MIA	Missing in Action
NSC	National Security Council
NSF	National Security File
NVN	North Vietnamese
OF	Office File
OFF	Office of Facts and Figures
OGR	Office of Government Reports
OWI	Office of War Information
PAVN	People's Army of North Vietnam
POW	Prisoner of War
PSF	President's Secretary's File
SHAEF	Supreme Headquarters Allies Expeditionary Force
SMOF	Staff Member and Office Files

UN	United Nations
UP	United Press
VC	Viet Cong
WHCF	White House Central Files
WIA	Wounded in Action
WMD	Weapons of Mass Destruction

NOTES

Introduction

1. Fletcher and Gerhart, "In Pre-Dawn Darkness, Obama Salutes Victims of War," *WP*, October 30, 2009; Meyer and Parsons, "Obama Honors Fallen Soldiers at Dover Base," *Chicago Tribune*, October 30, 2009; editorial, "The Commander's Duty Done," *NYT*, October 30, 2009.
2. "Liz Cheney Slams Obama Photo-Op," Free Republic, website, October 29, 2009; "Limbaugh: Obama Visit to Dover Base a 'Photo Op,'" Fox News, website, November 1, 2009.
3. Katz, "Public Opinion and Foreign Policy," 498.
4. Mueller, *Wars, Presidents, and Public Opinion*; and "Iraq Syndrome," 44. For a summary of recent literature and its impact on conventional wisdom, see Gelpi, Feaver, and Reifler, *Paying the Human Costs*, 1–2, although the book itself is a sustained challenge to the Mueller thesis.
5. See, for instance, Jentleson, "Pretty Prudent Public," 49–73; Feaver and Gelpi, *Choosing Your Battles*.
6. See, for instance, Larson, *Casualties and Consensus*.
7. See, for example, Gartner and Segura, "War, Casualties, and Public Opinion," 278–300.
8. One exception to this scholarly neglect is Giangreco, "'Spinning the Casualties,'" 22–29. But in chaps. 2 and 3 in this book I challenge this article in numerous ways.
9. Leland and Oboroceanu, "American War and Military Operations Casualties."
10. "Casualties Explained"; "Pentagon Gives Revised Listings," both in *NYT*, November 14 and December 4, 1952.
11. Faust, *This Republic of Suffering*, 14, 102–5, 118–22, 252–53; Sledge, *Soldier Dead*, 33, 37, 97.
12. Nenninger, *Leavenworth Schools and the Old Army*.
13. "History of the Dog Tag."

Chapter 1

1. Link, *Campaigns for Progressivism and Peace*, 106–11, 390–416; Cooper, *Wilson*, 375–97; Wilson, "An Unpublished Prolegomenon to a Peace Note," November 25, 1916, in Link, *Wilson Papers*, 40:67–70.
2. Tumulty, *Wilson As I Knew Him*, 256.
3. The general staff actually consisted of forty-one officers, but a law prevented more than half from being in the capital at any one time.
4. Of course this battle was short only in the World War I context. Civil War battles like Shiloh, Antietam, or Gettysburg had lasted just a few days.
5. Foster, *Studies in America's News*, 273.

6. Philpott, *Bloody Victory*, 94; Stevenson, *1914–1918*, 162, 168.

7. On Britain, see "Military Press Control: A History of the Work of MI7, 1914–19," WO 32/9304, UK National Archives, Kew [hereafter NA/UK]; Farrar, *News from the Front*, 13, 23, 44, 68; Thompson, *Politicians, the Press, and Propaganda*, 28–32; on France, see Collins, "Development of Censorship," 17–18; Rajfus, *La Censure*, 29–50; for general background, see Nafziger, "World War Correspondents," *Journalism Quarterly*, 229–31, 233–34; on Germany, see Goldfarb, "Words as Weapons," 470–86.

8. Collins, "Development of Censorship," 5.

9. Marquis, "Words as Weapons," 476.

10. "The Achievement on the Somme"; "German Exaggerations," both in *Times* (London), August 3, 1916, and November 22, 1916.

11. Farrar, *News from the Front*, 150; Wilson, *Myriad Faces of War*, 396.

12. Beurier, "Information, Censorship, or Propaganda?" 293–324; Reeves, "Film Propaganda," 468.

13. On American war correspondents at this time, see Crozier, *American Reporters on the Western Front*; Hohenberg, *Foreign Correspondence*, 234–37; Knightley, *First Casualty*, 116–17, 124–27.

14. Davis, "War that Lurks in the Forest of the Vosges," *NYT*, February 13, 1916. See also Stephens, "Shattered Windows," 65:66–68.

15. Link, *Campaigns for Progressivism and Peace*, 307–8; Kazin, *Godly Hero*, 247–48; "Efforts of American Pacifists to Avert War," *Literary Digest*, February 24, 1917.

16. House Diary, September 16, 1917, Link, *Wilson Papers*, 44:203; Beaver, *Baker*, 47–48; Chambers, *To Raise an Army*, 144, 150.

17. Spector, "'You're Not Going to Send Soldiers,'" 1–4.

18. Woodward, *Trial By Friendship*, 50–59; Chambers, *To Raise an Army*, 158.

19. Chambers, *To Raise an Army*, 164–67, 181–86.

20. Beaver, *Baker*, 48–49; Chambers, *To Raise an Army*, 149–50.

21. See, for instance, "The Allied Drive in Flanders"; "Why We are Not Downhearted," both in *Literary Digest*, August 11 and 25, 1917; "9,750,000 Killed, 23,500,000 Hurt, War Estimate," *Washington Times*, November 17, 1917.

22. Coffman, *War to End All Wars*, 67–68.

23. Mead, *Doughboys*, 153; Smythe, *Pershing*, 125, 142.

24. Pershing, *My Experiences*, 141–48; Stallings, *Doughboys*, 34–35; Coffman, *War to End All Wars*, 137.

25. Prior and Wilson, *Passchendaele*, 186; Stevenson, *1914–1918*, 377–85.

26. Bruce, *Fraternity of Arms*, 138; Smythe, *Pershing*, 56.

27. Stallings, *Doughboys*, 36–39; Mead, *Doughboys*, 159–64; Broun, *AEF*, 250–70.

28. Coffman, *War to End All Wars*, 144–47.

29. Nolan, Memorandum for the Chief of Staff, March 3, 1918, Entry 222, box 6110, RG 120, National Archives II.

30. Wilson, *Myriad Faces of War*, 127–28, 675.

31. Sweeney to Nolan, March 4, 1918, American Expeditionary Force (AEF), GHQ, G-2-D, Censorship Miscellaneous, Alphabetical File, Atrocities Folder, Entry 222, box 6110, RG 120; McCabe, Memo to Chief Censor, April 2, 1918, Entry 240, box 6207, RG 120.

32. Palmer, *With My Own Eyes*, 365; Mead, *Doughboys*, 163.

33. Wilson, "Bryce's Investigation," 374; Gullace, "Sexual Violence and Family Honor," 714–16.

34. McAdoo, *Crowded Years*, 374; Kennedy, *Over Here*, 105; Vaughn, *Holding Fast*, 72–81, 155–57.

35. Nolan to Chief of Staff, January 13, 1918; Sweeney to Whitney, May 31, 1918; both in AEF, GHQ, G-2-D, Censorship Miscellaneous, Alphabetical File, Atrocities Folder, Entry 222, box 6110, RG 120.

36. Wickes to Morgan, December 29, 1917, AEF, GHQ, Censorship, Press Publications Stopped Folder, Entry 221, box 6127, RG 120; Associated Press (AP), "Shells Kill More Pershing Men"; AP, "Pershing Visits Graves," both in *NYT*, November 18 and 19, 1917.

37. Smythe, *Pershing*, 3–4, 15, 25, 43.

38. Palmer, *With My Own Eyes*, 335–42; Palmer to Pershing, August 24, 1917, General Correspondence: Palmer Folder, box 153, Pershing Papers, LC; Palmer to Nolan, "Press Arrangements," undated, Entry 240, box 5913, RG 120.

39. Nolan to Chief of Staff, "Arrangements for accredited Correspondents with the U.S. Army," July 5, 1917; Palmer to Nolan, "Regulations for War Correspondents," July 7, 1917, both in Entry 240, box 5913, RG 120. "Organization of Correspondents' Camp," September 25, 1917, Entry 239, box 6212, RG 120. "Censorship Instructions for Censors," undated, Entry 221, box 6126, RG 120.

40. Palmer to Gibbons, October 31, 1917, Entry 239, box 6131, RG 120.

41. Nolan, Memorandum for the Commander in Chief, March 20, 1918, Entry 239, box 6195, RG 120.

42. Palmer, *With My Own Eyes*, 343.

43. Paragraph to Cable, attached to Nolan, Memorandum for the Chief of Staff, March 3, 1918, AEF, GHQ, G-2-D, Censorship Miscellaneous, Alphabetical File, Atrocities Folder, Entry 222, box 6110, RG 120; The British policy is summarized in Hampshire, Minute 45/Gen./4302, October 22, 1938, Publication of Lists in the Press, WO 32/15148, NA/UK.

44. Nolan, Memorandum for the Commander in Chief, March 20, 1918, Entry 239, box 6195, RG 120; "Holds Up Casualty Lists," *NYT*, April 25, 1918.

45. As the British pointed out, although the Germans could glean useful information from POWs, it was still vital not to give them confirmation in published casualty lists. General Staff, Memo on Publication of Casualties, February 29, 1916, Publication of Lists in the Press, WO 32/15148, NA/UK.

46. "Refuse to Issue Casualty Lists of Our Forces," *NYT*, March 9, 1918.

47. AP Superintendent to Frank McIntyre, March 22, 1918, C-3-7, box 9, Entry 149, RG 165.

48. Stevenson, *1914–1918*, 408–20.

49. "Casualty Lists Put Under Ban," *NYT*, April 3, 1918.

50. "Refuse to Issue Casualty Lists of Our Forces," *NYT*, March 9, 1918.

51. "The Casualty List Practice Illogical," *NYT*, March 25, 1918; *Congressional Record* 56, 3: 3754, 4110–11.

52. Corey to his Mother, November 21, 1917, box 2, Corey Papers, LC; Bass, "Notes on Mobilization of the American Press," undated [but attached to letter of December 8, 1917], Entry 222, box 6112, RG 120.

53. Williams, "Sins of the Censors," *Collier's*, January 12, 1918; editorial, "Censorship in France," *NYT*, January 15, 1918; Wickes to Morgan, February 4, 1918, Entry 240, box 5913, RG 120; Crozier, *American Reporters*, 191–93. The *NYT* hierarchy was less troubled by Williams's expulsion when they discovered that he had been moonlighting for other news organizations; see Ochs to Grasty, January 23, 1918, Grasty File, box 14, New York Times Company Records: Ochs Papers, New York Public Library.

54. Editorial, "An Inexplicable Order," *NYT*, April 4, 1918.

55. Roberts to House, December 6, 1917, General Correspondence: Roberts Folder, box 175, Pershing Papers; Barry, "Lodge Assails News Suppression," *NYT*, September 1, 1918.

56. McAdoo, *Crowded Years*, 408–9; Editorial, "Censorship in France," *NYT*, January 15, 1918; Long to Wilson, November 19, 1917, box 3, Creel Papers, LC.

57. "Cables Pershing for News of Drive," *NYT*, March 24, 1918. The actual casualty totals for each side on the first day of the offensive were just under 40,000, with the Germans suffering almost 11,000 KIA and the British a little over 7,500. See Stevenson, *With Our Backs to the Wall*, 55.

58. On rumor and casualties, see editorial, "Better Modify It," *NYT*, March 11, 1918, and "Keep Steady," *LA Times*, November 19, 1917. Senior officials also worried that the War Department was leaking stories of big impending casualties, fueling headlines like "Casualty List 'Very Large.'" See Chief Military Censor to the Adjutant General, April 11, 1918, C-3-8, box 9, Entry 149, RG 165.

59. "Give Casualty Addresses"; editorial, "A Wise Decision," both in *NYT*, May 2 and 3, 1918.

60. Palmer, *With My Own Eyes*, 368–69; Crozier, *American Reporters*, 17, 27, 29, 53, 160; Cornebise, *Stars and Stripes*, 4–5.

61. Lytton, *Press and the General Staff*, x–xi, 114; Farrar, *News from the Front*, 148, 168–74.

62. Watson to Nolan, November 21, 1917; Nolan to Chief Signal Officer, December 6, 1917, both in Entry 221, box 6126, RG 120; Watson to Sweeney, February 6, 1918; Wade to McCabe, both in July 3, 1918, Entry 221, box 6130, RG 120.

63. O'Keefe, *Thousand Deadlines*, 1.

64. Sweeney to Nolan, May 29, 1918, Entry 221, box 6130, RG 120.

65. *United States Army in the World War*, 16:87.

66. Parks to McCabe, June 27, 1918; Wade to McCabe, July 3, 1918; Nolan to Liggett, August 18, 1918; Reynolds, "Liaison in Time of Increased Activity," August 31, 1918; all in Entry 221, box 6130, RG 120.

67. Watson to Dengler, May 14, 1918, AEF, GHQ, G-2-D, Censorship Miscellaneous, Alphabetical File, Atrocities Folder, Entry 222, box 6110; "Censorship Instructions for Censors," undated, Entry 221, box 6126, both in RG 120.

68. Johnson, *Without Censor*, 292–93.

69. Mead, *Doughboys*, 252–64; Stevenson, *With Our Backs to the Wall*, 114–17.

70. This section is based on U.S. Congress, Senate, *Hearings before Military Affairs Committee: Delay in Casualty Lists*, 18–19; "Baker Asks for Casualty Lists," *LA Times*, July 27, 1918; "Report of Big Losses False," *Boston Globe*," August 4, 1918; "First Casualties from the Marne," *NYT*, August 5, 1918.

71. Smythe, *Pershing*, 185.

72. On these battles, see Braim, *Test of Battle*; Lengel, *To Conquer Hell*; Smythe, *Pershing*, 179–237; Grotelueschen, *AEF Way of War*.

73. Lengel, *To Conquer Hell*, 4, 192; Agwar to Washington, October 13, 1918, AEF Cables Sent File, Harbord Papers, LC.

74. Assistant Chief of Staff to Chief of Staff, First Army, "Summary Duties for Press Officer," November 18, 1918, (FAAEF) G-2 Folder, box 14, Drum Papers, Military History Institute, Carlisle, PA [hereafter MHI].

75. "1,453 Casualties, Largest Total for Day, Announced," *New York Herald*, October 22, 1918.

76. Pew to Reilly, October 31, 1918, Creel Correspondence, CPI-A1, Entry 1, box 20, RG 63; "Army Bureau Explains Big Casualty Lists," *San Francisco Chronicle*, October 21, 1918. See also Churchill to Kebler, October 10, 1918, Chief Military Censor Files, C-3-12, box 9, Entry 149, RG 165.

77. Watson, "Press Relations and Censorship in the AEF," January 1927, Army War College Curriculum Archives, MHI; Johnson, *Without Censor*, 154. For the closer relationship between the military and media around the battle zone, see also "The Lot of a Scribe in France Told by Philip Payne," *Editor and Publisher*, December 7, 1918; Nolan, "Draft of Unpublished History of World War I," January 17, 1935, Press-17, box 2, Nolan Papers, MHI.

78. Johnson, *Without Censor*, 176, 191; Tompkins, "News from the Front," 168–69. The War Department also asked the Adjutant General in Missouri "to refrain from giving publicity to unofficial statements" on casualties in the Thirty-fifth Division, after a stories appeared in the local press. See Churchill to Clark, October 31, 1918, N-3-649, box 23, Entry 149, RG 165.

79. "Allies Forcing Huns to Quit Belgium," *Cleveland Press*, October 2, 1918; "Battle Rages with Greatest Violence from Sea to Verdun," *New York Herald*, October 2, 1918. This paragraph is based on an analysis of a cross-section of U.S. newspapers, including the *Boston Globe, Chicago Tribune, Cleveland Press, New York Herald, NYT*, and *San Francisco Examiner*.

80. Johnson, *Without Censor*, 133.

81. "Republic Dawns in Germany," *Cleveland Press*, October 16, 1918; Benwick, "Germany Transformed Within a Week," *NYT*, November 11, 1918.

82. "Reply Offers to Quit Invaded Territory"; "President Wilson's Reply to Germany," both in *New York Herald*, October 22 and 24, 1918; "All We Fought for is Won, Says Wilson," *NYT*, November 12, 1918.

83. U.S. Congress, Senate, *Hearings before Military Affairs Committee: Delay in Casualty Lists*, 3–31.

84. "Casualties Held to Save Face of Army—Allen," *Chicago Tribune*, February 20, 1919. For background, see Ferrell, *Collapse at Meuse-Argonne*, 115–27.

85. U.S. Congress, House, *Hearings before Rules Committee: Losses of Thirty-fifth Division during the Argonne Battle,* 22, 36, 48–49; "Yanks Mowed Down by Own Artillery, Gov. Allen Charges," *Chicago Tribune,* February 18, 1919. For background, see Thirty-fifth Division Controversy Folder, box B54, Allen Papers, LC.

86. U.S. Congress, House, *Hearings before Rules Committee: Losses of Thirty-fifth Division during the Argonne Battle,* 66; Connor to Chief of Staff, April 2, 1919, Casualties Suffered by American Troops under French and American Command Folder, box 14, Drum Papers, MHI.

87. Grasty, Copy of Matter Sent to *NY Times,* January 22, 1919, box 84, Pershing Papers.

88. Palmer, *America in France,* 276; Kennedy, *Over Here,* 219–22; Huelfer, *The "Casualty Issue,"* 34–35.

89. These paragraphs are based on Leuchtenberg, *Perils of Prosperity,* 58; Knock, *To End All Wars,* 253–62; Cooper, *Wilson,* 499, 506; Huelfer, *The "Casualty Issue,"* 35.

90. *History of the American Graves Registration Service,* 12–32, 92–115; Piehler, *Remembering War,* 92–121; Meigs, *Optimism at Armageddon,* 147–48; Budreau, "Politics of Remembrance," 371–411.

91. Jonas, *Isolationism,* 1.

92. Roosevelt, *Public Papers,* August 14, 1936.

Chapter 2

1. Leff, "Politics of Sacrifice," 1296; Reynolds, *Rich Relations,* 44.

2. Dallek, *Roosevelt and American Foreign Policy,* 171–313; Farnham, *Roosevelt and the Munich Crisis,* 49–227; Casey, *Cautious Crusade,* 5–15; Reynolds, *From Munich to Pearl Harbor;* Borg, "Notes on Roosevelt's Quarantine Speech," 405–33.

3. Schneider, *Should America Go To War?* 19, 24, 37.

4. Reynolds, "1940," 325–50; Zahniser, "Rethinking the Significance of Disaster," 252–76.

5. Early to Roosevelt, August 16, 1940, box 24, Early Papers, Roosevelt Library; Cantril to Young, "America Faces the War—The Reaction of Public Opinion," undated [January 1941?], Chart 4, Office File (OF) 857, Roosevelt Papers, Roosevelt Library.

6. Cole, *Roosevelt and the Isolationists,* 380–82; Doenecke, *Storm on the Horizon,* 150–64.

7. Roosevelt, *Public Papers,* October 30, 1940; Divine, *Foreign Policy and U.S. Presidential Elections,* 65–68, 80–81.

8. Roosevelt, *Public Papers,* December 29, 1940.

9. Doenecke, *Battle Against Intervention,* 41, 139–41; Cole, *Roosevelt and the Isolationists,* 415.

10. Maris to Stimson, January 29, 1941; Marshall to Early, January 30, 1941, both in Stimson-OF, Entry 100, box 5, RG 107. AP, "Foolproof Tags to Tell All a Soldier Needs to Have Known," *WP,* January 29, 1941.

11. U.S. Senate, *Hearings before Foreign Relations Committee: To Promote the Defense of the United States,* 85, 117–21, 155–57; Edwards, "Bare More 'Steps to War'"; "Casualty Tags? Ask Brooks"; *Chicago Tribune,* January 30 and February 1, 1941.

12. Memo for Looker, "Trends of Major News and Editorial Comments, January 1–July 1 [1941]," Bureau of Public Relations (BPR): Press and News Analyses, Entry 350, box 8, RG 107.

13. On the administration's effort to keep the lend-lease hearings "as narrow as possible," see Kimball, *Most Unsordid Act,* 179–80.

14. "Evolution of the Minority," March 14, 1941, President's Secretary's File (PSF)-Dep-Treasury, Editorial Opinion, Roosevelt Papers; Kimball, *Most Unsordid Act,* 156, 228–29.

15. Gallup, "War Views of Families of Men Most Affected by Draft Shown No Different from Others in Survey," May 28, 1941, Stimson-OF, Entry 100, box 8, RG 107.

16. Bliss, *In Search of Light,* 31–44; Sevareid, *Not So Wild a Dream,* 176–79; Perisco, *Murrow,* 171–82; Calder, *Myth of the Blitz,* 209–27.

17. Sherry, *Rise of American Air Power,* 87; Reynolds, *Creation of the Anglo-American Alliance,* 50.

18. Barth to Kuhn, "Sense of Strain," June 13, 1941, PSF-Dep-Treasury, Editorial Opinion, Roosevelt Papers.

19. Roosevelt, *Public Papers*, September 11, 1941; Dallek, *Roosevelt and Foreign Policy*, 287–88.
20. Winfield, *FDR and the News Media*, 172, 191–93. For the navy's effort to stop the *New York Times* from printing details, see Sulzberger to Knox, December 10, 1941, Knox OF, 89-1-8, Entry 23, box 55, RG 80; Krock, Memo on Meeting with Hull, December 11, 1941, World War II Folder, box 274, NYT Company Records: Sulzberger Papers, New York Public Library.
21. War Department, BPR, Memorandum for the Press, December 8, 1941, Legislation and Policy Precedent Files, Casualties WW II Folder, Entry 390, box 42, RG 407.
22. War Department, BPR, "Whispering Campaign in Brooklyn, New York, Causes War Department to Issue Complete Denial," January 16, 1942, Legislative and Policy Precedent Files, Death-Notification Folder, Entry 390, box 1, RG 407.
23. Memo for Mitchell, "Columnists, January 4–10, 1942," January 26, 1942, BPR: Press and News Analyses, Entry 350, box 8, RG 107.
24. Roosevelt, *Public Papers*, December 9, 1941; Barth to Kuhn, "Meeting the Issue," December 19, 1941, PSF-Dep-Treasury, Morgenthau, Editorial Opinion, Roosevelt Papers.
25. Roosevelt, *Public Papers*, February 23, 1942; Office of Facts and Figures (OFF), "The President's 'Map' Speech Audience, March 30, 1942, OF 4619, Roosevelt Papers.
26. Kintner to MacLeish, January 21 and February 9, 1942, Office of War Information (OWI), Records of Historian, Subject File, box 11, RG 208.
27. Spector, *Eagle Against the Sun*, 100–139; Thorne, *Allies of a Kind*, 154–67; Weinberg, *World at Arms*, 310–27.
28. See, for instance, "Casualties: Just as Bloody," *Time*, August 3, 1942; Fischer, "U.S. Casualties for War, 48,956, Mostly Missing," *Chicago Tribune*, November 19, 1942. For the navy's private estimates, in which about a half of casualties were MIA, see Bureau of Naval Personnel, "War Casualties, December 7, 1941–July 1, 1942," Knox OF, 79-1-35, Entry 23, box 51, RG 80. The British also calculated that it took between 90 and 150 days to get a casualty name into the press "largely due to the choking of the channel by POWs." Kemble, Minute, January 30, 1943, Publication of Lists in the Press, WO 32/15148, NA/UK.
29. Larrabee, *Commander in Chief*, 155, 186–87; Winkler, *Politics of Propaganda*, 49.
30. Davis, "War Information and Military Security," November 19, 1942, Subject File: OWI, box 10, Davis Papers, LC.
31. AP, Wire to Editors, undated [December 1941], Censorship Folder, box 125, NYT Company Records: Sulzberger Papers; "Casualties: Just as Bloody," *Time*, August 3, 1942.
32. "Fortune Survey," [undated, but marked release on July 31, 1942] copy in PPF 5437, Roosevelt Papers; Office of Government Reports (OGR), "Weekly Analysis of Press Reaction," April 16, 1942, OF 788, Roosevelt Papers
33. OFF, Survey No.10, February 16, 1942, PSF-OFF, Roosevelt Papers; OFF, Intelligence Report, No.23, May 13, 1942, PSF-OWI, Survey of Intelligence, Roosevelt Papers. OFF, CWI, Board Meeting, April 10, 1942, OFF: Minutes of Meetings, box 52, MacLeish Papers, LC.
34. Barth to Kuhn, "The Nation Rallies," December 12, 1941, PSF-Dep-Treasury, Editorial Opinion, Roosevelt Papers; OGR, "Weekly Analysis of Press Reaction," March 6, 1942, OF 788, Roosevelt Papers.
35. OWI, Intelligence Report, Nos. 51 and 52, November 27 and December 4, 1942, PSF-OWI, Survey of Intelligence, Roosevelt Papers.
36. Reynolds, *From Munich to Pearl Harbor*, 185–86. See also Overy, *Why the Allies Won*, 190–98.
37. Matloff, *Strategic Planning*, 117; OWI, "Leading Editorial and Column Topics, December 15–21, 1942," December 22, 1942, Entry 171, box 1847, RG 44.
38. Stimson to Roosevelt, January 8, 1942; and Roosevelt's response January 13, 1942, both in PSF-Safe-War Department, Roosevelt Papers. Some senior officials worried that resulting the ninety-division army would be too small; see Matloff, "90-Division Gamble," 365–81.
39. Sainsbury, *North African Landings*, 20–21, 111; Stoler, *Politics of the Second Front*, 32–63.
40. Howe, *Northwest Africa*, 63–72, 277–83, 438–58; Atkinson, *Army at Dawn*, 33–39, 339–73; D'Este, *Patton*, 431–36, 456–58.

41. For example, Watson, "Press Relations and Censorship in the AEF," January 1927, Army War College Curriculum Archives, MHI. For a discussion of these colleges, see Winton, *Corps Commanders of the Bulge*, 13–30.

42. *Regulations for Correspondents Accompanying U.S. Army Forces in the Field*.

43. Watson, "Press Relations and Censorship in the AEF." For other efforts to digest the lessons of World War I, see the documents in Adjutant General's Office, Central Decimal File, 000.77, box 8, RG 407.

44. Censorship Office, *Code of Wartime Practices for American Broadcasters*, 3. On radio and censorship, see Sweeney, *Secrets of Victory*, 7–13, 20–21.

45. Vogel, *Pentagon*, xxii, 283–85, 296.

46. See, for instance, "The Press: Air Marker Fraud," *Time*, August 24, 1942; Surles to Hepburn, February 13, 1942, BPR File, 000.77, Entry 499, box 7, RG 165.

47. For the activities of these units, see Memoranda Re PL490, as Amended, compiled by Chief, Casualty Branch, Entry 34, box 184, RG 165; Steere and Boardman, *Final Disposition of World War II Dead*.

48. See, for instance, U.S. Congress, House of Representatives, *Hearings before Appropriations Committee, Subcommittee: Military Establishment Appropriation for 1944*, 129–31, 288–89; U.S. Congress, Senate, *Hearing before Military Affairs Committee: Veterans' Rights to Benefits*, 1–5, 17–37; U.S. Congress, House of Representatives, *Hearings before Military Affairs Committee: National Cemeteries*, 5–7.

49. "The ASF in World War II: Casualty Reporting," vol. 2, undated, box 522, Entry 97, RG 160.

50. Ibid.

51. "Army and Navy Lift Ban on Full Casualty Lists," *Editor and Publisher*, January 2, 1943. The navy also started to receive congratulations from Congress, when it began providing legislators with more up-to-date lists. See Vinson to Knox, November 2, 1943, Knox OF, 79-2-43, Entry 23, box 51, RG 80.

52. Pyle, "Attack So Sudden No One Believed It Real Thing," *Washington Daily News*, February 26, 1943. On Pyle's private views of the army, see Pyle, letter to his wife, February 21, 1943, Pyle Mss., II, Pyle Papers, Lilly Library, Indiana University. See also Tobin, *Ernie Pyle's War*, 82–83; Butcher, *My Three Years with Eisenhower*, 266.

53. AP, "Nation Steeled for Casualties by Stimson," *LA Times*, February 11, 1943; OWI, Intelligence Report, No. 64, February 26, 1943, PSF-Subject-OWI, Roosevelt Papers; Middleton, "Battle at Sbeitla," *NYT*, February 18, 1943.

54. Stimson, Address before Annual Meeting of American Society of Newspaper Editors, April 22, 1944; Radio Address, "Size of the Army," March 9, 1943; Stimson-OF, Entry 100, boxes 1 and 10, RG 107.

55. OWI, "Intelligence Report," No.63, February 19, 1943, PSF-OWI, Survey of Intelligence, Roosevelt Papers. See also Bailey to Byrnes, forwarded to Tully, February 10, 1943, PSF-Subject-EOP, Byrnes, Roosevelt Papers.

56. OWI, "Current Surveys," No.13, July 21, 1943, Entry 149, box 1715, RG 44.

57. Roeder, *Censored War*, 11–12; Board of War Information, "Minutes of Meeting," July 21, 1943, OWI, Records of Historian: Subject File, box 12, RG 208.

58. Davis, "Notes on First Day in Office," June 16, 1942; Davis, Report to the President, OWI, June 13, 1942 to September 15, 1945, 14–15, both in Subject File: OWI, box 10, Davis Papers.

59. Roeder, *Censored War*, 11–12; Surles to McClure, February 18, 1943, BPR File, 000.7, Entry 499, box 13, RG 165.

60. Roeder, *Censored War*, 11–12. See also Memorandum for Director of BPR, Pictorial Branch, September 3, 1943, BPR File, 062.1, Entry 499, box 23, RG 165; "Lifts Picture Ban on War's Realism," *NYT*, September 5, 1943; Stimson to Surles, December 7, 1943, Stimson: Safe File, Entry 499, box 11, RG 107.

61. Brinkley, *Publisher*, 205–15, 229–32, 282–83.

62. Crowl and Love, *Seizure of the Gilberts and Marshalls*, 12–17; Spector, *Eagle Against the Sun*, 256–67.

63. Knox, Press Conference, November 26, 1943, box 6, Mason Papers, Wisconsin Historical Society; "Tarawa Life Loss Heavy, Knox Warns," *NYT*, November 27, 1943.

64. "Part of Tarawa Becomes Forever a Part of America as Marine Dead are Buried," Navy Communiqué, December 6, 1943, Marine Corps, PI Division, Navy Releases, box 1, RG 127.

65. *With the Marines at Tarawa*, 1944. Pearlman, *Warmaking*, 250; Malowski, *Armed with Cameras*, 259–60.

66. Crowl and Love, *Seizure of the Gilberts and Marshalls*, 157–59.

67. Editorial, "Losses at Tarawa," *Chicago Tribune*, December 4, 1943.

68. Mason, Daily Log, December 6 and 10, 1943, Telephone Logs, box 4, Mason Papers.

69. Mason, Daily Log, December 10; "Navy Reports Cut in Tarawa Losses," *NYT*, January 6, 1944.

70. Sainsbury, *Turning Point*, 256.

71. McNaughton to Johnson, "500,000 Casualties," December 23, 1943, Time Dispatches, First Series, folder 116, Houghton Library, Harvard University.

72. McNaughton to Johnson, "500,000 Casualties"; OWI, Bureau of Special Services, "Prediction of War Casualties, December 23–31, 1943," Analysis of Public Opinion, No.30, Records of the Research Division, Entry 149, box 1712, RG 44; "Davis Says No One Knows," *WP*, December 23, 1943.

73. McNaughton to Johnson, "500,000 Casualties."

74. OWI, Bureau of Special Services, "Mediterranean Theater—Military and Political," September 29, 1943, Entry 107, box 1026, RG 44.

75. Tatman, Memorandum for the Director, WDHPR, "Supplementary Press Digest," December 21, 1943, BPR: Press and News Analyses, Entry 350, box 9, RG 107.

76. Pyle, *Brave Men*, 164–66.

77. Miller, *Story of Ernie Pyle*, 297–98; Tobin, *Pyle's War*, 137–39.

78. Flynn, *Draft*, 68–86.

79. "Selective Service as the Tide of War Turns: The 3rd Report of the Director of Selective Service, 1943–1944," 214–15, Annual Reports, Entry 43, box 1, RG 147.

80. State Department, "Public Attitudes on Foreign Policy," No.7, January 7, 1944, Foster Files, Entry 568J, box 1, RG 59. Peace Now material can be found in U.S. Congress, House of Representatives, Special Committee on Un-American Activities, *Investigation of Un-American Propaganda Activities in the U.S.: Report on the Peace Now Movement*, 7–9.

81. OWI, "Cairo and Tehran Conferences," December 7, 1943, Entry 108, box 1027, RG 44; State Department, "Public Attitudes on Foreign Policy: Increasing Demand for a More Positive Statement on Foreign Policy," No.16, March 20, 1944, Foster Files, Entry 568J, box 1, RG 59.

82. Cantril to Walker, May 8, 1944, OF 857, Roosevelt Papers.

83. *FRUS: Conference at Casablanca*, 781. See also Hastings, *Bomber Command*, 184–88; Overy, *Air War*, 1939–1945, 73–74, 204–5.

84. Craven and Cate, *Army Air Forces*, 2:277–79, 298–307; Sherry, *Rise of American Air Power*, 148–49; Miller, *Eighth Air Force*, 56–57.

85. Miller, *Eighth Air Force*, 45, 49.

86. Salisbury, *Journey for Our Times*, 195.

87. OWI Scripts, "This Is Official," July 11, 1943, Entry 146, box 765, RG 208.

88. Roosevelt to Sikorski, July 3, 1942, PSF-Diplomatic-Poland, Roosevelt Papers.

89. Schaffer, "American Military Ethics," 321; Schaffer, *Wings of Judgment*, 61; Crane, *Bombs, Cities, Civilians*, 28, 33; Sherry, *Rise of American Air Power*, 144; Roeder, *Censored War*, 84; Roosevelt, *Public Papers*, September 17, 1943.

90. OGR, "Weekly Analysis of Press Reaction," May 8, 1942, OF 788; "Weekly Analysis of Press Reaction," August 7, 1942, OF 5015, both in Roosevelt Papers. See also Sherry, *Rise of American Air Power*, 138–39.

91. OWI, "Intelligence Report," No.66, March 12, 1943, PSF-OWI, Survey of Intelligence, Roosevelt Papers.

92. Miller, *Eighth Air Force*, 7.

93. Eaker to Arnold, June 29, 1943, Eighth Air Force Correspondence: Arnold Folder, box I:17, Eaker Papers, LC.

94. Craven and Cate, *Army Air Forces*, 2:696–706; Sherry, *Rise of American Air Power*, 157–58.

95. These paragraphs are based on the detailed report, Lyon to Hoyt, undated [October 1943], BPR File, 000.7, Entry 499, box 16, RG 165.

96. Arnold to the BPR Director, "Proposed Revision of Policy on Release of Information of AAF Combat Missions," January 2, 1944, BPR File, 000.7, Entry 499, box 33, RG 165. Arnold had long pushed for a change to air force communiqués to shift the focus from U.S. losses; see Arnold to Eaker, June 29, 1943, Eighth Air Force Correspondence: Arnold Folder, box I:17, Eaker Papers. For the Eighth Army's broader reappraisal, see Craven and Cate, *Army Air Forces*, 2:712–20.

97. Director of the BPR to Commanding General, AAF, January 10, 1944, BPR File, 000.7, Entry 499, box 33, RG 165.

98. Fitzgerald to Surles, January 7, 1944, BPR File, 000.7, Entry 499, box 33, RG 165.

99. Westlake, Memo for Chief of Air Staff, March 7, 1944, BPR File, 000.7, Entry 499, box 39, RG 165.

100. Craven and Cate, *Army Air Forces*, 3:9–13, 43, 46–47.

Chapter 3

1. Churchill to Eisenhower, January 28, 1944, DF 000.7, box 2, RG 331.

2. Ambrose, *Supreme Commander*, 402–3.

3. Pinkley, "Correspondent Corps is Set for Invasion Coverage"; "Dailies Rush Extras on Big Invasion Coverage," both in *Editor and Publisher*, May 27 and June 10, 1944. "H-Hour, 1944," in box 1, Mueller Papers, Wisconsin Historical Society, gives transcript highlights of NBC's D-Day coverage.

4. McClure to Chief of Staff, "Guidance of Press in Initial Stage," April 26, 1944, Press and Radio Releases for Initial Plans of Overlord, Supreme Headquarters Allied Expeditionary Force (SHAEF), 000.71/5, box 3, RG331.

5. Braestrup, *Battle Lines*, 31; Address by Supreme Commander, undated [May 11, 1944], Press Correspondents File, SHAEF, 000.74, box 4, RG 331.

6. "History of U.S. and SHAEF Press Censorship in ETO, 1942–1945," box 2, Merrick Papers, MHI; Notes for War Correspondents Accredited to SHAEF, undated, Policy and Infractions of Press Censorship File, SHAEF, 000.73, box 4, RG 331. For background on SHAEF censorship, see also Pogue, *Supreme Command*, 90–91, 519–20.

7. These paragraphs are based on Harrison, *Cross-Channel Attack*, 269–335; Weigley, *Eisenhower's Lieutenants*, 78–91; Beevor, *D-Day*, 88–124; Pogue, *Pogue's War*, 83; Salaita, "Embellishing Omaha Beach," 531–34.

8. Bradley, *Soldier's Story*, 235–36; Harrison, *Cross-Channel Attack*, 278–84, especially fn 34.

9. Bradley, *Soldier's Story*, 238; AP, "Fixes Invasion Cost 150,000 U.S. Men 1st Month," *Chicago Tribune*, April 9, 1944.

10. McDonald, "Casualties Held Surprisingly Low"; "Weather Chief Cause of Beach Casualties"; "Forego Travel Plans,"; all in *NYT*, June 8, 9, and 11, 1944. Mueller's Fourth for Global Pool, June 7, 1944, Mueller's Pooled Scripts, microfilm, Wisconsin Historical Society.

11. SHAEF to War Department, S-54073, June 17, 1944, BPR File, 000.7, box 35, RG 165; Hansen, War Diary, June 17, 1944, Series II: Official Files, box 4, Hansen Papers, MHI; AP, "3,283 Killed and 12,600 Wounded U.S. Toll in Invasion, Bradley Says," *NYT*, June 18, 1944; Bradley, *Soldier's Story*, 299.

12. Marshall to Eisenhower, W-68072, July 21, 1944; Minutes of Public Relations Council, June 21, 1944, both in SHAEF General Staff, G-1 Administrative Section, DF 704, Entry 6, box 34, RG 331.

13. Surles to Davis, WARX 49631, WARZ-52988, and WARX 53942, June 12, 19, and 20, 1944, BPR File, 000.7, box 35, RG 165.

14. Davis, Memo to Assistant Chief of Staff, G-1, SHAEF, "Official Release of Statistics Concerning Casualties in Personnel," June 19, 1944, SHAEF General Staff, G-1 Administrative Section, DF 704, Entry 6, box 34, RG 331; Hansen, War Diary, June 21, 1944, Series II: Official Files, box 4, Hansen Papers.

15. War Cabinet, "Casualties in 'OVERLORD,'" August 1, 1944, Battle Casualties, Northern France, WO 32/11172, NA/UK. Stuart to Assistant Chief of Staff, G-1, SHAEF, "Publication of Casualty Lists," August 4, 1944; Bridges to Baker, August 29, 1944, both in Casualties: Release to the Press, WO 219/1534, NA/UK.

16. Buckland to Barker, "Casualty Reports," July 26, 1944, SHAEF General Staff, G-1 Administrative Section, DF 704, Entry 6, box 34, RG 331.

17. Dupuy, Memo for Assistant Chief of Staff, G-1, SHAEF, "Casualties," July 26, 1944, SHAEF General Staff, G-1 Administrative Section, DF 704, Entry 6, box 34, RG 331.

18. Nourse to Commanding General, 79th Infantry Division, Casualty Reports, July 18, 1944; Boyle, Report of Investigation Concerning Dissemination of Battle Casualty Information, July 26–August 25, 1944, both in SHAEF General Staff, G-1 Administrative Section, DF 704, Entry 6, box 34, RG 331.

19. Blumenson, *Breakout and Pursuit*, 175–76; Doubler, *Closing with the Enemy*, 31–62.

20. Blumenson, *Breakout and Pursuit*, 247–331, 528–58, 590–618.

21. Hodges to Corps, Division, and Separate Unit Commanders, "Casualty Reporting," August 12, 1944, SHAEF General Staff, G-1 Administrative Section, DF 704, Entry 6, box 34, RG 331.

22. Robertson to Griffin, August 15, 1944, SHAEF General Staff, G-1 Administrative Section, DF 704, Entry 6, box 34, RG 331; Beevor, *D-Day*, 359.

23. Griffin to Buckland, "Casualty and PW Reports," August 19, 1944, SHAEF General Staff, G-1 Administrative Section, DF 704, Entry 6, box 34, RG 331.

24. "Invasion Casualty Lists 3 July"; "American Casualties Reach 251,158 Total"; *NYT*, June 27 and 30, 1944.

25. "Casualties Reach 115,665 in France"; "Army's Invasion Casualties Rise to 174,780 in French Zones"; and "U.S Ground Casualties in West Reach 257,624," *NYT*, August 6, October 20, and December 19, 1944.

26. Millett, "The United States Armed Forces," 79.

27. Atkinson, *Day of Battle*, 106–10. This was the figure that subsequently appeared in the press. However, Matthew B. Ridgway, who commanded the airborne troops involved, later supplied the War Department with a total of only ninety-seven who were either KIA, died of wounds, or MIA, with a further eighty-two who had been wounded but had returned to active duty, and fifty more who had been so badly injured that they were lost to the division. See Ridgway to TAG, "Casualties, Sicilian Campaign, CT 504," May 19, 1944, BPR File, 000.7, Entry 499, box 36, RG 165.

28. Blumenson, *Breakout and Pursuit*, 228–36.

29. Lockett to Welch, "Army's News Policy," December 21, 1944, Folder 236, Time Dispatches, Houghton Library, Harvard University.

30. AP, "410 U.S. Paratroopers, Mistaken for Foe, Killed in Air Battle," *LA Times*, March 17, 1944; "Stimson Attacks Story of Laxity in Transports' Loss," *WP*, March 24, 1944.

31. Marshall, WARX 17749, April 2, 1944, BPR File, 000.7, box 33, RG 165.

32. Bradley, *Soldier's Story*, 348–49; "Army and Navy: From My Own Men," *Time*, August 14, 1944.

33. "Bombing of Troops in Error Explained," *NYT*, July 28, 1944. The PR-conscious air force was naturally concerned when these army statements led to much media criticism in the *New York Herald Tribune* and *NYT* and on NBC; see Westlake to Boyd, WARX-71643, July 27, 1944, BPR File 000.7, Entry 499, box 37, RG 165.

34. "Battle of France: Bradley Breaks Loose," *Time*, August 14, 1944; Boyle, AP Dispatch, August 12, 1944, Speeches and Writings File, box 2, Boyle Papers, Wisconsin Historical Society.

35. "Bombing of Troops in Error Explained," *NYT*, July 28, 1944.

36. Kenner, War Diary, May 1–August 31, 1944, SHAEF Special Staffs: Medical Division, Entry 68, box 8, RG 331.

37. M'Laughlin, "D-Day Wounded Got Care in 10 Minutes," *NYT*, July 31, 1944.

38. Blumenson, *Breakout and Pursuit*, 175–76; Doubler, *Closing with the Enemy*, 60–61, 242–43

39. Doubler, *Closing with the Enemy*, 60–61, 242–43.

40. Surles to ETOUSA, WX 30316, April 30, 1944, SHAEF General Staff, G-1 Administrative Section, DF 704, Entry 6, box 34, RG 331; Hall, "Plan of Coverage of Hospitals and Interviewing of Wounded Military Personnel Subsequent to D-Day," May 31, 1944, BPR File, 000.7, Entry 499, box 34, RG 165.

41. Surles to ETOUSA and Theater's Concerned, April 30, 1944, SGS, 000.7, box 2, RG 331.

42. Barker to Chief of Staff, "Release of Casualty Figures," September 7, 1944; Boehnke, "Casualty Reports," June 28, 1944, both in SHAEF General Staff, G-1 Administrative Section, DF 704, Entry 6, box 34, RG 331. Blumenson, *Breakout and Pursuit*, 175. For the media's intermittent interest in such casualties, see Huebner, *Warrior Image*, 32–37.

43. Horne, "Central States: Public, Sober but Confident, Prays for Invasion Troops," *NYT*, June 11, 1944. See also Ambrose, *D-Day*, 495.

44. Darilek, *Loyal Opposition*; Divine, *Foreign Policy*, 123.

45. For a summary of Dewey's initial charges, along with the White House response, see S[amuel] I. R[osenman], Memo for the President, October 2, 1944, Campaign 1944 Folder, box 25, Early Papers, Roosevelt Library. See also "Text of Dewey Speech Assailing F. D.'s Prewar 'Appeasement' Policies,'" *Washington Times-Herald*, October 25, 1944.

46. "Representative Clare Booth Luce's Speech before the Party Gathering," *NYT*, June 28, 1944. Background material can be found in Congressional File, Subject File: Roosevelt, box 599, Luce Papers, LC.

47. Editorial, "The Limits of Partisanship," *NYT*, June 29, 1944.

48. See, for instance, Barnes, Memo for the President, September 24, 1943; Cantril and Lambert to Roosevelt, May 8, 1944; H[adley] C[antril], July 5, 1944; all in OF 857, Roosevelt Papers, Roosevelt Library. Cantril to Rosenman, August 28, 1944, Material for FDR's Speeches, box 19, Rosenman Papers, Roosevelt Library.

49. Roosevelt, *Public Papers*, June 12, 1944. This theme was also emphasized in the government's Fifth War Loan Drive between June 12 and July 8, which included radio commercials with the following line: "The cost of invasion in dollars as well as lives comes high. So it's up to us, safe here at home, to raise the largest sum of money ever raised." See OWI, "Summary of Radio Campaign: Fifth War Loan," Entry 120, box 710, RG 208.

50. Roosevelt to Beaverbrook, July 20, 1944, PSF (Diplomatic): Britain, Roosevelt Papers.

51. James, *Years of MacArthur*, 2:526–36.

52. On these battles, see Cannon, *Leyte*, 60–80, 367–68; Spector, *Eagle Against the Sun*, 418–20, 426–44, 513–17; Murray and Millett, *War to be Won*, 362–73. On the press coverage, see Bentel, "Correspondents Killed at Aachen and Leyte," *Editor and Publisher*, October 27, 1944.

53. Roosevelt, *Public Papers*, October 20 and 27, 1944; Divine, *Foreign Policy*, 158.

54. Crowl, *Campaign in the Marianas*, 11–12, 15–20, 265; Murray and Millett, *War to be Won*, 353–62.

55. "Wheeler Says Saipan Battle Under-played," *Editor and Publisher*, July 29, 1944; Memo for Press Correspondents Accredited to Pacific Fleet, July 25, 1944, McCormick Papers, microfilm, Wisconsin Historical Society.

56. "Pacific Coverage Hits High Point at Saipan"; "Hits Wheeler Blast at Saipan Coverage," both in *Editor and Publisher*, August 19 and 26, 1944.

57. "The Significance of Saipan," Secretary of Navy Press Release, July 12, 1944, Marine Corps, PI Division, Navy Releases, box 2, RG 127.

58. "2,359 Yanks Die on Saipan," *Chicago Tribune*, July 13, 1944.

59. Cantril to Tully, July 26, 1944, PSF (Subject): Opinion Polls, Roosevelt Papers; H[adley] C[antril], August 22, 1944, OF 857, Roosevelt Papers.

60. For a recent analysis, see Hoenicke Moore, *Know Your Enemy*, 293–303.

61. Second Army to SHAEF, A-79, December 27, 1944, SHAEF General Staff, G-1 Administrative Section, DF 704, Entry 6, box 34, RG 331.

62. Atkinson, *Guns at Last Light*, 261–89; Weinberg, *World at Arms*, 701–2.

63. Lewis, "Morgenthau Plan Blamed for Stiffening of Nazis," *Washington Times-Herald*, September 30, 1944; Lindley, "Future of Germany: Reaction to Morgenthau Plan," *WP*, September 29, 1944.

64. Dewey, "This Must be the Last War," October 18, 1944, *Republican Party Pamphlets*. LC. See also "Text of Dewey's Address," *NYT*, November 5, 1944.

65. Niles to Tully, September 8, 1944, PSF (Subject): Opinion Polls, Roosevelt Papers.

66. See Maps dated September 24 and October 27, 1944, PSF (Subject): Opinion Polls, Roosevelt Papers.

67. Roosevelt, *Public Papers*, September 29, 1944.

68. Roosevelt was particularly sensitive to how war news was disseminated to reporters during the campaign, forbidding, for example, reports on the Philippines naval battles to be handed out on his "political" campaign train. See Early to Hopkins, October 27, 1944, Presidential Trips File, Map Room Papers, box 20, Roosevelt Papers.

69. Morgenthau, Jr., Diary, October 19, 1944, 783:153–56, Morgenthau Papers, Roosevelt Library; Stimson, Diary, November 4, 1944, Yale University.

70. "Stimson Again Cites Cost of Our Victory"; "Battle Casualties Pass 500,000 Mark," both in *NYT*, November 10, 1944. Editorial, "War Casualties," *NYT*, November 11, 1944.

71. Robinson to Early, November 2, 1944, OF 857, Roosevelt Papers.

72. Roosevelt, *Public Papers*, November 2, 1944.

73. Ferrell, *Dying President*, 94–97.

74. Weigley, *Eisenhower's Lieutenants*, 356–64.

75. MacDonald, *Battle of the Huertgen Forest*, 195–96; Weigley, *Eisenhower's Lieutenants*, 364–69; Atkinson, *Guns at Last Light*, 313–14.

76. Weigley, *Eisenhower's Lieutenants*, 370–75; Doubler, *Closing with the Enemy*, 246–47.

77. Matloff, "90 Division Gamble," 378.

78. Weigley, *Eisenhower's Lieutenants*, 375–77.

79. On the supply situation, see MacDonald, *Siegfried Line Campaign*, 10–14; Cole, *Lorraine Campaign*, 595–96.

80. Bissell to Betts, October 12, 1944, W-45374, BPR File, 000.7, Entry 499, box 38, RG 165. See also Butcher, *My Three Years with Eisenhower*, 688.

81. "Heavy Losses of American Troops Cited by Officers on Western Front," *NYT*, December 2, 1944.

82. Ibid.

83. Allen, "Publication of Casualty Figures," December 4 and 9, 1944, SHAEF General Staff, G-1 Administrative Section, DF 704, Entry 6, box 34, RG 331. This particular idea did not get very far because intelligence operatives still worried about divulging valuable information to the enemy.

84. "Heavy Losses of American Troops Cited by Officers on Western Front," *NYT*, December 2, 1944; "Heavy U.S. Casualties Reported in Europe," *Christian Science Monitor*, December 7, 1944.

85. Teletype Conference between General Henry and General Barker, December 19, 1944, BPR File, 000.7, box 35, RG 165. On Gallagher as "the bellwether," see Butcher, *My Three Years with Eisenhower*, 692.

86. "Thomas of House Military Affairs Committee Lists Six Factors Affecting Progress of War, Casualties, and Troops' Morale," *NYT*, December 19, 1944.

87. Teletype Conference between Henry and Barker, December 19, 1944, BPR File, 000.7, box 35, RG 165.

88. Parker, *Battle of the Bulge*, 45–56; Vogel, "German and Allied Conduct," 7:678–83.

89. Cole, *Ardennes*, 161–70

90. Winton, *Corps Commanders of the Bulge*, 101–6; Cole, *Ardennes*, 458–80; Atkinson, *Guns at Last Light*, 446–56.

91. "Newsmen Flare Up at Army Blackout," *Editor and Publisher*, December 23, 1944; Price, undated Memo [early January 1945], copy in Censorship Files, box 25, Early Papers, Roosevelt Papers; Kennedy, *Kennedy's War*, 148–49.

92. "The Penalties," *Time*, January 1, 1945; SHAEF, Press Briefing, December 23, 1944, Entry 83, box 25, RG 331.

93. AP, "SHAEF Gives No Data on Losses in West," *NYT*, January 4, 1945. See also United Press (UP), "Yank Casualties on West Front Still Secret," *LA Times*, January 4, 1945.

94. This angst was only heightened by publication of a German massacre of more than one hundred U.S. prisoners; see SHAEF, Press Release, December 31, 1944, SHAEF, Special Staff, PRD, Entry 83, box 30, RG 331; Stimson Diary, December 31, 1944. Officials also released photographs showing the Americans troops the Germans had killed after their surrender. See Roeder, "Censoring Disorder," 51.

95. *Congressional Record*, 1945, 91, 10:A336; State Department, Memo for the President, December 30, 1944, PSF, Departmental, State: Stettinius, Roosevelt Papers; OWI Correspondence Panels Section, to Foster, "Increasing Public Concern about International Affairs," January 23, 1945, Entry 149, box 1709, RG 44. This unease was also partly a product of early signs that postwar relations with the Soviets, and perhaps even the British, would be difficult. See Dallek, *Roosevelt and American Foreign Policy*, 503–6.

96. State Department Office of Public Affairs, "'Unconditional Surrender': From Casablanca to Yalta," Special Report, No.65, March 9, 1945, Entry 658J, box 1, RG 59. As this report made clear, 80 percent of Americans still supported unconditional surrender.

97. SHAEF, Press Briefing, December 16, 1944, Entry 83, box 25, RG 331. SHAEF, Press Censors Guidance, No. 718, "German Counteroffensive—Blackout," December 23, 1944; and No.741, "Cancellation of 36 Hour Time Lag," January 3, 1945, both in Entry 86, box 46, RG 331. "Newsmen Flare Up at Army Blackout," *Editor and Publisher*, December 23, 1944.

98. Boyle, AP Dispatch, December 23 and 29, 1944, Speeches and Writings File, box 2, Boyle Papers; Hill, "SHAEF a Headache to War Reporters," *Editor and Publisher*, January 13, 1945.

99. SHAEF, Press Briefing, December 23, 1944, Entry 83, box 25, RG 331

100. "U.S. Casualties in Belgium 40,000," *NYT*, January 16, 1945; "Casualties in 'The Bulge,'" *LA Times*, January 17, 1945.

101. "The Press: Early to the Rescue," *Time*, January 22, 1945.

102. Leigh, *Mobilizing Consent*, 105–9.

103. Davis, Report to the President, OWI, June 13, 1942 to September 15, 1945, 14–15, 28, 64, Subject File: OWI, box 10, Davis Papers, LC; Winkler, *Politics of Propaganda*, 56, 67, 70–71.

104. Davis and Dalton, Letter to Newspaper Editors, February 22, 1945, Press Folder, box 1067, Entry 220, RG 208; "Army and Navy to Give Press Consolidated Casualty Lists," *Washington Star*, February 24, 1945.

105. "Final Report on Activities of the Domestic News Bureau, OWI, July 13, 1942–September 15, 1945," box 1068, Entry 220, RG208. James to Sulzberger, February 23, 1945, World War II Folder, box 274, *NYT* Company Records: Sulzberger Papers, New York Public Library. The AP's position can be found in Casualties Folder, box 63, AP02A.3 Subject Files Listing, AP Archives.

106. OWI, "Final Report on Activities of the Domestic News Bureau, July 13, 1942–September 15, 1945," box 1068, Entry 220, RG208. Dalton to Bornstein, March 21, 1945; Milliken to Westling, March 24; Milliken to Salt, March 30, 1945; Dean to Davitt, June 27, 1945, all in Press Folder, box 1067, Entry 220, RG 208. James to Sulzberger, February 23, 1945.

107. Milliken to Conner, April 5 and 17, 1945, Press Folder, box 1067, Entry 220, RG 208; AP, "OWI Will Start Daily Printed Lists of Army, Navy Casualties Next Month," *NYT*, February 24, 1945.

108. UP, "14,664 Casualties Listed, Record for a Single Day," *NYT*, March 29, 1945; "Final Report on Activities of the Domestic News Bureau, OWI, July 13, 1942–September 15, 1945," box 1068, Entry 220, RG208.

109. Pyle, letter to his wife, February 2, 1945, Mss., II, Pyle Papers, Lilly Library, Indiana University.

110. Dickinson, "Ideal Press Setup for Luzon"; Price, "Navy Plans Help Cameramen in Speedy Coverage on Iwo"; *Editor and Publisher*, January 27 and February 24, 1945.

111. "Story of Luzon: A Slow, Brutal, Costly Advance in Jungle Scrub," *New York Herald Tribune*, February 12, 1945; AP, "Third of Tiny Island Won Despite Fierce Resistance by Jap Forces," *Chicago Tribune*, February 21, 1945.

112. Beaufort, "Iwo Struggle Fiercer Than Even Tarawa," *Christian Science Monitor*, February 20, 1945; Bigart, "Reporter Learns Why the Cost was High and Why Victory Will be Worth It," *New York Herald Tribune*, March 9, 1945. For the battle, see Dyer, *Amphibians Came to Conquer*, 2:997.

113. For the battle, see Appleman, Burns, Guergeler, and Steven, *Okinawa*, 68–70, 163–73; Frank, *Downfall*, 70. For Pyle, see "Without Carnage," *Washington Daily News*, April 9, 1945; Tobin, *Pyle's War*, 240. For the press coverage, see Bigart, "3-Month Battle is Predicted to Clear Okinawa"; "Okinawa Knoll Stormed after 3 Costly Days," both in *New York Herald Tribune*, April 10 and 25, 1945. Smith, "Casualties Grown on Okinawa," *Chicago Tribune*, April 10, 1945. Moscow, "Sugar Loaf Taken," *NYT*, May 20, 1945.

114. Smith, "Japanese Fight Harder as War Pushes Closer," *Chicago Tribune*, April 12, 1945; AP, "Okinawa Costliest of Pacific Battles," *NYT*, June 22, 1945. On Palmer, see Chappell, *Before the Bomb*, 41.

115. Frank, *Downfall*, 27–37.

116. UP, "Battle Toll Above Civil War's Total"; AP, "Our War Losses Reach 1,002,887," *NYT*, March 30 and June 1, 1945.

117. On these stories, see Shalett, Memo for Whitney, August 16, 1944, World War II Folder, box 274, NYT Company Records: Sulzberger Papers; Loftus, "Atrocities Bared," *NYT*, September 6, 1945.

118. "On To Tokyo and What?" *Life*, May 21, 1945; OWI, "Current Surveys," No.7, February 23, 1945, Entry 149, box 1719, RG 44.

119. Blair, "New England"; Baldwin, "The Battle for Iwo-I," *NYT*; February 25 and March 5, 1945. *Congressional Record, 1945*, 91, 11, A2666. Chappell, *Before the Bomb*, 76–77.

120. As Lawrence complained, the navy held his story of the loss of the *Indianapolis* until the day of Truman's announcement that Japan had agreed to surrender; it then held his exclusive about large naval losses until the day the surrender was signed. See Lawrence to Sulzberger, September 16, 1945, Censorship Folder, box 125, NYT Company Records: Sulzberger Papers. Lawrence, "334 U.S. Ships Hit in Okinawa Battle," *NYT*, September 3, 1945.

121. Pearlman, *Warmaking*, 268.

122. *Foreign Relations of the United States: Conference at Potsdam*, 1:903–10; Frank, *Downfall*, 132–48; Giangreco, *Hell to Pay*, 58–60.

123. For a good summary of these debates, see Walker, "Decision to Use the Bomb," 11–37.

124. Miscamble, *Most Controversial Decision*, 70–71; Bernstein, "Understanding the Atomic Bomb," 73–74.

125. Hershberg, *Conant*; Bernstein, "Seizing the Contested Terrain, 35–72.

126. On Truman's private views, see Ferrell, *Dear Bess*, 519; Miscamble, *From Roosevelt to Truman*, 178–79.

127. Truman, *Public Papers*, September 1, 1945.

128. Berger, "400,000 in Silent Tribute as War Dead Come Home," *NYT*, October 27, 1947; Colley, *Safely Rest*, 1–6; Bodnar, *"Good War,"* 100–103.

Chapter 4

1. Gould, "Solider, Mother Meet at a TV Show," *NYT*, September 22, 1950.

2. Holloway, *Stalin and the Bomb*, 272–78.

3. For the best brief summary, see Stueck, *Rethinking*, 69–77.

4. *Foreign Relations of the United States, 1950*, 7:158, and 1:325–26, 330, 337–38; Foot, *Wrong War*, 57; Gaddis, "Korea in American Politics," 281–83.

5. For a detailed account of this first week, see Paige, *Korean Decision*, 79–270.

6. State Department, PA, "Daily Opinion Summary," June 26, 1950, Entry 658K, box 4, RG 59.

7. State Department, PA, "Daily Opinion Summary," June 28, 1950, Entry 658K, box 4, RG 59; Sevareid broadcast reprinted in Radio Reports, Special for Guylay, July 3, 1950, 1950 Campaign: Radio Reports Folder, box 276, Taft Papers, LC.

8. MacArthur to Department of Army, July 10, 1950, RG 9, box 26 MacArthur Papers, MacArthur Memorial Library.

9. DOD, Press Branch, "Casualty Releases," August 10, 1950; DOD, OPI, Memo for the Press, "Summary of Casualty Reporting Procedure," August 11, 1950, both in Entry 149A, box 1, RG 330.

10. See, for instance, "First U.S. Casualties in Korea," *NYT*, July 3, 1950.

11. DOD, Press Branch, "Casualty Releases," August 10, 1950; DOD, OPI, Memo for the Press, "Summary of Casualty Reporting Procedure," August 11, 1950, both in Entry 149A, box 1, RG 330. OPI, 'Activity Reports', July 6, 1950, Entry 134, box 152, RG 330.

12. Witsell, "Casualty Report," 7–10. "Army Tells How Casualty Report Is Speeded Up," *Editor and Publisher*, December 9, 1950.

13. Dean, *Dean's Story*, 14; Blair, *Forgotten War*, 93.

14. Blair, *Forgotten War*, 91–97, 121–22; Millett, *War for Korea*, 78–84.

15. Appleman, *South to the Naktong*, 179–81, 262, 391.

16. Ibid., 82–86, 94, 146–80.

17. Blair to Bermingham, "Box Scores," July 28, 1950, Time Dispatches, Folder 589, Houghton Library, Harvard University.

18. On MacArthur's pre–Korean War publicity activities, see James, *Years of MacArthur*, 1:130–35 and 2:89, 164–65, 277–78, 708–9.

19. SCAP GHQ, PIO, Press Releases, July 11, 13 and 20, 1950, Entry 1102, box 27, RG 331.

20. SCAP GHQ, PIO, Communiqué No.99, July 20, 1950, Entry 1102, box 27, RG 331. For the battle itself, see Appleman, *South to the Naktong*, 146–80.

21. Higgins, "Newswoman Tells Harrowing Tale of Night Infiltration Raid on U.S. Command Post," *WP*, August 4, 1950.

22. "Death of Wounded Reduced in Korea," *NYT*, November 10, 1950. Far East Command, PIO, "Amazingly Low Death Rate in Korea," October 23, 1950, Entry 429, box 362, RG 407.

23. On partisanship during this period, see Caridi, *Korean War and American Politics*; Kepley, *Collapse of the Middle Way*. On Taft and McCarthy, see Reeves, *McCarthy*, 308–11; Patterson, *Mr. Republican*, 446–51.

24. On MacArthur's Korean War press system and the reasoning behind it, see Echols to Correspondents, July 2, 1950, RG 6, box 4, MacArthur Papers; Echols to Dabney, July 31, 1950, Official Correspondence Folder, box 2, Echols Papers, MHI; Erwin, "Voluntary Censorship Asked in Korean War," *Editor and Publisher*, July 8, 1950; Echols, "Information in the Combat Zone," 61–64.

25. McCartney, "Survivors Describe 4 Hour Clash Near Osan," *Chicago Tribune*, July 6, 1950. Higgins, "Death of First Infantryman"; Bigart, "From a Foxhole in Korea," both in *New York Herald Tribune*, July 6 and 12, 1950.

26. "Angry U.S. Girds for Rough War," *Newsweek*, July 24, 1950.

27. "Why Are We Taking a Beating?" *Life*, July 24, 1950; Caridi, *Korean War and American Politics*, 95.

28. DOD, OPI, Memorandum for the Press, "Summary of Casualty Reporting Procedure," August 11, 1950, Entry 149A, box 1, RG 330.

29. "Unproved Casualties Handed to Congress," *NYT*, August 12, 1950.

30. "100 Seek War Beat Despite Privations"; "Communications Snag for War Reporters," both in *Editor and Publisher*, August 12 and 26, 1950. DOD, OPI, "Activity Reports," August 8, 1950, Entry 134, box 152, RG 330.

31. "U.S. Army Confirms 2,616 Casualties"; "Casualty Gap Denied," both in *NYT*, August 8 and 11, 1951.

32. CINCFE to Department of Army, July 12, 1950, box 149, MacArthur Papers; Far East Command, PIO, Communiqué No.72, July 13, 1950, Entry 1102, box 27, RG 331. See also Johnston, "GI's of 'Lost' Battalion Say Odds Against Unit Were 15-1," *NYT*, July 11, 1950; "Needed: A Rule Book," *Time*, July 24, 1950.

33. "News Executives Prefer Voluntary Censorship Now," *Editor and Publisher*, August 19, 1950.

34. White, "Truman Terms Contemptible Wherry Attack on Acheson," *NYT*, August 18, 1950.

35. McFarland and Roll, *Johnson*, 341–45; Pearlman, *Truman and MacArthur*, 93.

36. Booth to Bermingham, "Politics—II," October 13, 1950, Folder 609, Time Dispatches. Minutes, RNC Meeting, September 14, 1950, microfilm 10, frames 234, 373–74, RNC Papers, LC.
37. Shu, *Mao's Military Romanticism*, 95–107; Halberstam, *Coldest Winter*, 42.
38. "Calls Korea Issue," *NYT*, November 5, 1950; McNaughton, "The Election," November 10, 1950, Folder 616, Time Dispatches.
39. Griffith, *Politics of Fear*, 122–31; Hulsey, *Dirksen*, 26–29.
40. Appleman, *Disaster in Korea*, 262–336; Marshall, *River and the Gauntlet*, 251–348.
41. Appleman, *Escaping the Trap*, 24, 319–44.
42. "MacArthur's Own Story," *U.S. News & World Report*, December 8, 1950; AP Report, December 2, 1950, copy in OF 584, box 1397, Truman Papers, Truman Library; James, *Years of MacArthur*, 1:540–41.
43. MacArthur to Army Commanders, December 10, 1950, RG 9, box 53, MacArthur Papers. On the reported casualty figures, see AP, "6,886 Casualties in Korea Notified Through Aug. 25"; AP, "20,756 Casualties Reported to Date"; AP, "Casualties in Korea Reach 27,610 for U.S."; AP, "U.S. Casualties at 31,028"; AP, "U.S. Casualties Rise in Korea to 33,878"; AP, "U.S. Casualties Reach 40,176 in Korean War," in *NYT*, September 2, October 5, November 3, November 30 and December 14, 1950, and January 5, 1951.
44. Bigart, "Ghastly Night Put in by Yanks," *WP*, November 28, 1950; Sparks, "Nightmare Valley Ahead of Yanks," *Chicago Daily News*, December 6, 1950.
45. Moore, "Wounded GIs Burned Alive, Survivors Say," *WP*, December 3, 1950.
46. Sherrod to Bermingham, "Heavy Casualties II," and "Add Heavy Casualties," December 9 and 11, 1950, Folders 621 and 622, Time Dispatches.
47. "Marine Losses 'Heavier Than Tarawa,'" *WP*, December 11, 1950.
48. *U.S. Marine Corps Personnel Casualties in World War II.*
49. "The Battle," December 6, 1950, Folder 620, Time Dispatches. For other speculation, see "Rise in Casualties Noted"; "3,000 Casualties Held Marine Toll," both in *NYT*, December 11 and 12, 1950.
50. Sherrod to Bermingham, "Add Heavy Casualties," December 11, 1950, Folder 622, Time Dispatches.
51. Eighth Army, PIO Command Report, December 1950, Entry 429, box, 1140, RG 407; Korean Release, Number 749, December 21, 1950, Entry 50, box 2, RG 319.
52. Korean Release, Number 749, December 21, 1950, Entry 50, box 2, RG 319.
53. Pearlman, *Truman and MacArthur*, 1–16, 140.
54. Editorial, "MacArthur's Disaster," December 6, 1950.
55. Echols, "Information in the Combat Zone," 61.
56. Higgins, "On the Battlefront in Korea," *New York Herald Tribune*, December 6, 1951.
57. Patterson, *Mr. Republican*, 485–86.
58. Lucas, "We Have Lost More Men Than Rest of UN Sent," *Washington News*, February 16, 1951.
59. Aiken to Wetherhead, Foreign Affairs File, Crate 39, box 1, Aiken Papers, University of Vermont.
60. Gallup, "Public Favors Withdrawing from Korea by Nearly 3 to 1," *WP*, January 21, 1951. This same week the Pentagon's Office of Public Information also noted that casualties were the "principal press interest." DOD, OPI, "Activity Reports," January 24, 1951, Entry 134, box 155, RG 330.
61. For the argument that citizens from communities who experience a higher loss of life are more likely to oppose a war, see Gartner, Segura, and Wilkening, "All Politics are Local," 673–76.
62. "Casualties Forcing Army to Add 50,000 Draftees"; "Educators Favor Draft Proposals," both in *NYT*, January 12 and 20, 1951.
63. Flynn, *Hershey*, 180–87; and Flynn, *Draft*, 114–25.
64. "Draft 'Delinquents,'" January 26, 1951, Folder 629, Time Dispatches.
65. "Casualties Forcing Army to Add 50,000 Draftees," *NYT*, January 12, 1951. Parks to Collins, February 26, 1951, Unclassified Decimal File 000.7, box 54, Entry 206A, RG 319.
66. Parks, Memo for Deputy Chief, March 15, 1951; Parks to Hickey, March 21, 1951; Hickey to Parks, April 1, 1951, all in Unclassified Decimal File 000.7, box 54, Entry 206A, RG 319.

Quirk, Memo for Ridgway, March 17, 1951, Korean War Folder 2, box 1, Quirk Papers, Truman Library.

67. Quirk, Memo for Ridgway, March 17, 1951, Korean War Folder 2, box 1, Quirk Papers.
68. Appleman, *Ridgway Duels for Korea*, 162–348. James, *Refighting the Last War*, 58–60.
69. James, *Refighting the Last War*, 70–71.
70. Ridgway, *Korean War*, 111.
71. DOD, OPI, Minutes: National Society of Professional Engineers Conference, March 2, 1951, Entry 146, box 723 RG 330.
72. Halberstam, *Coldest Winter*, 5.
73. U.S. Congress, Senate, *Hearings before Armed Services and Foreign Relations Committees: Military Situation in the Far East*, 44, 65–66, 30.
74. U.S. Congress, Senate, *Hearings before Armed Services and Foreign Relations Committees: Military Situation in the Far East*, 610–11, 937, 950, 1278–79, 1286–88. *Congressional Record*, 97:5418, 5778, 6605, 6623–28, A3122.
75. *Congressional Record*, 97:12537–39; 98:1598–1600.
76. CBS, "People's Platform," May 6, 1951, copy in Folder 16, box 195A, Marshall Papers, Virginia Military Institute; Taft to Smith, May 23, 1951, Subject File: Foreign Policy, box 968, Taft Papers; State Department, PA, "Daily Opinion Summary," July 23, 1951, Entry 658K, box 6, RG 59.
77. "Loss Ratio in Korea 1–36 in UN's Favor," *NYT*, May 22, 1951.
78. Foot, *Substitute for Victory*, 208.
79. Blair, *Forgotten War*, 947; Braim, *Will to Win*, 239; Jackson, "Lost Chance," 275.
80. Millett, *War for Korea*, 453; James, *Refighting the Last War*, 73–74; Hermes, *Truce Tent*, 176–77.
81. Duff, "Statement at Pentagon Briefing," July 27, 1951, DOD OPI Files, 000.78, box 70, RG 330.
82. Fisher, "Gen. Van Fleet Rips Truman Policy in War"; Norman, "Reveal Van Fleet Warning"; both in *Chicago Tribune*, March 6 and 23, 1953; U.S. Congress, Senate, *Hearings before the Armed Services Committee: Ammunition Supplies in the Far East*, 12–33.
83. Adams to Larkin, May 14, 1951, Folder 4, box195A, Marshall Papers; "Hearing Is Told of Drop in U.S. Casualties," *NYT*, May 13, 1951.
84. Army Department, PI Division, "Briefing Notes from Discussion of Korean Casualties by the Surgeon General," February 2, 1951, Entry 50, box 2, RG 319. See also Pearson, "Casualty Figures Held Faulty," *WP*, March 7, 1951.
85. U.S. Congress, Senate, *Hearings before Armed Services and Foreign Relations Committees: Military Situation in the Far East*, 1286–87.
86. Memo Re Marshall Testimony, undated, Hearings Materials, Series 12, box 7, Russell Papers, University of Georgia.
87. Swindells, "Marine Correspondents in Korea"; "Sparks Hits K-War Coverage at Home," *Editor and Publisher*, March 22, 1952.
88. "Military Censorship Imposed by MacArthur," *Editor and Publisher*, December 23, 1950; Parks to Echols, December 21, 1950, Chief of I&E, UCD 092 (Korea), box 17, RG319; Parks to Echols, December 23, 1950, Chief of I&E, UCD 000.74, box 5, RG 319.
89. Hermes, *Truce Tent*, 80–103; Blair, *Forgotten War*, 947–50.
90. Korean Release, Unnumbered, September 5, 1951, Entry 50, box 5, RG 319. "18-Day Fight Won!" *Chicago Daily News*, September 5, 1951; "U.S. Troops Battle for Weeks," *WP*, September 5, 1951; "U.S. Forces Win Korea Ridge in 17-Day Battle," *New York Herald Tribune*, September 6, 1951.
91. State Department, PA, "Monthly Survey on American Opinion," January and February 1952, Entry 568L, box 12, RG 59. Russell, "Comparison of American Popular Opinion on Foreign Policy a Year Ago and Today," January 2, 1952; Foster to Sargeant, "Late March Opinion Survey," April 3, 1952; both in Entry 568N, box 20, RG 59.
92. Young, "Hard Sell," 130–31; "Korea: The 'Forgotten' War," *U.S. News & World Report*, October 5, 1951.
93. Marshall, "Statement," September 10, 1951; Lovett, "Statement," September 20, 1951; DOD, OPI, Military Production News, September 10, 1951; PR Progress Report, October

1 to November 1, 1951, all in Staff Member and Office Files (SMOF): Jackson, box 21, Truman Papers.

94. Clarvoe to Howard, October 5, 1951, City File (San Francisco): SF News, box 251, Howard Papers, LC.

95. Poster, undated, SMOF: Jackson, box 21, Truman Papers.

96. Casey, *Selling the Korean War*, 286–89. As well as the propaganda value of this policy, Truman firmly believed that communist POWs should not be forcibly returned to face either death or the gulag.

97. For an excellent account of the fate of these POWs, see Latham, *Cold Days in Hell*.

98. Bridges, Cain, and Dirksen, Press Release, July 30, 1951, Senate Armed Services Committee Papers, Correspondence: Bridges File, box 187, RG 46.

99. Barrett to Matthews, February 4, 1952, PA Assistant Secretary of State Memos, box 2, RG 59.

100. Phillips to Tubby, July 3, 1952; Sargeant to Boughton, July 9, 1952; PA Assistant Secretary of State Memos, box 2, RG 59. State Department PA, "Opinion and Activities of American Private Groups and Organizations," August 18, 1952, Entry 568M, box 17, RG 59.

101. Eisenhower, Campaign Speeches, September 15 and 22, October 23, 1952, Speeches and Statements, Campaign File, 1952, boxes 2 to 7, Benedict Papers, Eisenhower Library. See also David Lawrence, "6,000 U.S. Boys Dead in Korea Called Real Issue of Campaign," *New York Herald Tribune*, September 30, 1952.

102. Hermes, *Truce Tent*, 303–18; Blair, *Forgotten War*, 970.

103. "Then He Was Dead"; "Bloodshed in the Hills," both in *Time*, October 6 and 27, 1952.

104. "An Old Pattern," *Time*, November 3, 1952. See also, "Relationship of Friendly Casualties to Enemy Fire," undated, copy in Whitman File: Administrative Series, Wilson Folder, box 40, Eisenhower Papers, Eisenhower Library.

105. State Department, PA, "Monthly Survey of American Opinion," January, October, and November 1952, Entry 568L, box 12, RG 59.

106. Lubell, *Revolt of the Moderates*, 39–40.

107. Blair to Beshoar for NA, November 14, 1952, Folder 732, Time Dispatches.

108. "Casualties Explained"; "Pentagon Gives Revised Listings," both in *NYT*, November 14 and December 4, 1952.

109. Blair to Beshoar for NA, November 14, 1952, Folder 732, Time Dispatches.

110. Medhurst, "Text and Context," 469.

111. Casey, *Selling the Korean War*, 347–49.

112. Eisenhower, *Public Papers*, July 26, 1953.

113. Young, "POWs," 320; Piehler, *Remembering War*, 320.

114. Pearlman, *Warmaking*, 332; McMaster, *Dereliction of Duty*, 10.

115. Herring and Immerman, "Eisenhower, Dulles, and Dienbienphu," 350, 353.

Chapter 5

1. May, "U.S. Government," 217–18.

2. Eisenhower, *Public Papers*, January 17, 1961.

3. McMaster, *Dereliction of Duty*, 5–7.

4. Stanton, *Rise and Fall*, 24–25.

5. "Briefing Sheet on Press Relations of the U.S. Mission in Saigon," March 4, 1966, Policy—Press Relations Folder, USIA, IAF-VN, Entry 67, box 71, RG 276.

6. For an excellent account of this earlier phase of the Vietnam War, which ends with the first U.S. casualties, see Logevall, *Embers of War*, 699–701.

7. Freedman, *Kennedy's Wars*, 326–34; Jones, *Death of a Generation*, 440–41.

8. Beschloss, *Taking Charge*, 248–50, 262–63, 266–67; McMaster, *Dereliction of Duty*, 70.

9. OSD, "Public Affairs Policy Guidance for Personnel Returning from South Vietnam," undated [late March 1962], National Security File (NSF)-Countries-VN, box 196, Kennedy Papers, Kennedy Library; Hammond, *Public Affairs*, 1:15, 45–46; Jones, *Death of a Generation*, 169.

10. Halberstam, "Curbs in Vietnam Irk U.S. Officers," *NYT*, November 22, 1962; Wyatt, *Paper Soldiers*, 93–96.

11. DOD, Press Conference, February 13, 1963, Press Conferences Folder, PR 18-2, File 847, Kennedy Papers; Hammond, *Public Affairs*, 1:17; Prochnau, *Once Upon A Distant War*, 24.

12. Jones, *Death of a Generation*, 144, 168, 239; DeBenedetti, *American Ordeal*, 83.

13. "A Captain's Last Letters from Vietnam," *U.S. News & World Report*, May 4, 1964; Mecklin, *Mission in Torment*, 115–16.

14. "Dead Reported in Vietnam War," *WP*, October 5, 1963.

15. Dietz, *Republicans and Vietnam*, 35; Johns, *Vietnam's Second Front*, 15.

16. Republican Leadership, Press Release, April 21, 1964, Remarks and Releases File, Dirksen Papers, Dirksen Congressional Center; Allett to Shank, April 21, 1964; clipping, "U.S. Counts Rising Toll in Latest Vietnam Setback," *Chicago Sun-Times*, April 16, 1964, both in Correspondence File, box 77, Halleck MSS., Lilly Library, University of Indiana; Trussell, "GOP Says Role of U.S. in War is Concealed by Administration," *NYT*, April 22, 1964.

17. Beschloss, *Taking Charge*, 364–65; Johnson, *Public Papers*, April 21, 1964.

18. AP, "Casualty Figures Updated," *NYT*, May 17, 1964.

19. "Why? Why?" *Washington Star*, May 12, 1964.

20. Perlstein, *Before the Storm*, 341, 494.

21. According to one poll, eight out of ten Americans opposed Goldwater's policy positions. See "The Harris Survey," July 13, 1964, White House Central File (WHCF)-NF-Harris, box 120, Johnson Papers, Johnson Library; see also Matthews, "To Defeat a Maverick," 670–73.

22. Moyers to Johnson, October 3, 1964, WHOF-Aides-Moyers, box 10, Johnson Papers.

23. Johnson, *Public Papers*, October 9, 1964; McMaster, *Dereliction of Duty*, 117–18; Bundy, "Position Paper on Expanding the South Vietnamese Conflict to the North," July 30, 1964, vol.14, NSF-CF-VN, box 6, Johnson Papers; Jorden to Bundy, "President Johnson's Foreign Policy Positions as Developed in the 1964 Election Campaign," October 29, 1964; Jorden, "Why We're in Southeast Asia," September 4, 1964, both in NSF-SF, box 41, Johnson Papers.

24. CBS Script, *Vietnam: The Deadly Decision*, April 1, 1964, box 4, Collingwood Papers, Wisconsin Historical Society. See also Brinkley, *Cronkite*, 300.

25. Hammond, *Public Affairs*, 1:69.

26. VanDeMark, *Into the Quagmire*, 153–54.

27. Beschloss, *Taking Charge*, 369.

28. "Meeting on Vietnam, 10:40," July 21, 1965, Meetings Notes File, box 1, Johnson Papers.

29. "Meeting on July 21, 1965, 2:45 p.m.," Meetings Notes File, box 1, Johnson Papers.

30. Gravel, *Pentagon Papers*, 3: 687–91.

31. McMaster, *Dereliction of Duty*, 58, 64–65, 74–75, 100; Gravel, *Pentagon Papers*, 3: 467; Gibson, *Perfect War*, 97. On McNamara's views, see Memo of Meeting with the President, February 17, 1965, Meetings Notes File, box 1, Johnson Papers; McNamara to Johnson, July 28, 1965, WHCF, ND19 CO312, box 215, Johnson Papers. On Johnson's view, see Moyers to Jensen, September 4, 1965, WHCF-SF, SP 3–101, box 168, Johnson Papers.

32. McNaughton, "Action for South Vietnam," March 10, 1965, Vietnam Memos, vol. 30, NSF-CF-VN, box 14, Johnson Papers.

33. McMaster, *Dereliction of Duty*, 294–95; McNamara, *In Retrospect*, 204. In April 1965 McNamara had estimated that it would take at least six months for North Vietnam to respond to graduated pressure, and perhaps as long as a year or two; see Gravel, *Pentagon Papers*, 3:705–6.

34. McMaster, *Dereliction of Duty*, 100–101, 261; Herring, *LBJ and Vietnam*, 32–34; Bator, "No Good Choices," 320.

35. VanDeMark, *Into the Quagmire*, 211–13; Bator, "No Good Choices," 321–25; Herring, *LBJ and Vietnam*, 121, 131.

36. "Meeting on Vietnam, 3:00," July 22, 1965, Meetings Notes File, box 1, Johnson Papers.

37. "Meeting on Vietnam, 10:40," July 21, 1965, Meetings Notes File, box 1, Johnson Papers.

38. Cited in Jones, *Death of a Generation*, 7.

39. Westmoreland, *Soldier Reports*, 119, 410; Pearlman, *Warmaking*, 354–55.

40. Gibson, *Perfect War*, 112–13. For a summary of how the "kill ratio" was computed, see MACV to OASD PA, November 11, 1965, Office of the Chief of Administration: Messages, Entry 1150, box 7, RG 319.

41. According to one estimate, battalion commanders had a 30 to 50 percent chance of being relieved if they were deemed a failure, and failure was determined by body counts. Gibson, *Perfect War*, 112–16.

42. As Stanton points out, "American losses were subject to manipulation as well. For instance, dying soldiers put aboard medical evacuation hospitals were often counted as only wounded in unit after-action tables." Stanton, *Rise and Fall*, xx.

43. Gibson, *Perfect War*, 124.

44. MACV to OASD PA, November 21, 1965, Office of the Chief of Administration: Messages, Entry 1150, box 7, RG 319. Hammond, *Public Affairs*, 1:207.

45. George Ball, "Public Affairs Policy Guidance for Vietnam," June 30, 1964; Dean Rusk to Saigon Embassy, July 6, 1964, both in USIA, IAF-VN, Entry 67, box 67, RG 276. Senate, *News Policies in Vietnam*, 90–91; Cull, *Cold War*, 245–54; Hammond, *Public Affairs*, 1:80–83, 93, 107; Wyatt, *Paper Soldiers*, 46–47, 158.

46. Minutes, Public Affairs Policy Committee for Vietnam, August 23, 1965, USIA, IAF-VN, Entry 67, box 67, RG 276; Westmoreland, History Notes, September 5, 1965, box 8, Westmoreland Papers, Center of Military History; Hammond, *Public Affairs*, 1:138–39, 143–45, 159–61, 193–95

47. Newsom, Confidential Memo, May 7, 1965, WHCF, ND19 CO312, box 215, Johnson Papers.

48. "Briefing Sheet on Press Relations of the U.S. Mission in Saigon," March 4, 1966, Policy—Press Relations Folder, USIA, IAF-VN, Entry 67, box 71, RG 276; Hammond, *Public Affairs*, 1:179–80.

49. MACV, "Weekly Summaries," 1965–71, MACV HQ, Information Office: PI Division, Entry 305, boxes 1–7, RG 472.

50. U.S. Congress, Senate, *Hearings before Foreign Relations Committee: News Policies in Vietnam*, 83–84. The Pentagon was also primed to respond promptly to all manner of media inquiries about casualties, from discrepancies in announcements about helicopter losses to deaths from disease. See, for instance, Smith, "Defense Marketing Service," January 24, 1967; Army Department, PI Division: News Branch, "Query/Personnel," January 16, 1967, both in Army-OCINFO, PI: News Branch, Press Queries Folder, Entry D-2, box 5, RG 319.

51. Lippmann, "Stalemate in Vietnam," *Hartford Courant*, September 30, 1965.

52. MACV, "Weekly Summary," November 24, 1965, MACV HQ, Information Office: PI Division, Entry 305, box 1, RG 472.

53. These paragraphs are based on Carland, *Stemming the Tide*, 95–150; Hammond, *Public Affairs*, 1:210–13. See also, MACV to OASD PA, November 21, 1965, Office of the Chief of Administration: Messages, Entry 1150, box 7, RG 319.

54. Moore, *We Were Soldiers Once*, 306.

55. Sheehan, "Battalion of GI's Battered in Trap," *NYT*, November 19, 1965. For Sheehan's account of how he covered the battle, see *Bright Shining Lie*, 577–79.

56. Sheehan, "Battalion of GI's Battered in Trap," *NYT*, November 19, 1965; "More U.S. Troops Join Worst Battle Yet of Viet Conflict," *WP*, November 17, 1965.

57. Reston, "The Casualty Controversy," *NYT*, November 26, 1965; Westmoreland, History Notes, November 20, 1965, box 8, Westmoreland Papers.

58. MACV, "Weekly Summary," November 17 and 24, 1965, MACV HQ, Information Office: PI Division, Entry 305, box 1, RG 472. Salazar, "Week's Losses Highest of War for Americans," *LA Times*, November 18, 1965.

59. Paul to White, August 11, 1965; Vance to Johnson, August 26, 1966, both in WHCF-SF-ND 9-2, Casualties File, box 44, Johnson Papers; Carmody, "It's a Job You'll Never Like Doing," *WP*, February 20, 1966; "Pentagon Says Casualties' Kin Get 'Immediate Notification,'" *NYT*, August 27, 1966. For a detailed description of such notification efforts, see Davis, *Long Road Home*, 138–41; Longley, *Grunts*, 119–23.

60. Moore, *We Were Soldiers Once*, 323–25; "Army Official Defends Casualty Notice Setup," *Columbus* (GA) *Ledger*, November 20, 1965. This was not Western Union's first brush with controversy; see Marvin [Watson] to Johnson, July 20, 1965, WHCF-SF-ND 9-2, Casualties File, box 44, Johnson Papers.

61. "'Next of Kin' Slated for ABC Tonight," *NYT*, November 27, 1965. Six months later ABC aired another shows about Ia Drang casualties, this time because one its correspondents, Howard K. Smith, had a son who was still recovering from a wound sustained in this battle. See "ABC News Commentator Smith Interviews Own Soldier Vietnam Casualty," July 1, 1966, OSD: Public Affairs Projects, 1961–71, Entry 464, box 1, RG 330.

62. Hallin, *The "Uncensored War,"* 129–30; Lichty and Fouhy, "Television Reporting," 585.

63. Prochnau, *Once Upon A Distant War*, 29–30; Doherty, *Cold War, Cool Medium*, 60–69. On the culture of war correspondents, see Pedelty, *War Stories*, 29–30, 130; and Laurence, *Cat from Hué*, 141–42, 667–68.

64. Chief, TV Production to Smith, August 23, 1966, Chronological File, OSD: Public Affairs Projects, 1961–71, Entry 464, box 1, RG 330; Laurence, *Cat from Hué*, 288–89.

65. CBS, "Battle of Ia Drang," YouTube video. On Cronkite's thinking about the war in the fall of 1965, see Brinkley, *Cronkite*, 349–50.

66. Dallek, *Flawed Giant*, 506.

67. Moyers, News Conference, November 24, 1965, PSNC 216A, White House Press Office Files, box 9, Johnson Papers; Semple, "Johnson Grieves over Toll in War," *NYT*, November 25, 1965.

68. Logan, "President Pays Surprise Visit to U.S. Troops in Morocco," *NYT*, January 27, 1943; Atkinson, *Army at Dawn*, 290–91.

69. "Truman at Hospital, Asks about Wounded," *NYT*, September 12, 1950.

70. Valenti to Johnson, September 1, 1965; Johnson to Muller, March 1, 1965, WHCF, ND 19, CO312, boxes 217 and 214, Johnson Papers.

71. McNamara to Johnson, "Courses of Action in Vietnam," November 3, 1965, Vietnam Memos (B), Folder, vol.42, NSF-CF-VN, box 24; "Meeting with Foreign Policy Advisers on Bombing Pause," December 18, 1965, Meeting Notes File, box 1, both in Johnson Papers; McNamara, *In Retrospect*, 220–25.

72. "Meeting with Foreign Policy Advisers on Vietnam, 9:41," December 17, 1965, Meeting Notes File, box 1, Johnson Papers; Johnson, *Vantage Point*, 233–39; Johnson, *Public Papers*, January 12, 1966.

73. Kirby, "Public Affairs Policy Cable: SecDef Background Briefing," February 10, 1966, Press Briefings—DOD Folder, Entry 67, USIA, IAF-VN, box 71, RG 276.

74. Thomson and Ropa to Bundy, "The Week in Asia," November 10, 1965, Vietnam Memos (A), vol.42, NSF-CF-VN, box 14, Johnson Papers; "The Draft: The Unjust vs. The Unwilling," *Newsweek*, April 11, 1966; Jeffrey-Jones, *Peace Now*, 14; Small, *Johnson, Nixon, and the Doves*, 62.

75. "Harris Survey," February 28, 1966, WHCF-NF-Harris, box 120, Johnson Papers.

76. "No Exit," "Dissent and Defeat," *Time*, February 25 and March 11, 1966; Woods, *Fulbright*, 106–23; Fulbright, *Arrogance of Power*, 107–9; Fry, "To Negotiate or Bomb," 518–20.

77. NBC News, "Brinkley, First Spot," June 30, 1965, Brinkley Scripts Folder, box 28, Brinkley Papers, Wisconsin Historical Society.

78. "The Worries of Washington," *Newsweek*, April 18, 1966; "GOP Says Johnson Deceives on War," *NYT*, September 21, 1966. Van Atta, *With Honor*, 112–13. See also Roche to Watson, "1966 Election Outlook," January 27, 1966, WHCF-SF, PL 2, box 85, Johnson Papers.

79. Clark and Reynolds, "Dirksen Interview," ABC Transcript, January 9, 1966, Remarks and Releases File, Dirksen Papers.

80. Johns, *Vietnam's Second Front*, 120; Hulsey, *Dirksen*, 65–67, 209.

81. Bator, "No Good Choices," 336.

82. Garfinkle, *Telltale Hearts*, 48; Jeffreys-Jones, *Peace Now!*, 46–47; Isserman and Kazin, *America Divided*, 7–22.

83. Chancellor to Zorthian, September 8, 1966, Defense Folder, USIA, IAF-VN, Entry 67, box 68, RG 276. On Westmoreland's strategy, see MacGarrigle, *Taking the Offensive*, 3–17.

84. Mohr, "U.S. Casualties in Vietnam Increasing Sharply in '66," *NYT*; "American Casualties in Week Reported Higher Than Saigon's"; Sheehan, "Casualties Show How Vietnam Differs from Earlier Wars"; Apple, "Casualties of U.S. During Last Week the War's Highest; *NYT*, March 3, September 9, and October 7, 1966, and January 20, 1967.

85. Muste to Lovell, February 28, 1966, Correspondence Folder, box 2, Fifth Avenue Vietnam Peace Parade Committee Records, Wisconsin Historical Society.

86. "Do GIs Have a Right to Know," undated, Flyers Folder, box 1, Fifth Avenue Vietnam Peace Parade Committee Records.

87. Ad Hoc Committee of Veterans for Peace in Vietnam, "Support the November 27 March on Washington for Peace in Vietnam," Students for Democratic Society Papers, Wisconsin Historical Society.

88. Ad Hoc Committee of Veterans for Peace in Vietnam, "Support the November 27 March on Washington for Peace in Vietnam"; The Vietnam Day Committee, Berkeley, "Reservists and Men of Draft Age," undated, both in Students for Democratic Society Papers.

89. Foley, *Confronting the War Machine*, 6–7, 14; Appy, *Working-Class War*, 36; "Statement of Support for Those Burning Their Draft Cards on November 6, 1965," Press Releases, 1965–71 Folder, box 2, Fifth Avenue Vietnam Peace Parade Committee Records.

90. Appy, *Working-Class War*, 18. See also "The Draft: The Unjust vs. the Unwilling," *Newsweek*, April 11, 1966.

91. Redmon to Moyers, November 20, 1965, WHCF-ND 9-2, Conscription File, box 148, Johnson Papers. Spector, *After Tet*, 29–32.

92. Capozzola, *Uncle Sam Needs You*, 34, 63–64. See also Barbeau and Henri, *Unknown Soldiers*, 10–11, 34–36; Wynn, *Afro-American*, 28–29.

93. "Huns Beaten Back by Our Boys," *Chicago Defender*, July 6, 1918; "Our Marines at Saipan," *Pittsburgh Courier*, July 8, 1944.

94. "Terrific 24th Keeps Fighting," *New York Amsterdam News*, September 9, 1950. For the issues and allegations surrounding this regiment, see MacGregor, *Integration of the Armed Forces*, 437–39; Bowers, Hammond, and MacGarringle, *Black Soldier, White Army*, 263–70; Blair, *Forgotten War*, 147–52, 683–84.

95. Wynn, *Afro-American and the Second World War*, 35.

96. MacGregor, *Integration of the Armed Forces*, 433–35, 457.

97. Taylor, "There is No Color Line for Heroes"; CASUALTIES HIGH IN 24TH REGIMENT: BLOOD FOR DEMOCRACY, both in *New Journal and Guide*, August 26, 1944, and October 7, 1950.

98. Booker to Martin, August 13, 1965, WHCF, ND 19 CO312, box 215, Johnson Papers; Westheider, *Fighting on Two Fronts*, 8–9; Huebner, *Warrior Image*, 184.

99. Scott, "Segregation is Peculiar," *Philadelphia Tribune*, November 16, 1918. According to a media inquiry in 1967, the military kept no casualty statistics by race during World War II and Korea. See Army Department, PI Division: News Branch, "Query Vietnam Personnel," February 14, 1967, Army-OCINFO, PI: News Branch, Press Queries Folder, Entry D-2, box 5, RG 319.

100. Negro Casualties, undated, WHCF-SF-ND 9-2, Casualties File, box 44, Johnson Papers.

101. "Negroes, Poor Whites Chief Victims Says Columnist Alsop," *Philadelphia Tribune*, October 1, 1966. On Stewart Alsop's attitude to Vietnam, see Merry, *Taking on the World*, 447–55.

102. On the NAACP stance, and the growing rank-and-file discontent, see, for instance, Wilkins to Wallace, January 10, 1966, and Smith to Wilkins, March 14, 1966, Vietnam Correspondence, 1966; Morsell, April 18, 1967, Vietnam Correspondence 1967 Folder, all in Group IV, box A88, NAACP Papers, LC.

103. "King, Powell, and Maclom X on the Vietnam War," [undated], Flyers Folder, box 1, Fifth Avenue Vietnam Peace Parade Committee Records; Williams, *Unwinding the War*, 427–40.

104. Mullen, *Blacks and Vietnam*, 16; "King, Powell, and Maclom X on the Vietnam War," [undated], Flyers Folder, box 1, Fifth Avenue Vietnam Peace Parade Committee Records.

105. Panzer to Johnson, October 6 and 24, 1967, WHCF-NF-Gallup, box 18, Johnson Papers.

106. "Notes of President's Meeting," October 23, 1967, Tom Johnson's Notes of Meetings, box 1, Johnson Papers.

107. Panzer to Johnson, May 26, 1967, June 27, 1968 (for student attitudes), and October 17, 1967 (for those personally affected by the war), WHCF-NF-Gallup, box 18, Johnson Papers.

108. DeBenedetti, *American Ordeal*, 203; Wells, *War Within*, 204–12.

109. "Westmoreland's Challenge to Critics," *Denver Post*, April 25, 1967; Panzer to Christian, April 25, 1967, WHCF-SF, PR 18 (Publicity), box 359, Johnson Papers; Westmoreland, *Soldier Reports*, 225–26.

110. Herring, *LBJ and Vietnam*, 143–44.

111. Laurence, *Cat from Hué*, 442.

112. Transcript, Stag Dinner for House Members (Democratic), November 2, 1967, Congressional Briefings on Vietnam, box 1, Johnson Papers.

113. Westmoreland-Rowan Interview, CBS, November 17, 1967, COMACV Public Statements Folder, Folders 1–50 box, Westmoreland Papers.

114. One problem, which later formed the basis for a high-profile court case, was whether these claims were knowingly based on manipulated intelligence. See Berman, *Johnson's War*, 74–75, 111–12.

115. "Safer, Cam Ne," YouTube video.

116. Clodfelter, *Limits of Air Power*, 126–27.

117. Small, *Johnson, Nixon, and the Doves*, 31–37; Small, *At the Water's Edge*, 48–47; Maraniss, *They Marched*, 69–75.

118. Salisbury, "A Visitor to Hanoi Inspects Damage Laid to U.S. Raids," *NYT*, December 25, 1966.

119. Hamilton, Lawrence, and Cozma, "The Paradox of Respectability," 83.

120. Wells, *War Within*, 101, 155; Gravel, *Pentagon Papers*, 4:171–72.

121. U.S. Congress, House, *Hearings before Subcommittee on Government Information*, April 20, 1967, 15–16; "U.S. Will Report Its Losses in War in Exact Figures," *NYT*, March 6, 1967.

122. Westmoreland, *Soldier Reports*, 273–74; Christian to Johnson, February 23, 1967, WHCF-SF, ND 19/CO312, box 224, Johnson Papers.

123. "The War: Casualties Pass 100,000," *LA Times*, October 8, 1967.

124. "Meeting with Advisers," October 5 and 15, 1967, Tom Johnson's Notes of Meetings, box 1, Johnson Papers; Westmoreland, *Soldier Reports*, 273–74. According to a Pentagon analysis, 70 percent of troops hospitalized between January 1965 and May 1967 had been returned to duty; see Nitze to Rusk, August 3, 1967, WHCF-SF, ND 9-2 (Casualties), box 44, Johnson Papers.

125. Califano to Johnson, June 10, 1966, WHCF-SF, ND 19/CO312, box 221, Johnson Papers; Lippmann, "The Credibility Gap-I," *WP*, April 21, 1967; Panzer to Johnson, October 24, 1967, WHCF-NF-Gallup, box 18, Johnson Papers; Turner, *Johnson's Dual War*, 176–77.

126. Califano to Johnson, June 10, 1966, WHCF-SF, ND 19/CO312, box 221, Johnson Papers.

127. Panzer to Johnson, January 26, 1968, WHCF-NF-Gallup, box 18, Johnson Papers.

128. Herring, *America's Longest War*, 226–32.

129. Spector, *After Tet*, 55; Braestrup, *Big Story*, 75–118.

130. Turner, *Johnson's Dual War*, 230–31, 234–35.

131. Kennedy, Speech, March 18, 1968, http://www.jfklibrary.org/; Schmitz, *Tet Offensive*, 138–40.

132. Panzer to Johnson, February 12, and March 12 and 29, 1968, WHCF-NF-Gallup, box 18, Johnson Papers.

133. Johnson, *Public Papers*, February 12 and March 16, 1968.

134. "Luncheon Meeting," March 22, 1968, Meeting Notes File, box 2, Johnson Papers.

135. "Meeting with Senior Foreign Policy Advisers," March 4, 1968, Tom Johnson's Notes of Meetings, box 1, Johnson Papers.

136. Johnson, *Public Papers*, March 31, 1968.

137. See, for instance, Nixon, September 20, 1968, PPS 208, Speech File, box 208, Nixon Papers; Kimball, *Nixon's Vietnam War*, 55–56.

138. Kimball, *Nixon's Vietnam War*, 82–83.

Chapter 6

1. Spector, *After Tet*, 144–45, 231–34; Sorley, *Better War*, 20–21; Stanton, *Rise and Fall*, 269–70; Hammond, *Public Affairs*, 2:34–39; Clarke, *Advice and Support*, 361–62.
2. Spector, *After Tet*, 319; "U.S. Vietnam Toll Was 14,500 in '68," *WP*, January 3, 1969.
3. MACV, "Weekly Summary," 6, 13, 20, and March 27, 1969, MACV HQ, Information Office: PI Division, Entry 305, box 2, RG 472. Reston, "Mr. Nixon and the Vietnam Casualties," *NYT*, March 7, 1969.
4. Zaffiri, *Hamburger Hill*, 16, 27–28; Sorley, *Better War*, 139–41; Stanton, *Rise and Fall*, 284–86. These were the casualties the U.S. military attributed specifically to the capture of the hill; overall losses for the operation were listed as 78 KIA and 546 WIA. Wheeler to Laird, May 21, 1969, Hamburger Hill Folder, National Security Council (NSC)-VN-SF, box 67, Nixon Papers, Nixon Library.
5. Just, "The Reality of War on Hamburger Hill," *WP*, May 21, 1969.
6. Sharbutt, "Americans Stained with Blood, Sweat, and Mud," *Washington Star*, May 19, 1969.
7. UPI wire No.144, undated [May 21, 1969], Hamburger Hill Folder, NSC-VN-SF, box 67, Nixon Papers; "Laird Defends U.S. Vietnam Tactics," *NYT*, May 26, 1969.
8. "Hamburger Hill Given Up after Bloody Victory," *Chicago Tribune*, May 28, 1969; "Mondale Hits Strategy on Viet Hill," *WP*, May 29, 1969; "War Scored by Mansfield," *Baltimore Sun*," May 30, 1969.
9. "Television Report," May 30–31, 1969, WHSF-SMOF, Annotated News Summaries, box 30, Nixon Papers.
10. On *Life's* circulation problems, see Brinkley, *The Publisher*, 454–55. *Time* had also turned against Vietnam, see Landers, *Weekly War*, 130–31.
11. "Vietnam: One Week's Dead," *Life*, June 27, 1969. For the magazine's earlier stance, see "A Town's Troubled Mood as War Comes Home," *Life*, August 12, 1966; Pachios to Moyers, September 2, 1966, WHCF-SF, ND 19/CO312, box 222, Johnson Papers, Johnson Library.
12. Small, *Presidency of Nixon*, 74; Dallek, *Nixon and Kissinger*, 183.
13. Kimball, *Nixon's Vietnam War*, 76–86; Burr and Kimball, "Nixon's Secret Nuclear Alert," 113–56; Shawcross, *Sideshow*, 19–30; Beecher, "Raids in Cambodia by U.S. Un-protested," *NYT*, May 9, 1969.
14. Nixon, *RN*, 382.
15. Kissinger to Nixon, "Impact of American Casualties on your Vietnam Policy," June 21, 1969, ND 8-1 (Casualties), box 26, Nixon Papers.
16. Butterfield to Laird, June 11, 1969, Hamburger Hill Folder, NSC-VN-SF, box 67, Nixon Papers.
17. Haldeman, *Diaries*, 48; Reston, "Edward Kennedy's Challenge to President Nixon," *NYT*, May 21, 1969. Within two months Chappaquiddick would end Kennedy's new position as the Democratic spearhead. For Nixon's response to Kennedy's speeches, see "Television Report," May 30–31, 1969, WHSF-SMOF, Annotated News Summaries, box 30, Nixon Papers.
18. Nixon, *Public Papers*, June 19, 1969.
19. Abrams to Wheeler, March 19, 1969, MAC 3806; and March 30, 1969, MAC 4035, both in Abrams Messages, CMH; Sorley, *Vietnam Chronicles*, 162. From April on, Washington did place more pressure on Abrams to reduce battlefield casualties; see Hammond, *Public Affairs*, 2:80–82.
20. Kissinger to Nixon, "Impact of American Casualties on your Vietnam Policy," June 21, 1969, ND 8-1 (Casualties), box 26, Nixon Papers.
21. Haldeman, *Diaries*, 69–70; Hammond, *Public Affairs*, 2:138; Kimball, *Nixon's War*, 151.
22. Wilson, "Laird Discloses Policy Designed to Cut Casualties," *WP*, July 16, 1969; Beecher, "U.S. Studies Shift of Tactics in War," *NYT*, July 25, 1969. On the lack of a specific public statement, see Hammond, *Public Affairs*, 2:137.
23. Cosmas, *MACV, 1968–73*, 256–57.
24. Spector, *After Tet*, 95–100; Sorley, *Better War*, 68–79.

25. Kissinger, *White House Years*, 1480–81.
26. Van Atta, *With Honor*, 113, 136, 313.
27. Laird to Nixon, "Trip to Vietnam and CINCPAC," March 13, 1969, Laird's Vietnam Trip Folder, NSC-VN-SF, box 70, Nixon Papers; Willbanks, *Abandoning Vietnam*, 16.
28. Scheider to Kissinger, "Background Briefing for Legislative People," April 15, 1969, Vietnam (General Files) Folder, NSC-VN-SF, box 129, Nixon Papers. Haldeman, *Diaries*, 69–70; Hanhimäki, *Flawed Architect*, 42–43; Willbanks, *Abandoning Vietnam*, 22.
29. Nixon, *Public Papers*, June 8, 1969.
30. Kissinger, *Ending the Vietnam War*, 84.
31. Nixon, Memo, October 10, 1970, President's Desk, PPF, box 185, Nixon Papers.
32. Nixon, *Public Papers*, January 20, 1969.
33. Laird to Nixon, "Trip to Vietnam and CINCPAC," March 13, 1969, Laird's Vietnam Trip Folder; Laird to Nixon, May 13, 1969, Speech Planning and Misc. Folder, both in NSC-VN-SF, box 70, Nixon Papers.
34. "The Politics of Polarization," *Time*, November 21, 1969.
35. MACV, "Weekly Summary," August 23, September 6 and 27, and October 4, 1969, Information Office: PI Division, box 2, RG 472.
36. Nixon to Kissinger, October 27, 1969, Notes of November 3, 1969 Speech Folder, NSC-VN-SF, box 79, Nixon Papers.
37. Nixon, *Public Papers*, November 3, 1969.
38. Small, *At the Water's Edge*, 141–42.
39. These paragraphs are based on DeBenedetti, *American Ordeal*, 252–63; Wells, *War Within*, 389–95; Small, *Nixon, Johnson, and the Doves*, 182–89; Van Atta, *With Honor*, 230–31.
40. Haldeman, *Diaries*, 107–8.
41. Mason, *Nixon and the Quest for a New Majority*, 62–63; Wells, *War Within*, 379–89.
42. Nixon, *Public Papers*, November 3, 1969.
43. "Gallup Telephone Poll—The President's Speech," undated [November 4, 1969], Notes of November 3, 1969 Speech Folder, NSC-VN-SF, box 79, Nixon Papers. See also Pach, "Our Worst Enemy," 556–57.
44. Flynn, *The Draft*, 245–49; Van Atta, *With Honor*, 246–47.
45. Nixon, *Public Papers*, April 20, 1970.
46. "Special Report: Television Commentary following the President's Speech," April 20, 1970; Wire Service Stories, April 21, 1970, both in President's April 20 Vietnam Speech Folder, NSC-VN-SF, box 124, Nixon Papers.
47. Wells, *War Within*, 403–9; Reeves, *President Nixon*, 176; Shawcross, *Sideshow*, 135–36.
48. Kimball, *Nixon's War*, 197–210; Dallek, *Nixon and Kissinger*, 163, 191–96; Willbanks, *Abandoning Vietnam*, 69–83.
49. Reeves, *President Nixon*, 200.
50. McManis to Kissinger, "Congressional Reaction to the President's Speech," May 1, 1970, President's Cambodia Speech Folder, NSC-Cambodia Operations, box 583, Nixon Papers
51. Nixon, *Public Papers*, April 30, 1970.
52. Abrams to Wheeler, May 1, 1970, MAC5871, Abrams Messages.
53. RNC, "Courageous Move to Save American Lives," May 4, 1970, President's Cambodia Speech Folder, NSC-Cambodia Operations, box 583, Nixon Papers.
54. De Onis, "Nixon Denounces 'Bums' on Campus," *NYT*, May 2, 1970.
55. Reeves, *President Nixon*, 200; DeBenedetti, *American Ordeal*, 279–80, Wells, *War Within*, 424–30. "Television Report," May 7, 1970, Reaction to President's Cambodia Speech Folder, NSC-Cambodia Operations, box 584, Nixon Papers.
56. Greenberg, *Nixon's Shadow*, 90.
57. "Tele Review: Part of the Family," *Variety*, June 2, 1971.
58. "Television Report," May 6, 1970, Reaction to President's Cambodia Speech Folder, NSC-Cambodia Operations, box 584, Nixon Papers.
59. "O'Brien Sees Cambodia Thrust Raising Deaths," *WP*, May 10, 1970.
60. "Spiking the Loot," *Newsweek*, May 18, 1970; Sigal, *Reporters and Officials*, 31–32; Hammond, *Public Affairs*, 2:326–27.
61. Heineman, *Campus Wars*, 245–49, 253; Reeves, *President Nixon*, 216.

62. The most controversial consequence of Nixon's new mood was the Huston Plan to gather intelligence on the antiwar movement. See Kuter, *Wars of Watergate*, 96–101.
63. "Television Report," May 8, 1970, Reaction to President's Cambodia Speech Folder, NSC-Cambodia Operations, box 584, Nixon Papers; Nixon, *Public Papers*, May 8, 1970.
64. "Television Report," May 7 and 8, 1970, Reaction to President's Cambodia Speech Folder, NSC-Cambodia Operations, box 584, Nixon Papers.
65. MACV, "Weekly Summary," and May 7, 14, 21 and 28, 1970, MACV HQ Information Office: PI Division, Entry 305, box 3, RG 472.
66. Nixon, *Public Papers*, June 30, 1970.
67. *Congressional Record*, 116, 34: 30567; Longley, "Congress and the Vietnam War," 302–3; Johns, *Vietnam's Second Front*, 283–87.
68. Reeves, *President Nixon*, 74.
69. Kissinger, *White House Years*, 453–56; Reeves, *President Nixon*, 177; Hammond, *Public Affairs*, 2:272–79; Finney, "U.S., Reacting to Senate Critics, to List Losses in Area Separately," *NYT*, March 10, 1970.
70. Stern and Kaiser, "'Zero Contact' Offensive Falls Short of Goals," *WP*, May 10, 1970; "Just How Important are Those Caches," *Time*, June 1, 1970; Hammond, *Public Affairs*, 2:327–28, 333–35.
71. Sterba, "U.S. War Deaths Cut by Half in Last Year," *NYT*, September 18, 1970.
72. "Casualty Figures Put at 5-Year Low," *NYT*, November 3, 1970.
73. MACV, Memo for Correspondents, "Explanation of Casualty Reports," November 19, 1970, box 3; Memo for the Press, August 26, 1969, box 2, both in MACV HQ Information Office: PI Division, Entry 305, box 3, RG 472.
74. Blumenthal, "Casualty Reports by U.S. Again Raise Skepticism," *NYT*, February 16, 1971.
75. Schmidt, "Pentagon Denies a Numbers Game," *NYT*, April 30, 1971.
76. McGovern, *American Journey*, 20, 128–32.
77. Miroff, *Liberals' Moment*, 13, 84–97.
78. Reeves, *President Nixon*, 497.
79. Hammond, *Public Affairs*, 2:458–62, 487–88; Haldeman, *Diaries*, 262; Davis, *Long Road Home*, 425–26.
80. Wells, *War Within*, 389–95; Dallek, *Nixon and Kissinger*, 305–6.
81. Nixon, *Public Papers*, January 25, 1972; Berman, *No Peace, No Honor*, 112–13.
82. Nixon, *Public Papers*, April 26, 1972. See also Hughes, "Fatal Politics," 498–500.
83. Randolph, *Powerful and Brutal Weapons*, 27, 120, 177–78, 183, 209; Andradé, *America's Last Vietnam Battle*, 25–26.
84. Berman, *No Peace, No Honor*, 133–34, 155–57, 215–18, 228–29, 246–47; Asselin, *A Bitter Peace*, 79–85,112–13, 163–73; Lien-Hang, *Hanoi's War*, 258–99.
85. "No U.S. Combat Deaths—First Time in Seven Years," *WP*, September 22, 1972.
86. Katz, "Public Opinion and Foreign Policy," 498.
87. Lord to Kissinger, "President's Speech," April 5, 1971, President's April 7, 1971 Speech Folder, NSC-VN-SF, box 124, Nixon Papers.
88. Ronder to Hatch, October 5, 1970; Stevens, Memo for Director of Defense Information, October 14, 1970, both in NET Doc on Next of Kin Folder, OSD: PA Projects, 1961–71, Entry 464, box 1, RG 330.
89. Small, "Nixon and the War at Home," 145.
90. Davis, *Long Road Home*, 229–45. For a more skeptical account of Nixon's motives, see Franklin, *M.I.A.*, 46–48.
91. Allen, "'Help Us Tell the Truth about Vietnam,'" 253–68; Davis, *Long Road Home*, 419–26.
92. Nixon, *Public Papers*, March 13, 1971, and October 16, 1972.
93. Nixon, *RN*, 868.
94. Hammond, *Public Affairs*, 2:382–85.
95. Johnson and Wilson, "The U.S. Army: A Battle for Survival," *WP*, September 12, 1971; "GI Jitters on the Home Front," *LA Times*, October 17, 1971; Hammond, *Public Affairs*, 2:382–88.
96. "Pentagon Reports 10,000 Died in War of Noncombat Causes," *NYT*, June 5, 1973.
97. Randolph, *Powerful and Brutal Weapons*, 125.
98. Clodfelter, *Limits of Air Power*, 195.

99. Oliver, *My Lai*, esp. 134–37.
100. Kimball, *Nixon's War*, 365–66; Wells, *War Within*, 561; DeBenedetti, *American Ordeal*, 345.
101. Nixon, *RN*, 889.
102. Isaacs, *Without Honor*, 500–501.
103. Kuter, *Wars of Watergate*, 155–59; Olson, *Watergate*, 9–21.
104. Hagopian, *Vietnam War in American Memory*, 32, 49.
105. Mueller, *Wars, Presidents, and Public Opinion*; Gelpi, Feaver, and Reifer, *Paying the Human Costs*, 9.
106. Reagan, *Public Papers*, August 18, 1980, and June 12, 1981.
107. Wilcox, *Waiting for an Army to Die*, ix; Scott, *Politics of Readjustment*, 75–97.
108. Shephard, *War of Nerves*, 348; Scott, *Politics of Readjustment*, 9.
109. Reagan, *Public Papers*, November 10, 1981. Hagopian, *Vietnam War in American Memory*, 202–3, 101–2, 348–97.
110. Cohen, *Empire Without Tears*, 70–75.
111. Hagopian, *Vietnam War in American Memory*, 44–45. Reagan cited in Sobel, *Impact of Public Opinion*, 114.
112. Braestrup, *Battle Lines*, 88–104.
113. "Pentagon Aide Vows Press Plan"; "Pentagon's Panel on Press Coverage to Meet"; "Key Sections of Panel's Report on the Military and the Press"; "Pentagon Issues New Guidelines for Combat Zones"; *NYT*, December 9, 1983, February 5, and August 24, 1984.
114. Weisskopf, "Media Pool is Activated by Pentagon," *WP*, April 22, 1985; "Pentagon Says Secret Press Plan Went Awry," *NYT*, April 23, 1985.
115. Shenon, "Handling of Press During Libya Fighting Faulted," *NYT*, April 7, 1986.
116. Wilson, "Army Study Plays Down Media's Vietnam-Era Impact," *WP*, August 29, 1989.
117. Powell, *Soldier's Way*, 303.

Chapter 7

1. http://www.alternet.org/asoldierspeaks/49368/; http://iraqmemorial.org/
2. Mueller, *Wars, Presidents, and Public Opinion*; Morlin, "How Much War Will Americans Support?" *WP*, September 2, 1990.
3. Friedman and Karsh, *Gulf Conflict*, 285.
4. Weiser, "Computer Simulations: Attempting to Predict the Price of Victory," *WP*, January 20, 1991.
5. Oreskes, "A Debate Unfolds about Going to War against the Iraqis," *NYT*, November 12, 1990.
6. Bush, *Public Papers*, November 30, 1990.
7. Friedman and Karsh, *Gulf Conflict*, 285–86; Gordon and Trainor, *Generals' War*, 379–80.
8. Woodward, "The Rules of the Game," 12–13; Taylor, *War and the Media*, 35–36, 50–54; Carruthers, *Media at War*, 134–36, 143.
9. Friedman and Karsh, *Gulf Conflict*, 408–9. Bush, *Public Papers*, March 1 and 2, 1991,
10. Hagopian, *Vietnam War in American Memory*, 411.
11. Clinton, *Public Papers*, March 24, 1999; Harris, *Survivor*, 367–68.
12. These paragraphs are based on Kristol and Kagan, "National Interest," 6–7; Ehrenberg et al., *Iraq Papers*, 19–20, 22–23, 26–27; Chernus, *Monsters to Destroy*, 29–31, 41.
13. McNaughton, "Action for South Vietnam," March 10, 1965, Vietnam Memos, vol. 30, NSF-CF-VN, box 14, Johnson Papers.
14. Halper and Clarke, *America Alone*, 26–27; Ehrenberg et al., *Iraq Papers*, 22–23; Kagan and Kagan, *While America Sleeps*, 426–29.
15. Mann, *Rise of the Vulcans*, ix–x, 254–55, 272–73; Halper and Clarke, *America Alone*, 14, 112–28.
16. "NYT/CBS Poll," *NYT*, September 25, 2001; Mann, *Rise of the Vulcans*, 299.
17. Cited in Woodward, *Bush at War*, 37.
18. Bush, *Public Papers*, September 14, 2001.
19. Woodward, *Bush at War*, 96.
20. Wright, et al., *Different Kind of War*, 2–3; Woodward, *Bush at War*, 38.

21. Rumsfeld-Myers, Press Conference, October 18, 2001, DOD News Transcripts, website; Gordon, "A Direct Engagement," *NYT*, October 20, 2001.

22. Wright et al., *Different Kind of War*, 35–40; Bergen, *Longest War*, 59.

23. Woodward, *Bush at War*, 278; Wright et al., *Different Kind of War*, 113–20; *U.S. Special Operations Command History*, 93–101.

24. Smucker, "How Bin Laden Got Away," *Christian Science Monitor*, March 4, 2002; Gellman and Ricks, "U.S. Concludes that Bin Laden Escaped at Tora Bora Fight," *WP*, April 17, 2002. Bergen, *Longest War*, 80–81.

25. Merkle, "Poll Shows Growing Concern About Terror War," November 8, 2001; Gary Langer, "Poll Finds Support for Bush, War on Terrorism Isn't Fading," March 11, 2002; both at ABC Poll Vault, website.

26. Dillon, "'He's a Hero,' Says Widow of Green Beret Killed in Afghan Combat," *NYT*, March 5, 2002.

27. Rumsfeld, *Known and Unknown*, 408–9; Herspring, *Rumsfeld's Wars*, 24–31, 71, 86–87; Bush, *Public Papers*, December 11, 2001.

28. Rumsfeld, September 10, 2001, DOD Speech Archive, website.

29. Herspring, *Rumsfeld's Wars*, 71.

30. Mann, *Rise of the Vulcans*, 332–58; Bush, *Public Papers*, February 26, 2003.

31. Gordon and Trainor, *Cobra II*, 28–30, 53, 76–77, 99–89, 95–96; Herspring, *Rumsfeld's Wars*, 114–29; Ricks, *Fiasco*, 121–22, 127–29; Rumsfeld, *Known and Unknown*, 425–42; Woodward, *Plan of Attack*, 36–37, 102.

32. Seib, *Beyond the Front Lines*, 51–54; Brewer, *Why America Fights*, 252–53.

33. Project for Excellence in Journalism, "Embedded Reporters."

34. Hamdy and Mobarak, "Iraq War Ushers in Web-based Era," 246–50; Kaye and Johnson, "Weblogs as a Source of Information," 294–96.

35. Jasperson and El-Kikhia, "CNN and al Jazeera's Media Coverage," 118–19, 126–27.

36. Gould, "Solider, Mother Meet at a TV Show," *NYT*, September 22, 1950; Hallin, "Uncensored War," 124–26, 138–39.

37. Gamson, *Claims to Fame*, 42–43; Project for Excellence in Journalism, "State of the News Media, 2006"; Stetler, "AP Says It Wants to Know Everything About Britney Spears," *NYT*, January 14, 2008; Seib, *Beyond the Front Lines*, 4.

38. Gordon and Trainor, *Cobra II*, 79, 360, 498–99; Woodward, *Plan of Attack*, 401–9.

39. U.S. Army, "Official Report on 507th Maintenance Company"; Gordon and Trainor, *Cobra II*, 240.

40. Yardley, "TV Images Confirm Fears of Prisoners' Kin," *NYT*, March 25, 2003; Seib, *Beyond the Front Lines*, 108.

41. Davey, "For 1,000 Troops, There is No Going Home," *NYT*, September 9, 2004; Hillman, "The Female Shape of the All-Volunteer Force," 150–61.

42. Jehl and Blair, "Rescue in Iraq and a 'Big Stir' in West Virginia," *NYT*, April 3, 2003.

43. Chinni, "Jessica Lynch"; Jehl and Blair, "Rescue in Iraq and a 'Big Stir' in West Virginia," *NYT*, April 3, 2003.

44. Wilgoren and Nagourney, "While Mourning Dead, Many Americans Say Level of Casualties is Acceptable," *NYT*, April 8, 2003.

45. AP, "Kerry Says U.S. Now has 'Backdoor Draft,'" June 3, 2004, MSNBC, website.

46. Gibbs and Thompson, "A Soldier's Life," *Time*, July 21, 2003.

47. "How Local Newspapers Reported Latest Deaths in Iraq," *Editor and Publisher*, October 12, 2006.

48. *NYT*, web edition; *WP*, web edition.

49. "Reading the Polls on Iraq"; Wilgoren and Nagourney, "While Mourning Dead, Many Americans Say Level of Casualties is Acceptable," *NYT*, February 23 and April 8, 2003.

50. Bush, *Public Papers*, May 1, 2003.

51. These paragraphs are based on Gordon and Trainor, *Cobra II*, 435, 455, 461–62, 498–99; Ricks, *Fiasco*, 163, 195, 217.

52. Rumsfeld-Myers, Press Conference, April 11, 2011; Rumsfeld-Garner, Press Conference, June 18, 2003; both in DOD News Transcripts. Rohde, "Deadly Attacks on GI's Rise," *NYT*, June 10, 2003.

53. Broder, "War for Public Opinion"; Kaufman, "Day's Death Toll for U.S. Troops is Highest Since March," *WP*, November 2 and 3, 2003.
54. Stevenson, "Public's Doubt Vs. Bush's Vows"; Bumiller, "Issue for Bush: How to Speak of Casualties?" *NYT*, November 3 and 5, 2003.
55. Milbank, "Curtains Ordered for Media Coverage of Returning Coffins," *WP*, October 21, 2003.
56. Bumiller, "Issue for Bush: How to Speak of Casualties?" *NYT*, November 5, 2003; B. Woodward, *State of Denial*, 319–20, 482.
57. Bumiller, "Issue for Bush: How to Speak of Casualties?" *NYT*, November 5, 2003.
58. Rosenthal, "Accounting for the Invisible Casualties Shouldn't Be a Matter of Politics"; Justice, "Bush Meets Families of 26 Killed in Iraq," both in *NYT*, November 14 and 25, 2003. Milbank, "Curtains Ordered for Media Coverage of Returning Coffins," *WP*, October 21, 2003.
59. Brewer, *Why America Fights*, 243; B. Woodward, *State of Denial*, 278.
60. Wilgoren and Nagourney, "While Mourning Dead, Many Americans Say Level of Casualties is Acceptable"; Davey, "For Those Who Question the War, Complications Amid the Pain of Loss," both in *NYT*, April 8 and 14, 2003.
61. Loeb, "In Iraq, Pace of Casualties has Accelerated," *WP*, December 28, 2003. WP-ABC Polls, 2003–2007.
62. Gelpi, Feaver, and Reifler, *Paying the Human Costs*, 142; WP-ABC Polls, 2003–2007.
63. Helm, "Turner Joy: Veterans Draw Parallels between Vietnam, Iraq," *Bremerton Sun*, August 8, 2004.
64. Broder, "The War for Public Opinion," *WP*, November 2, 2003.
65. "Powell, Roberts, Levin Interviewed on CBS' *Face the Nation*," *CQ Newsmaker Transcripts*, October 19, 2003, CQ.com, LC; Sachs, "Postwar GI Death Toll Exceeds Wartime Total," *NYT*, October 30, 2003.
66. Project for Excellence in Journalism, "Jessica Lynch."
67. U.S. Congress, House, *Oversight and Government Reform Committee Report: Misleading Information from the Battlefield*.
68. Ibid., 47.
69. Herbert, "Truth and Deceit," *NYT*, June 2, 2005; Morford, "The Big Lie of Jessica Lynch," *San Francisco Chronicle*, September 5, 2003. The distinction between "real heroes" and manufactured celebrities stems from Borstin's seminal book *Image*, 61.
70. Woodward, *Plan of Attack*, 203; Kornblut, "Kennedy to Assail Bush over Iraq War," *Boston Globe*, October 16, 2003.
71. Justice, "Bush Meets Families of 26 Killed in Iraq," *NYT*, November 25, 2003; Clark, "A New Course Needed in Iraq," *Boston Globe*, November 6, 2003.
72. Ricks, *Fiasco*, 331–32; ABC News Videos, "Blackwater Hangings," March 31, 2004.
73. Gelpi, Feaver, and Reifler, *Paying the Human Costs of War*, 162; Anselmo, "Uneasy Republicans at Bush's Side as Insurgency in Iraq Intensifies," *CQ Weekly—Defense*, April 10, 2004, CQ.com.
74. "Every Death Should be on the Front Page," *Daily Kos*, April 1, 2004.
75. Dobbs, "Kerry in Vietnam: Two Conflicting Tales," *WSJ*, August 24, 2004; Swift Vets and POWs for Truth, website.
76. Schlesinger, "Citing War's Costs, Kerry Goes after Bush," *WSJ*, September 9, 2004; Apple, "In Ohio, Unexpected Stumble from Kerry," *NYT*, September 12, 2004.
77. AP, "Kerry Rips Bush, Cheney Defends President," March 17, 2004, MSNBC, website.
78. "Transcript of the Candidates' First Debate," *NYT*, October 1, 2004.
79. Nagourney and Elder, "Bush Opens Lead Despite Unease Voiced in Survey," *NYT*, September 18, 2004; Ricks, *Fiasco*, 333–46.
80. Ricks, *Fiasco*, 359–61, 424–26; "AP Explains Its Iraq Coverage," *Editor and Publisher*, August 25, 2005.
81. Nagourney and Elder, "Bush Opens Lead Despite Unease Voiced in Survey," *NYT*, September 18, 2004; WP-ABC Polls, 2003–2007, website.
82. Davey, "For 1,000 Troops, There is No Going Home," *NYT*, September 9, 2004.
83. Bush, *Public Papers*, January 20, 2005.

84. Ricks, *Gamble*, 45–48, 55; iCasualties.org, website.
85. Kesler, "Is the Press Covering the Iraq War on the Cheap?"; "The 'Peculiar' Disappearance of Iraq Coverage"; "Number of Embeds Drops to Lowest Level in Iraq," *Editor and Publisher*, April 25, 2005, July 29, 2006, October 10, 2006.
86. "How News Outlets Reported U.S. Toll in Iraq Hitting 4,000," *Editor and Publisher*, March 23, 2008; iCasualties.org, website.
87. Fletcher, "Cindy Sheehan's Pitched Battle," *WP*, August 13, 2005; Griffin, "Cindy Sheehan Doesn't Speak for Me," *WSJ*, August 18, 2005; Rich, "The Swift Boating of Cindy Sheehan," *NYT*, August 21, 2005.
88. Saad, "Americans Sympathize."
89. Gelpi, Feaver, and Reifler, "Success Matters," 7-46.
90. Baker and Balz, "Bush Words Reflect Public Opinion Strategy," *WP*, June 30, 2005; Shane, "Bush's Speech on Iraq War Echoes Voice of an Analyst," *NYT*, December 4, 2005; Brewer, *Why We Fight*, 268–69; Woodward, *State of Denial*, 397–98.
91. Ricks, *Gamble*, 58; Sanger, "Bush Declares Sacrifice in Iraq to be 'Worth It,'" *NYT*, June 29, 2005.
92. "Seven Lawmakers Ask Bush for Explanation of Underreporting of Casualties in Iraq."
93. Bush, *Public Papers*, October 21, 2006. Rumsfeld, Interview on the O'Reilly Factor, December 12, 2005, DOD News Transcripts; Cloud, "Rumsfeld Says the Media Focus Too Much on Negatives in Iraq," *NYT*, December 6, 2005.
94. Rich, "Dying to Save the GOP Congress," *NYT*, October 29, 2006.
95. Blimes, "The Battle of Iraq's Wounded," *LA Times*, January 5, 2007; Grady, "Agency Says Higher Casualty Total Was Posted in Error," *NYT*, January 30, 2007.
96. Grady, "Agency Says Higher Casualty Total Was Posted in Error," *NYT*, January 30, 2007; "Casualties in Iraq," Antiwar.com, website.
97. "Rall Cartoon: U.S. Deaths in Iraq Uncounted," *Editor and Publisher*, August 8, 2005.
98. Hedges, "Parties Wage a Proxy War: It's Rumsfeld," *Chicago Tribune*, November 4, 2006. Kriner and Shen, *Casualty Gap*, 173.
99. Ricks, *Gamble*, 114–22, 141, 159, 167, 179.
100. Bauder, "Iraq Disappears as TV Story," *USA Today*, March 17, 2008; "Journalists in Iraq Defend Coverage," *Editor and Publisher*, November 27, 2007.
101. Ricks, *Gamble*, 188, 248.
102. Ibid., 79.
103. Remnick, *Bridge*, 344–49; "Senator Obama Interviewed on MSNBC," *CQ Newsmaker Transcripts*, January 23, 2007, CQ.com.
104. "Obama's Speech on Iraq, March 2008."
105. Woodward, *Obama's Wars*, 159–60, 178, 206.
106. Ibid., 247.
107. Obama, *Public Papers*, December 1, 2009.
108. http://iCasualties.org/, website; CBS-*NYT* Polls, 2010–11, website.
109. Obama, *Public Papers*, May 1, 2011.

Conclusion

1. "Bush Delivers Reading at Ground Zero on 9/11 Anniversary," YouTube.
2. Lincoln, *Public Papers*, November 19, 1863.
3. Roosevelt, *Public Papers*, June 12, 1944.
4. See, for instance, Casey, *Selling the Korean War*, especially 279–89. The concept of "remobilization" is developed by Horne, "Remobilizing for 'Total War,'" 195–211.
5. Bush, *Decision Points*, 263–64, 357–58, 369–70.
6. Robertson to Griffin, August 15, 1944, SHAEF General Staff, G-1 Administrative Section, DF 704, Entry 6, box 34, RG 331.
7. "Briefing Sheet on Press Relations of the U.S. Mission in Saigon," March 4, 1966, Policy—Press Relations Folder, USIA, IAF-VN, Entry 67, box 71, RG 276; Hammond, *Public Affairs*, 1:179–80.

8. Kriner and Shen, *Casualty Gap*, 9.
9. Halberstam, *Coldest Winter*, 5.
10. Gelpi, Feaver, and Reifler, "Success Matters," 7–46, and *Paying the Human Costs of War*, 162.
11. Editorial, "An Inexplicable Order," *NYT*, April 4, 1918.
12. "Angry U.S. Girds for Rough War," *Newsweek*, July 24, 1950.
13. Johnson, *Without Censor*, 176, 191; Seib, *Beyond the Front Lines*, 64.
14. Pogue, *Marshall*, 316.

BIBLIOGRAPHY

Primary Sources

NATIONAL ARCHIVES, COLLEGE PARK, MD

RG 44. Office of Government Reports (World War II)
RG 59. State Department (World War II and Korean War)
RG 65. Committee on Public Information (World War I)
RG 80. Office of the Secretary of the Navy (World War II)
RG 107. Office of the Secretary of War (World War I and II)
RG 120. American Expeditionary Force (World War I)
RG 127. Marine Corps (World War II and Korean War)
RG 147. Selective Service (World War II)
RG 160. Army Service Forces (World War II)
RG 165. War Department (World War I and II)
RG 208. Office of War Information (World War II)
RG 319. Army Chief of Staff (Korean War and Vietnam War)
RG 330. Office of Secretary of Defense (Korean War and Vietnam War)
RG 331. Supreme Headquarters Allied Expeditionary Forces (World War II and Korean War)
RG 407. Adjutant General's Office (World War I and II, Korean War)
RG 472. Military Assistance Command Vietnam (Vietnam War)

NATIONAL ARCHIVES, UK, KEW GARDENS, LONDON

WO, War Office Files (World War I and II)

PRIVATE PAPERS

Abrams, Creighton. Center of Military History, Washington, DC
Acheson, Dean. Truman Presidential Library, Independence, MO
Aiken, George S. Bailey/Howe Library, University of Vermont, Burlington, VT
Allen, Henry J. Library of Congress, Washington, DC
Alsop, Joseph, and Stewart Alsop. Library of Congress, Washington, DC
Army War College Curriculum Archives. Military History Institute, Carlisle, PA
Associated Press Archives. New York, NY
Baker, Newton D. Library of Congress, Washington, DC
Benedict, Stephen. Eisenhower Presidential Library, Abilene, KS
Bigart, Homer. Wisconsin Historical Society, Madison, WI
Boyle, Harold V. Wisconsin Historical Society, Madison, WI

Bradley, Omar. Military History Institute, Carlisle, PA
Brinkley, David. Wisconsin Historical Society, Madison, WI
Carroll, Raymond G. Library of Congress, Washington, DC
Collingwood, Charles. Wisconsin Historical Society, Madison, WI
Collins, J. Lawton. Eisenhower Presidential Library, Abilene, KS
Corey, Herbert. Library of Congress, Washington, DC
Creel, George. Library of Congress, Washington, DC
Davis, Elmer. Library of Congress, Washington, DC
Dirksen, Everett. Dirksen Congressional Center, Pekin, IL
Drum, Hugh A. Military History Institute, Carlisle, PA
Eaker, Ira. Library of Congress, Washington, DC
Early, Stephen. Roosevelt Library, Hyde Park, NY
Echols, Marion P. Military History Institute, Carlisle, PA
Eisenhower, Dwight D. Eisenhower Presidential Library, Abilene, KS
Fifth Avenue Vietnam Peace Parade Committee. Wisconsin Historical Society, Madison, WI
Halleck, Charles A. Lilly Library, Indiana University, Bloomington, IN
Hansen, Chester B. Military History Institute, Carlisle, PA
Harbord, James G. Library of Congress, Washington, DC
Howard, Roy W. Library of Congress, Washington, DC
Hughes, Emmett. Mudd Library, Princeton University, Princeton, NJ
Johnson, Lyndon B. Johnson Presidential Library, Austin, TX
Kennedy, John F. Kennedy Presidential Library, Boston, MA
Knox, Frank. Library of Congress, Washington, DC
Krock, Arthur. Mudd Library, Princeton University, Princeton, NJ
Luce, Clare Booth. Library of Congress, Washington, DC
MacArthur, Douglas. MacArthur Memorial Library, Norfolk, VA
MacLeish, Archibald. Library of Congress, Washington, DC
March, Peyton. Library of Congress, Washington, DC
Marshall, George C. Virginia Military Institute, Lexington, VA
Mason, Frank E. Wisconsin Historical Society, Madison, WI
McCormick, Robert. Wisconsin Historical Society, Madison, WI
Merrick, Richard H. Military History Institute, Carlisle, PA
Morgenthau, Jr., Henry. Roosevelt Presidential Library, Hyde Park, NY
Mueller, Merrill. Wisconsin Historical Society, Madison, WI
NAACP. Library of Congress, Washington, DC
New York Times Company Records: Adolph S. Ochs Papers. New York Public Library
New York Times Company Records: Arthur H. Sulzberger Papers. New York Public Library
Nixon, Richard M. Nixon Presidential Library, Yorba Linda, CA
Nolan, Dennis. Military History Institute, Carlisle, PA
Palmer, Frederick. Military History Institute, Carlisle, PA
Patton, George S. Library of Congress, Washington, DC
Pershing, John. Library of Congress, Washington, DC
Pyle, Ernie. Lilly Library, Indiana University, Bloomington, IN
Quirk, James T. Truman Presidential Library, Independence, MO
Republican Party, National Committee. Library of Congress, Washington, DC
Ridgway, Matthew B. Military History Institute, Carlisle, PA
Roosevelt, Franklin D. Roosevelt Presidential Library, Hyde Park, NY
Rosenman, Samuel I. Roosevelt Presidential Library, Hyde Park, NY
Russell, Richard B. University of Georgia, Athens, GA
Salisbury, Harrison. Butler Library, Columbia University, New York, NY
Sevareid, A. Eric. Library of Congress, Washington, DC
Smith, H. Alexander. Mudd Library, Princeton University, Princeton, NJ
Stimson, Henry. Yale University, New Haven, CT

Students for Democratic Society. Wisconsin Historical Society, Madison, WI
Taft, Robert A. Library of Congress, Washington, DC
Tobey, Charles W. Dartmouth College, Hanover, NH
Time Magazine Dispatches. Houghton Library, Harvard University, Cambridge, MA
Truman, Harry S. Truman Presidential Library, Independence, MO
Viskniskki, Guy T. Military History Institute, Carlisle, PA
Westmoreland, William. Center of Military History, Washington, DC

NEWSPAPERS AND MAGAZINES

Boston Globe
Bremerton Sun
Chicago Daily News
Chicago Tribune
Christian Science Monitor
Cleveland Press
Collier's
Columbus Ledger-Enquirer
Editor and Publisher
Life
Literary Digest
Los Angeles Times (LA Times)
New York Herald
New York Herald Tribune
New York Times (NYT)
Newsweek
San Francisco Chronicle
San Francisco Examiner
Time
Times (London)
U.S. News & World Report
USA Today
Variety
Wall Street Journal (WSJ)
Washington Daily News
Washington Post (WP)
Washington Star
Washington Times
Washington Times-Herald

PUBLISHED DOCUMENTS

Beschloss, Michael R., ed. *Taking Charge: The Johnson White House Tapes, 1963–1964*. New York: Simon and Schuster, 1997.
Bliss, Edward, ed. *In Search of Light: The Broadcasts of Edward R. Murrow, 1938–1961*. New York: Da Capo, 1997.
Ehrenberg, John, J. Patrice McSherry, José Ramón Sánchez, and Caroleen Marji Sayej, eds. *The Iraq Papers*. New York: Oxford University Press, 2010.
Ferrell, Robert H., ed. *Dear Bess*. New York: W. W. Norton, 1983.
Four Minute Men Bulletin. Washington, DC: Committee on Public Information, 1917–1918.
Gravel, Mike, ed. *The Pentagon Papers: The Defense Department History of United States Decision-making on Vietnam*. 3 vols. Boston: Beacon Press, 1971.
Haldeman, H. R. *The Haldeman Diaries: Inside the Nixon White House*. New York: G. P. Putnam, 1994.
Link, Arthur, ed. *The Papers of Woodrow Wilson*. 69 vols. Princeton: Princeton University Press, 1966–94.

McGovern, George. *An American Journey: The Presidential Campaign Speeches of George McGovern.* New York: Random House, 1974.

Pyle, Ernie. *Brave Men.* Lincoln, NE: Bison Books, 2001.

Republican Party Pamphlets. Washington, DC: Library of Congress.

Sorley, Lewis, ed. *Vietnam Chronicles: The Abrams Tapes, 1968–1972.* Lubbock: Texas Tech University Press, 2004.

United States Army in the World War, 1917–1919. Vols. 10–17. Washington, DC: Center of Military History, 1988.

U.S. Army. Adjutant General's Office, Statistical and Accounting Branch. *Army Battle Casualties and Non-Battle Deaths in World Two: Final Report.* Washington, DC: Department of the Army, 1946.

U.S. Censorship Office. *Code of Wartime Practices for American Broadcasters.* Washington, DC: GPO, 1942.

U.S. Congress. *Congressional Record.* Washington, DC: GPO, 1917–2011.

U.S. Congress. House of Representatives. *Hearings before Appropriations Committee, Subcommittee: Military Establishment Appropriation for 1944.* Washington, DC: GPO, 1943.

———. *Hearings before Military Affairs Committee: National Cemeteries.* Washington, DC: GPO, 1945.

———. *Hearings before Rules Committee: Losses of Thirty-Fifth Division during the Argonne Battle.* Washington, DC: GPO, 1919.

———. *Hearings before Special Committee on Un-American Activities: Report on the Peace Now Movement.* Washington, DC: GPO, 1944.

———. *Oversight and Government Reform Committee Report: Misleading Information from the Battlefield: The Tillman and Lynch Episodes.* Washington, DC: GPO, 2008.

U.S. Congress, Senate. *Hearings before the Armed Services and Foreign Relations Committees: Military Situation in the Far East.* Washington, DC: GPO, 1951.

———. *Hearings before the Armed Services Committee: Ammunition Supplies in the Far East.* Washington, DC: GPO, 1953.

———. *Hearings before Foreign Relations Committee: News Policies in Vietnam.* Washington, DC: GPO, 1966.

———. *Hearings before Foreign Relations Committee: To Promote the Defense of the United States.* Washington, DC: GPO, 1941.

———. *Hearings before Military Affairs Committee: Delay in Casualty Lists.* Washington, DC: GPO, 1918.

———. *Hearings before Military Affairs Committee: Veterans' Rights to Benefits.* Washington, DC: GPO, 1944.

U.S. State Department. *Foreign Relations of the United States: Conference at Potsdam.* 2 vols. Washington, DC: GPO, 1960.

———. *Foreign Relations of the United States: The Conferences at Washington, 1941–1942, and Casablanca, 1943.* Washington, DC: GPO, 1968.

———. *Foreign Relations of the United States: Korea, 1950.* Vol. 7. Washington, DC: GPO, 1976.

U.S. War College Division, General Staff Corps. *The Proper Relationship Between the Army and the Press in War.* Washington, DC: GPO, 1916.

U.S. War Department. *Regulations for Correspondents Accompanying U.S. Army Forces in the Field.* Washington, DC: GPO, 1941.

———. *U.S. Army Field Service Regulations, 1914, Corrected to April 15, 1917.* Washington, DC: GPO, 1917.

MEMOIRS

Bradley, Omar N. *A Soldier's Story.* New York: Modern Library, 1999.

Broun, Heywood. *The AEF: With General Pershing and the American Forces.* New York: D. Appleton, 1918.

Bush, George W. *Decision Points.* New York: Modern Library, 2010.

Butcher, Harry C. *My Three Years with Eisenhower*. New York: Simon and Schuster, 1946.

Dean, William F. *General Dean's Story*. New York: Viking, 1954.

Johnson, Lyndon B. *Vantage Point: Perspectives of the Presidency, 1963–1969*. New York: Holt, Rinehart, and Winston, 1971.

Johnson, Thomas M. *Without Censor*. Indianapolis: Bobbs-Merrill, 1928.

Kennedy, Ed. *Ed Kennedy's War: V-E Day, Censorship, and the Associated Press*. Baton Rouge: Louisiana State University Press, 2012.

Kissinger, Henry. *Ending the Vietnam War: A History of America's Involvement in and Extrication from the Vietnam War*. New York: Simon and Schuster, 2003.

———. *White House Years*. London: Weidenfeld and Nicolson, 1979.

Laurence, John. *The Cat from Hué: A Vietnam War Story*. New York: Public Affairs, 2002.

Lytton, Neville. *The Press and the General Staff*. London: W. Collins, 1920.

McAdoo, William G. *Crowded Years*. Boston: Century, 1931.

McNamara, Robert. *In Retrospect: The Tragedy and Lessons of Vietnam*. New York: Crown, 1995.

Mecklin, John. *Mission in Torment*. Garden City, NY: Doubleday, 1965.

Middleton, Drew. *Where Has Last July Gone?* New York: Quadrangle/New York Times Books, 1973.

Moore, Harold G., and Joseph L. Galloway. *We Were Soldiers Once . . . And Young: Ia Drang: The Battle that Changed the War in Vietnam*. New York: Random House, 1992.

Nixon, Richard M. *RN: The Memoirs of Richard Nixon*. London: Book Club, 1978.

Palmer, Frederick. *America in France*. New York: Dodd, Mead, 1918.

———. *With My Own Eyes*. New York: A. L. Burt, 1932.

Pershing, John J. *My Experiences in the World War*. London: Hodder and Stoughton, 1931.

Pogue, Forrest C. *Pogue's War: Diaries of a WWII Combat Historian*. Lexington: University Press of Kentucky, 2001.

Powell, Colin. *A Soldier's Way: An Autobiography*. London: Random House, 1995.

Ridgway, Matthew B. *The Korean War*. Garden City, NY: Doubleday, 1967.

Rumsfeld, Donald. *Known and Unknown: A Memoir*. New York: Sentinel, 2011.

Salisbury, Harrison. *A Journey for Our Times: A Memoir*. New York: Harper and Row, 1983.

Sevareid, Eric. *Not So Wild a Dream: A Personal Story of Youth and the American Faith*. New York: Atheneum, 1976.

Tumulty, Joseph. *Wilson As I Knew Him*. Garden City, NY: Literary Digest, 1921.

Westmoreland, William. *A Soldier Reports*. Garden City, NY: Doubleday, 1976.

INTERNET DOCUMENTS AND DATABASES

ABC News Vault. http://abcnews.go.com/sections/politics/PollVault/pollvault

ABC News Videos. "Blackwater Hangings," March 31, 2004. http://abcnews.go.com/Archives/video/march-31-2004-blackwater-hangings-9719071.

Antiwar.com. http://www.antiwar.com/casualties/

CBS-*New York Times* Polls, 2010–2011. http://www.pollingreport.com/afghan.htm

CQ.com. Library of Congress.

Daily Kos. http://www.dailykos.com/

Fox News. http://www.foxnews.com/

Free Republic. http://www.freerepublic.com/home.htm

Helm, Elaine. "*Turner Joy*: Veterans Draw Parallels between Vietnam, Iraq." August 28, 2004. http://www.vfp109rcc.org/uss_turner_joy_rally_by_vfp.htm.

"History of the Dog Tag." http://www.173rdairborne.com/dogtag.htm.

iCasualties.org. http://icasualties.org/Iraq/ByMonth.aspx

Johnson, Lyndon B. Tapes. Miller Center for Public Affairs. http://millercenter.org/scripps/archive/presidentialrecordings/johnson

Kennedy, Robert. Speech, 18 March 1968. http://www.jfklibrary.org/

MSNBC. http://www.msnbc.msn.com/

New York Times, web edition. http://projects.latimes.com/wardead/; http://www.nytimes.com/ref/us/20061228_3000FACES_TAB2.html

Nixon, Richard M. Tapes. http://nixontapes.org/

"Obama's Speech on Iraq, March 2008." *Council on Foreign Relations: Essential Documents.* http://www.cfr.org/us-election-2008/obamas-speech-iraq-march-2008/p15761

Project for Excellence in Journalism. "Embedded Reporters: What Are Americans Getting?" April 3, 2003. www.journalism.org/resources/briefing/archive/.

———. "Jessica Lynch: Media Mythmaking in the Iraq War." June 23, 2003. http://www.journalism.org/print/223

———. "The State of the News Media, 2006." http://stateofthemedia.org/2006/journalist-survey-intro/commentary/

Public Papers of the Presidents. American Presidency Project. http://www.presidency.ucsb.edu/index.php

Saad, Lydia. "Americans Sympathize with Protesting Mum." *Gallup News Service.* September 2, 2005. http://www.gallup.com/poll/18355/Americans-Sympathize-Protesting-Mom.aspx.

"Seven Lawmakers Ask Bush for Explanation of Underreporting of Casualties in Iraq." http://www.ufppc.org/us-a-world-news-mainmenu-35/3785-news-seven-lawmakers-ask-bush-for-explanation-of-underreporting-of-american-casualties-in-iraq.html.

Swift Vets and POWs for Truth. http://www.swiftvets.com/

U.S. Army. Official Report on the 507th Maintenance Company: An Nasiriyah, Iraq. http://www.why-war.com/files/article07102003a.pdf

U.S. Defense Department. DOD News Transcripts Archive. http://www.defense.gov/transcripts/archive.aspx

———. DOD Speech Archive. http://www.defense.gov/speeches/archive.aspx

U.S. Marine Corps Personnel Casualties in World War II, www.history.navy.mil/faqs/faq11-1.htm.

Washington Post, web edition. http://projects.washingtonpost.com/fallen/

Washington Post-ABC Polls, 2003–2007. http://www.washingtonpost.com/wp-srv/politics/polls/postpoll_060307.html

YouTube Video. "The Battle for Ia Drang." *CBS.* 1965. http://www.youtube.com/watch?v=25x53ibwp7A

———. "Bush Delivers Reading at Ground Zero on 9/11 Anniversary." *PBS Video.* 2011. http://www.youtube.com/watch?v=mCBP6Rus93o

———. "Safer Cam Ne." 1965. http://www.youtube.com/watch?v=hNYZZi25Ttg

———. "With the Marines at Tarawa." Marine Corps-Warner Brothers. 1944. http://www.youtube.com/watch?v=lSzIohU1Zj4

Secondary Sources

BOOKS

Ambrose, Stephen E. *D-Day: The Climactic Battle of World War II.* New York: Simon and Schuster, 1994.

———. *The Supreme Commander: The War Years of Dwight D. Eisenhower.* Jackson: University Press of Mississippi, 1970.

Andradé, Dale. *America's Last Vietnam Battle: Hanoi's 1972 Easter Offensive.* Lawrence: University Press of Kansas, 2001.

Appleman, Roy E. *Disaster in Korea: The Chinese Confront MacArthur.* College Station: Texas A&M University Press, 1989.

———. *Escaping the Trap: The U.S. Army X Corps in Northeast Korea, 1950.* College Station: Texas A&M University Press, 1990.

———. *Ridgway Duels for Korea.* College Station: Texas A&M University Press, 1990.

———. *South to the Naktong, North to the Yalu.* Washington, DC: Center of Military History, 1961.

Appleman, Roy E., James M. Burns, Russell A. Guergeler, and John Steven. *Okinawa: The Last Battle.* Washington, DC: Center of Military History, 2005.

Appy, Christian G. *Working-Class War: American Combat Soldiers and Vietnam.* Chapel Hill: University of North Carolina Press, 1993.

Asselin, Pierre. *A Bitter Peace: Washington, Hanoi, and the Making of the Paris Peace Agreement.* Chapel Hill: University of North Carolina Press, 2002.

Atkinson, Rick. *An Army at Dawn: The War in North Africa, 1942–1943.* New York: Henry Holt, 2002.

———. *The Day of Battle: The War in Sicily and Italy, 1943–1944.* New York: Henry Holt, 2007.

———. *The Guns at Last Light: The War in Western Europe, 1944–1945.* New York: Henry Holt, 2013.

Axelrod, Alan, *Selling the Great War: The Making of American Propaganda.* New York: Macmillan, 2009.

Barbeau, Arthur E., and Florette Henri. *The Unknown Soldiers: African-American Troops in World War I.* New York: Da Capo, 1996.

Beaver, Daniel R. *Newton D. Baker and the American War Effort, 1917–1919.* Lincoln: University of Nebraska Press, 1966.

Beevor, Antony. *D-Day: The Battle for Normandy.* London: Penguin, 2009.

Bergen, Peter L. *The Longest War: The Enduring Conflict between America and al-Qaeda.* New York: Free Press, 2011.

Berman, Larry. *Lyndon Johnson's War.* New York: W. W. Norton, 1989.

———. *No Peace, No Honor: Nixon, Kissinger, and Betrayal in Vietnam.* New York: Free Press, 2001.

Blair, Clair. *The Forgotten War: America in Korea, 1950–1953.* Annapolis, MD: Naval Institute Press, 1987.

Blumenson, Martin. *Breakout and Pursuit.* Washington, DC: Center of Military History, 1961.

Bodnar, John. *The "Good War" in American Memory.* Baltimore, MD: Johns Hopkins University Press, 2010.

Boritt, Gabor. *The Gettysburg Gospel.* New York: Simon and Schuster, 2006.

Borstin, Daniel J. *The Image: A Guide to Pseudo-Events in America.* New York: Vintage, 1992.

Bowers, William T., William M. Hammond, and George L. MacGringle. *Black Soldier, White Army: The 24th Regiment in Korea.* Washington, DC: Center of Military History, 1996.

Braestrup, Peter. *Battle Lines.* New York: Priority Press, 1985.

———. *Big Story.* New York: Anchor Press, 1978.

Braim, Paul. *The Test of Battle: The AEF in the Meuse-Argonne Campaign.* Newark: University of Delaware Press, 1987.

———. *The Will to Win: The Life of General James A. Van Fleet.* Annapolis, MD: Naval Institute Press, 2001.

Brewer, Susan A. *Why America Fights: Patriotism and War Propaganda from the Philippines to Iraq.* New York: Oxford University Press, 2009.

Brinkley, Alan. *The Publisher: Henry Luce and the American Century.* New York: Knopf, 2010.

Brinkley, Douglas. *Cronkite.* New York: HarperCollins, 2012.

Bruce, Robert B. *A Fraternity of Arms: America and France in the Great War.* Lawrence: University Press of Kansas, 2003.

Calder, Angus. *The Myth of the Blitz.* London: Pimlico, 1991.

Cannon, Hamlin. *Leyte: Return to the Philippines.* Washington, DC: Center of Military History, 1954.

Capozzola, Christopher. *Uncle Sam Needs You: World War I and the Making of the Modern American Citizen.* New York: Oxford University Press, 2008.

Caridi, Ronald J. *The Korean War and American Politics: The Republican Party as a Case Study.* Philadelphia: University of Pennsylvania Press, 1968.

Carland, John M. *Stemming the Tide, May 1965 to October 1966.* Washington, DC: Center of Military History, 2000.

Carruthers, Susan L. *The Media at War.* Basingstoke: Palgrave, 2000.

Carson, Clayborne. *In Struggle: SNCC and the Black Awakening of the 1960s.* Cambridge, MA: Harvard University Press, 1995.

Casey, Steven. *Cautious Crusade: Franklin D. Roosevelt, American Public Opinion, and the War against Nazi Germany.* New York: Oxford University Press, 2001.

————. *Selling the Korean War: Propaganda, Politics, and Public Opinion in the United States, 1950–1953*. New York: Oxford University Press, 2008.

Chambers, John Whiteclay. *To Raise an Army: The Draft Comes to Modern America*. New York: Free Press, 1987.

Chappell, John D. *Before the Bomb: How America Approached the End of the Pacific War*. Lexington: University of Kentucky Press, 1997.

Chernus, Ira. *Monsters to Destroy: The Neoconservative War on Terror and Sin*. Boulder, CO: Paradigm, 2006.

Clarke, Jeffrey J. *Advice and Support: The Final Years, 1965–1973*. Washington, DC: Center of Military History, 1988.

Clodfelter, Mark. *The Limits of Air Power: The American Bombing of North Vietnam*. Lincoln, NE: Bison Books, 2006.

Coffman, Edward M. *The War to End All Wars: The American Military Experience in World War I*. Madison: University of Wisconsin Press, 1986.

Cohen, Warren I. *Empire Without Tears: America's Foreign Relations, 1921–1933*. Philadelphia: Temple University Press, 1987.

Cole, Hugh M. *Ardennes: The Battle of the Bulge*. Washington, DC: Center of Military History, 1965.

————. *The Lorraine Campaign*. Washington, DC: Office of the Chief of Military History, Department of the Army, 2007.

Cole, Wayne S. *Roosevelt and the Isolationists, 1932–45*. Lincoln: University of Nebraska Press, 1983.

Colley, David P. *Safely Rest*. New York: Berkeley Publishing Group, 2004.

Cooper, John Milton. *Woodrow Wilson: A Biography*. New York: Knopf, 2009.

Cornebise, Alfred E. *The Stars and Stripes: Doughboy Journalism in World War I*. Westport, CT: Greenwood Press, 1984.

Cosmas, Graham A. *MACV: The Joint Command in the Years of Withdrawal, 1968–1973*. Washington, DC: Center of Military History, 2007.

Crane, C. Conrad. *Bombs, Cities, Civilians: American Airpower Strategy in World War II*. Lawrence: University Press of Kansas, 1993.

Craven, Wesley Frank, and James Lea Cate. *The Army Air Forces in World War II*. 7 vols. Washington, DC: GPO, 1983.

Crowl, Philip A. *Campaign in the Marianas*. Washington, DC: Center of Military History, 1995.

Crowl, Philip A., and Edmund G. Love. *Seizure of the Gilberts and Marshalls*. Washington, DC: Center of Military History, 1955.

Crozier, Emmet. *American Reporters on the Western Front, 1914–1918*. New York: Oxford University Press, 1959.

Cull, Nicholas J. *The Cold War and the United States Information Agency: American Propaganda and Public Diplomacy, 1945–1989*. Cambridge: Cambridge University Press, 2008.

Dallek, Robert. *Flawed Giant: Lyndon Johnson and His Times, 1961–1973*. New York: Oxford University Press, 1998.

————. *Franklin D. Roosevelt and American Foreign Policy, 1932–1945*. New York: Oxford University Press, 1979.

————. *Nixon and Kissinger: Partners in Power*. New York: HarperCollins, 2007.

Darilek, Richard E. *A Loyal Opposition in Time of War: The Republican Party and the Politics of Foreign Policy from Pearl Harbor to Yalta*. Westport, CT: Greenwood Press, 1976.

Davis, Vernon E. *The Long Road Home: U.S. Prisoner of War Policy and Planning in Southeast Asia*. Washington, DC: Office of Secretary of Defense, Historical Office, 2000.

DeBenedetti, Charles. *An American Ordeal: The Antiwar Movement of the Vietnam Era*. Syracuse, NY: Syracuse University Press, 1990.

Desmond, Robert W. *Windows on the World: The Information Process in a Changing Society, 1900–1920*. Iowa City: University of Iowa Press, 1980.

D'Este, Carlo. *Patton: A Genius for War*. New York: HarperCollins, 1995.

Devlin, Patrick. *Too Proud to Fight: Woodrow Wilson's Neutrality*. New York: Oxford University Press, 1975.

Dietz, Terry. *Republicans and Vietnam, 1961–1968*. Westport, CT: Greenwood Press, 1986.

Divine, Robert A. *Foreign Policy and U.S. Presidential Elections, 1940–1948*. New York: New Viewpoints, 1974.

Doenecke, Justus D. *The Battle Against Intervention, 1939–1941*. Malabar, FL: Kreiger, 1997.

———. *Storm on the Horizon: The Challenge to American Intervention, 1939–1941*. Lanham, MD: Rowman and Littlefield, 2003.

Doubler, Michael M. *Closing with the Enemy: How GIs Fought the War in Europe, 1944–1945*. Lawrence: University Press of Kansas, 1994.

Dyer, George C. *The Amphibians Came to Conquer*. 2 vols. Washington, DC: GPO, 1969.

Farnham, Barbara Rearden. *Roosevelt and the Munich Crisis: A Study of Political Decision-Making*. Princeton: Princeton University Press, 1997.

Farrar, Martin J. *News from the Front: War Correspondents on the Western Front, 1914–1918*. Stroud, UK: Sutton Publishing, 1998.

Faust, Drew Gilpin. *This Republic of Suffering: Death and the American Civil War*. New York: Knopf, 2008.

Feaver, Peter D., and Christopher Gelpi. *Choosing Your Battles: American-Civil Relations and the Use of Force*. Princeton: Princeton University Press, 2004.

Ferrell, Robert H. *Collapse at Meuse-Argonne: The Failure of the Missouri-Kansas Division*. Columbia: University of Missouri Press, 2004.

———. *The Dying President: Franklin D. Roosevelt, 1944–1945*. Columbia: University of Missouri Press, 1998.

Flynn, George Q. *The Draft, 1940–1973*. Lawrence: University Press of Kansas, 1993.

———. *Lewis B. Hershey: Mr. Selective Service*. Chapel Hill: University of North Carolina Press, 1985.

Foley, Michael S. *Confronting the War Machine: Draft Resistance during the Vietnam War*. Chapel Hill: University of North Carolina Press, 2003.

Foot, Rosemary. *Substitute for Victory: The Politics of Peacemaking at the Korean Armistice Talks*. Ithaca, NY: Cornell University Press, 1990.

———. *The Wrong War: American Policy and Dimensions of the Korean Conflict, 1950–1953*. Ithaca, NY: Cornell University Press, 1985.

Foster, H. Schuyler. *Studies in America's News of the European War*. PhD diss., University of Chicago, 1932.

Frank, Richard E. *Downfall: The End of the Imperial Japanese Empire*. New York: Penguin Press, 1999.

Franklin, H. Bruce. *M.I.A or Mythmaking in America*. Chicago: University of Chicago Press, 1992.

Freedman, Lawrence. *Kennedy's Wars: Berlin, Cuba, Laos, and Vietnam*. New York: Oxford University Press, 2000.

Freedman, Lawrence, and Efraim Karsh. *The Gulf Conflict, 1990–1991: Diplomacy and War in the New World Order*. London: Faber and Faber, 1993.

Fulbright, J. William. *The Arrogance of Power*. London: Pelican, 1970.

Gamson, Joshua. *Claims to Fame: Celebrity in Contemporary America*. Berkeley: University of California Press, 1994.

Garfinkle, Adam. *Telltale Hearts: The Origins and Impact of the Vietnam Antiwar Movement*. Basingstoke: Palgrave, 1995.

Gelpi, Christopher, Peter Feaver, and Jason Reifler. *Paying the Human Costs of War: American Public Opinion and Casualties in Military Conflicts*. Princeton: Princeton University Press, 2009.

Giangreco, D. M. *Hell to Pay: Operation Downfall and the Invasion of Japan, 1945–1947*. Annapolis, MD: Naval Institute Press, 2009.

Gibson, James William. *The Perfect War: Technowar in Vietnam*. New York: Atlantic Monthly Press, 1986.

Gordon, Michael, and Bernard Trainor. *Cobra II: The Inside Story of the Invasion and Occupation of Iraq*. London: Pantheon, 2006.

———. *The Generals' War: The Inside Story of the First Gulf War*. London: Little, Brown, 1995.

Greenberg, David. *Nixon's Shadow: The History of an Image*. New York: W. W. Norton, 2004.

Griffith, Robert. *The Politics of Fear: Joseph R. McCarthy and the Senate.* 2nd ed. Amherst: University of Massachusetts Press, 1987.

Grotelueschen, Mark E. *The AEF Way of War: The American Army and Combat in World War I.* Cambridge: University of Cambridge Press, 2007.

Hagopian, Patrick. *The Vietnam War in American Memory: Veterans, Memorials, and the Politics of Healing.* Amherst: University of Massachusetts Press, 2009.

Halberstam, David. *The Coldest Winter: America and the Korean War.* London: Pan, 2008.

Hallin, Daniel C. *The "Uncensored War": The Media and Vietnam.* Berkeley: University of California Press, 1986.

Halper, Stefan, and Jonathan Clarke. *America Alone: The Neo-Conservatives and the Global Order.* Cambridge: University of Cambridge Press, 2004.

Hammond, William M. *Public Affairs: The Military and Media, 1962–1973.* 2 vols. Washington, DC: Center of Military History, 1990–1996.

———. *Reporting Vietnam: Media and Military at War.* Lawrence: University Press of Kansas, 1998.

Hanhimäki, Jussi. *The Flawed Architect: Henry Kissinger and American Foreign Policy.* New York: Oxford University Press, 2004.

Harris, John F. *The Survivor: Bill Clinton in the White House.* New York: Random House, 2005.

Harrison, Gordon A. *Cross-Channel Attack.* Washington, DC: Center of Military History, 1951.

Hastings, Max. *Bomber Command: The Myths and Realities of the Strategic Bomber Offensive, 1939–1945.* New York: Dial Press, 1979.

Heineman, Kenneth J. *Campus Wars: The Peace Movement at American State Universities in the Vietnam Era.* New York: NYU Press, 1993.

Hermes, Walter G. *Truce Tent and Fighting Front.* Washington, DC: Center of Military History, 1992.

Herring, George C. *America's Longest War: The United States and Vietnam, 1950–1975.* 4th ed. New York: McGraw-Hill, 2002.

Hershberg, James G. *James B. Conant: Harvard to Hiroshima and the Making of the Nuclear Age.* New York: Knopf, 1993.

Herspring, Dale R. *Rumsfeld's Wars: The Arrogance of Power.* Lawrence: University Press of Kansas, 2008.

Hildebrand, Robert. *Power and the People: Executive Management of Public Opinion on Foreign Affairs, 1897–1921.* Chapel Hill: University of North Carolina Press, 1981.

History of the American Graves Registration Service. Washington, DC: Adjutant General Center, 1976.

Hoenicke Moore, Michaela. *Know Your Enemy: The American Debate on Nazism, 1933–1945.* Cambridge: University of Cambridge Press, 2010.

Hohenberg, John. *Foreign Correspondence: The Great Reporters and Their Times.* New York: Columbia University Press, 1964.

Holloway, David. *Stalin and the Bomb: The Soviet Union and Atomic Energy, 1939–1956.* New Haven, CT: Yale University Press, 1994.

Howe, George F. *Northwest Africa: Seizing the Initiative in the West.* Washington, DC: Office of the Chief of Military History, Department of the Army, 1957.

Huebner, Andrew J. *The Warrior Image: Soldiers in American Culture from the Second World War to the Vietnam Era.* Chapel Hill: University of North Carolina Press, 2008.

Huelfer, Evan A. *The "Casualty Issue" in American Military Practice: The Impact of World War I.* Westport, CT: Greenwood Press, 2003.

Hulsey, Byron C. *Everett Dirksen and His Presidents: How a Giant Shaped American Politics.* Lawrence: University Press of Kansas, 2000.

Isaacs, Arnold R. *Without Honor: Defeat in Vietnam and Cambodia.* Baltimore, MD: Johns Hopkins University Press, 1983.

Isserman, Maurice, and Michael Kazin. *America Divided: The Civil War of the 1960s.* Oxford: Oxford University Press, 2000.

James, Clayton D. *Refighting the Last War: Command and Crisis in Korea, 1950–1953.* New York: Free Press, 1993.

———. *The Years of MacArthur.* 3 vols. Boston: Houghton Mifflin, 1970–1985.

Jeffreys-Jones, Rhodri. *Peace Now! American Society and the Ending of the Vietnam War.* New Haven, CT: Yale University Press, 1999.

Johns, Andrew L. *Vietnam's Second Front: Domestic Politics, the Republican Party, and the War.* Lexington: University Press of Kentucky, 2010.

Jonas, Manfred. *Isolationism in America, 1935–1941.* Ithaca, NY: Cornell University Press, 1966.

Jones, Howard. *Death of a Generation: How the Assassinations of Diem and JFK Prolonged the Vietnam War.* Oxford: Oxford University Press, 2003.

Kagan, Donald, and Frederick W. Kagan. *While America Sleeps: Self-Delusion, Military Weakness, and the Threat to Peace Today.* New York: St. Martin's Press, 2000.

Kazin, Michael. *A Godly Hero: The Life of William Jennings Bryan.* New York: Knopf, 2006.

Keene, Jennifer D. *Doughboys, the Great War, and the Remaking of Modern America.* Baltimore, MD: Johns Hopkins University Press, 2001.

Kennedy, David M. *Over Here: The First World War and American Society.* New York: Oxford University Press, 1980.

Kepley, David R. *The Collapse of the Middle Way: Senate Republicans and the Bipartisan Foreign Policy, 1948–1952.* Westport, CT: Greenwood Press, 1988.

Kimball, Warren F. *The Most Unsordid Act: Lend-Lease, 1939–1941.* Baltimore, MD: Johns Hopkins University Press, 1969.

Knightley, Philip. *The First Casualty. From the Crimea to the Falklands: The War Correspondent as Hero, Propagandist and Myth Maker.* Rev. ed. London: Pan, 1989.

Knock, Thomas J. *To End All Wars: Woodrow Wilson and the Quest for a New World Order.* Princeton: Princeton University Press, 1992.

Kriner, Douglas L., and Francis X. Shen. *The Casualty Gap: The Causes and Consequences of American Wartime Inequalities.* New York: Oxford University Press. 2010.

Kuter, Stanley I. *The Wars of Watergate: The Last Crisis of Richard Nixon.* New York: Random House, 1992.

Landers, James. *The Weekly War: Newsmagazines and Vietnam.* Columbia: University of Missouri Press, 2004.

Larrabee, Eric. *Commander in Chief: Franklin D. Roosevelt, His Lieutenants, and Their War.* New York: Harper and Row, 1987.

Larson, Eric V. *Casualties and Consensus: The Historical Role of Casualties in Domestic Support for U.S. Military Operations.* Santa Monica, CA: Rand, 1996.

Latham, Jr., William Clark. *Cold Days in Hell: American POWs in Korea.* College Station: Texas A&M University Press, 2012.

Leigh, Michael. *Mobilizing Consent: Public Opinion and American Foreign Policy, 1937–1947.* Westport, CT: Greenwood Press, 1976.

Lengel, Edward G. *To Conquer Hell: The Meuse-Argonne, 1918.* New York: Henry Holt, 2008.

Leuchtenberg, William E. *The Perils of Prosperity, 1914–32.* Chicago: University of Chicago Press, 1958.

Lien-Hang, T. Nguyen. *Hanoi's War: An International History of the War for Peace in Vietnam.* Chapel Hill: University of North Carolina Press, 2012.

Link, Arthur S. *Wilson: Campaigns for Progressivism and Peace.* Princeton: Princeton University Press, 1965.

Logevall, Frederick. *Embers of War: The Fall of an Empire and the Making of America's Vietnam.* New York: Random House, 2012.

Longley, Kyle. *Grunts: The American Combat Soldier in Vietnam.* Armonk, NY: M. E. Sharpe, 2008.

Lubell, Samuel. *Revolt of the Moderates.* New York: Harper and Brothers, 1956.

MacDonald, Charles B. *The Battle of the Huertgen Forest.* Philadelphia: University of Pennsylvania Press, 1963.

————. *The Siegfried Line Campaign*. Washington, DC: Center of Military History, 1963.

MacGarrigle, George L. *Taking the Offensive, October 1966 to October 1967*. Washington, DC: Center of Military History, 1998.

MacGregor, Morris J. *Integration of the Armed Forces, 1940–1965*. Washington, DC: Center of Military History, 1981.

Mann, James. *Rise of the Vulcans: The History of Bush's War Cabinet*. New York: Viking, 2004.

Maraniss, David. *They Marched Into the Sunlight: War and Peace in Vietnam and America, October 1967*. New York: Simon and Schuster, 2004.

Marshall, S. L. A. *The River and the Gauntlet: Defeat of the Eighth Army by the Chinese Communist Forces, November 1950*. New ed. New York: Time, 1962.

Marszalek, John J. *Sherman's Other War: The General and the Civil War Press*. Kent, OH: Kent State University Press, 1999.

Mason, Robert. *Richard Nixon and the Quest for a New Majority*. Chapel Hill: University of North Carolina Press, 2004.

Matloff, Maurice. *Strategic Planning for Coalition Warfare, 1943–1944*. Washington, DC: Center of Military History, 1959.

Matthews, Joseph J. *Reporting the Wars*. Minneapolis: University of Minnesota Press, 1957.

May, Ernest R. *The World War and American Isolation, 1914–197*. Cambridge, MA: Harvard University Press, 1963.

McFarland, Keith D., and David L. Roll. *Louis Johnson and the Arming of America: The Roosevelt and Truman Years*. Bloomington: Indiana University Press, 2005.

McMaster, H. R. *Dereliction of Duty: Lyndon Johnson, Robert McNamara, The Joint Chiefs of Staff, and the Lies that Led to Vietnam*. New York: HarperCollins, 1997.

Mead, Gary. *The Doughboys: America and the First World War*. London: Allen Lane, 2000.

Meigs, Mark. *Optimism at Armageddon: Voices of American Participants in the First World War*. Basingstoke: Palgrave, 1997.

Merry, Robert W. *Taking on the World: Joseph and Stewart Alsop—Guardians of the American Century*. New York: Viking, 1996.

Miller, Donald L. *Eighth Air Force: The American Bomber Crews in Britain*. London: Aurum Press, 2006.

Miller, Lee G. *The Story of Ernie Pyle*. New York: Viking Press, 1950.

Millett, Allan R. *The War for Korea, 1950–1951: They Came from the North*. Lawrence: University Press of Kansas, 2010.

Miroff, Bruce. *The Liberals' Moment: The McGovern Insurgency and the Identity Crisis of the Democratic Party*. Lawrence: University Press of Kansas, 2007.

Miscamble, Wilson. *From Roosevelt to Truman: Potsdam, Hiroshima, and the Cold War*. Cambridge: Cambridge University Press, 2007.

————. *The Most Controversial Decision: Truman, the Atomic Bomb, and the Defeat of Japan*. Cambridge: Cambridge University Press, 2011.

Mock, James R. *Censorship–1917*. Princeton: Princeton University Press, 1941.

Mueller, John. *Wars, Presidents, and Public Opinion*. New York: Wiley, 1973.

Mullen, Robert W. *Blacks in Vietnam*. Washington, DC: University Press of America, 1981.

Murray, Williamson, and Allan R. Millett. *A War to be Won: Fighting the Second World War*. Cambridge, MA: Harvard University Press, 2000.

Nenninger, Timothy. *The Leavenworth Schools and the Old Army: Education, Professionalism, and the Officer Corps of the United States Army*. Westport, CT: Greenwood Press, 1978.

O'Keefe, Kevin J. *A Thousand Deadlines: The New York City Press and American Neutrality, 1914–1917*. The Hague: Martinus Nijhoff Publishers, 1972.

Oliver, Kendrick. *The My Lai Massacre in American History and Memory*. Manchester, UK: Manchester University Press, 2006.

Olson, Keith W. *Watergate: The Presidential Scandal That Shook America*. Lawrence: University Press of Kansas, 2003.

Osgood, Kenneth, and Andrew K. Frank, eds. *Selling War in a Media Age: The Presidency and Public Opinion in the American Century*. Gainesville: University Press of Florida, 2010.

Overy, Richard. *The Air War, 1939–1945*. London: Europa, 1980.

———. *Why the Allies Won*. London: Jonathan Cape, 1995.

Paige, Glenn D. *The Korean Decision, June 24–30, 1950*. New York: Free Press, 1968.

Parker, Danny S., ed. *The Battle of the Bulge, The German View: Perspectives from Hitler's High Command*. Mechanicsburg, PA: Stackpole, 1999.

Patterson, James T. *Mr. Republican: A Biography of Robert A. Taft*. Boston: Houghton Mifflin, 1972.

Paul, Christopher, and James J. Kim. *Reporters on the Battlefield: The Embedded Press System in Historical Context*. Santa Monica, CA: Rand, 2004.

Pearlman, Michael D. *Truman and MacArthur: Policy, Politics, and the Hunger for Honor and Renown*. Bloomington: Indiana University Press, 2008.

———. *Warmaking and American Democracy: The Struggle over Military Strategy, 1700–Present*. Lawrence: University Press of Kansas, 1999.

Pedelty, Mark. *War Stories: The Culture of Foreign Correspondents*. New York: Routledge, 1995.

Perlstein, Rick. *Before the Storm: Barry Goldwater and the Unmaking of the American Consensus*. New York: Hill and Wang, 2001.

Perisco, Joseph E. *Edward R. Murrow: An American Original*. New York: Da Capo, 1997.

Philpott, William. *Bloody Victory: The Sacrifice on the Somme*. London: Abacus, 2009.

Piehler, G. Kurt. *Remembering War the American Way*. Washington, DC: Smithsonian Institute Press, 1995.

Pogue, Forrest C. *George C. Marshall: Organizer of Victory, 1943–1945*. New York: Viking Press, 1973.

———. *The Supreme Command*. Washington, DC: Office of the Chief of Military History, Department of the Army, 1954.

Ponder, Stephen. *Managing the Press: Origins of the Media Presidency, 1897–1933*. Basingstoke: Palgrave, 2000.

Prior, Robin, and Trevor Wilson. *Passchendaele: The Untold Story*. 2nd ed. New Haven: Yale University Press, 2002.

Prochnau, William. *Once Upon a Distant War: David Halberstam, Neil Sheehan, Peter Arnett— Young War Correspondents and Their Early Vietnam Battles*. New York: Vintage, 1995.

Rajfus, Maurice. *La Censure: militaire et policière*. Paris: Le Cherche midi, 1999.

Randolph, Stephen P. *Powerful and Brutal Weapons: Nixon, Kissinger, and the Easter Offensive*. Cambridge, MA: Harvard University Press, 2007.

Reeves, Richard. *President Nixon: Alone in the White House*. New York: Simon and Schuster, 2001.

Reeves, Thomas C. *The Life and Times of Joe McCarthy*. New York: Stein and Day, 1982.

Reister, Frank A., *Battle Casualties and Medical Statistics: U.S. Army Experience in the Korean War*. Washington, DC: Surgeon General, Department of the Army, 1973.

Remnick, David. *The Bridge: The Life and Rise of Barack Obama*. New York: Vintage, 2010.

Reynolds, David. *The Creation of the Anglo-American Alliance: A Study in Competitive Cooperation*. Chapel Hill: University of North Carolina Press, 1982.

———. *From Munich to Pearl Harbor: Roosevelt's America and the Origins of the Second World War*. Chicago: University of Chicago Press, 2001.

———. *Rich Relations: The American Occupation of Britain, 1942–1945*. London: HarperCollins, 1995.

Ricks, Thomas E. *Fiasco: The American Military Adventure in Iraq*. New York: Penguin Press, 2007.

———. *The Gamble: General Petraeus and the Untold Story of the American Surge in Iraq*. New York: Penguin Press, 2009.

Roeder, George H. *The Censored War: American Visual Experience during World War II*. New Haven: Yale University Press, 1993.

Sainsbury, Keith. *The North African Landings, 1942: A Strategic Decision*. London: Davis-Poynter, 1976.

———. *The Turning Point: Roosevelt, Stalin, Churchill, and Chiang Kai-shek, 1943*. Oxford: Oxford University Press, 1986.

Schaffer, Ronald. *Wings of Judgment: American Bombing in World War II*. New York: Oxford University Press, 1985.

Schmitz, David F. *The Tet Offensive: Politics, War, and Public Opinion*. Lanham, MD: Rowman and Littlefield, 2005.

Schneider, James C. *Should America Go To War? The Debate over Foreign Policy in Chicago, 1939–1941*. Chapel Hill: University of North Carolina Press, 1989.

Scott, Wilbur J. *The Politics of Readjustment: Vietnam Veterans Since the War*. New York: Aldine De Gruyter, 1993.

Seib, Philip. *Beyond the Front Lines: How the News Media Cover a World Shaped by War*. Basingstoke: Palgrave, 2004.

Shawcross, William. *Sideshow: Kissinger, Nixon, and the Destruction of Cambodia*. London: André Deutsch, 1979.

Sheehan, Neil. *A Bright Shining Lie: John Paul Vann and America in Vietnam*. New York: Vintage, 1988.

Shephard, Ben. *A War of Nerves: Soldiers and Psychiatrists in the Twentieth Century*. Cambridge, MA: Harvard University Press, 2003.

Sherry, Michael S. *The Rise of American Air Power: The Creation of Armageddon*. New Haven: Yale University Press, 1987.

Shu, Guang Zhang. *Mao's Military Romanticism: China and the Korean War*. Lawrence: University Press of Kansas, 2005.

Sigal, Leon V. *Reporters and Officials: The Organization and Politics of Newsmaking*. Lexington, MA: Lexington Books/D. C. Heath, 1973.

Sledge, Michael. *Soldier Dead: How We Recover, Identify, Bury, and Honor Our Military Fallen*. New York: Columbia University Press, 2005.

Small, Melvin. *At the Water's Edge: American Politics and the Vietnam War*. Chicago: Ivan R. Dee, 2005.

———. *Johnson, Nixon, and the Doves*. New Brunswick, NJ: Rutgers University Press, 1988.

———. *The Presidency of Richard Nixon*. Lawrence: University Press of Kansas, 2003.

Smith, Jeffery A. *War and Press Freedom: The Problem of Prerogative Power*. New York: Oxford University Press, 1999.

Smythe, Donald. *Pershing: General of the Armies*. Bloomington: Indiana University Press, 1986.

Sobel, Richard. *The Impact of Public Opinion on U.S. Foreign Policy since Vietnam*. New York: Oxford University Press, 2001.

Sorley, Lewis. *A Better War: The Unexamined Victories and Final Tragedy of America's Last Years in Vietnam*. New York: Harcourt Brace, 1999.

Spector, Ronald H. *After Tet: The Bloodiest Year in Vietnam*. New York: Free Press, 1993.

———. *Eagle Against the Sun: The American War with Japan*. New York: Vintage, 1985.

Stallings, Laurence. *The Doughboys: The Story of the AEF, 1917–1918*. New York: Harper and Row, 1963.

Stanton, Shelby L. *The Rise and Fall of an American Army*. New York: Dell, 1985.

Steere, Edward, and Thayer M. Boardman. *Final Disposition of World War II Dead 1945–51*. Washington, DC: Historical Branch, Office of Quartermaster General, 1957.

Stevenson, David. *1914–1918: The History of the First World War*. London: Allen Lane, 2004.

———. *With Our Backs to the Wall: Victory and Defeat in 1918*. London: Allen Lane, 2011.

Stoler, Mark. *The Politics of the Second Front: American Military Planning and Diplomacy in Coalition Warfare*. Westport, CT: Greenwood Press, 1977.

Stueck, William. *Rethinking the Korean War: A New Diplomatic and Strategic History*. Princeton: Princeton University Press, 2002.

Sweeney, Michael S. *The Military and the Press: An Uneasy Truce*. Evanston, IL: Northwestern University Press, 2006.

———. *Secrets of Victory: The Office of Censorship and the American Press and Radio in World War II*. Chapel Hill: University of North Carolina Press, 2001.

Taylor, Philip M. *War and the Media: Propaganda and Persuasion in the Gulf War*. Manchester, UK: Manchester University Press, 1992.

Thompson, J. Lee. *Politicians, The Press, and Propaganda: Lord Northcliffe and the Great War, 1914–1919*. Kent, OH: Kent State University Press, 1999.

Thorne, Christopher. *Allies of a Kind: The United States, Britain and the War Against Japan, 1941–1945*. Oxford: Oxford University Press, 1978.

Tobin, James. *Ernie Pyle's War*. New York: Free Press, 2006.

Tulis, Jeffrey. *The Rhetorical Presidency*. Princeton: Princeton University Press, 1990.

Turner, Kathleen J. *Lyndon Johnson's Dual War: Vietnam and the Press*. Chicago: University of Chicago Press, 1985.

United States Special Operations Command History. 6th ed. Tampa, FL: USSOCOM, History and Research Office, 2008.

Van Atta, Dale. *With Honor: Melvin Laird in War, Peace, and Politics*. Madison, WI: University of Wisconsin Press, 2008.

VanDeMark, Brian. *Into the Quagmire: Lyndon Johnson and the Escalation of the Vietnam War*. New York: Oxford University Press, 1991.

Vaughn, Stephen. *Holding Fast the Inner Lines: Democracy, Nationalism, and the Committee on Public Information*. Chapel Hill: University of North Carolina Press, 1980.

Vogel, Steve. *The Pentagon: A History*. New York: Random House, 2007.

Weigley, Russell F. *Eisenhower's Lieutenants: The Campaign of France and Germany, 1944–1945*. Bloomington: Indiana University Press, 1981.

Weinberg, Gerhard L. *A World at Arms: A Global History of World War II*. Cambridge: Cambridge University Press, 1994.

Wells, Tom. *The War Within: America's Battle over Vietnam*. Berkeley: University of California Press, 1994.

Westheider, James E. *Fighting on Two Fronts: African Americans and the Vietnam War*. New York: NYU Press, 1997.

Wilcox, Fred A. *Waiting for an Army to Die: The Tragedy of Agent Orange*. New York: Vintage, 1983.

Willbanks, James H. *Abandoning Vietnam: How America Left and South Vietnam Lost Its War*. Lawrence: University Press of Kansas, 2008.

Williams, Reese. *Unwinding the War: From War into Peace*. Seattle, WA: Real Comet Press, 1987.

Wilson, Trevor. *Myriad Faces of War: Britain and the Great War, 1914–1918*. Oxford: Oxford University Press, 1986.

Winfield, Betty Houchin. *FDR and the News Media*. New York: Columbia University Press, 1994.

Winkler, Allan M. *The Politics of Propaganda: The Office of War Information*. New Haven: Yale University Press, 1978.

Winton, Harold R. *Corps Commanders of the Bulge: Six Generals and Victory in the Ardennes*. Lawrence: University Press of Kansas, 2007.

Woods, Randall Bennett. J. *William Fulbright, Vietnam, and the Search for a Cold War Foreign Policy*. Cambridge: Cambridge University Press, 1998.

Woodward, Bob. *Bush at War*. New York: Simon and Schuster, 2002.

———. *Obama's Wars*. New York: Simon and Schuster. 2010.

———. *Plan of Attack*. New York: Simon and Schuster, 2004.

———. *State of Denial*. New York: Simon and Schuster. 2006.

Woodward, David R. *Trial By Friendship: Anglo-American Relations, 1917–1918*. Lexington: University Press of Kentucky, 1993.

Wright, Donald P., James R. Bird, Steven E. Clay, Peter W. Connors, Scott C. Farquhar, Lynne Chandler Garcia, and Dennis F. Van Wey. *A Different Kind of War: The United States Army in Operation ENDURING FREEDOM, October 2001–September 2005*. Fort Leavenworth, KS: Combat Studies Institute Press, 2010.

Wyatt, Clarence R. *Paper Soldiers: The American Press and the Vietnam War*. New York: W. W. Norton, 1993.

Wynn, Neil A. *The Afro-American and the Second World War*. New York: Holmes and Meier, 1975.

Zaffiri, Samuel. *Hamburger Hill, May 11–20, 1969*. Novato, CA: Presidio Press, 1988.

ARTICLES

Allen, Michael J. "'Help Us Tell the Truth about Vietnam': POW/MIA Politics and the End of the American War." In *Making Sense of the Vietnam Wars: Local, National, and Transnational Perspectives*, edited by Mark Philip Bradley and Marilyn B. Young, 251–75. Oxford: Oxford University Press, 2008.

Bator, Francis M. "No Good Choices: LBJ and the Vietnam/Great Society Connection." *Diplomatic History* 32 (2008): 309–40.

Berg, Manfred. "Guns, Butter, and Civil Rights: The NAACP and the Vietnam War, 1964–1968." In *Aspects of War in American History*, edited by David K. Adams and Cornelis A. Van Minnen, 213–38. Keele: Keele University Press, 1997.

Bernstein, Barton J. "Seizing the Contested Terrain of the Early Nuclear History: Stimson, Conant, and Their Allies Explain the Decision to Use the Atomic Bomb." *Diplomatic History* 17 (1993): 35–72.

———. "Truman and the A-Bomb: Targeting Noncombatants, Using the Bomb, and His Defending the 'Decision.'" *Journal of Military History* 62 (1998): 547–70.

———. "Understanding the Atomic Bomb and the Japanese Surrender: Missed Opportunities, Little-Known Near Disasters, and Modern Memory." In *Hiroshima in History and Memory*, edited by Michael J. Hogan, 38–79. Cambridge: Cambridge University Press, 1996.

Beurier, Joëlle. "Information, Censorship, or Propaganda? The Illustrated French Press in the First World War." In *Untold War: New Perspectives in First World War Studies*, edited by Heather Jones, Jennifer O'Brien, and Christoph Schmidt-Supprian, 293–324. Boston: Brill, 2008.

Borg, Dorothy. "Notes on Roosevelt's Quarantine Speech." *Political Science Quarterly* 72 (1957): 405–33.

Brown, Charles H. "Press Censorship in the Spanish-American War." *Journalism Quarterly* 42 (1965): 581–90.

Budreau, Lisa M. "The Politics of Remembrance: The Gold Star Mothers' Pilgrimage and America's Fading Memory of the Great War." *Journal of Military History* 72 (2008): 371–411.

Collins, Ross F. "The Development of Censorship in World War I France." *Journalism Monographs* 131 (1992): 1–25.

Echols, Marion P. "Information in the Combat Zone." *Army Information Digest* 6 (1951): 60–64.

Fry, Joseph A. "To Negotiate or Bomb: Congressional Prescriptions for Withdrawing U.S. Troops from Vietnam." *Diplomatic History* 34 (2010): 517–28.

Gaddis, John Lewis. "Korea in American Politics, Strategy and Diplomacy, 1945–1950." In *The Origins of the Cold War in Asia*, edited by Yonosuke Nagai and Akira Iriye, 277–98. Tokyo, 1977.

Gartner, Scott, and Gary M. Segura. "War, Casualties, and Public Opinion." *Journal of Conflict Resolution* 42 (1998): 278–300.

Gartner, Scott, Gary Segura, and Michael Wilkening. "All Politics are Local: Local Losses and Individual Attitudes toward the Vietnam War." *Journal of Conflict Resolution* 41 (1997): 669–94.

Gelpi, Christopher, Peter D. Feaver, and Jason Reifler. "Success Matters: Casualty Sensitivity and the War in Iraq." *International Security* 30 (2005/6): 7–46.

Giangreco, D. M. "'A Score of Bloody Okinawas and Iwo Jimas': President Truman and Casualty Estimates for the Invasion of Japan." *Pacific Historical Review* 72 (2003): 93–132.

———. "'Spinning the Casualties': Media Strategies during the Roosevelt Administration." *Passport: The Newsletter of the Society for Historians of American Foreign Relations* 35 (2004): 22–29.

Gullace, Nicoletta F. "Sexual Violence and Family Honor: British Propaganda and International Law during the First World War." *American Historical Review* 102 (1997): 714–47.

Hamdy, Naila, and Radwa Mobarak. "Iraq War Ushers in Web-Based Era." In *Global Media Go To War: Role of News and Entertainment Media during the 2003 Gulf War*, edited by Ralph D. Berenger, 245–54. Spokane, WA: Marquette Books, 2004.

Hamilton, John Maxwell, Regina G. Lawrence, and Raluca Cozma. "The Paradox of Respectability: The Limits of Indexing and Harrison Salisbury's Coverage of the Vietnam War." *International Journal of Press/Politics* 15 (2010): 77–103.

Herring, George C., and Richard H. Immerman. "Eisenhower, Dulles, and Dienbienphu: 'The Day We Didn't Go To War' Revisited." *Journal of American History* 71 (1984): 343–63.

Hillman, Elizabeth L. "The Female Shape of the All-Volunteer Force." In *Iraq and the Lessons of Vietnam*, edited by Lloyd C. Gardner and Marilyn B. Young, 150–61. New York: New Press, 2007.

Horne, John. "Remobilizing for 'Total War': France and Britain, 1917–1918." In *State, Society, and Mobilization in Europe during the First World War*, edited by John Horne, 195–211. Cambridge: University of Cambridge Press, 1997.

Hughes, Ken. "Fatal Politics: Nixon's Political Timetable for Withdrawing from Vietnam." *Diplomatic History* 34 (2010): 497–506.

Humphrey, Carol Sue. "Coming of Age: The Growth of the American Media in the Nineteenth Century." In *The Rise of Western Journalism, 1815–1914*, edited by Ross F. Collins and E. M. Palmegiano, 194–200. Jefferson, NC: McFarland, 2007.

Jackson, Colin F. "Lost Chance or Lost Horizon? Strategic Opportunity and Escalation Risk in the Korean War, April–July 1951." *Journal of Strategic Studies* 33 (2010): 255–89.

Jasperson, Amy E., and Mansour O. El-Kikhia. "CNN and al Jazeera's Media Coverage of America's War in Afghanistan." In *Framing Terrorism: The News Media, the Government, and the Public*, edited by Pippa Norris, Montague Kern, and Marion Just, 113–32. New York: Routledge, 2003.

Jentleson, Bruce. "The Pretty Prudent Public: Post-Vietnam Opinion on the Use of Military Force." *International Studies Quarterly* 36 (1992): 49–73.

Katz, Andrew Z. "Public Opinion and Foreign Policy: The Nixon Administration and the Pursuit of Peace with Honor in Vietnam." *Presidential Studies Quarterly* 27 (1997): 496–513.

Kaye, Barbara K., and Thomas J. Johnson. "Weblogs as a Source of Information about the 2003 Iraq War." In *Global Media Go To War: Role of News and Entertainment Media during the 2003 Gulf War*, edited by Ralph D. Berenger, 291–301. Spokane, WA: Marquette Books, 2004.

Kristol, William, and Robert Kagan. "National Interest and Global Responsibility." In *Present Dangers: Crisis and Opportunity in American Foreign and Defense Policy*, edited by William Kristol and Robert Kagan, 3–24. San Francisco: Encounter Books, 2000.

Leff, Mark H. "The Politics of Sacrifice on the American Home Front in World War II." *Journal of American History* 77 (1991): 1296–1318.

Leland, Anne, and Mari-Jana Oboroceanu. "American War and Military Operations Casualties: Lists and Statistics." *Congressional Research Service*, February 26, 2010.

Leonard, Thomas C. "The Uncensored War." *Culturefront* 7 (1998): 59–62.

Lichty, Laurence W., and Edward Fouhy. "Television Reporting of the Vietnam War; or Did Walter Cronkite Really Lose the War." *World and I* (1987): 581–85.

Link, Arthur S. "The Cobb Interview." *Journal of American History* 72 (1985): 7–17.

Longley, Kyle. "Congress and the Vietnam War: Senate Doves and Their Impact on the War." In *The War That Never Ends: New Perspectives on the Vietnam War*, edited by David L. Anderson and John Ernst, 289–310. Lawrence: University Press of Kansas, 2007.

Mander, Mary S. "Pen and Sword: Problems of Reporting the Spanish-American War." *Journalism History* 9 (1982): 2–9, 28.

Marquis, Alice Goldfarb. "Words as Weapons: Propaganda in Britain and Germany during the First World War." *Journal of Contemporary History* 13 (1978): 467–98.

Matloff, Maurice. "The 90-Division Gamble." In *Command Decisions*, edited by Kent Roberts Greenfield, 365–81. Washington, DC, 2000.

Matthews, Jeffrey J. "To Defeat a Maverick: The Goldwater Candidacy Revisited, 1963–64." *Presidential Studies Quarterly* 27 (1997): 662–78.

May, Ernest R. "The U.S. Government, A Legacy of the Cold War." In *The End of the Cold War: Its Meaning and Implications*, edited by Michael J. Hogan, 217–43. Cambridge: Cambridge University Press, 1992.

Medhurst, Martin. "Text and Context in the 1952 Presidential Campaign: Eisenhower's 'I Shall Go to Korea' Speech." *Presidential Studies Quarterly*. 30 (2000): 464–84.

Miles, Rufus E. "Hiroshima: The Strange Myth of Half a Million Lives Saved." *International Security* 10 (1985): 121–40.

Millett, Allan R. "The United States Armed Forces in the Second World War." In *Military Effectiveness*. Vol. 3, *The Second World War*, edited by Allan R. Millett and Williamson Murray, 116–56. Boston: Allen and Unwin, 1988.

Mueller, John. "The Iraq Syndrome." *Foreign Affairs* 84 (2005): 44–54.

Nafziger, Ralph O. "World War Correspondents and Censorship of the Belligerents." *Journalism Quarterly* 14 (1937): 226–43.

Nenninger, Timothy K. "American Military Effectiveness in the First World War." In *Military Effectiveness*. Vol. 1, *The First World War*, edited by Allan R. Millett and Williamson Murray, 116–56. Boston: Allen and Unwin, 1988.

Neumann, Brian. "A Question of Authority: The March-Pershing 'Feud' in World War I." *Journal of Military History* 73 (2009): 1117–42.

Pach, Chester. "'Our Worst Enemy Seems to Be the Press': TV News, the Nixon Administration, and U.S. Troop Withdrawal from Vietnam, 1969–1973." *Diplomatic History* 34 (2010): 555–65.

Reeves, Nicholas. "Film Propaganda and Its Audience: The Example of Britain's Official Films during the First World War." *Journal of Contemporary History* 18 (1983): 463–94.

Reilly, Tom. "Newspaper Suppression during the Mexican War, 1846–1848." *Journalism Quarterly* 54 (1977): 262–70.

Reynolds, David. "1940: The Fulcrum of the Twentieth Century?" *International Affairs* 66 (1990): 325–50.

Roeder, Jr., George H. "Censoring Disorder: American Visual Imagery of World War II." In *The War in American Culture: Society and Consciousness during World War II*, edited by Lewis A. Erernberg and Susan E. Hirsch, 46–70. Chicago: University of Chicago Press, 1996.

Salaita, George D. "Embellishing Omaha Beach." *Journal of Military History* 72 (2008): 531–34.

Schaffer, Ronald. "American Military Ethics in World War II: The Bombing of German Civilians." *Journal of American History* 67 (1980): 318–34.

Small, Melvin. "Containing Domestic Enemies: Richard M. Nixon and the War at Home." In *Shadow on the White House: Presidents and the Vietnam War, 1945–1975*, edited by David L. Anderson, 130–51. Lawrence: University Press of Kansas, 1993.

Spector, Ronald. "'You're Not Going to Send Soldiers Over There Are You!': The American Search for an Alternative to the Western Front, 1916–17." *Military Affairs* 36 (1972): 1–4.

Steere, Edward. "Genesis of American Graves Registration, 1861–1870." *Military Affairs* 12 (1948): 149–61.

Stephens, Rodney. "Shattered Windows, German Spies, and Zigzag Trenches: World War I Through the Eyes of Richard Harding Davies." *Historian* 65 (2002): 43–73.

Tompkins, Raymond S. "News from the Front." *American Mercury* 14 (1928): 168–69.

Vogel, Detlef. "German and Allied Conduct of the War in the West." In *Germany and the Second World War*, edited by Horst Boog, Gerhard Krebs, and Detlef Vogel, 7:459–702. Oxford: Oxford University Press, 2006.

Walker, J. Samuel. "The Decision to Use the Bomb: A Historiographical Update." In *Hiroshima in History and Memory*, edited by Michael J. Hogan, 11–37. Cambridge: Cambridge University Press, 1996.

Wilson, Trevor. "Lord Bryce's Investigation into Alleged German Atrocities in Belgium 1914–15." *Journal of Contemporary History* 14 (1979): 369–83.

Witsell, Edward F. "The Casualty Report Tells the Story." *Army Information Digest* 11 (November 1950): 7–10.

Woodward, Gary C. "The Rules of the Game: The Military and the Press in the Persian Gulf War." In *The Media and the Persian Gulf War*, edited by Robert E. Denton, Jr., 1–26. Westport, CT: Greenwood Press, 1993.

Young, Charles S. "POWs: The Hidden Reason for Forgetting Korea." *Journal of Strategic Studies* 33 (2010): 317–32.

Young, Marilyn B. "The Hard Sell: The Korean War." In Osgood and Frank, *Selling War*, 113–39.

Zahniser, Marvin R. "Rethinking the Significance of Disaster: The United States and the Fall of France in 1940." *International History Review* 14 (1992): 252–76.

INDEX

kamikaze attacks, 100
Kasserine Pass, Battle of, 38, 52–53, 56, 58, 152
Kay, David, 224
Kennedy, Edward (Ted), 177, 179, 226
Kennedy, John F.
  and military, 138
  and Vietnam, 140–41, 170
Kennedy, Robert, 172, 173
Kent State, 186–88
Kerry, John, 194, 227–29
Khe Sanh, Battle of, 172, 175
kill ratio, 126, 148
killed in action (KIA), 150, 185, 219, 244
  U.S. totals, 6–7, 77, 151, 159, 178, 188–89,
    198, 228, 234
Killer, Operation, 123–24
Kim Il Sung, 105
King, Ernest, 49
King, Martin Luther, 164
Kiplinger, Walter, 60
Kirk, Norman T., 80
Kissinger, Henry, 179–80, 181, 182, 194
Knox, Frank
  and Pearl Harbor, 47
  and Tarawa, 58–60
Korean War
  casualties in, 108, 113, 116, 119, 125, 126,
    128, 130, 131, 133–35
  censorship in, 111, 129–30
  United Nations and, 105–6, 120–21
  U.S. battles in, 108–10, 111–12, 114–20,
    123–24, 129–30, 133–34, 162–63
  U.S. intervention, 105–6
Korean Syndrome, 135–37, 139–40, 145,
    173–74, 178, 245
Kosovo, 208
Krause, Allison, 186–87
Kristol, William, 208
Kunu–ri, Battle of, 115, 118

Laird, Melvin, 181, 182, 183, 185, 188, 190, 197, 247
Laos, 176, 179, 185, 190, 194
Lawrence, William H., 100, 264n120
League of Families, 197
League of Nations, 36
Leff, Mark H., 38
Lehrer, Jim, 211, 225, 228
Lend-lease, 42–43, 48. *See also* "arsenal of
    democracy"
Libya, 203
Life
  in Korean War, 112
  in Vietnam War, 178, 183, 219
  in World War II, 58, 83, 100
  See also images of casualties
Liggett, Hunter, 30
Limbaugh, Rush, 4
Lincoln, 172, 238

Lippmann, Walter, 150
Los Angeles Times, 99, 169, 219, 233
Lubell, Samuel, 134
Luce, Clare Booth, 83–84
Ludendorff Offensive, 8, 22–23, 25, 27, 30, 246
Lugar, Richard, 235
Lyon, George, 93
Lynch, Jessica, 218, 225, 226

MacArthur, Douglas, 6, 241
  in World War II, 85, 97
  in Korean War, 106–9, 111, 113–14, 115–17,
    119–21, 124–28
MacArthur Hearings, 124–26, 128
Mansfield, Mike, 177, 185, 199
Mao Zedong, 105, 114, 125
March, Peyton, 28, 31–32, 34
March, William, 36
Market–Garden, Operation, 87–88
Marshall, George C., 29, 58, 74, 79, 90, 99, 101,
    247–48
Mason, Frank, 60
"Massacre Valley," 123
May, Ernest, 225
McAdoo, William, 25
McCain, John, 235
McCarthy, Eugene, 172, 173
McCarthy, Joseph, 110
McCarthyism. *See* Red scare
McGovern, George, 5, 177, 189, 192,
    194, 196
McNair, Lesley J., 79
McNamara, Robert
  and casualties, 145, 148–49, 170, 209
  pessimism about Vietnam, 155, 168
  and statistics, 138, 147
  and strategy, 145
media
  challenges official casualty figures, 8, 23–25,
    28, 50–51, 112–14, 119–21, 190–91,
    233–34
  criticizes censorship, 23–25, 78–79, 49–51,
    84, 93–94, 120, 190–91, 264n120
  emphasizes casualties, 35–36, 50–51, 61–63,
    93–95, 96, 98–100, 111–14, 116–18,
    123, 133–34, 141–42, 144, 152–54, 159,
    169–70, 177–78, 188, 190–91, 198, 199,
    216, 218–20, 230–31, 235
  evolution of, 9, 44, 54, 104–5, 153–54,
    215–17, 243
  importance of casualties to, 8, 63, 96, 222
  over-optimism of, 56–58, 90–91
  publishes enemy estimates, 48–50, 93–94,
    119, 243
  speculation about casualties, 25, 47–48,
    61–62, 93–94, 99, 111, 117–20, 218
  See also Internet; press; radio; television;
    war correspondents